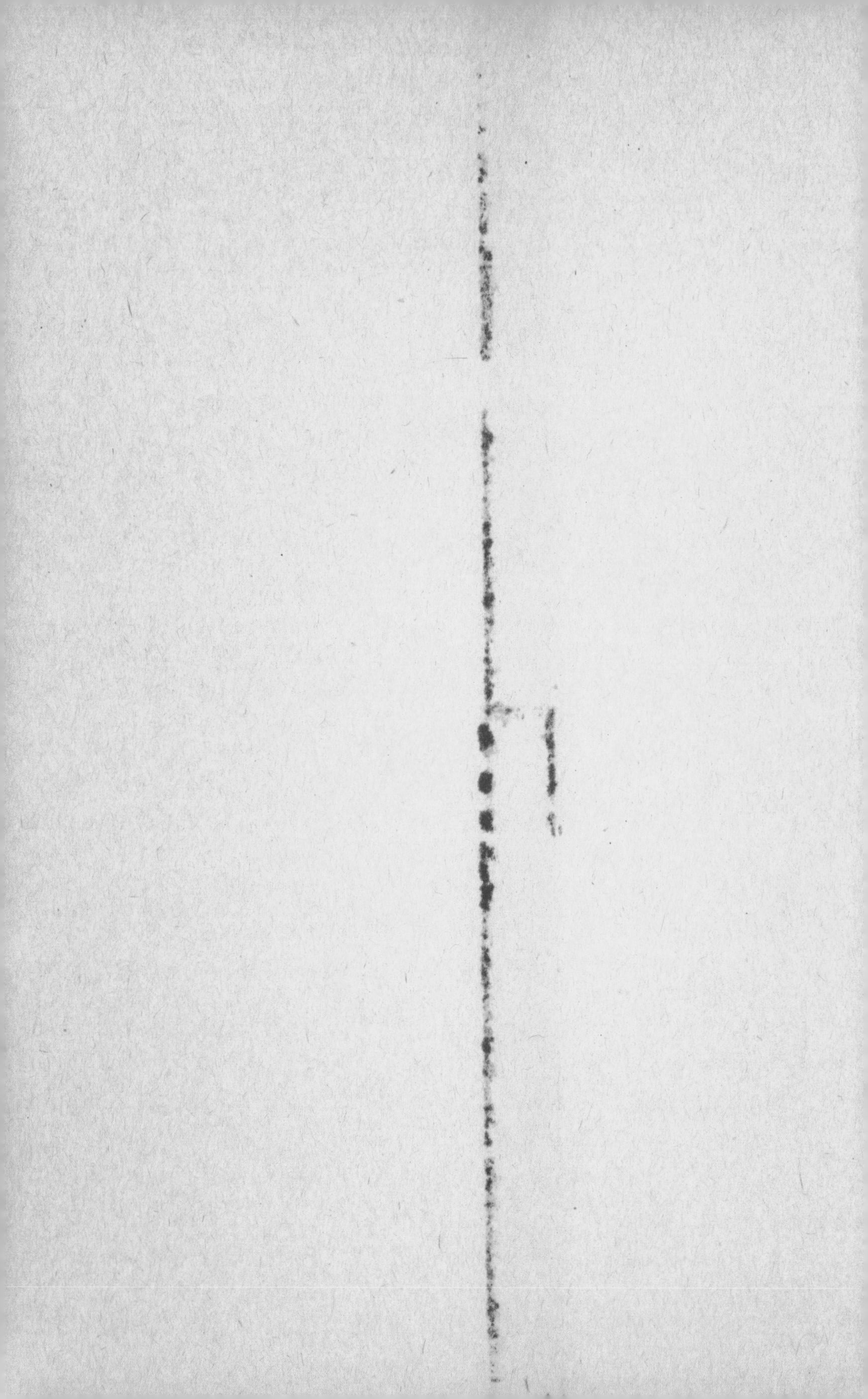

THE *American Conscience*

THE American Conscience

by Roger Burlingame

NEW YORK

Alfred · A · Knopf

1960

L.C. catalog card number: 56–5782

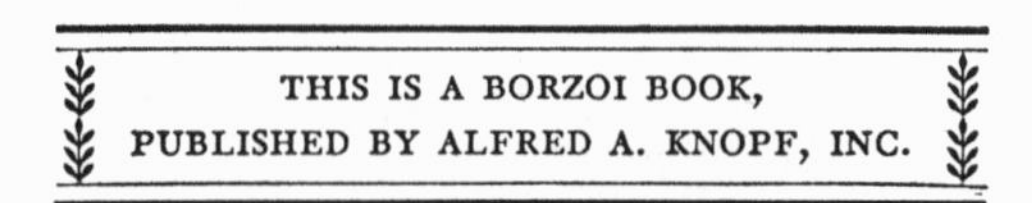
THIS IS A BORZOI BOOK,
PUBLISHED BY ALFRED A. KNOPF, INC.

PUBLISHED MARCH 18, 1957
SECOND PRINTING, FEBRUARY 1960

To my wife

Acknowledgments

I AM GRATEFUL for the assistance given me by the staffs of the Harvard College Library and the Yale University Library. The patient help by librarians in the New York Public Library—especially Mr. Robert W. Hill, Mr. F. Ivor D. Avellino, Mrs. Moritia-Leah Fredericks, and Mrs. Shirley Springer—has been indispensable.

I want to thank Professor Arthur Meier Schlesinger of Harvard for the exceedingly useful suggestions resulting from his careful reading of the manuscript and Mr. Harold Strauss for abundant editorial contributions which have been both meticulous and sympathetic.

I have had inspirational encouragement from my old friend Henry Irving Brock of *The New York Times* and from my long-time guide and companion, Kenneth Littauer. For bibliographical, indexing, and stenographic contributions, my thanks go to Mrs. Louis Richard Keeffe and Mrs. Russell Loring.

Most of all, as usual, my wife has helped. I thank her not only for her forbearance during my occasional creative tantrums but for her remarkable understanding of what I was trying to do in this book. The value to me of her constructive criticism will be recognized by those many authors to whom as "Ann Watkins" she has given intuitive judgment combined with a rare comprehension of craftsmanship.

Contents

PART VI: THE NATIONAL CONSCIENCE

THE *American Conscience*

Chapter I

Introduction

THIS BOOK IS AN INQUIRY into three centuries of American behavior and the moral judgments of the people upon themselves. It tries to interpret the cycles of extravagance and restraint through which we have passed in the light of events or conditions of our peculiar history. It inquires into the flux of public opinion under religious compulsions and economic pressures. It will try to discover why religions and philosophies flowing in from the Old World became transmuted in our wilderness, and how the promises of rich, virgin land altered the concepts of sin and heaven.

Unless American history were indeed peculiar, there would be no justification for a special study of the American conscience. If the American people had followed an orthodox historical pattern, the reasons for their behavior would be easy to trace in analyses of the ethics of a hundred other societies. But the American character was not cast in an orthodox matrix. Its mold is unique.

It is the premise of this study that American moral attitudes differed from those of the peoples from which we sprang because of a set of special determinants in the formation of our national thought. These were, first, isolation both physical and spiritual—by an ocean and by acts of will; second, the movement of the frontier and of social institution behind it; and, third, the natural wealth encountered in the transcontinental march. There were other factors, such as the religious reformers and separatists whose migrations to America resulted in a shower of splinter sects; there were the so-called Great Awakening and Enlightenment, both stemming largely from overseas—but, in the main, the American conscience has had three reference points: isolation, the frontier, and the abundance of natural resources.

The moving frontier came to an end between 1880 and 1890. Actual isolation ended between the Spanish War in 1898, when "manifest destiny" carried us across the Pacific, and 1914, when a variety of causes, including the national conscience, took us to Europe. Meanwhile, other forces, monstrous in appearance, seemed to take possession of the American scene. The abundance of "free" land had somehow become enclosed by impersonal corporation ownership. It was no longer cleared and plowed by hardy individuals, but put into vast mechanized production. A reversal of the agricultural economy had sent most of a generation away from the land, recalling Jefferson's warning that "when we get piled upon one another in cities, we shall become corrupt as in Europe and go to eating one another as they do there." The wealth, so long apparently available to the citizen of humblest origin—provided he was "smart" enough—was now segregated by strange new devices which, to the people, seemed to be financial fictions.

Thus, from a long period in which the stresses derived from physical environment, we had emerged into one in which social problems prevailed. From the effect of living widely apart, alone with nature, we turned to the difficulties of living close-packed with one another. Since then the new forces have increased pressures of a leveling kind. Intensive urbanization, the power age, and mass production have exerted strains no longer unique but common to whatever part of mankind participates in what we call civilization. It is not surprising that the dark look of these factors contrasting with the glow of frontier promise has led many of us into the belief that, however strong the pioneer influences may have been in their time, they are wholly obscured by the later shadows.

Yet, as we pursue our inquiry through the new environment, we encounter more and more evidences that American moral attitudes may be traced back to the formative period. Often we cling to an ideal which events and social overlays have rendered obsolete, or to convictions which obstruct the machinery of our new prosperity, or even to political behavior which assumes that frontier conditions continue.

We insist, for instance, upon a "free competitive enterprise" which has been largely inoperative for seventy years; on "rugged individualism" which the organizing impulses inherent in our later society work constantly to suppress; on freedom of thought, speech, and press against the paralyzing pressure of mass advertising; on the rights of man while group absorption or labor division forces his anonymity; on "grass roots" under a tight network of communications designed to nullify local interests; on the "dignity" of labor which not only no longer requires skill but has become nearly unconscious; on the horrors of socialism after all the Owenite, Fourierist, and Marxist propaganda has been almost instinctively rejected by American masses; on fear of monopoly when some form or degree of monopoly is essential to the proper function of mass production; on a minimum of government planning below the social needs of the new community; and, even in the face of our late central position in the world complex, on the dangers of "foreign entanglements." These insistences, of course, are far from universal even among American businessmen, yet they are still emotional enough to cause perennial legislation, and they are not merely questions of economic or political philosophy. They are matters of conscience.

Whether these conscientious prejudices are desirable in a changing world is a question for the social moralist, not for the historian of moral attitudes. Most of them have their source in the frontier phase of American history. They are recognizable even by foreign observers as stemming from that experience. But they are "ideals." What foreigners often fail to note is that the faults they so freely condemn have the same place of origin. Our naïve foreign policies, our crude national propaganda, our apparent greed, our concentration on money, our contempt for law, our indifference toward predatory operations in business or finance, our tolerance of corruption in government—these and many other lapses which made us what Kipling called "the scandal of the elder earth," and which keep us under suspicion overseas, are frontier products. Some began before the era of the westward-moving frontier. The American who Kipling said was goaded by "the cynic devil in his blood" to "flout the law he makes" and "make the law he flouts" was goaded by no such thing. He simply inherited a legacy from a generation of his colonial forefathers who were able to survive only by "flouting" British customs regulations. Later, western-frontier "vigilantes" who took law into their own hands in the absence of constituted authority buttressed the flouting attitude until, in the dark days of national prohibition, Europeans again held up their hands in amazement at our "cynical" scorn of our own homemade constitutional amendment.

It is true that American writers have been inclined to romanticize the frontier as the molder of democracy and the builder of our sterner virtues. Much American literature is concerned with the "American dream" of frontier days; more than one generation of boys derived its sense of the frontier spirit from Fenimore Cooper, and the latest, as we write, is acutely moved by televised reflections of the open range. These images have been carried, via Hollywood, to Europe with such insistence that they are almost impossible to extricate from uninformed European thinking.

Our own moralists, on the other hand, tend to ascribe our lapses to foreign influence. At the height of our immigration, they spoke of the flood of corruption which entered with the foreigners. It was the immigrants, they said, who caused the crime waves, and they pointed to notorious gangsters with foreign names. Yet these criminals came from countries in which law was far more rigidly enforced than in the United States, and in which a greater respect for law prevailed. It is permissible to believe that, had these persons stayed at home, they would have lived at peace with their communities. But, reared in fear of the police, they came to a land accustomed to license where police and courts were purchasable and legal machinery was slow to convict. Unless they were men and women of considerable stability, is it surprising that they ran amuck and used their talents to take advantage of every non-social or antisocial frontier inheritance?

But it is only necessary to explore our own native behavior at the peaks of frontier activity to find intervals of immorality from which it seemed recovery would be impossible. In the high, wide, and handsome days after the Civil War when the infallible Constitution itself had suspended operation over a large part of the country, there was a lapse of public conscience far greater than any of later occurrence. But this was the result of sudden wealth, of the fabulous success of new industry and new finance in the North and West, of the daily news of bonanzas when the streets of the frontier mining towns ran with a naïve mixture of blood and champagne and, in sinister New York, such bandits as Gould, Fisk, and Drew paraded unmolested through admiring cordons of police to a subservient court. No Al Capone or Dutch Schultz inspired this debacle of conscience to which Brooks and Henry Adams saw no hope of effective resistance.

Yet when, as the frontier closed and opportunity no longer knocked on every American's door, reform set in, this too was an effect of wholly American forces. The true virtues which had marked an earlier way of life simply returned after the orgy. A moral core which had solidified in the tougher, lonelier days again became visible and was found, to the surprise of many, not to have been eaten away.

These cycles, the crises and recoveries, are American: their origins were protected by our isolation. Often the evil seems to have been drained out into the enormous empty spaces. And on lonely frontier farms with their long winter nights of enforced meditation, those who did not go insane built up resistances to fight such evil as in a more compact society was potentially more damaging.

2

This study cannot—must not—review the current scene or attempt to appraise the problems of the future. Its concern is with history. The bearing of history upon the here and now is obviously important. But the historian must recognize his limitations. The events of the past fifty years were not instrumental in forming the basic American character. Most of them were concerned with other societies after our isolation had become a memory—no longer a fact. What they contributed to American motivations, impulses, and behavior was not uniquely or primarily American. On the contrary, they tended to confuse the native moral concepts. Whether their eventual effect will be to destroy those concepts, to replace them with others, or to blend them into some new "one-world" design is a question for the historian of the future.

There was one curious hangover of earlier behavior in the decade of the 1920's. Here we see the American people trying in a sort of blind frenzy to crawl back into its mother's womb. It was our last effort not to wake from the frontier dream. The great pacifist hope (into which we drew several reluctant European nations), the coincident paradoxical repudiation of "foreign entanglements," and national prohibition were pure products of the isolationism caused by the disappearing fact of isolation. Prohibition was also a frontier product with industrialist window-dressing. But the product which industry truly contributed to the frontier revival was the automobile. Ford, indeed, reopened the closed frontier; with his revolutionary machine he renewed nearly every frontier experience. And with the development of this new frontier came the mirage of vast new wealth. The wealth turned momentarily into money, and at the end of the decade the money turned into paper—paper doodled with pictures of gold mountains in a never-never frontier West. We waked, then, and we have hardly slept again.

Except for that romantic aftermath, then, this history will close with the close of the nineteenth century. The world wars and the cold war are outside its scope.

The American Conscience is not written for scholars. There are parts of it that scholars may not like. It takes no account of the fads and vogues in historical appraisal that are continually passing through the shadows of the academy. It is written for the "lay reader" if, in this age of specialization, there remains such a creature. It is meant to be a kind of springboard for the American who wants to dive into a sea of thought about the morals and behavior of his countrymen. If he comes up out of that sea with a wholly different pattern of belief, he will at least have taken the dive, and so, in part, the aim of the study will have been attained.

PART I

THE Provincial Conscience

Chapter II

The Mayflower Pilgrims

THE STORY OF the American conscience begins in a cluster of villages in northeastern England at the end of Elizabeth's reign. Gainsborough, Bawtry, Babworth, Austerfield, and Scrooby were near together at the place of meeting of the three counties of Lincoln, Nottingham, and York; the Idle River wandered among them. The people were yeoman sheep farmers. They were simple, straight-thinking folk, for the most part—stubborn, sure of their faith, enduring: courageous in the certainty that they had found the truth. But as the truth they had found was not the truth that resounded in the cathedrals, intoned by pompous prelates in vestments and accompanied by choirs and the music of organs, they lived in fear.

In the time of Elizabeth they had been watched and questioned by the magistrates.[1] Stories had drifted in about men who thought as they thought being hanged in other places because they would not let their children be baptized in the Queen's church and because they said Scripture gave no warrant for lace-surpliced bishops and prayers out of a book. They had said further that it was unlawful for the Queen to be head of the church, for the Word of God spoken by Paul allowed only apostles, prophets, teachers, elders, and deacons. They had said that the Queen had merely taken the place of the Pope, so that the Church of England was not a reformed church. But as church and state were close-locked together, a heretic was a traitor. Six men had been publicly executed. Numberless others had died in prison.

In this time, however, the people of the north-county villages had

[1] William Bradford: *Of Plymouth Plantation*, S. E. Morison, editor (New York, 1952), p. 8.

only been spied upon or jeered at and held in contempt by their upright, orthodox neighbors. They had committed no open, no formal, crime. On Sundays they would go quietly to some house where an educated man would read the Bible and explain how Calvin and his disciples had evolved from it their complex and somber theology. These were clandestine meetings which often escaped the notice of the royal agents. Then the Queen died and the people's sufferings "were but as flea-bitings in comparison of these which now came upon them." [2]

From the throne that Elizabeth had made secure, the disorderly James I, beset by his uncertainties, exercised a captious, despotic rule. The day of his accession was hardly past when he announced that he would "harry" those who did not conform to his church "out of the land." [3] James had been king of Scotland before he was king of England. The presbyterian Scots would never admit him as head of the Kirk. Coming to the new throne, therefore, and finding the English church already committed to his headship, he resolved to strengthen resistance to any new reform. If he could prevent it, the great Anglican institution should never slip out of his grasp. He was confronted, however, by the sporadic uprisings and rebellions of dissident subjects scattered all the way from the Humber to the tip of Devon.

2

In the past century Europe had been swept by Reformation. The Bible, coming out of its hiding in the dark cloisters of the medieval church, emerging from the language of scholars into vernaculars common folk could understand, and issuing at last, in that new form, by the thousand from the new printing presses, had broken the Roman power. Luther and Calvin, Zwingli and Beza had shown how far the church of Rome had moved away from the word of Christ and the fellowship of the apostles. From Saint Augustine these teachers had drawn a picture of the primitive Christian church, simple, devout, following in the footsteps of Paul. No pope, they said, no bishops or robed priests directed the worship of those dedicated folk in the days when the echo of Christ's voice could still

[2] Bradford: op. cit., p. 10.

[3] William Barlow: *The Summe and Substance of the Conference . . . at Hampton Court, Jan. 14, 1603* (London, 1605).

be heard. There was nothing in the teachings of Jesus or the letters of Paul about transubstantiation, extreme unction, purgatory, or indulgences, and there was clearly no justification in any part of Scripture for the vast lands, monasteries, cathedrals, and a priesthood living in corrupt luxury. These things, some of which had drained the wealth of princes and worked hardship on frightened sinners among the poor, were "human" inventions which, according to the newly revealed Word, must be repugnant to the living Christ.

Through Germany from Wittenberg, through the Swiss Federation from Geneva, into the Low Countries the rebellion had spread, meeting persecution and inquisition on the way. And it had come with John Knox to Scotland, where a scathing manifesto had swept away the church and dogma of Rome. These things had been good, the dissidents in East Anglia had thought: why, then, must England lag behind?

In theory, England was also "reformed." Henry VIII had declared that the Pope no longer controlled the church in his realm. He had then violated the sacrament of matrimony and been excommunicated. Announcing himself as the new head of the English church, he had confiscated the lands and monasteries, recouping the ebbing royal funds and throwing thousands of unemployables into vagabondage on the roads. Yet the church had not changed. In priesthood, in ritual, in "corrupt" practice it had not changed. Incense still burned, holy water was still sprinkled, the sign of the cross still made. Nor did it greatly change under the frail boy Edward VI. After him it lapsed back when Henry's daughter Mary, thirsting for revenge for Henry's persecution of her mother, tried to bring back the full Roman power.

In the reign of Bloody Mary, many prelates of the Church of England sought exile on the continent. When the five terrible years were over and Elizabeth had restored Henry's church, these clergymen returned, many of them in a different mood. They had seen the true Reformation. They had read the words of Calvin and Luther and heard them repeated everywhere. They saw, therefore, the Anglican hierarchy and ceremony in a new light. And they turned their efforts toward removing all the lingering taint and smell of Rome from the Church of England.

They succeeded in introducing a new theology. The famous Thirty-nine Articles, adopted in 1571, contained the doctrines of both Calvin and Luther. They acknowledged that "Holy Scripture containeth all things necessary to salvation. . . ." They rejected "Purgatory, Pardons, Worshipping and Adoration, as well of Images as of Reliques, and also invocation of Saints. . . ." [4] But the reformers did not succeed in eliminating the organization of archbishops, bishops, vicars, rectors, and other prelates appointed by the Queen and supported—still in luxury—by the taxpayers. Elizabeth was jealous of her prerogatives. She might listen to Mary's exiles for a time. But if they pressed her too far to subdue the grandeur or power of her church, she might resort to the common royal practice of her time and send them to the scaffold.

The restless consciences of these awakened people would not, however, be suppressed. A few such rebels could be found in nearly all parts of England. Most of them were in the ancient kingdom of East Anglia. The University of Cambridge rocked with the sound of their protest. They insisted they were not renegades. They loved the church. They had no intent of abandoning it. But they wanted to purge it from the inside.

These people were called Puritans. Their presence made Elizabeth uneasy. They were even more troubling to James. More and more of them were finding seats in Parliament. Already there were signs that such insurgent spirits might one day split the kingdom apart.

Meanwhile, there developed what we should call a left wing of the Puritan movement. These radicals despaired of changing the church from within. They had embraced Calvinism entire. They believed a congregation was sufficient in itself without priests to command it. They believed in the rights and privileges of laymen in the church body. They rejected the Book of Common Prayer, saying that man's communion with the Holy Ghost could not be formulated or limited. They wished at last to separate wholly from the Church of England. The people of the left wing were called Separatists.

It was the Separatists in the villages of York, Lincoln, and Nottingham who were building the cradle of the American conscience.

[4] *Book of Common Prayer, Church of England.*

3

A boy of Austerfield was fourteen when James I came to the English throne in 1603. He was the child of prosperous yeoman farmers. Unlike most of the community, he had learned to read. At twelve he had found the Bible. It was the Geneva Bible, called familiarly the "breeches Bible" because its translator had seen Adam, in his shame, making breeches from the leaves in the Garden. The boy had been carried away by the reading from all his family's tradition into a burning zeal for a new religion. Finally, at fourteen he had joined the congregation that met Sundays at the manor house in Scrooby. Remembering and writing later in a freer land, he preserved for us nearly all our knowledge of these north-country beginnings. His name was William Bradford.[5]

Bradford has introduced us to some of the moving spirits of his time and place. There was William Brewster, who had worked in Elizabeth's diplomatic circles, who had been abroad, who knew the world that the farmers had hardly dreamed about. Brewster had every quality that might charm a boy. He was rich and educated, a "gentleman," with wide experience. In 1603 he was postmaster at Scrooby, a position of much importance, as Scrooby was a relay station on the post road. He lived in the old manor house, once the palace of the archbishop of York—decaying, Bradford says, in that time, but a welcome *foyer* for the Separatists. Brewster had seen the light. That is why, to his peril, he entertained a congregation of rebels on the Lord's Days. Bradford idolized him. "He was wise and discreet," Bradford wrote of him, "and well spoken, having a grave and deliberate utterance, of a very cheerful spirit, very sociable and pleasant amongst his friends, of an humble and modest mind. . . ." [6]

And there was John Robinson, the learned pastor of Gainsborough, who had spent some seven years at Corpus Christi College in Cambridge, who talked to the people at Scrooby and instructed them in the Calvinist doctrines of predestination and grace, of Adam's fall, and of man's helplessness to redeem himself. It is probable that the sturdy farmers never became sure precisely what the

[5] Bradford Smith: *Bradford of Plymouth* (Philadelphia, 1951), *passim.*
[6] Bradford: op. cit., p. 327.

theology meant, and that they continued to behave as if their wills were free; yet Robinson's magnetism heartened their faith at a time when they sorely needed it, and in Bradford's memory that personal inspiration remained very much alive. And there was Richard Clyfton, "a grave and reverend preacher, who by his pains and diligence had done much good, and under God had been a means of the conversion of many." [7]

It would have been safer if the congregation at Scrooby had kept their gatherings informal, but their consciences would not let them. In the maturity of their worship and study, they had become, in the view of their leaders, a church, and they must stand as such before the world. They did, therefore, what all good Calvinists did and "joined themselves (by a covenant of the Lord) into a church estate, in the fellowship of the gospel, to walk in all His ways . . . according to their best endeavours, whatsoever it should cost them. . . . And," Bradford adds at the beginning of his classic book, in characteristic understatement, "that it cost them something this ensuing history will declare." [8]

It was then that their troubles of hounding and persecution (beside which their former afflictions were but "flea-bitings") began. Now they were hauled from their beds at night and taken away to prison at Newgate or to the dreaded London Clink, where they retched in the stinking air, fought off the vermin, starved, and often died of what was known as "jail fever." And they were separated from wives and children, they were stoned in the streets, their precious Bibles were confiscated, until the weaker ones fled or capitulated.

Those who were supported by "God's grace and Spirit" were patient even under these persecutions. They were deeply preoccupied by their mission—their task to bring back the living Christ from the exile into which the medieval church had sent him. Such a dedication eased hardship, quieted fear, and brought a reconciliation even with death.

Yet the Scrooby folk had no morbid desire to burn for their faith. Their great wish was to live for their faith to the end that, as Bradford remembered, "one small candle may light a thousand" [9] and their little church spread their gospel far over the earth. Unhap-

[7] Ibid., pp. 9, 10.
[8] Ibid., p. 9.
[9] Ibid., p. 236.

pily, the greater their zeal, the more frustrated they became. By 1607, as the fifth year of James began, they were convinced that their church could not endure in beloved England: that they must abandon either their faith or their homes.

4

The exile which beckoned them lay across the North Sea. Thence other persecuted men had gone before them. In the Low Countries, they had heard, there was a new kind of freedom unprecedented in any world they knew. In Holland, the most dynamic, independent, and stridently fighting province of the Netherlands, a recent decree had provided that no inquiries "should be made into any man's belief or conscience" and that no "injury or hindrance should be offered to any man on account of his religion." [1] Perhaps it was a dangerous policy, that freedom for all, but if it meant liberty for *them*, then there Robinson and Clyfton and Brewster decided they should go. It was a difficult decision, for the men and women were attached to the English village ways. They loved their thatched houses, their little gardens, and all the customs and ethics and neighborliness of home. But if God had chosen them to do his work—and they believed this as firmly as the Israelites had believed it—then choice for themselves was out of their hands.

No sooner was the hard decision made, however, than the difficulties of carrying out their promise appeared. Though James had sworn to harry the dissenters out of the land, that vacillating King now refused the Scrooby folk license to leave, and his agents cruelly interfered with their attempts to sail into exile.

Their first try was in the fall of 1607. After many weeks of planning and after chartering a ship, they were betrayed by the ship's captain to the King's police, who captured them, confiscated their precious goods, "searching to their shirts for money, yea even the women further than became modesty; and then carried them back into the town and made them a spectacle and wonder to the multitude which came flocking on all sides to behold them." [2]

In the following spring they arranged with a Dutch captain to

[1] J. L. Motley: *The Rise of the Dutch Republic,* (London, 1904) III, 8.
[2] Bradford: op. cit., p. 12.

take them in his ship to Amsterdam. He was to meet them in a secret place between Grimsby and Hull on the Humber. The men went to the rendezvous overland, the women and children in a small bark by water. The Dutchman came and took some of the men on board. The women had to wait for a change of tide. Suddenly there appeared "a great company, both horse and foot . . . for the country was raised to take them." [3] The frightened captain pulled up his anchor, hoisted his sails, and sailed away, thus splitting the company in two, separating—it seemed forever—a part of the men from their friends and families! The men and women who were left on shore "were hurried from one place to another and from one justice to another" until the magistrates and constables "were glad to be rid of them in the end upon any terms for all were wearied and tired with them."

Eventually "their cause became famous" because of their "godly carriage and Christian behavior" and they were secretly aided and supported so that "they all gat over at length, some at one time and some at another, and met together again according to their desires, with no small rejoicing." [4]

The place in which they came together was Amsterdam. From then on they called themselves the Pilgrims.

5

For some forty years, on and off, the Dutch had fought the tremendous power of Spain with heroic courage. The Spanish had occupied that part of the Netherlands which became Belgium, and made continual raids into the northern provinces, of which Holland had returned the most stubborn resistance. Not only had the Spanish armies slaughtered the people of the areas they had conquered, but they had tortured and killed many thousands of nonconforming Dutch in the name of the Holy Roman Church. Now, however, the power of Spain was on the ebb. Beaten on the sea by the English fleet in 1588 and losing their American wealth in captured galleons, the Spanish could no longer afford to combat the Dutch with their old vigor. They agreed, therefore, to a twelve-year armistice—beginning in 1609, the year after the Pilgrims arrived.

[3] Ibid., pp. 14, 15. [4] Ibid.

When the northern provinces had formed the Dutch Republic in 1579, they had decreed the extraordinary injunction against religious bigotry which for many years afterward had no parallel in Europe. Even in the most advanced reformed countries uniformity of faith had been insisted on, and such heretics as Servetus in Calvin's Geneva had been punished with a fiery death. It seems strange to citizens of the American republic, whose constitutional provision of tolerance followed that of their Dutch precursors by more than two centuries, that this was once thought a radical and dangerous practice.

The wide-eyed, clod-hopping Pilgrim yokels, who had never been more than a few miles from their primitive native villages, soon encountered, amid the glitter and sound of the great city, the dangers of freedom. Other groups of dissenters who had preceded them had made shocking departures from the rigid Calvinist dogmas. Under the English persecution they had been stanch in their faith. In a common danger the opponents of the Established Church had remained united. Now, in the land of their first liberty, a branch had broken off and run, in the opinion of Brewster's and Robinson's Pilgrims, amuck. The theological tangents on which they had moved are, for the most part, too subtle for our casual examination, though we may note one: the sinful error that a man might be saved through his own righteousness without the assistance of Christ. The newly arrived Pilgrims were stunned by this "novelty" their former friends had come to embrace, and they leaped into such violent contention with them that the peace and unity of the entire reform-in-exile were threatened.

John Robinson, a person of gentle and pacific wisdom, determined, therefore, that his flock must move. He and Brewster chose Leyden, a smaller university town with a history perhaps braver than that of any community of its size in the whole of Christendom.

It is possible that the sojourn of these exiled people in this milieu of great national patriotism and advanced liberal thought affected the future civilization of New England and perhaps, indeed, of all America. It is usual to think of Dutch influences coming directly from the settlements of New Netherland, yet the Pilgrims could hardly have helped making a contribution from the culture they had absorbed in Leyden.

Thirty-five years before they arrived, the Spaniards had laid siege to the town. At the end of two months the inhabitants were starving. Eight thousand people died of hunger and pestilence. The survivors ate weeds and grass, dogs, cats, and vermin. Yet even then, when the Spanish outside the walls sent an insulting demand for surrender, they hurled back an answer which has echoed ever since in the ears of Dutch patriots:

> Ye call us rat-eaters and dog-eaters and it is true. So long, then, as ye hear dog bark or cat mew within the walls, ye may know that the city holds out. And when all has perished but ourselves, be sure that we will each devour our left arms, retaining our right to defend our women, our liberty, and our religion against the foreign tyrant. . . . When the last hour has come, with our hands we will set fire to the city, and perish, men, women, and children together, in the flames, rather than suffer our homes to be polluted, and our liberties to be crushed.[5]

These words may have begun a new thought in the minds of some of the Pilgrims. They understood men dying for faith. They had said "Amen" to long prayers for deliverance into freedom of their church. But this cry of defiance of men with their backs to the wall, promising to burn in fires of their own lighting for abstract liberty—liberty for its own sake—was a sound which had not penetrated the villages of Lincolnshire, Nottinghamshire, and Yorkshire in the memory of the exiles. The example of courage was needful and good for those far gone in homesickness or doubt of their own strength.

The more serene of the flock enjoyed "much sweet and delightful society and spiritual comfort together in the ways of God." [6] Robinson loved the university and startled the Dutch professors with his powers of theological disputation. Bradford, who as a boy of nineteen had fallen in love at Amsterdam with twelve-year-old Dorothy May, went back four years later and brought his young bride to Leyden, where, it is hoped, they lived in happiness because the tragedy which later befell this girl, still in her early twenties, is one of the most poignant in our colonial history.

In these years more and more Separatists came from England to join the congregation until at last the Scrooby nucleus had become a minority. Some of the first comers had weakened and gone home. Thus, the complexion of the body changed somewhat though the spirit remained steadfast.

[5] Motley: op. cit., II, 592, 593. [6] Bradford: op. cit., p. 17.

Finally, restlessness grew among the lesser folk. Some were disturbed to feel age coming on them. Many found their children drifting away from them, even from the English language, even from the faith. Bradford writes of the great licentiousness of the Dutch and the temptations for youth. As we read his words, we think naturally of the fleshpots and fornication so often mentioned in sermons of the time and wonder at the prevalence of such things among the hard-pressed Hollanders. Looking further into it, however, we find that the real fear of the Pilgrim pastors was not of such corruptions but of the effect on their boys and girls of Dutch desecration of the Sabbath, which in Leyden was a day of feasting and games!

By 1619 this peril, added to the other dangers (which seem to us more real), had moved the "sagest members" to apprehension of the future. The greatest menace of all, of course, was the imminence of renewed war with Spain. In another two years the truce signed in 1609 would terminate, and the possibility of a Spanish inquisition with death for non-Catholics loomed large. Finally, economic conditions were becoming nearly intolerable. "And therefore," wrote Bradford, they "thought it better to dislodge betimes, to some place of better advantage and less danger, if any such could be found." [7]

In the twelve years since a hopeful little group of Englishmen had gone to Virginia, news had come of the Jamestown settlement there, which seemed now to have a solid, enduring foundation. But news had come, too, of the suffering of the emigrants in the first terrible years. The Virginia colonists of 1607 had not, to be sure, been inspired by religious zeal. They had gone in the hope of finding gold (as the Spaniards two thousand miles south had found it) and under that persistent European delusion, the hope of finding a "northwest passage" up the James River to the Indies. Yet the tales of starving times, pestilence, and the barbarities of Indians which had drifted back were enough to shake the faith of the stoutest believers.

There ensued, then, one of the most moving conflicts between conscience and fear that we may find in the background of the American tradition. The argument was long remembered, and those who won it and survived began the growth of that American moral core which in the three centuries that followed stood against even greater attack than the Pilgrims knew.

[7] Ibid., p. 24.

6

> The place they had thoughts on [William Bradford tells] was some of those vast and unpeopled countries of America, which are fruitful and fit for habitation, being devoid of all civil inhabitants, where there are only savage and brutish men which range up and down, little otherwise than the wild beasts of the same. This proposition being made public and coming to the scanning of all, it raised many variable opinions amongst men and caused many fears and doubts among themselves.[8]

The argument of the doubters heaped fear upon fear in the manner of those in all ages who try to restrain reckless adventurers. If they should survive, they said, the perils of the sea—which for the women and the aged was unlikely—the "miseries of the land" would probably "utterly . . . ruinate them." These were famine, nakedness, and disease due to change of air, diet, and the dangerous necessity of the "drinking of water" instead of wholesome beer or cider. Finally, if by God's extreme mercy they should still live, there would be continual danger from

> the savage people, who are cruel, barbarous and most treacherous . . . not being content only to kill and take away life, but delight to torment men in the most bloody manner that may be; flaying some alive with the shells of fishes, cutting off the members and joints of others by piecemeal and broiling on the coals, eat the collops of their flesh in their sight whilst they live. . . .[9]

Truly there had already been long and lurid tales from Virginia! Bradford, though full of courage and hope himself, had to admit in sympathy for those less brave that

> the very hearing of these things could not but move the very bowels of men to grate within them and make the weak to quake and tremble.[1]

Yet the pastors answered the questions and quieted some of the fears. Reading their words, we cannot escape the sense of heartening they must have borne. Even in print their eloquence is kin to that of the most comforting exhortations in all our history. Spoken in the voices of men who were loved almost to the point of worship,

[8] Ibid., p. 25.
[9] Ibid., p. 26.
[1] Ibid.

they must have fallen like balm on those who trembled in the chill of their fears.

> The difficulties were many, but not invincible. For though there were many of them likely, yet they were not certain. It might be sundry of the things feared might never befall; others by provident care and the use of good means might in a great measure be prevented; and all of them, through the help of God, by fortitude and patience, might either be borne or overcome. True it was that such attempts were not to be made and undertaken without ground and reason, not rashly or lightly as many have done for curiosity or hope of gain. . . . But their condition was not ordinary, their ends were good and honourable, their calling lawful and urgent; and therefore they might expect the blessing of God in their proceeding. Yea, though they should lose their lives in this action, yet might they have comfort in the same and their endeavours would be honourable.[2]

Even so, by the time the long and secret negotiations for the departure were completed, less than a third of the congregation were hardy enough to take the chance. The "sagest" had decided, though the Dutch then had an American settlement, to sail under the English rather than the Dutch flag. Two envoys to England secured, after many delays, the "connivance" of the harassed King, permission from the Virginia Company to settle in its vast domain, and the financial backing of a group of London merchants. So the men and their valiant women—some with tiny babies, some pregnant—left for England in July 1620 and, after further disheartening vicissitudes, sailed in September from the Devonshire port of Plymouth into the unknown where Satan and the Lord God contended for the mastery of the waves.

The story from here to the other Plymouth on Cape Cod Bay has been too often told to need repeating, nor do the events of the voyage concern the growth of the American conscience. On the crowded little ship with the gay name the Pilgrims were in God's hands and their destiny was foreordained. In the storms the theological subtleties must have seemed of little importance, and the passengers were too frightened or too sick to sin had any unlikely opportunities arisen. It was only at the end, when they lay in the harbor at Provincetown, that trouble came because some of the laborers and servants these people had brought with them threatened

[2] Ibid., p. 27.

to break loose on landing and escape from their commitments. And this detail might never have been remembered but that it brought about what has been called the first written constitution in the world.

This celebrated Mayflower Compact formed the group into a "civil body politic" empowered to make laws, and it exacted an oath from every signer to obey them. Landing was conditional upon signing this solemn covenant, and the rebels, who had no wish to return to England, capitulated and withdrew their threats.

And then did Dorothy May Bradford sin there for the last time in her brief life? While the *Mayflower* lay at anchor and William had gone exploring in a shallop, his wife fell overboard and was drowned. Did she fall, late historians have asked? [3] Or did the terrible bleakness of the Massachusetts shore make the homesick girl forget that her life was dedicated to Christ and not at her own disposal?

Thus began the first colony of Englishmen who had left their homes for reasons of conscience.

[3] E.g., Samuel Eliot Morison in introduction to Bradford: op. cit., p. xxiv.

Chapter III

The *New England Calvin*

THESE PEOPLE, the Pilgrims, landed in mid-December after weeks of exploring the coast in small boats. It is not easy for us to imagine the starkness of their prospect. After the coast of England, green to the water's edge, the next land they had seen was this waste of rocks. It had the hostile look of country in which there is no human life. It was cold with high, bitter winds. There could be no shelter on shore until the Pilgrims built it. The only protection was the ship on which they had lived two months in crowded discomfort: the men below decks forward, the women and children in the high poop aft. The *Mayflower* was redolent of tedium and sickness, heavy with the smell of confined animals, somber with the memory of late death. Yet it was home, it was a floating piece of England, and the company was loath to leave it. Now, as never before, these driven people needed the heartening of faith, the nearness of a protecting God.

Theirs was a grim religion—or so it seems to us. It held that man was by nature corrupt to the core. He inherited a seed of sin from which nothing he could do would save him. His mind, said Calvin, "is so utterly alienated from the righteousness of God that he cannot conceive, desire, or design anything but what is wicked, distorted, foul, impure, and iniquitous. . . ." [1] His only hope of escape from eternal condemnation lay in the extension to him of God's grace. This "election" to salvation was an arbitrary act to which no human effort could move the Almighty. In a timeless infinity, the inscrutable wisdom had chosen; the divine finger had touched an individual here and there, and nothing could change his destiny.

[1] John Calvin: *Institutes of the Christian Religion,* Book II, Chap. 5, Sec. 19.

The question that doubters have always asked is: how can one tell whether or not he has been elected? The answer Calvinists gave was that, although you could never be sure because God made no personal revelations, good works and righteousness were evidence of grace. Thus, if a person was seen to walk continually in the ways of the Lord it was assumed he was of the elect and he was called a "saint."

These convictions were fundamental to the faith of those *Mayflower* passengers who had been members of a Separatist church in England or Holland. To today's Protestant faithful, most of whom believe that God is benevolent and forgiving and that heaven is the reward of the good life, this doctrine seems a negation of true Christianity. Yet in the darkness of the seventeenth-century dawn, among folk whose ways were inevitably hard, it was logical enough.

The doors had not yet opened on that long vista of scientific enlightenment down which we are still marching. The mass of the people were tormented by superstitious fears. Men and women—and even children—were often "possessed" by demons. Sorcerers and witches practiced charms, enchantments, and soothsaying. Satan was everywhere, stalking through storms or, in muted voice, persuading to sin in the back lots. Lightning, thunder, tempests of wind and wave testified to God's wrath. Men had not learned the reasons for natural phenomena or their control. It was logical to believe one was wholly in God's hands and that God was inexorable. The Catholics, to be sure, were taught that the divine will could be softened by penance, repentance, invocation of the saints, or the attainment of absolution, but for that very reason the Separatists hardened their minds and hearts against these things.

Yet the faith of the Pilgrims had aspects which supported them in their hardships. They had come to believe, in their exile, that they were themselves—the "brethren"—a chosen group. They had entered into a "covenant of the Lord" in establishing their church; since then they had felt increasingly near to God until at last, with the decision to migrate to the new world, they had come to believe they were true instruments of God's will to spread the gospel—perhaps even among the heathen. It was probable, therefore, that each and all had received the grace, the election, the promise of salvation after death.

Perhaps a sense of distinction came to the Pilgrim church members from the fact that many of the *Mayflower*'s passengers were not in the covenant. Among these were the indentured servants—bonded to service until they had paid their passage—and skilled workers who had been hired by the financing merchants to accompany the expedition. Neither Myles Standish, for instance, nor John Alden, both of whom were so important to Bradford's colony, were members of the Leyden congregation. There were also children aboard and boys old enough to work: these were orphans or paupers assigned to some member of the group to be brought up as apprentices or servants. Technically, all these, not being saints, were "strangers."

As the slow landing began, Bradford records that

> which way soever they turned their eyes (save upward to the heavens) they could have little solace or content in respect of any outward objects. For summer being done, all things stand upon them with a weather-beaten face, and the whole country, full of woods and thickets, represented a wild and savage hue. If they looked behind them, there was the mighty ocean which they had passed and was now as a main bar and gulf to separate them from all the civil parts of the world.[2]

But in the midst of this despairing contemplation, there comes, in Bradford's words, the high note of courage from faith:

> What could now sustain them but the Spirit of God and His grace? May not and ought not the children of these fathers rightly say: "Our fathers were Englishmen which came over this great ocean, and were ready to perish in this wilderness; but they cried unto the Lord, and He heard their voice and looked upon their adversity. . . ."[3]

2

In the first winter fifty of the hundred and two who landed died of cold, hunger, and scurvy. The half-dozen who remained healthy were heroic in their care of the sick:

> fetched them wood, made them fires, dressed them meat, made their beds, washed their loathsome clothes, clothed and unclothed them . . . did all the homely and necessary offices for them which dainty and queasy stomachs cannot endure to hear named. . . .[4]

[2] Bradford: op. cit., p. 62.
[3] Ibid., pp. 62, 63.
[4] Ibid., p. 77.

Bradford leaves us to imagine the details—the burials, for instance, in the frozen ground; the long pulls back and forth to the *Mayflower*, which lay all winter at anchor nearly two miles out in the harbor, to get the last of the supplies—for which they had to fight the seamen aboard; and the constant repairs of the "cottages," which were mere wigwams or the crudest of frame huts.

Through this grievous time the Lord continued to support those he did not take away. A merit in the Calvinist congregationalism must have been that it took a man's mind off himself. With his spiritual destiny predetermined, there was no need for the kind of brooding introspection characteristic of those faiths in which salvation depends upon behavior. Also, the doctrines were concerned with the glorification of God. Every good thing a man did, he did not for himself, not to secure a place for himself in the next world's sun, but in dedication to the Lord, in worship or praise. In Calvin's concept, man—loathsome man—counted for nothing; whatever he might do was in the divine service. In Plymouth, therefore, Calvinism, filtered through stalwart English minds, made extroverts of the Pilgrims.

The spring smiled at last and "the sick and lame recovered apace." After a few sharp encounters, a messenger of peace had come from the Indians—the famous Pawtuxet Squanto, who had been kidnapped by an English explorer, carried to England, where he had learned the language, and brought back. With his help a kind of treaty was made with the "great Sachem," Massasoit, and the native corn was planted. In April the *Mayflower* weighed anchor and left, and though it must have been a sore sight to see her go, not one of the brethren climbed aboard to sail back into the comfort of England. The Separatist conscience had become an American conscience.

In the summer "there was no want" but a great quantity of game of all kinds and a harvest of corn for which, in the fall, they gave thanks—the first Thanksgiving.[5] In November an unexpected ship, the *Fortune*, arrived with reinforcements of men and a few provisions. Finally, when the second winter came, they were secure in frame houses behind a palisade. From then on the Plymouth plantation—with occasional hungry and distressed intervals—moved toward prosperity.

[5] Ibid., p. 90.

It is curious that, with their zeal for the spread of the Gospel, so little serious effort was made to convert the Indians. We know that this had been an intent when migration was first thought of. Yet, though non-aggression treaties were made and though the friendly Squanto taught the Pilgrims much about the workings of nature in the wilderness, the "savages" were left pretty much alone to worship their own austere Father in their own "heathen" manner. The Pilgrims were, therefore, like the other Englishmen who had preceded them in Virginia and were to follow them throughout the colonies. They were unlike the Spaniards or the French to the north, who not only made many converts to the Catholic faith but married the Indian women with the church's blessing. The English distrusted the natives, met them with distrust—though, in the interests of trading and peace, it was often concealed—and the Indians were quick to respond in kind. Finally, the initial distrust must have been greatly aggravated by the news of the disastrous failure of Indian missions in Virginia.

Some fourteen years after the landing the Pilgrims had comfort in the fact that "it pleased God to visit these Indians with a great sickness and such a mortality that of a thousand above nine and a half hundred of them died, and many of them did rot above the ground for want of burial." [6] Bradford goes into graphic detail about the horrors of the disease and records that their case was so pitiful that, finally, the English "did what they could for them. . . . But by the marvellous goodness and providence of God, not one of the English was so much as sick or in the least measure tainted with this disease. . . ." [7] And if, as most authorities agree, the disease was smallpox, the outcome in that pre-vaccine age seems close to miraculous. In any case, a sigh of relief must have gone up behind the Plymouth stockade at the Lord's removal of the constant dread of attack.

3

In England, while Plymouth was maturing in its community conscience, the Puritans were entering a new phase. King James died in 1625 and his son Charles, who would one day lose his head in a Puritan rebellion, began to pave the way for that event by stubborn

[6] Ibid., p. 270. [7] Ibid., p. 271.

resistance to church reform. The Puritans, who were becoming numerous and influential, still refused to "separate" from the Established Church and only wanted to purge it from within of its "corruptions." James had tolerated these purifiers. Charles would have none of them. As his instrument of persecution he chose the high churchman William Laud, who became, in the eyes of all nonconformists, a veritable antichrist.

All over England, then, dissenting clergymen began to be relieved of their offices. Under this pressure the Puritans divided into two groups. One aimed at that control of Parliament which ended in civil war. The other—in which we are interested—lost hope in reforming the church in England and turned its eyes westward toward a "wilderness Zion." In the free new world they could do as they liked, have their Anglican church without bishops, altars, organs, or stained glass, and be unmolested in the kind of worship their conscience dictated. That, at least, was what they thought. In the late 1620's, therefore, what is known in American history as the Great Migration began.

With the news of success coming from Plymouth, accompanied, in ships which had gone there and returned, by good cargoes of lumber, beaver skins, and other material evidences of profitable industry, it was becoming increasingly easy to find financial support for enterprises in the North. In 1628 a company called the Massachusetts Bay Company was organized to exploit a royal patent covering territory between the Charles and the Merrimac rivers. A pious Puritan with executive ability named John Endecott was named temporary governor, pending the drawing of the company's charter, and sent over in command of a group of scouts to choose a site for a new "plantation." Endecott landed on Cape Anne, where some fishermen had established a headquarters, moved to the Indian village of Naumkeag, to which he gave the Hebrew name of Salem, decided that there was the site, began clearing and building, and then made friends with Bradford and others in Plymouth.

It was customary for Puritans to disparage and distrust the Separatists. This was because in Holland the Separatists had been fractured—perhaps by Dutch liberty—into a number of quarreling sects, and ugly rumors had come back to England of their instability and scandalous contentions. In the New World, however, where Englishmen were few and far apart and friendly assistance sometimes seemed more important than theology, Endecott quickly forgot all this and was soon on as warm terms with the Plymouth elders as was possible for a man of his stiffness and chill. A few months later, when a second expedition arrived, he had become, in all but name, as thoroughly Separatist as Brewster or Bradford.

The second group of immigrants included two ministers, Francis Higginson and Samuel Skelton, both insistent in their protest that they would never abandon the "mother church." Indeed, as Higginson's ship, the *Talbot*, cleared Land's End in England, the minister delivered an affectionate, sentimental, and tearful farewell in these words:

> We will not say, as the Separatists were wont to say at their leaving of England, Farewell Babylon, Farewell Rome! But we will say, farewell dear England! Farewell the Church of God in England, and all the Christian friends there! We do not go to New England as Separatists from the Church of England, though we cannot but separate from the corruptions in it, but we go to practise the positive part of church reformation, and propagate the gospel in America.[8]

Endecott met Higginson on his arrival, took him to his house, and refreshed him after the long voyage. We do not know what he said, but within a month Higginson and Skelton were elected teacher and pastor of the First Church of Salem and ordained by the elders—ceremonies completely foreign to the Anglican church. Soon after, two unhappy members of the group who wanted to have the Book of Common Prayer of the Church of England read in the "meetings" were forcibly sent back to England on the next ship! Thus the religious dictatorship which has been called theocracy, oligarchy, and Bible rule in Massachusetts Bay began.

Next to come was the settlement's real founder, the deeply religious but exceedingly practical John Winthrop—one of the true heroes of our colonial history. From the time he was first associated with the company of emigrants, he was wholly dedicated to the public good. This dedication must often have been opposed by his private disposition and at times even by his private conscience, for his ways were gentle and his heart turned more toward forgiveness than stern necessity demanded of his conduct.

[8] Cotton Mather: *Magnalia Christi Americana,* Book III, Part II, Chap. 2, Sec. 12.

The company of which he was the most eminent shareholder—the Massachusetts Bay Company—received its charter in the spring of 1629, and soon after, the prime movers decided that control must be forever removed from England, that the charter must be transferred and carried bodily to Massachusetts, there to become the basis, not of a commercial enterprise as the backers had planned, but of a religious commonwealth. Therefore, those who planned to migrate gathered in secret meeting apart from the stockholders who were to stay at home and made a compact that they would not go unless the transfer was made. In short, there would be no plantation unless these drastic terms were agreed to! It was a business coup of a shrewdness we rarely associate with such dedicated folk. It has since been pronounced wholly illegal. But it was successful, and it put the new plantation on a firmer and more independent foundation than that of any colony yet established by the English, the Spanish, the French, or the Dutch in the western hemisphere. It set the stage on which the first act of the American conscience—the New England conscience—could be played.

Winthrop was chosen governor. Those who had signed the compact were Richard Saltonstall, Thomas Dudley, William Vassall, Nicholas West, Kellam Browne, Isaac Johnson, John Humfry, John Sharpe, Increase Nowell, William Pinchon, and William Colbron. These may be called the founding fathers of Massachusetts. Most of them left England with some seven hundred emigrants in six ships in the first week of April 1630. The Reverend John Cotton, who came over later and played a dynamic part in the commonwealth's history, delivered a parting sermon in which he said that these migrants, like the Israelites, were a chosen people going to a promised land, a place the Lord had especially prepared for them in which they would live and work for the glory of God. Winthrop then delivered almost precisely the same farewell to the Church of England that Higginson had done, dated his journal "Easter Monday" in conformity with the Anglican custom, and underwent, when he arrived, the same total conversion to that congregationalism which was to dominate New England for a hundred years.[9]

[9] *Winthrop's Journal*, J. K. Hosmer, editor (New York, 1908), Introduction, *passim,* and I, 23n.

4

To the discomfiture of Endecott, the new governor rejected Salem as the headquarters of the commonwealth. Instead, he chose the Indian village of Shawmut, which some homesick Lincolnshireman renamed Boston. As reinforcements came from England, they branched out, forming new towns with new churches. All the churches were formed in the same way, with the ministers elected by the congregations, and all professed the same doctrines.

It has been said that this election of pastors was a democratic beginning. It is true that Puritans believed all members of a congregation to be equal in the sight of God. But there the democracy stopped. Winthrop's government was an oligarchy. Only church *members* had a vote.[1] Though everyone was required to go to church, only the elect—the "saints"—had the franchise. The saints were a small minority. Hundreds of workers—artisans, laborers, servants of all kinds—had no voice at all in the government, though they paid taxes to support both magistrates and church. In theory, God picked the voters, though in practice, ministers and members decided who, as evidenced by their "good works," had been given grace and might therefore become freemen.[2]

In ten years, twenty thousand people came to New England from distressed England.[3] As this "Great Migration" got under way, the New England conscience began to require protection from the individual consciences that presently came into conflict with it. This community conscience was a very concrete thing. The people who had come over with Endecott, Higginson, and Winthrop had made a covenant *as a body*—as had the Pilgrims—with the Lord. This was a solemn contract with the Almighty which committed the group to certain ways of thought and conduct. In return, the community received divine protection and favor. Any fortune or catastrophe which affected the society as a whole, such as a plentiful harvest or an epidemic, was evidence that it had or had not kept its part in the

[1] T. J. Wertenbaker: *The Puritan Oligarchy* (New York, 1947), p. 65.

[2] John G. Palfrey: *History of New England* (Boston, 1858–90), III, 41, 41n.

[3] Raymond P. Stearns: "The Great Migration," in *Dictionary of American History* (New York, 1940), II, 418.

bargain. To show their recognition of God's responses, the people had days of general thanksgiving or "humiliation." [4]

As the covenant covered ministers, congregations, and civil magistrates, the union of church and government was total. The church depended on the courts and on the law-enforcement officers to keep the religious practice orthodox. A person who expressed such a deviation, for example, as a belief in adult baptism might well be forcibly expelled by the police. Such heresy could not be allowed, for it undermined not merely the church but the entire body politic. Not a single theological tenet could be attacked without putting the civil government in danger, while any criticism of government was a criticism of the church and, indirectly, of Providence and would very likely incur the divine wrath.

In the first year the governor handled what conscientious disagreements there were with fine diplomacy. If in one of the churches a minister fell into "error," Winthrop would send some orthodox cleric to "dispute" or debate with him. Usually the delinquent preacher would see his mistake and recant. He might be sincerely convinced, or he might be afraid of losing his job if he persisted in his heresy. There were several cases at the very start of such lapses, and every breach was healed without recourse to action by the magistrates. Then along came Roger Williams.

This extraordinary person to whom we owe much of the liberal thought which has come to inform our American progress arrived early in 1631. Although he was still in his middle twenties, he was a learned minister and a Puritan of importance in England. He was a protégé of the great lawyer Edward Coke, and a graduate of Charterhouse school and Pembroke College, Cambridge.[5] But his radical views had brought him to the attention of Laud, now Archbishop of Canterbury, and England had become too hot for him.

He was welcomed in Massachusetts Bay as any educated minister was in that day when such persons were rare and greatly needed. He was invited to assist at the Boston church and immediately shocked ministers and congregation by declining on the grounds that they weren't sufficiently "Separatist" and had not repented of

[4] Perry Miller: *The New England Mind: From Colony to Province* (Cambridge, Mass., 1953), p. 24.

[5] S. H. Brockunier: *The Irrepressible Democrat, Roger Williams* (New York, 1940), Chap. 1.

their onetime connection with the Church of England.[6] He was called then to the church at Salem (whose congregation was farther to the left), but within a few months he decided that even there the views were not radical enough to suit him. So he went to Plymouth, where the declared Separatists Bradford and Brewster promised an understanding of his convictions.

The tolerant Bradford thought him "a man godly and zealous, having many precious parts," and Williams seems to have gained friends and disciples during his first year there. Then, however, he "began to fall into some strange opinions" [7] to which uneasy members of the congregation called Bradford's attention. The first and most radical opinion was that civil magistrates should have no power in spiritual matters—a direct blow at the very heart of the alliance of church and state. As Williams put it, there was no Scriptural authority for enforcement by the civil government of the commandments of the "first table." [8] This table held the first four commandments of the decalogue—namely, those dealing with the unique God, with idolatry, with blasphemy, and with the Sabbath. If Williams's opinion were accepted, therefore, no judge might sentence a man to punishment for profane speaking or Sabbath-breaking—two of the most heinous crimes in the list! In such a case, of what use were the stocks, pillories, "bilbowes," whipping-posts, or even the magistrates themselves? If sins of this deep dye should go unpunished, the entire Bible commonwealth would dissolve in corruption!

Perhaps, however, even this might have been forgiven by the advanced thinker Bradford had it been a mere opinion. There is much evidence that the Plymouth governor respected convictions that differed sharply from his own. But when, as certain church members alleged, Williams went "from opinion to practice" and tried to "impose" some of his revolutionary views upon his congregation, it was upsetting and "for a time the church here went under some hard censure by his occasion." [9] So he left Plymouth, and Salem, despite the cloud he was now under, took him back.

Before he left, however, he committed what was probably the most disturbing "error" of his career—this time not religious but po-

[6] Narragansett Club Publications, VI, 356.
[7] Bradford: op. cit., p. 257.
[8] Winthrop: op. cit., I, 62, 154.
[9] Bradford: op. cit., p. 257.

litical. He had come to know and love the Indians. He was one of the very few New England clerics who was concerned about the welfare and happiness of the natives. He looked upon them as human beings entitled to certain rights and privileges—not as an inferior race of unredeemable heathen. He even learned certain of the tribal languages. Finally he was so stirred by what he considered the unjust treatment of these aboriginal Americans by the English that his conscience overcame his discretion.

He wrote, then, a treatise maintaining that the English king had no right to give grants and patents to land that belonged to the Indians, and that in doing it James had "told a solemn public lie." [1] Nothing could have been more unfortunate than such a word at that time. New England was already under suspicion among orthodox Englishmen. It seemed to the people of Plymouth and the Bay that such a criticism of royalty might do them great harm in the mother country. Furthermore, it was a blow at the very existence of the New England settlements.

In his Journal, Winthrop states that Williams tried to make amends for this essay, saying that it had been written for Bradford's private consideration; but he never repented of his belief, which he reiterated in later writings.

In July 1635, Williams was haled before the General Court and charged with his dangerous opinions. In September, when he still refused to recant, the sentence of banishment was pronounced against him.[2]

Historians ever since have been arguing about the justice of this verdict. Yet it is hard to see how, in the context, anything else was possible. In any case, we may feel profound gratitude for the outcome. For this great zealot established in his exile what became the colony of Rhode Island and introduced there the principle of religious liberty, the New World's greatest tradition. In Providence, which he founded in the first year after his banishment, even Jews, Quakers, and Anabaptists were not molested in their religious exercise. If Roger Williams had been tolerated or ignored in Massachusetts Bay, a signal reform in Puritan thinking might have been long delayed. If his teaching had prevailed among many people,

[1] Winthrop: op. cit., I, 116.

[2] *Records of the Governor and Company of the Massachusetts Bay in New England*, N. B. Shurtleff, editor (Boston, 1853–4), I, 161.

Massachusetts might have been split by a destructive schism. That he should have built a new "Zion" in the wilderness from which, in the course of time, the light of freedom would go out to illumine a continent and make America a haven for all the world's oppressed was a far happier circumstance.

5

Roger Williams posed the first threat to the security of theocracy in New England. The second was, in some ways, so puzzling in its detail as to be almost incomprehensible to the modern mind. It followed so close on the heels of the heretical behavior of Williams that it made the Fathers fear for the very existence of the Bible state.

The second heretic was a woman. This fact in itself gave rise to special scandal in a day when the feminine mind was not expected to express itself in public. She was not a witch. She seems, indeed, to have been a person of godly and spiritual disposition with a most urgent conscience and a strong missionary sense and, by the unlettered and otherwise unprivileged part of the population, greatly loved.

Anne Hutchinson came with her husband, William, in 1634. In her first year in Boston she was known for her charity, her kind offices to the sick, and her general helpfulness to all troubled souls. In the second year, however, it was rumored that she talked too much about theology. The elders, pastors, and teachers of the churches were expected to control in matters of doctrine, and no mere member of a congregation—and a woman at that—was supposed to "intermeddle" in that realm.[3]

The alarming thing, however, was that by 1636 she had quietly acquired a very considerable following. Many women and a sprinkling of men used to gather at her house to hear her "prophesy." She seems to have had a gift of language and a convincing wit. It became her practice to comment each week on the sermon of the previous Sabbath, and when her drastic revisions of the accepted tenets began to arouse her disciples to personal vilification of the ministers, there was fear in the high places.

[3] For full details of this "Antinomian controversy," see Charles Francis Adams: *Three Episodes of Massachusetts History* (Boston, 1892), Vol. I, Part II.

The doctrinal issues are almost impossible for the modern reader to disentangle from the theological jargon of the period. Actually it is not necessary to make the effort, as the true conflict was more concerned with politics than with religion. The doctrines were so easy to misunderstand and misinterpret, and even the Scriptural documentation so varied and so often contradictory, that only the learned could be sure what the orthodox faith really was. In Massachusetts the ministers in power, therefore, had been obliged to specify the dogma that was right and that which was wrong after they had worked it out with long study and longer prayer.

The point was—though the issues were far vaguer than in the case of Williams—that any deviation from the line laid down by the clergy in power was an instant danger to the state. The potential dissent among the people was so strong that any change of emphasis in the doctrines of "grace" and "good works" was likely to split the church wide open, providing personal antagonism was present. In Boston, Anne's following grew menacingly large. Her appeal was to the humble, the lowly, the unreflective, the actual illiterate. As Samuel Eliot Morison says, her meetings "fed the belief, dear to religious fanatics in all ages, that God was more likely to reveal his truth to an ignorant than to an educated person." [4] This was precisely the opposite view to that of the erudite clergy at that very moment helping to found Harvard College. As always, it was possible to arouse among the masses contempt for the intellectuals—in later days called "braintrusters," "highbrows," or "eggheads"—and Mistress Hutchinson aroused it. Thus, in the election year of 1637 there were two angrily contending parties and the wilderness Zion—already proud, aloof, and extremely snobbish—was on the brink of real disaster.

The threat was the re-election of the young governor, Harry Vane, who—to the astonishment and chagrin of the ministers and magistrates—had revealed sympathy for Anne. It was certain that at the election, always held in Boston, his party and Anne's would win—so great had become her following there among the regenerate as well as among the crowds. Thus, at the last minute the Fathers decided that if the end was to save the state, the end would justify any means. The means they decided upon was to move the election to

[4] Samuel E. Morison: *Builders of the Bay Colony* (Boston, 1930), pp. 119, 120.

Newtown (Cambridge)—so far away in 1637 that the Boston voters could not get there in time to vote. There, surrounded by their own cohorts, the "good" Puritans overthrew Harry Vane and salvaged the commonwealth intact for the glory of God.

What followed was the sort of purge that always becomes necessary from time to time in an authoritarian state. Anne was put on trial. In it she talked some of the most eloquent nonsense that had so far been heard in the Bible state. Perhaps not twenty people on each side knew what she was talking about—only that in some foggy way she had strayed from the "line." Probably only a small proportion of the people of both parties knew what the doctrinal words meant. They were aligned, as many political parties have since been, behind slogans. The phrases "Covenant of Grace" and "Covenant of Works" meant as much or as little as the "Cross of Gold" meant to the supporters of Bryan in 1896 or the "Four Freedoms" to those of Roosevelt in 1940. But in the 1630's the cards were stacked.

For a while the magistrates and ministers conducting the trial were lost in the flood of dialectic. But then Anne Hutchinson gave them something hard and concrete to work upon. God, she said, had revealed himself to her in ecstatic visions. Although this was accepted procedure a few generations later, it was held blasphemy by the hierarchy of Massachusetts Bay in the first decade of its settlement, especially when described by a wicked, female schismatic. So Anne Hutchinson, like Roger Williams, was banished and, like him, went to a Rhode Island plantation. Six years later, after she had moved to Pelham Bay, "it pleased God" that she and all but one of her family should be brutally massacred by Indians.[5]

In the same season the Reverend Wheelwright, who had supported her, was also banished with two of his followers and, moving north, founded new, freer communities in New Hampshire.

Thus, radiating out from the rigid Puritan colony, other, more liberal consciences moved into new, fallow places in the vast emptiness. The realization was growing that in this wonderful land there was room for everything; that freedom for every shade of faith, for every color of belief in God and worship, lay just beyond some sector of the horizon.

[5] Charles Francis Adams: *Antinomianism* (Boston, 1894), pp. 93, 94.

6

The behavior of both the Pilgrims and the Puritans is particularized in the court records. From them we may gain a fair understanding of the prevailing morality and of the ethical attitudes of clergy and magistrates. In appraising these things, however, we must remember how the community was divided. The "saints"—the minority—were, in general, law-abiding, sincere in their professions of belief, and truly devoted to their churches and their ministers. The black marks in the books are mostly against the "strangers" who came, like camp-followers, with the expeditions for economic rather than religious reasons. These workers, professional soldiers, and servants were necessary to the community, but they constituted a disorderly element. They committed most of the crimes and misdemeanors and received the most severe punishments. While lapses by the "saints" were overlooked or lightly punished, the hand of the law came down heavily on the unredeemed majority.

Many of the workers were apprentices—boys bound for a term of years to an artisan who lodged, clothed, and fed them. A number of the children and adolescents—boy and girl servants and apprentices—had been kidnapped in the streets of London and other cities and shipped across to help fill the pressing needs of the scantily populated, hard-working colonial communities. This "spiriting away" of young people grew eventually into a highly profitable business, and it became a natural target for the reformers. Meanwhile, it is hardly surprising that persons so treated should have been wanton or criminal in their conduct.

Drunkenness and theft were at the top of the list. Murder was rare. Special sins against the religious code were common among the "strangers": sentences of whipping, branding, pillory, and stocks were given at every session of the courts for swearing and for breaches of the Sabbath. Sexual crimes ran from simple fornication to sodomy and bestiality. Lurid details of the sins against nature appear on the Plymouth court records, and a section of Bradford's history is devoted to "Opinions of the Ministers on Unnatural Vice," in which certain of the more sensational terms are couched in Latin.[6]

[6] Bradford: op. cit., pp. 404–13. See also *Plymouth Colony Records*, N. B. Shurtleff, editor (Boston, 1855–61), I, 64.

It seems to us that there was unnecessary cruelty in the punishment of some of the lapses. For example, there are many charges of "fornication" based solely on the fact that babies were born seven months or less after marriage. For this, men were whipped while their humiliated and agonized wives were set in the stocks to watch the whipping. There were other cases of fornication which had no consequences, yet they were discovered and punished. It is a cause of wonder how so many of these incidents came to light until we realize that the communities were exceedingly small, that everyone could (and did) watch everyone else, that the houses had but one room so that privacy was difficult, and that many persons were so frightened of hellfire that they confessed in the hope that even a Calvinist God would forgive. Nevertheless, sexual delinquency must have been frequent indeed, assuming that for every published episode there were many others that remained unrevealed.

For common civil offenses, public mortification was the usual punishment. Stocks, pillories, and whipping-posts were in central places in the towns so that culprits were at the mercy of insulting crowds. This was a strong deterrent to members of the upper classes, and for the wealthy and highborn the magistrates often substituted fines for public shame. But the miserable petty thief, the drunkard, the boys and girls whose desires were too urgent had to bear the leers of the multitude. In addition to their hours in the stocks or the lashes ("stripes") of the whip, a scarlet letter was often ordered to be worn for months or a year: D for drunkard, T for thief, A for adulterer.

The death penalty was prescribed for murder, rape, adultery, or filial disobedience by adolescents over sixteen, and, in Massachusetts Bay, for persistent blasphemy of a certain degree. Except for murder and "bestiality," however, execution was rare, virtually nonexistent. Unlike old England, where men and women and even children in this time were put to death for stealing a loaf of bread, New England valued human life far too much to exact the capital penalty if it could be avoided. The land was too big, the population too small, labor too scarce, and death by accident or sickness too common to allow for any unnecessary sacrifice.

Crimes against church and state were punished with a severity which reflects the fears of the theocratic ruling class. Thus, for instance, Henry Lynn was "whipped and banished the plantation . . .

for writing into England falsely and maliciously against the government. . . ."[7] John Lee was whipped and fined "for calling Mr. Roger Ludlow false-hearted knave" and other similar names,[8] and the punishment was repeated a few months later for speaking reproachfully of the governor, saying that he "was but a lawyer's clerk," "had no more understanding than himself," and that the court made "laws to pick men's purses." To demonstrate his contempt, Lee enticed the governor's maid into a cornfield and "abused" her.[9] Philip Ratcliffe, a servant, "being convict . . . of most foul, scandalous invectives against our churches and government, was censured to be whipped, lose his ears, and be banished the plantation. . . ."[1]

In spite of the coarse and mean crimes, however, and the brutal punishments, and in spite of an increasingly morbid attitude toward certain normal human weaknesses, the towns and farms of New England were far more moral and wholesome than most of their counterparts in Europe. Difficult as the bonded element might be, once the indentured term was finished, large numbers of the servants settled on lands of their own, and their descendants produced some of our most honored families. Some ran away from their masters to find freedom and adventure in the wilds of the frontier. Even the convicts that were deported from England into the colonies to get rid of them were somehow purged in the wilderness away from the crowding and poverty of a "wearied" Old World.

Somber stories are told of the Massachusetts Puritans, and we have been given ugly pictures. Macaulay, writing some two centuries later, described the English Puritans from whom they came as "pharisees," loathing all fun and sport, enemies of the arts and of music, drab in dress and sour of face,[2] and this portrait was magnified by American historians, who laid many of our latter-day sins at the door of these ancestors and predecessors. Later, diligent researches by "objective" writers found fallacies in the picture and, rushing to the other extreme, glorified the New England Puritans

[7] *Records of the Court of Assistants of Massachusetts Bay* (Boston, 1901–28), II, 19.

[8] Ibid., II, 43.

[9] Ibid., II, 49.

[1] Winthrop: op. cit., I, 64.

[2] *History of England,* I, 60, 61.

beyond reason. Somewhere between the two appraisals lies the truth.

We cannot judge these people outside the context of ignorance, superstition, cruelty, despotism, bigotry, coarseness, and ugly manners of seventeenth-century England. Nor can we escape repugnance in the backward look at the dreary Lord's Days, the stocks, pillories, and whipping-posts, the absence of dance and show and sport which seem so essential to modern American living. The best we can do is to accept the Puritan faults where we find them, and to believe that with all of them they established a moral basis upon which a goodly part of our later society has been built.

Chapter IV

New Wildernesses

IT IS POPULARLY believed among Americans that religious toleration in this country stemmed from an original and unique concept held by Roger Williams. Yet as we go back over the sequence of phases through which English society was passing in the seventeenth century, liberty of conscience appears to us as a historical necessity. The wide reading of Scripture in the vernacular gave rise to a whole spectrum of doctrinal colors that shaded subtly from one into another. But simultaneously with this divergence the Protestant world was taking on many other than religious concerns. For England, the commercial horizon was widening. According to some writers, the Protestant ethic was a factor in the march toward capitalism.[1]

In England, moreover, the political crisis made tolerance expedient among Puritans. Already in the 1630's the forces which would one day overthrow Charles I were consolidating and gaining power. As Puritan numbers increased in Parliament, and the line of cleavage grew more distinct, the various kinds of Protestants forgot their hostility to become "Roundheads" together. If revolution should come, even the hated Anabaptists and all sorts of extreme Separatists would be needed in the line-up against king and aristocracy. Thus, Puritans could forgive the hated extremists to enlist them against a king they hated more.

This urgency in England was not felt across the ocean. In Massachusetts Bay and the new settlements in the Connecticut Valley, the radical sects remained despised and persecuted. As has frequently happened in history, the former radicals among the Puritans became ultra-conservative. This part of New England set its face stolidly against every liberal gesture, against any leniency toward those

[1] R. H. Tawney: *Religion and the Rise of Capitalism* (New York, 1926), *passim.*

who diverged in doctrine from the "saints." After banishing Roger Williams and Anne Hutchinson, the divines and magistrates of the Bay colony became more bitter than ever in their fight against heresy.

In the 1640's the isolation was beginning that was to make New England a separate nation. It was a new kind of isolation. In the beginning there had been the isolation of distance, the isolation caused by a perilous ocean whose long crossing had made an interval when the immigrants had seemed out of the world, in the hands of God. Yet it was the God of home, England's God, in whose hands they were, and, once landed, once suffering and dying on the alien soil, hearts and minds turned toward that special God and country in terrible nostalgia.

The Puritan colonists had first thought of New England only as an extension of England.[2] In this remote place—but still England—they could work out their reform, their purification in peace; from there, in time, it would spread back all over the homeland. This was the thinking of the founding divines: of John Cotton, of Winthrop, and of Richard Mather. They echoed the words of Higginson: "We do not go to New England as Separatists from the Church of England . . . but we go to practice the positive part of church reformation." [3] They did, in fact, establish another church, but their homesickness would not let them admit divorce from the old.

Keeping these feelings alive was the constant stream of immigrants through the 1630's. These were the Puritans who had been hounded by Archbishop Laud with the support of the increasingly arbitrary Charles I. The relentless drive was directed toward solidifying the episcopacy of the Church of England and forcing the observance of those rites and ceremonies that the Puritans most hated. The unhappy folk seeking refuge in the New World from religious persecution were, therefore, intensely zealous for reform. Then, suddenly, the migration stopped and the Puritans in New England were cut off from their fellows in the mother country.

The migration stopped when the Puritans in England—Puritans of all shades and tempers—began to rally round the Long Parliament in 1640. From being outcasts and victims of the cruelties inflicted by Charles and by Laud in the King's tyrannical years the

[2] Miller: *The New England Mind: From Colony to Province,* pp. 4–6.
[3] See p. 31 *supra.*

Puritans had come, at last, into control. Their cause was now in England itself. Escape was finished. And the new Parliament, with its new army in which Oliver Cromwell was rising to leadership, would need all of them.

With this steady, heartening flow of reinforcement for their purpose interrupted, the New England Puritans began to think of their church as standing on its own and so of their colony's having achieved a spiritual independence of England. In such a mood, they could withdraw more deeply into their intolerance, repudiating the English liberals who, under pressure of the crusade, favored liberty of conscience within the Protestant framework. The Williams and Hutchinson episodes had already scared them away from independent thought. In 1640 we see the distinction in sharp clarity: in England tolerance was consolidating the forces of political reform; in New England it was a peril to the political structure.

There were, to be sure, other factors in the growing sense of separation. The suffering that had kept alive the homesickness was over. The American land had been almost unbelievably responsive: testimony to the Lord's satisfaction with the colonists' behavior. There was an abundance of good things as rich and sweet as the milk and honey of Canaan. Finally, a new generation was growing up, American-born: children who knew of the early hardships only secondhand from stories told at their fathers' knees. Thus there came about a new American integrity and, for the first time, a separate American conscience.

2

It was not the idea that conscience should be free that caused the banishment of Roger Williams. Only later did the concept come to him, though it was a natural outgrowth of certain of his other beliefs. He was sent into exile because he preached the separation of church and state—removing from the magistrates the power to enforce religious conformity; because he preached total separation from the Church of England; because he denied the power of the King to grant American lands without consent of the Indian owners; and because he preached against accepting the oaths of the "unregenerate." There was nothing particularly liberal about all this, and he insisted on his doctrines with a stubborn fanaticism greater than that of the Massachusetts clerics.[4]

Then, in the long loneliness, the bitter hardship, of his winter trek to the Narragansett country other thoughts came to him. We know little of the journey and only those results of his meditations which appear in his later writings. From the inarticulate, illiterate boy, Thomas Angell, who went with him we have learned nothing. Angell seems almost to have been a part of Roger or a satellite reflecting the light and heat of him but without words.

All along the frozen overland trail there was a constant spiritual intimacy between Williams and the Indians. He learned their language, making his notes into a kind of dictionary or grammar valuable to ethnologists ever since. Evidently he was greatly beloved by these natives. They took him into their primitive homes—wigwams with fires burning in the center and the smoke moving uncertainly through holes in the tops: "filthy," he said, writing later in the mood of a cleanly Englishman [5]—and he was deeply moved by the warm friendship emanating along with the stink from the crowded naked bodies sharing their shelter with the alien white.

One would expect a religious fanatic with Williams's charm to try to convert these friends. But his conscience would not let him press the Christian God upon the Indians with any but the gentlest presentation. Though he did not say so, he was probably impressed with their own serene faith. He was certainly moved by their tolerant attitude—so different from the harsh bigotry he had lately known—and this must have confirmed him in any thought of liberty he entertained.

> They have a modest religious persuasion [he wrote] not to disturb any man, either themselves, English, Dutch or any, in their conscience and worship; and therefore say, "Peace, hold your peace." [6]

It must have been a relief to Williams after the loud, complex arguments of Boston and Salem to hear these words spoken in the forest hush. In this same time, apart from all the civilization he had ever known, he found among the savages not only a disposition against disturbing the worship of "any man" but an eager willing-

[4] Perry Miller: *Roger Williams* (Indianapolis, 1953), *passim.*
[5] Ibid., p. 50.
[6] Narragansett Club Publications (Providence, 1866), I, 153.

ness to listen to a man talking of another faith than theirs. Telling later of his experience in the wilderness, and explaining that "little could I speak to their understanding" because of the variety of their dialects, he added:

> Yet so much (through the help of God) I did speak, of the true and living only wise God, of the creation, of man, and his fall from God, &c., that at the parting many burst forth, "Oh when will you come again, to bring us more news of this God?" [7]

It is probable that as much of Williams's fascination for these Indians lay in the spell of his personality as in what he said, for even his enemies have given testimony to an appeal that often disarmed them. Certainly much of his doctrinal exposition and even of his passionate diatribe against bigotry is tedious with an overloading of words and surfeit of repetition, and even in a day when such things were current in theological debate they would have bored and irritated his listeners but for the bright fire which seemed to play round him, the unfailing warmth of his presence, the reaching out of his sympathy and friendship to followers and opponents alike.

He and Angell came, in the spring, to the estuary of Narragansett Bay called Great Salt River, and there, according to his scruple, he arranged with two Indian sachems to buy from them the land for a settlement. He named it Providence in gratitude for his survival; presently he was joined by other exiles and by his own wife and children, who had made their way overland in the summer.

There was nothing exceptional about the physical fact of the little community of one street along the river, surrounded by wilderness unexplored but by the red hunters. Little settlements of the sort were springing up everywhere: along the Connecticut and the Hudson and the Kennebec—wherever that urgent impulse of the migrant English to get away from one another, to escape crowded society, was operating. So Roger Williams set no landmark of history with his Providence. But in its law he set a milestone in the history of the American conscience for which he must be honored while there is still freedom in our land.

The order echoed the Indian words "Peace, hold your peace." No man must be molested for his religion. Whatever faith he might

[7] Ibid., I, 49.

choose, that he must be allowed to hold, be he Jew or Turk or pagan. The magistrates should have no power to intervene in the affairs of any church except in order to keep the civil peace. They were empowered, however, to act against violators of Williams's decree. A year after the founding of Providence one of its citizens lost his franchise "for restraining of the libertie of conscience." [8]

As we have seen, the concept was neither original nor unique with Roger Williams. It had been of long tenure in Holland; it was held by the Dutch in America, and it was spreading among the "Independents" in England. It is not probable that the Indians gave Williams the idea, though no doubt they strengthened the thought which had evolved from his belief in the separation of church and state. But Providence saw its first application in the English colonies of North America. From there the practice spread, slowly through New England, more rapidly through the middle and southern colonies, until, at last, no American could deny it and the concept was crystallized a century and a half later in the words of the federal Bill of Rights.

In another particular, Providence was a departure from colonial custom. While it was true that sporadic settlements were occurring through the backwoods, all were attached to some established and chartered colony owing allegiance specified in words written on parchment to the English crown. But Providence was attached to nothing. On the contrary, it represented a definite gesture of disattachment from Massachusetts Bay. It was an outlawed community, a refuge, legally speaking, from justice. It had no charter. No royal patent appeared to specify the Narragansett country.

The result of this uncertainty was continual conflict. Even before Williams had settled on the bank of Great Salt River, he had been pushed away from the first site he had chosen by Governor Winslow of Plymouth, who claimed the territory and was afraid of "displeasing the Bay" by letting him squat there.[9] It was a time when the gentler Plymouth people felt obliged to watch their *p*'s and *q*'s in regard to their strong, rigid Massachusetts neighbors. Now the communities of Warwick, Portsmouth, and Newport, formed of various sorts of Massachusetts dissidents, were growing up in the

[8] *Rhode Island Colonial Records,* compiled by J. R. Bartlett (Providence, 1856–1865), I, 16.

[9] Miller: *Roger Williams,* p. 229.

unchartered territory. The arguments over the rights involved were carried on by such vigorous exiles as William Coddington and the heretic Samuel Gorton, who was sheltering the devil's advocate, poor Anne Hutchinson. So Roger Williams was forced to go to England to secure some sort of legal instrument for his community, and there, from 1640 to 1644, in the midst of the great English Civil War, he conducted his classic fight for the liberty of the American conscience.

England, grown liberal to Protestant diversification, was good ground for his work. He had the sympathy and friendship of two of the most prominent Englishmen of the day, Milton and Cromwell, though he went further than either in his tolerance, being lenient even toward Catholics and opposed to the persecution of the Anglicans. But though his propaganda was printed in England, it was directed against the theocracy of Massachusetts Bay and the minister John Cotton in particular. It was not only concerned with religion; it advocated democracy in advance of prevailing acceptance even by radicals, and in these writings we have what is probably the first suggestion of the sovereignty of the people in American literature. The climax of his effort was a pamphlet, which today's reader finds exceedingly difficult, called *The Bloudy Tenant of Persecution.* It found ready response in England and turned English eyes with disapproval across the Atlantic to Massachusetts Bay, the target of the attack.

He secured his charter to "Providence Plantations." Whatever his enemies might think about a political motive in discountenancing powerful Massachusetts, which was trying to lay claim to his territory, the fact was that he wrote from pure zeal for his cause, not for his land.

To Governor John Winthrop he was so astonishingly forgiving that it seems there must have been some secret understanding between them, dangerous to confess but compensating to both their consciences. Williams stated that Winthrop even secretly connived at the Narragansett exile.[1] Throughout the governor's life they continued to correspond with full measure of affection at the heads and tails of their letters. And Williams, in his turn, furnished Winthrop valuable intelligence about the moves of hostile Indian tribes toward the bitter conflicts that laid waste much prospering New Eng-

[1] Massachusetts Historical Society Collections, 1st Series, I, 276.

land country. In his heart Winthrop undoubtedly felt occasional misgivings about the theocratic dicta, yet he knew that if he relaxed the rule, his colony, deeply dedicated to the principle of the "national" covenant, would fall apart.

When he returned, even the parliamentary charter was disputed. It was fought by the Bay colony to the north and by William Coddington of Portsmouth and Newport to the south. In all this difficulty Williams was far from the adroit antagonist or practical organizer. His community suffered poverty and dissent. It was invaded by Baptists, Jews, and Quakers, who could find no refuge elsewhere. Williams was unable to cope with the physical conditions consequent upon the influx. He was constantly preoccupied with his communion with God, with his personal theology, becoming, after other experiments, a "seeker"—an astonishing sect among the complacent groups whom God had so positively assured, in its admission that it did not know all of the truth. There were times when he thought of leaving the group of planters for a forest hermitage; again, he thought of devoting his life to the Indians.[2] Yet in the end he worked persistently, if not always effectively, for his community's welfare, and on a second visit to England won a second charter guaranteeing his independence of Coddington and endowing the whole of "Rhode Island Colony and Providence Plantations" with legal rights.

Perhaps no American hero has been so variously appraised as Roger Williams. Some of the estimates are obviously biased by theological prejudice. Adherents of the old Congregational polity have slighted his importance. Others have endowed him with qualities and concepts to which he never pretended, explaining him, for example, as a forerunner of Deism, or, with Vernon Parrington, maintaining that he followed a social rather than a theological direction in his thinking. There has been a strange mélange of opinion. In the residue of fact we can find only that he was the pioneer of the practice of religious liberty, that he was one of the first Englishmen who reached and moved the American aborigines, that he understood practical democracy ahead of his time, that he was dedicated to the search for truth rather than to its Scriptural revelation, that he read the Bible as allegory rather than as history and that he was a person

[2] C. M. Andrews: *The Colonial Period of American History* (New Haven, 1936), II, 5–6.

of compelling warmth and—for all the high fury of his writing—of great personal gentleness.[3]

3

While the American conscience was finding its first freedom on Narragansett Bay and the island of Aquidneck, the theocracy was expanding in another direction, carrying with it its covenants, its fasts and thanksgivings, its stocks, bilboes, pillories, ducking-stools, whipping-posts, and other equipment of the church state.

The great river whose sources were in the mountains of the territory that was then New Hampshire, which ran south through Massachusetts and the wilderness beyond into Long Island Sound, had been explored and advertised by Dutch and English. It had been called by various names in an attempt to reproduce the Indian designation. The easiest of these was "Connecticut." The wilderness valley of it, southwest of Boston, was said to be fertile. Also, in 1634 it had pleased God to wipe out most of its Indian population by a second epidemic of smallpox. It appeared that the divinely inspired affliction had infected the more peaceable tribes, sparing the warlike Pequots, who eventually had to be suppressed with arms. However, the Lord's apparent good office in the first instance seemed to suggest that the valley was another Promised Land.

The impulse this time does not seem to have been religious. In the towns of Newtown (Cambridge) and Dorchester, where the migrations began, the discontent seems to have had economic and political rather than conscientious causes, though these things are not always easy to separate. These towns, so near Boston, had grown crowded. The productiveness of the soil had ebbed.[4] Over their people, the shadow of Massachusetts Bay's General Court had apparently become irksome. The magistrates had too much arbitrary power. Newtown's spiritual leader, Thomas Hooker, though conservative in religion, was politically radical. He did not think it necessary to be a church member—one of God's elect—to be able to vote for civil officers, and many folk in the fringe of Boston held to this view.

[3] Vernon Parrington: *Main Currents in American Thought* (New York, 1927), I, 67. Miller: *Roger Williams*, p. 27.

[4] *Connecticut Colonial Records*, compiled by J. H. Trumbull and C. J. Hoadly (Hartford, 1850–90), I, 582.

In any case, there was much fasting and prayer before the decision. The overland trek was not easy. The women and children would be exposed to severe hardship. The consciences of these people had to be satisfied that they were not being disloyal to Massachusetts. They were, indeed, accused by the stay-at-homes of "turning their backs upon us" and seeking "the good of their cattle more than of their commonwealth." [5]

They moved in 1635 and 1636. They called the river towns they established Hartford, Wethersfield, and Windsor. Beyond the ambiguous process of purchase from the Indians, they had no title to the land. This may have disturbed the more honorable among them as well as those who feared eviction on this account, for when an independent group of settlers arrived from England with what looked like a patent, they accepted its authority. In the end they let a commission appointed by the Boston court draw up a scheme of government for them.

This separation from the parental flock was not considered a grave offense even though its reasons were economic. The Lord, after all, had meant his chosen to prosper. If the land round Boston was sandy and not fit for large populations, then Boston was no longer Canaan; the milk and honey flowed somewhere else. This justification for moving into vacant land where prosperity was forecast runs all through American history. It has often been accounted a sin not to use God's benefits to the full even if one accumulates great riches by so doing. In the migrations to the Connecticut valley we see one of the early expressions of what came to be a tradition and, in the ripeness of our golden age, was called "manifest destiny."

That the migrants had not, however, separated from the church polity of Massachusetts Bay was soon evident. The laws laid down by the new government, in which John Winthrop, Jr., was governor in 1636, were as strict as those of Massachusetts itself. The punishments prescribed and the general discipline exacted were even more stringent. Through the 1640's the legislation became progressively more severe until in 1650 it was assembled into the code which has since acquired the epithet of the "blue" laws of Connecticut. The strictures on nonconformity were based on the old intolerance. Heretics were to be hounded out of the colony as certainly as in the old theocracy. The only difference was a political one: it was decreed

[5] Massachusetts Historical Society Collections, 4th Series, VII, 25.

that all freemen might vote and that church membership was not required. The new colony was, however, far enough from democracy to satisfy the Puritans, who had much the same horror of that philosophy that Americans in the 1950's have of communism. The General Court soon shut down on any approach to a universal franchise by decreeing that a man must be approved of by the court in order to vote.

In 1642 twelve "capital laws" were established. In each the punishment was mandatory; each was given Scriptural sanction. Here they are, with their Old Testament references:

> 1. If any man after legal conviction shall have or worship any other God but the Lord God he shall be put to death. *Deut. 13:6, 17:2; Ex. 22:20.*

The ambiguity here is in the arrangement (as is often the case in early American rhetoric); the meaning being, of course, that the death sentence shall be executed after legal conviction.

> 2. If any man or woman be a witch (that is) hath or consulteth with a familiar spirit, they shall be put to death. *Ex. 22:18; Lev. 20:27; Deut. 18:10, 11.*
>
> 3. If any man shall blaspheme the name of God the Father, Son or Holy Ghost, with direct, express, presumptuous or high-handed blasphemy, or shall curse God in like manner, he shall be put to death. *Lev. 24:15, 16.*
>
> 4. If any person shall commit any wilful murder, which is manslaughter committed upon malice, hatred or cruelty, not in a man's necessary and just defence, nor by mere casualty against his will, he shall be put to death. *Ex. 21:12, 13, 14; Num. 35:30, 31.*
>
> 5. If any person shall slay another through guile, either by poisonings or other such devilish practice, he shall be put to death. *Ex. 21:14.*
>
> 6. If any man or woman shall lie with any beast or brute creature, by carnal copulation, they shall be put to death, and the beast shall be slain and buried. *Lev. 20:15, 16.*
>
> 7. If any man lieth with mankind as he lieth with a woman, both of them have committed abomination, they both shall surely be put to death. *Lev. 20:13.*
>
> 8. If any person commiteth adultery with a married or espoused wife, the adulterer and the adulteress shall surely be put to death. *Lev. 20:10, 18, 20; Deut. 22:23, 24.*

> 9. If any man shall forcibly and without consent ravish any maid or woman that is lawfully married or contracted, he shall be put to death. *Deut. 22:25.*
>
> 10. If any man stealeth [kidnaps] a man or mankind, he shall be put to death. *Ex. 21:16.*
>
> 11. If any man rise up by false witness, wittingly and of purpose to take away any man's life he shall be put to death. *Deut. 19:16, 18, 19.*
>
> 12. If any man shall conspire or attempt any invasion, insurrection or rebellion against the commonwealth, he shall be put to death.[6]

To these were added, in 1650, two statutes against children in accordance with Mosaic law:

> 13. If any child or children above sixteen years old and of sufficient understanding shall curse or smite their natural father or mother, he or they shall be put to death, unless it can be proved, etc.,

the proof being of extreme provocation or self-defense. The fourteenth law is similar, prescribing death for incorrigibly disobedient sons.[7]

These "capital laws" are characteristic of American Calvinist legislation. They had to be written on the books. Once they were coded, the Lord presumably would be satisfied. When the persons charged with the capital offenses came to trial, some extenuating circumstance was nearly always found. The little river towns could not afford to have their populations reduced by these punitive methods practiced by the Hebrews when men were expendable. Yet if they had not coded them, the wrath of God might have descended upon these covenanted Puritans in storm and drought, flood and pestilence.

This insistence upon legislation, whether or not it was enforced, was to become an American characteristic. The custom of disregarding the law—which has so horrified Europeans—came later. These so-called capital laws were for the most part obeyed, not from fear of the "mandatory" sentence, but from the general and natural fear of the substitute punishments: the fines, stocks, whippings, and brandings which were, in fact, abundantly administered.

When the court began writing sumptuary laws on their books, however, evasion and nullification began. Smoking, after tobacco

[6] *Connecticut Colonial Records,* I, 77, 78.

[7] Ibid., I, 515.

was found to be an abundant natural product of the Connecticut valley, was abjured for Connecticut citizens. The other uses of tobacco—chewing and snuffing—were equally abhorrent to the General Court unless a physician advised them for their famous medicinal properties! Out of such distaste came this extraordinary statute in 1647:

> It is ordered that no man within this colony, after the publication hereof, shall take any tobacco publicly in the street, nor shall any take it in the fields or woods, unless when they be on their travel or journey at least ten miles, or at the ordinary time of . . . dinner, or if it be not then taken, yet not above once in the day at most, and then not in company with any other. Nor shall any . . . take any tobacco in any house in the same town where he liveth with, and in the same company of, any more than one who useth . . . the same weed with him at that time. . . .[8]

Disentangled from its complicated verbiage, this order appears to encourage secret vice. The use of tobacco is permitted—though only just permitted—if it is not observed by more than one person. The limit here to one (indoors) is evidently designed to avoid the possibility of pleasure in the pursuit of this noxious exercise—the sight of a group laughing and talking while they smoked being, evidently, a horror to the court. This statute, obviously unenforceable as well as ludicrous, lasted only long enough to show the people that evasion was the only possible answer.

The legislation of private morals reached its ultimate in the separate colony of New Haven, founded by Theophilus Eaton and John Davenport in 1638. The New Haven "blue laws"—often stricter than those of Connecticut—were sometimes of a morbid nature that was almost neurotic, especially where they dealt with sex. The preoccupation of the New Haven clergy and magistrates with sin is graphically described by Charles M. Andrews:

> Drunkenness and sexual misdemeanors were "horrible miscarriages," for which those guilty were held accountable before God as well as the courts, and they were inquired into with a minuteness of scrutiny that has made it necessary in the case of sexual misdeeds, for the editors of the town and colony records to omit from the printed pages several portions of the original text. . . . Many lesser indulgences, such as cardplaying, dancing, and singing, were

[8] *Connecticut Colonial Records,* I, 153.

> frowned on and in part at least forbidden . . . but they were enjoyed on the sly. . . .[9]

In this short-lived but zealous colony which John Davenport thought of as an establishment of Christ's kingdom on earth, the denial of the franchise to those who were not church members was rigidly adhered to. This fact led to the abolition of the ancient institution of trial by jury, for, as Isabel M. Calder points out:

> a jury of non-church-members would have been an anomaly. Yet some of the towns of the colony were so small, and the church members so few, that after the elimination of interested parties and officers, a jury of twelve church-members could not have been impaneled.[1]

Such tyranny naturally led to discontent, and had not the colony been dissolved after the Restoration in England, there might have been a strong and open rebellion. New Haven was, however, absorbed by Connecticut in 1662.

4

By mid-century, New England designated an ecclesiastical rather than a geographical area. From the United Colonies of New England, a confederation adopted in the 1640's for defense and for spiritual consolidation, Rhode Island and New Hampshire were excluded as too liberal and Maine as Anglican. This nucleus of religious cohesion—Plymouth, Massachusetts Bay, Connecticut, and New Haven—grew more solidly together as defection and toleration surrounded it. Already, however, we see at the central core the threat of corruption. Already we see conscience leading in different directions. But we cannot ignore the importance of that core in the later history of American morality. The Puritan impulse was too strong to be defeated. It could be battered and altered, modified and mellowed. But all through the march of the frontier, in lonely outposts and crowded cities, in the drunken orgies of mining camps and the whorehouses of bonanza towns as well as in the vast diversity of churches, we shall sense its recurrence: sharp, acrid, and unmistakable, like a familiar smell.

[9] Andrews: op. cit., II, 180, 181.

[1] Isabel M. Calder: *The New Haven Colony* (New Haven, 1934), pp. 125, 126.

Chapter V

Mission in Virginia

PERHAPS more than other peoples Americans are prone to a sense of guilt in hindsight. In long aftermath, things seem wrong that were scarcely questioned when they happened. This may be because we have been given to extreme action on extreme impulses and events have moved too quickly for reflection. A few doubters have always spoken out: they have been shouted down—their voices drowned in the din following the swing of our emotional pendulum to the limit of its arc. This has been sporadically true, of course, of all sections of mankind. The mob outcry that screamed "Crucify him!" during Pilate's hesitation was merely the classic example. But in America there has been such haste in our history that thoughtless mass action has been more frequent and the regrets more acute than in slower-moving societies where there has been time to seek a balance.

Much of our thought today, in our more thoughtful maturity, is interlaced with misgivings about the Mexican War, the Reconstruction, the Spanish War, the Philippine Insurrection, the Panama Canal, the concentration camps for Japanese-Americans in the 1940's, the Yalta conference, the bombs of Hiroshima and Nagasaki—to recall only a handful—when in the fevered instants of action all these things seemed inevitable or patriotic. We have had time to figure out how they might all have been avoided. And this long afterthought has colored even some of the histories, so that it becomes difficult to recall events in the light of the mores, tempers, fears, and external pressures of the times in which they occurred.

Almost first on our recent agenda of remorse stands the American Indian. If we can believe the expressions of the late American conscience about this "noble savage," our English colonial ancestors treated him from the beginning with a subtle cruelty that was unprovoked; they exploited him with ruthless selfishness; when they could not annihilate him by force of arms, they corrupted him with liquor; they cheated him in every business deal, every treaty, every contract; they gave him diseases that decimated the tribes; he endured these things with long-suffering patience, and his occasional retaliation in massacres that have left indelible bloodstains on our history books was a justified revenge. These are twentieth-century concepts. Even when they are applied to our nineteenth-century behavior they tend to ignore legacies of emotion that have descended through generations of white Americans from the earliest times.

What we have done is to collect fragments of truth, divorce them from other fragments of an opposite color but equally true, and sew them into a fabric that bears little if any resemblance to the moral patterns of the times. Surely such sentiments as these would surprise the councilmen of the colonizing companies in seventeenth-century England. They would be incomprehensible to the trembling women of the Massachusetts Bay, shielding their children behind the palisades while their men were the targets of arrows shot from the dark woods by invisible raiders. And they would outrage the people of Jamestown as they contemplated the streams of blood flowing from their loved ones in March 1622 to stain the waters of Falling Creek.

There is truth, to be sure, in many items of our self-accusation. But three centuries ago there was little of the sense of the brotherhood of all mankind that we boast today. Inferior races were there to be exploited. If they impeded the European (especially the Englishman) in his march into the promised land God had prepared for him, they must either help him or be dealt with in such a way that they could not hinder him. We are shocked when a twentieth-century demagogue proclaims himself leader of a "master race," but in the early days of England's colonial activity this was becoming an accepted concept—at least among the "merchant adventurers" who staked the settlers. And even the notion of the "white man's burden" built up through long, successful colonial experiences had not yet occurred to the entrepreneurs of America.

There was a striking contrast in attitude between Anglo-Saxon and Latin colonizers. From both the Indian ultimately suffered, but the French and Spanish approaches left the white man with fewer regrets. First, the Latin colonists spent great effort on conversion; next, they practiced intermarriage. From the time of the sixteenth-century explorations when priests accompanied the explorers of the St. Lawrence, the French conscience was deeply concerned with religious missions. As with the Spaniards to the south, the spiritual conquest of the Indian went hand in hand with the acquisition of territory. The explorers reported their conquests to the king; the priests theirs to a cardinal.

At the same time that the souls of the redskin converts were being saved to the great credit of the Catholic Church, the race was being absorbed by the Europeans. Interracial sex relations were universal. There was scarcely a French *voyageur* in the Canadian woods without Indian blood. Among the Spaniards of Latin America the pure Indian race virtually disappeared. Before this, however, the Indians were used for the benefit of the Europeans. The Spanish exploited them as cheap—sometimes forced—labor and persecuted them if they rejected conversion; the French used them as front-line troops against the English or treated them unfairly in the fur trade. In the end the Indians were always submerged.

But they were not annihilated as they were by the English and those who lived under the English ægis. They were not immediately and deeply hurt in their pride as they were by Anglo-Saxon contempt. To the English, almost from the first, what we call "coexistence" was impossible. To the English, with rare exceptions—one in particular becoming part of our folklore—sex relations were taboo. And, also with a few exceptions, conversion to Christianity was neglected. In some of the earliest of the colonizing ventures, there was a good deal of propaganda beforehand about "preaching the Gospel to the heathen," but for the most part these intentions faded out when the Christians came face to face with their infidel neighbors.

It is the exceptions, however, to these rules that point up the Indian story in an exceedingly dramatic manner and introduce curious elements into our conscientious reflection. As we consider them in their romantic or macabre detail we become less sure that the deceit, the treachery, and the brutality were all on one side and the nobility all on the other.

2

When we review the tragic history of the first North American settlement at Jamestown, we see a strange interplay of friendly desire and suspicious fear on both sides. On their first landing, the Englishmen were attacked. After a day of exploring among "faire meadows and goodly tall Trees":

> At night, when wee were going aboard, there came the Savages creeping upon all foure, from the Hills, like Beares, with their Bowes in their mouthes, charged us very desperately in the faces, hurt Captaine Gabrill Archer in both his hands, and a sayler in two places of the body very dangerous. After they had spent their Arrowes, and felt the sharpnesse of our shot, they retired into the Woods with a great noise and so left us.[1]

At their next landing, however, Captain Newport faced the threatening savages unarmed and put his hand on his heart, whereupon the Indians laid down their bows, guided the Englishmen to their town, and put on a show of welcome with feasting, dancing, and religious ceremony that lasted several days. There seems indeed to have been a conflict between the kings of two tribes as to which should have the honor of entertaining the English. Yet all this time the English, remembering the first encounter and knowing of the Indians' extraordinary skill in forest fighting and ambuscade, were wary of treachery. And there seems to have been reason for their fears. Whatever the hospitality, the peace pipes, the gifts, the thanks, and the vows of friendship, the red men were always armed [2] and naturally dubious about the intents of a shipload of utter aliens with loud, explosive weapons marching into their territory. To Newport and Percy and Archer and to the other bold and wise people of the Virginia Company, understanding neither the speech, the grimaces, nor the inarticulate shouts of the natives, a battle seemed possible round every turn of the James River as they pursued their exploration.

[1] "Observations by George Percy," in *Narratives of Early Virginia,* Lyon G. Tyler, editor (New York, 1907), p. 10.

[2] Much has been made of the enormous advantage of the English arms. This seems to be based on an appraisal of much later developments. The effect of the English muskets on the Indians was mainly psychological because of the noise and smoke. But an Indian could shoot a dozen deadly arrows while the Englishman was reloading his inaccurate piece.

The whole sequence of events in Virginia suggests what we call psychological warfare or "cold war." There were bluffs, feints, appeasement, sparring for advantage on both the English and the Indian sides. To both, the fact of invasion must generally have been in mind. The alien white man was on land consecrated for centuries to native hunting and intertribal intercourse or conflict. He necessarily felt the Indian's prior possession either on his conscience or as an impediment to be removed as safely as possible. The Indians, scared by the noise of the gunpowder and the size of the ships, hoped by their welcomes, their ceremonies, their kings' messengers, their feasts, their gifts of venison and corn to stave off attack. The English, taking quick advantage of their impact, made further show of their strength with a fort and cannon, target practice, and arrow-proof mail.

But then a strange thing happened. In June, a month after the landing on James River, Captain Newport sailed away for England, "leaving us (one hundred and foure persons) verie bare and scantie of victualls, furthermore in warres and in danger of the Savages. . . ." [3] In August came the awful epidemic of dysentery. Day after day, men died.

> Our men were destroyed with cruell diseases, such as Swellings, Flixes, Burning Fevers, and by warres, and some departed suddenly, but for the most part they died of meere famine. There were never Englishmen left in a forreigne Country in such miserie as we were in this new discovered Virginia.[4]

Surely in this "starving time," as it was called, the savages surrounding the settlement in enormous quantity might easily have wiped out the little community. Yet in its extremity they saved it. Percy says that God "put a terrour in the Savages hearts" to keep them from attacking. But "after a while" he tells that

> It pleased God . . . to send those people which were our mortall enemies to releeve us with victuals, as Bread, Corne, Fish, and Flesh in great plentie, which was the setting up of our feeble men, otherwise we had all perished. Also we were frequented by divers Kings in the Countrie, bringing us store of provision to our great comfort.[5]

[3] *Narratives*, p. 20.
[4] Ibid., p. 21.
[5] Ibid., p. 22.

Captain John Smith, writing of the same time, also attributes the Indians' action to divine inspiration:

> But now was all our provision spent, . . . all helps abandoned, each houre expecting the fury of the Salvages; when God, the patron of all good indeavours, in that desperate extreamity, so changed the harts of the Salvages, that they brought such plenty of their fruits and provision, as no man wanted.[6]

Is the necessarily skeptical historian to accept the explanation that God so loved the English that he turned the enmity of the natives into a desire to save the invaders? This is, to be sure, the kind of reasoning that imbued all the effort of Britain's conquest of the North American East and the later conquest by the Americans of their own West. In Virginia, God turned the hearts of the savages to save the English. In Massachusetts and Connecticut, it pleased God to visit the Indians with a decimating epidemic of smallpox so that the English, for a time at least, need not worry. When in King Philip's and the Pequot wars God turned the hearts of the survivors against the Puritan settlers, it was on account of the New Englanders' sins. But when, fifteen years after their generous act, the hearts of the Pamunkens of the Tidewater turned violently against the Virginians, it is difficult to see God anywhere in the picture except, indeed, as a victim of Indian malice.

It is this phase that we are about to explore through some three acts of its drama and, as its curtain falls on both God and man, we see reasons for later English attitudes which cannot but relieve some of the severest twinges of our historical conscience.

3

The drama begins with the outstanding and celebrated exception to the English taboo of interracial sex relations: the marriage of the Emperor Powhatan's daughter to the Englishman who created the Virginia tobacco staple. From the beginning of the Jamestown settlement this charming and talented child, Pocahontas, seems to have felt drawn toward the white men. As John Smith and Christopher Newport paid their ceremonial visits to her father, she conceived a passion for Captain Smith which led her to help him in

[6] "The Proceedings of the English Colony in Virginia," in *Narratives*, p. 128.

many ways, even to the point of saving his life,[7] and though the captain never returned her love, he wrote of her as

> a child . . . which, not only for feature, countenance, and proportion, much exceedeth any of the rest of his people: but for wit and spirit, the only Nonpareil of his [Powhatan's] country.[8]

She is said, also, to have played near the Jamestown fort, turning handsprings with the English boys.[9] In any case, she seems to have undertaken a powerful liaison with the white men and to have had a profound influence for peace upon her proud father. And this great chieftain, in spite of some hostile acts, seems to have been one of the "good" Indians of Virginia's Tidewater history. In 1614, when Pocahontas married John Rolfe, Powhatan regarded it as a diplomatic union and, as a result of its successful conclusion, swore never during his lifetime to break the peace between his federation and the Virginia colony.

In England the marriage and Powhatan's oath brought about our second great exception to the English attitude: the determination on a large-scale conversion of the Indians, their baptism and indoctrination in the Anglican faith. There were, of course, later missionaries, such as Roger Williams and John Eliot; but this first truly zealous effort ended in a tragedy so spectacular that its failure may be partly responsible for the general abortion of English evangelism among the American natives.

Rolfe took his young bride to England. She was received there with recognition of her royal blood. The English in England had little understanding of what an American Indian really was, and to them a king's daughter was a king's daughter, be she red or white. In London she was received by the nobility and presented at court as a princess, and she seems to have behaved with a decorum that never betrayed her barbaric origin. But to the churchmen the most impressive fact of all was her baptism and her total renunciation of the idolatry of her race. If you could convert a king's daughter, why not all his subjects to the eternal glory of the church?

[7] As is the case with many historical incidents which have a romantic color, this celebrated episode, when she shielded Smith's body with her own as he was about to be executed by Powhatan's men, has been much debated; but the weight of opinion is with Smith's story. *Narratives*, pp. 28, 326, 327.

[8] Ibid., p. 69.

[9] William Strachey: *Historie of Travaile into Virginia Britannia* (Hakluyt Society, Publications, London, 1849), p. 111.

The movement consequent upon this reasoning was greatly stimulated by Pocahontas's untimely death at Gravesend in 1617, just as she and John Rolfe were about to sail back to Virginia. Now God had received his own, rescued by the pious English from the eternal damnation to which her heathen race was doomed! When her body was buried in the chancel of the Gravesend church,[1] those who had come to mourn were exalted. As Smith afterward wrote,

> shee made not more sorrow for her unexpected death, than joy to the beholders to heare and see her make so religious and godly an end.[2]

The missionary movement crystallized in the endowment of a college to be established in Virginia for the education of Indians and Indian missionaries. The promoters of the plan had become convinced that the peace sworn by Powhatan, already unbroken for some four years, would be consecrated by Pocahontas's death and would make possible a long, happy collaboration of the races to build Virginia into a great and holy colony. Already the colonists' defenses had been let down. From the tight, huddled community ever on the alert for attack, the colony had spread out into the extensive pattern that was to characterize the tobacco colonies—the plantations, as Smith said, "placed straglingly and scatteringly, as a choice veine of rich ground invited them, and further from neighbours the better." [3]

But then, a year after the death of his daughter, Powhatan died. Had the English known their neighbors as well as they later through bitter experience came to know them, they would have realized that the behavior of a tribe or federation of tribes depended largely on the will and prejudices of its chief or king, and that the duration of tranquillity had been far too brief to establish a tradition which might not be broken at the whim of a new potentate. But the "stupid" English, as Smith afterward called them, were so deeply preoccupied with their good works that when the new emperor bearing the formidable name of Opechancanough promised to keep Powhatan's promises they believed him.

By 1621, three years after Powhatan's death, the money for the

[1] Thomas J. Wertenbaker: "Pocahontas," in *Dictionary of American Biography*.
[2] John Smith: *Generall Historie*, in *Narratives*, p. 330.
[3] Ibid., p. 358.

college had all been raised. An exceedingly gentle and deeply religious Englishman, George Thorpe, was in charge of the plans. The site had been chosen—in Henrico across the river from Jamestown—and the school's staff, with the exception of the rector, had arrived. The relations between Thorpe and Opechancanough were almost unbelievably cordial: Thorpe built the king an English house with a lock and key that so fascinated him that he locked and unlocked it a hundred times a day. All over the plantations there was peace, contentment, and cheerful intercourse. The planters' houses were "generally open to the Salvages, who were alwaies friendly fed at their tables, and lodged in their bedchambers. . . ." [4]

Then, early in 1622, there was a flare-up which almost immediately died down. A favorite of the king's—a picturesque megalomaniac known as Jack of the Feather—treacherously murdered a planter named Morgan and was killed in reprisal by Morgan's servants. For a moment Opechancanough lost his temper and sent threats of revenge to the English, who replied in kind, though they had been so lulled by the decade of peace that they had lost the posture of defense. Then, almost instantly, the King appeared to repent and gave "the greatest signs of love and peace." [5] He conferred at length with Thorpe about religion, said the English God was better than the Indians', and seemed to want to bring his people to the Christian missionaries for conversion. In mid-March he declared that "the sky should fall" before he broke the peace.

The sky fell on the 22nd. All the week before, the Indians had shown exceptional good will and kindness, guiding the white men in the woods, and in return had asked the loan of the English boats to get their own men in quantity across the river. The night of the 21st "they came unarmed into our houses with Deere, Turkies, Fish, Fruits, and other provisions to sell us: yea, in some places sat downe at breakfast with our people. . . ." [6] All over the plantations they came that night, smiling, bowing, laughing. Then, suddenly, in the morning every Indian turned on the nearest English and with the English axes killed them. As Smith told it,

> immediately with their own tooles they slew most barbarously, not sparing either age or sex, man woman or childe; so sudden in their execution, that few or none discerned the weapon or blow. . . . In

[4] Ibid.
[5] Ibid.
[6] Ibid.

which manner also they slew many of our people at severall works in the fields, well knowing in what places and quarters each of our men were. . . .[7]

The weeks of friendliness had been for the purpose of spying. The meals at the settlers' houses, the night shelter they had sought there, were only devices to learn the habits of the planters. The whole affair was planned with such care, such attention to the smallest detail, and such brilliant dissimulation that it was worthy, technically, of a general long trained in the subtlest strategy. It implied, too, a degree of discipline as well as a depth of barbarity in every participant that might well remove English trust in any Indian.

There died,

that fatall morning under the bloudy and barbarous hands of that perfidious and inhumane people, three hundred and forty seven men, women and children; mostly by their owne weapons; and not being content with their lives, they fell againe upon the dead bodies . . . defacing, dragging, and mangling their dead carkases into many peeces and carrying some parts away in derision, with base and brutal triumph.[8]

Apparently, from the beginning Opechancanough had nursed resentment of the white man's coming. Whether he foresaw the ultimate victory of the English over the Indians and the annihilation of tribal power,[9] or whether his secret hatred was the result of a series of supposed personal injuries, his performance remains the first and perhaps the most loathsome masterpiece of large-scale treachery in our colonial history and stands as one of the offsets to our conscience pains.

The circumstances of this massacre and its place in the sequence of events were such as to impress it indelibly on the minds of seventeenth-century Englishmen. The most skillful of dramatists would be hard put to it to construct a tragedy with as powerful an emotional impact in the crescendo of its successive acts. Even the striking coincidence of the last scene occurring on Good Friday (if, indeed, it was coincidence) suggests an adroit contrivance of the playwright's art.

[7] Ibid., pp. 358, 359.

[8] Ibid., p. 359. Smith has been accused—sometimes quite justly—of exaggeration and inaccuracy. His account of the massacre, however, is abundantly corroborated by other documents, notably the *Records* (see note below).

[9] *Records of the Virginia Company*, Susan M. Kingsbury, editor (Washington, 1933), III, 556.

The missionary movement never recovered from the shattering blow. Thorpe and some seventeen college tutors having been killed and the college property destroyed, its continuance seemed hopeless even to some of the most ardent zealots. As the mists cleared over the grisly scene and the deep, recurrent, implacable antagonism was revealed, many a missionary must have wondered if his good works in the name of Christ could ever be worth the price.

Preserved in the colonial records is a document prepared soon after the massacre by one Edward Waterhouse for the instruction of the Council for Virginia in England. This paper tells the story, often using almost the same words as those in John Smith's *Generall Historie*, but the conclusions drawn by Waterhouse are especially significant. Nothing is more instructive as to the origin of the English colonial attitude toward the Indians than these bitter and eloquent words. It is quite obvious that some of the resolutions listed here for the future had already been favored by a good many of the settlers, but they had been suppressed by conscience, the sense of fair play, and the hope of missionary achievement. Now the restraints were gone. The Indians themselves had broken them. The Indians had cut the knot that tied the white men's hands "with gentlenesse and faire usage." Those hands were now

> set at liberty. . . . So that we, who hitherto have had possession of no more ground than their waste, and our purchase at a valuable consideration to their own contentment, gained; may now by right of Warre, and law of Nations, invade the country, and destroy them who sought to destroy us. . . . Now their cleared lands . . . shall be inhabited by us. . . .[1]

The policy hitherto observed of keeping hands off the Indian hunting would be ended; from now on, English conservation rules would be applied to Virginia game. From now on, the policy of "divide and conquer" would be applied to the savages, and tribe would be pitted against tribe. Finally, enslaving the Indians became legitimate, and they "who before were used as friends, may now most justly be compelled to servitude and drudgery."

In this year of 1622 there was no other English settlement in North America except that of the Pilgrims in Plymouth, who had not yet come into any real conflict with the natives. It is well, when we are inclined to blame our ancestors for striking the first blows,

[1] *Records of the Virginia Company*, III, 556–7.

to remember how exceedingly early in our colonial history this tragedy occurred. From Virginia, Governor Bradford of Plymouth received the news in a letter from a stranger named John Huddleston early in 1623.

> . . . I do intreat you [Huddleston wrote] (although not knowing you) that the old rule which I learned when I went to school may be sufficient; that is, Happy is he whom other men's harms doth make to beware.[2]

In the summer, Virginian visitors told the Pilgrims more. There can be no doubt that the story was told with varying degrees of color to later colonists, so that the disposition to friendliness with the Indians was considerably tempered.

If, then, the people of New England were cynical toward their "pagan" neighbors, if they hesitated to preach to them, if they took occasional advantage of them, if they refused them firearms, if they protected their women from Indian advances or stood their men in the pillory for sleeping with squaws, their distrust may have had other causes than mere Anglo-Saxon bullheadedness and contempt. Nearly half a century later even the gentle Roger Williams, after half a lifetime of missionary work, was obliged to give his countrymen warning against the hostile intent of certain Connecticut and Rhode Island tribes.

There had, by that time, inevitably been shocking episodes in which English treachery came close to matching that of the natives. The extermination of the New England tribes after King Philip's War did not leave the colonists with anything like clean hands, notwithstanding the atrocities of Haverhill and Deerfield. The unfair weapon of liquor was used in New York and Pennsylvania in the eighteenth century to the point where Franklin declared that

> if it be the design of Providence to extirpate these savages in order to make room for cultivators of the earth, it seems not improbable that rum may be the appointed means. It has already annihilated all the tribes who formerly inhabited the sea-coast.[3]

Throughout our history there have been terrible incidents and practices on both sides. The Pennsylvania frontier raids—inspired, to be sure, by the French but gratifying to the most brutal impulses

[2] Bradford: op. cit., p. 110.

[3] Benjamin Franklin: "Autobiography," in *Writings*, Albert H. Smyth, editor (New York, 1907), I, 376.

of the natives—were far from pretty. But all of it has been in the pattern of territorial conquest and development. How it might have been otherwise leads us into that dangerous game of "the if's of history." In our sensitive moments we repent our acts without, however, fully appraising the means by which we arrived at that hilltop from which remorse is convenient. Yet there is something peculiarly American in our worry, as if the very Puritan impulses that wrought the first of our sins were now turning to bewail them. Even in our "sophistication" the strange Calvinist abasement, humiliation, and guilt stick exasperatingly with us.

PART II

Awakening and Enlightenment

Chapter VI

Decline of the Bible State

IN THE VERY TIME of its founding, the Bible state of New England had contained the germs of its own destruction. Rigid, class-conscious, introspective, and ascetic, it could adjust neither to the changing intellectual climate of England nor to the rich material growth of America. Its structure had not the resiliency, the give, the constant balancing movement of its parts, that enables—for example—a great steel bridge to take the stresses of weather and traffic. The builders of the Bible state had focused so narrowly on their own sainthood that they had failed to see the growing discontent and power of the large unsanctified majority within their gates. They had ignored the profound impact of the Long Parliament on religion in England. They had purged themselves of those doubters whose troubled eyes had seen visions of tolerance, brotherhood, or equality. Safe in their walled isolation, they had turned from dynamic, radical dissent to a sterile conservatism of orthodoxy. Finally, when compromise was forced upon them by a new generation and by a new English king, their inflexible political structure cracked.

Insidiously, gnawing away from inside at the core of the body politic was a growing mercantile success. Agriculture in New England had not provided a surplus for trade over and above subsistence needs. Long winters brought farming to a standstill: other gainful occupations became necessary. The more enterprising of Massachusetts Bay, New Haven, and Connecticut men had taken to the sea. They became good fishermen. They built good ships. They carried their fish and their lumber to southern Europe and the West Indies, and they brought back, along with the fruit and oil, salt and sugar, ideas that were at variance with the pattern God had revealed to Cotton, Davenport, Eaton, Shepard, or even the gentler Winthrops.

The ships were owned, sure enough, by respectable, God-fearing, churchgoing merchants, such as John Hull, who was often on his knees among the bales of his cargo glorifying God, sometimes confusing his prayers with his bills of lading, but of unfailing piety. Yet the ships disgorged into Boston the riff-raff of their crews, bringing drunkenness and whoredom to the very steps of the temple.

And the merchants got rich. It has been said and partially proved that the Protestant ethic is allied to the spirit of capitalism.[1] Yet even Tawney, champion of that hypothesis, distinguishes between early and later practices of New England Calvinism.[2] In the first years of the Plymouth and Bay colonies many sermons were preached against avarice and "oppression," which in those days meant profiteering. "This evil," Governor Winthrop wrote in 1640, "was very notorious among all sorts of people, it being the common rule that most men walked by in all their commerce, to buy as cheap as they could, and to sell as dear." [3] And in 1632, twelve years after the founding of the Plymouth Colony, Governor Bradford saw results of increasing prosperity which he prophesied "will be the ruin of New England, at least of the churches of God there, and will provoke the Lord's displeasure. . . ." [4]

In the court records we find severe censures imposed on what was considered shrewd trading practice. There was the classic case of shopkeeper Robert Keane, "a man of eminent parts . . . Having come over for conscience' sake, and for the advancement of the gospel," [5] who nevertheless had commonly made the outrageous profit of sixpence in the shilling and sometimes even eightpence. Keane was humiliated and reduced to tears by the court, which also fined him two hundred pounds. And there was also Taylor, who "fell distracted" because he was accused in a sermon of cornering the milk market. Arriving on a ship with a cow in milk when all the Boston cows were dry, he had taken advantage of the disaster by

[1] Max Weber: *The Protestant Ethic and the Spirit of Capitalism* (London, 1930).

[2] R. H. Tawney: *Religion and the Rise of Capitalism* (New York, 1926), pp. 127–132.

[3] *Winthrop's Journal*, II, 20.

[4] William Bradford: *Of Plymouth Plantation*, 254.

[5] Winthrop: op. cit., I, 316.

charging twopence a quart.[6] There were many such lapses. In the early days they were scandals, and the court drew up rules of trading pitched in the somber key sounded by Calvin in Geneva.

But, as we have found, the code fitted the tough times. Men and women in common poverty and common hardship naturally distrusted the riches that could not be theirs, and called upon their God to bear witness against them. To them, also, the way of thrift was the way of self-abnegation. Desire was suppressed by necessity, leaving the mind open to total preoccupation with the glory of God. As Tawney says:

> Calvinism . . . distrusted wealth, as it distrusted all influences that distract the aim or relax the fibers of the soul, and, in the first flush of its youthful austerity, it did its best to make life unbearable for the rich. Before the Paradise of earthly comfort it hung a flaming brand, waved by the implacable shades of Moses and Aaron.[7]

Nevertheless, as the century advanced, the earthly comfort became more and more accessible. In fact, the austere code had worked so well that, in spite of magistrates and sermons, wealth accumulated. The code had insisted that a part of the glorification of God came in the diligence with which men worked at their "calling." In response, the land and the sea yielded up their plenty; the diligent and courageous merchants carried it far to opulent markets and in places remote from Boston's pulpits and New Haven's meetings sold dearer and bought cheaper than the general courts need ever know.

As the century wore well into its second half, the complaints of the clergy—the "jeremiads," as Perry Miller calls them—grew louder and more desperate. "*New England*," declared John Higginson in his "election sermon" of 1663, "*is originally a plantation of Religion not a plantation of trade*. Let Merchants and such as are increasing *Cent per Cent* remember this." [8] These sermons at the same time confessed failure to the Almighty and pressed the urgency for reform before it was too late. As Perry Miller says,

[6] Ibid., II, 20.
[7] Tawney: op. cit., p. 132.
[8] "The Cause of God, etc.," quoted in Lindsay Swift: *The Massachusetts Election Sermons* (Colonial Society of Massachusetts Publications), I, 398. Italics Higginson's.

They tell the story, and tell it coherently, of a society which was founded by men dedicated, in unity and simplicity, to realizing on earth eternal and immutable principles—and which progressively became involved with fishing, trade, and settlement.[9]

2

In Massachusetts Bay—the nucleus or hard core of the church state—the vote was still restricted, in 1660, to "church members." And the church members were still the "elect of God," those who were able to convince the clergy that they had received the Grace and, before all worlds, had been predestined to salvation. There was no evidence that God wanted the "strangers" to be saved. Among the strangers were the servants, voluntary and enslaved, whose number increased with the general prosperity. Some of them, judging by the court records, were low fellows indeed, guilty not only of dishonesty and normal sexual incontinence but of that horror of horrors, "bestiality." They were thorns in the flesh of the godly and, as their number grew while simultaneously the godly died out, it became urgent that both ministers and magistrates take thought for the threatening morrow.

The Bay Puritans had been prolific folk. In their day they had to be. The infant mortality was sometimes decimating. In the diary of John Hull, for instance—a man able to afford every care—we find child after child dying within the first month. Milk fever, smallpox, the "flux," and many unnamed distempers multiplied the tiny graves. It was a burdensome life for the women, but they expected it, and it was a means of glorifying God, who had enjoined his chosen to "increase and multiply." A goodly number of the children, however, had been sturdy or lucky and had survived. The question of what God would do about their souls and the effect of this on the colonial politics tore the people apart and ended in a compromise. And as there were no organs or nerve system in the physiology of the Bible state through which compromise could function, decay immediately set in. In the new climate of prosperity the germs of decay found a rich culture.

The question was whether the children of the elect were themselves automatically elect or whether they must individually receive

[9] Perry Miller: *The New England Mind: From Colony to Province*, p. 40.

the Grace. The realists, who were alarmed at the dwindling churches, pointed eagerly to the passage in Genesis in which the Lord established his covenant with Abraham "to be a God unto thee, and to thy seed after thee." [1] "Yes," said the objectors, "but did that mean the inner invisible Grace given to individuals or was it a mere outward investment of that degree of holiness which would make the later Grace possible?" So, after a great deal of argument and many jeremiads by the ancient Fathers, a synod was held which established the "Half-Way Covenant." This provided that the children of God's elect might become church members upon baptism and that when they came of age they could vote. They could not, however, partake of the Lord's Supper until they had experienced the actual ecstasy of conversion. They were, therefore, "half-way" members; they maintained the franchise, keeping it in more or less godly hands, but it was confidently expected by the optimistic promoters of the scheme that in their ripeness of years they would confess and prove that they had become saints.

This, in their ripeness, they failed to do. Whether comforts and proud garments had corrupted them; whether their inquiring minds had reached out to England and seen the profound changes which had come about between the beheading of the first Charles and the enthroning of the second; whether they needed the incentive of persecution which had spurred their fathers; or whether they failed to grasp the extremely complex theology which had evolved, in the wilderness, out of Calvinism—most of the children seemed immune to conversion. Furthermore, they refused—most of them—to look with loathing on the other sects: the Anabaptists, the Brownists, the Antinomians, the Familists, and even the Quakers, who were tolerated not only in Rhode Island but in New York and Pennsylvania. Plainly the compromise was failing to preserve the theocratic integrity.

The confidence of the saintly aristocracy was also failing. The dreaded democratic trend so inevitable in a wide, thinly peopled wilderness was beginning to break down the Lord's predestined hierarchy. The outstanding among the native-born sons of the godly, Increase Mather and his son Cotton, kept uttering assurances in the midst of their lamentations that conversion must eventually come to the children of the elite. As late as 1678, when the Half-Way Cove-

[1] Gen. 17:7.

nant was sixteen years old and the babies hopefully baptized under its ægis were just ripening into maturity, the elder Mather proclaimed:

> Now God hath seen meet to cast the line of Election so, as that it doth (though not wholly and only, yet) for the most part run through the loyns of godly parents. . . . And there are some Families that the Lord hath Chosen above others and therefore poured his Spirit upon the Offspring in such Families successively.[2]

Again and again in these years of foreboding, as Edmund Morgan has pointed out, the sentence "God casts the line of election in the loins of godly parents" [3] was reiterated from the pulpits, and the devout plutocrat John Hull copied the words in his notebook; yet, as the years went on, the offspring of God's nobility continued—sometimes with protesting tears—to maintain that they could not feel the spirit that was being poured upon them.

3

In another aspect, too, the rigid pattern broke. The Fathers had believed, along with their master, Calvin, that God had predestined some to poverty, others to goodly "outward estates" if not riches. There are records of punishment for those who, by wearing good clothes or jewelry, trespassed on the privileges of the rich. "One end of Apparel," said Samuel Willard, "is to distinguish and put a difference between persons according to the Places and Conditions." [4] William B. Weeden tells us that in Newbury in 1653 two women were tried for wearing silk hoods and scarves but, when it was shown that their husbands were worth two hundred pounds each, they were discharged.[5]

By the time William Hubbard preached in 1676, however, on "The Happiness of a People," saying that "it is not then the result of time or chance, that some men are mounted on horse-back, while others are left to travell on foot" and that God had appointed kings

[2] Increase Mather: *Pray for the Rising Generation* (Boston, 1678), quoted in Edmund S. Morgan: *The Puritan Family* (Boston, 1944), p. 102.

[3] Morgan: op. cit., p. 102.

[4] Quoted in Miller: op. cit., p. 48.

[5] William B. Weeden: *Economic and Social History of New England* (Boston, 1890). I, 227.

and workers,[6] the hierarchy had already been broken in New England. Everywhere men were bearing the fruit of that "diligence" to which all had been exhorted from the beginning. Men who had begun as apprentices or indentured servants, blacksmiths or tailors, had become property owners and were bequeathing large estates to their children. John Hull himself had been a poor farm boy, then a goldsmith's apprentice. At the same time several "gentlemen," unable to compete with the increasingly efficient business practice of the self-made adventurers, had lost their estates. The rigid design, adaptable enough to a tight little homogeneous community in isolation, had broken in a land where freedom was inherent in vast empty spaces and democracy inevitable with universal access to unbounded natural treasure. As Miller says:

> The social structure refused to stay fixed, and classifications decreed by God Himself dissolved. Pious industry wrecked the city on a hill, in which it had been assumed men would remain forever in the stations to which they were born, and inferiors would eternally bow to gentlemen and scholars.[7]

And now fewer and fewer in the congregations were moved by the heavy nostalgia of the older preachers. Where was the golden age that so recently flourished? The repetition in the pulpit was so constant that many must have drowsed through these laments. By the 1670's they had become stylized; in them we find no original thought, no gleam of light for the future.

> Truly so it is [wailed Samuel Torrey in his election sermon for 1674] the very heart of *New England* is changed, and exceedingly corrupted with the sins of the Times; there is a Spirit of Profaneness, a Spirit of Pride, a Spirit of Worldliness, a Spirit of Sensuality, a Spirit of Gainsaying and Rebellion, a Spirit of Libertinism, a Spirit of Carnality, Formality, Hypocrisy, and Spiritual Idolatry in the Worship of God.[8]

One can almost hear the accompaniment of snores to this rhythmic rhetoric poured into the static air of the meetings. One may imagine the dreams of the sumptuously attired, well-fed, unregenerate, herded by persistent law into the pews: dreams of warm Caribbean airs, of heady smells in Cádiz harbor, of smuggled fruits and

[6] Miller: op. cit., p. 48.
[7] Ibid., p. 49.
[8] Quoted in Lindsay Swift: op. cit., I, 402.

spices from French or Dutch or Portuguese islands, of the rich scent of naked black slave bodies from African coastal rendezvous and the aromatic fragrance of Medford rum from casks broken into by the painted Gold Coast chieftains or of the pungent effluvium from a hold packed with the sacred cod that would raise so high a price from the hungry Catholics of southern Europe. Or, perhaps, for him whose days of adventure were being replaced by more mature home comforts, dreams of the spacious new house a-building on Beacon Hill, product of all the salt fish, rum, pipe staves, and dubiously acquired Spanish bullion of the past: a home to be forever furnished with casks of Madeira brought into Boston harbor by his own fleet of sail. Where then was the voice of Calvin's Hebrew God warning the Libertines against the hope of heaven? Was not heaven already here?

4

The isolation from England that had lasted some twenty years ended in 1660 with the restoration of a king to the English throne. It had been a fruitful time both for the theocracy and for the people of New England. It had strengthened the independent political power of the church, yet at the same time it had helped build the forces that would destroy that power. By cutting off the profitable stream of immigrants who had fled from Charles I and his angry archbishop, the English civil war had forced New Englanders to find new means of prosperity through world trade. In the years of the commonwealth, New England had enjoyed special privileges under the Navigation Acts—a license not given to the other colonies. Thus, the corrupting fortunes grew parallel with the growth of Bible rule: the opposing giants waxed together and were ready for their conflict as Charles II came out of his exile.

The blissful ignorance of a changed Puritan temper in England had allowed the reactionary New England clergy to withdraw into deeper entrenchment behind their wall of bigotry. While in England the Long Parliament and the wars had provided a melting-pot for the Puritan sects, Anabaptists and Arminians, Brownists and Seekers were banished from Boston and Quakers were whipped at the cart tail. In the year of the Restoration, four Quakers, including the fanatic martyr Mary Dyer, were brutally executed at Boston.

The whippings and the hangings were watched with disgust by the growing crowds of the unregenerate. To many self-made businessmen who with their ships had broken out of the isolation, the church dictatorship was already anathema. Respectable property owners—and often devout men, too, according to their lights—chafed at being denied the franchise because of some esoteric theological technicality. Though they might once have been bonded boys, today they were pillars supporting the very church state that shut them out of government participation. It was not that they were democrats, God forbid. They simply favored a more realistic hierarchy.

At first it seemed as if the new Charles would look favorably upon the liberal group. In his declaration at Breda in April 1660, he announced

> We do declare a liberty to tender consciences; and that no man shall be disquieted, or called in question, for differences of opinion in matters of religion which do not disturb the peace of the kingdom.[9]

In December of the same year he wrote to the Massachusetts General Court a reiteration of that promise. His message must have disturbed the magistrates and assistants while it was encouraging to the dissidents.

> . . . neither shall we forget [he wrote] to make you and all our good people in those parts equal partakers of those promises of liberty and moderation to tender consciences expressed in our gracious declarations.[1]

Two years later the King granted to Connecticut a charter so generous that it almost seemed to confer autonomy on the colony. It later developed that this act was designed to strengthen Connecticut against the Dutch and that when, in 1664, New Amsterdam surrendered to the English without resistance, the King regretted it. By that time, however, rumors had reached him that roused his wrath against the proud government of "the Massachusetts," center of his northern colonies.

Through the remainder of his reign—which became a period of tyranny—this restored Stuart suffered recurrent spasms of rage at

[9] Lord Clarendon: *History of the Rebellion in England* (Boston, 1827), VI, 3015.

[1] Thomas Hutchinson: *The Hutchinson Papers* (Prince Society edition, Albany, 1865), II, 52.

the behavior of the Bible state. Before his death in 1685 the people as well as the government of the Bay colony had turned against him. But the antagonism began and grew because of the arrogance and intolerance of the theocrats—the governor, the magistrates, and the ruling elite—and it was fed by the growing body of anti-theocrats in Massachusetts, New Hampshire, Connecticut, and Maine (annexed by Massachusetts Bay). This "fifth column," as we should call it, gave the King's commissioners much of the information he used to defeat the theocracy.

How is this political history germane to a history of the American conscience? The answer comes in the pulpit lamentations of those transition years. It comes in the study of the confusion growing in the minds of the ministers between individual conscience and the evolving community conscience. Nothing is more striking to the student of that unique merger of church and state than the strange dichotomy of the "invisible" covenant of Grace and the so-called "national" or "federal" covenant. In one, the individual made a secret contract with God by which God promised salvation and the individual promised faith. In the other, the churches made an open contract by which God would take the whole community under his protection in return for worship, obedience and righteousness. The horrors of the Pequot War, in which enraged Indians scalped women and children and laid waste villages and farms down nearly the whole valley of the Connecticut, came in the eyes of the colonists not because they had exasperated the Indians beyond endurance through insult and deceit but because they had failed to keep their part of the bargain with the Deity!

Finally, in this critical interval we see the split in the covenanted body itself when the prosperous, traveled men of business and sea trade, and the unregenerate majority bewildered by the interference with their lives of a church aristocracy whose theology they could not understand, broke with the Fathers. The Fathers said that sin, at this point, riddled the community, but the records show more offenses against church codes than derelictions of the flesh.

In the upheaval we see—looking at it from here—the makings of a new community conscience which should be closer to the individual conscience than the federal covenant was to the invisible one. We see evidences of public opinion judging between right and wrong not on the basis of what the church said the Bible said, or because God had given the power to see such things only to his elect, but because the deep, intuitive, inner discomfort of individuals had prodded them into concert. We see, in short, an ethical sense emerging from the dogma and jargon of revealed religion—the same ethical sense which has regulated human conduct through all the ages, but which had been obscured for the Puritans by the doctrinal mists that had risen from the Reformation. It is permissible, nevertheless, to see values accruing to the core of our eventual national conscience from the very paradoxes of New England Puritanism.

5

The first round with the King was won by Massachusetts Bay. It is difficult not to admire the intransigence of these sturdy folk who were to become Yankees. The independence, the refusal to subject themselves to any master in the land they had abandoned, foreshadowed the stubborn fight for freedom of a later century. Although in 1664 their precious so-called "Body of Liberties"—which was their body of law—contained anything but liberties for the people, it was nevertheless fashioned out of God's Word, and God was the only sovereign who might subjugate them. So they received the King's commissioners in 1664 with high disdain. The commissioners returned to England admitting defeat but full of information about Massachusetts subversion—much of it contributed, of course, by the disaffected. The commissioners' report dealt especially with the colonial laws at variance with English law, the denial of the franchise on religious grounds, violation of the Navigation Acts, and the assumption of total autonomy.

Wars with Holland and other matters deterred the King for a decade from further action against the colony. Then in 1675 a number of interested persons, including the heirs of Mason and Gorges, the original patentees of Maine, persuaded the King that the time was again ripe to strike at New England. The ripeness of the time derived from the fearful ravages of King Philip's War, which were supposed to weaken Massachusetts into a mood of submission.

A querulous, self-seeking troublemaker who has been called "the evil genius of New England" [2] was chosen to carry a new royal letter to the Bay's General Court. This Edward Randolph arrived in Boston in July 1676 and, despite the season, immediately felt the chill which went out to greet him from the governor's council. He was invited to read the King's letter to this august body, a special chair having been placed for him to sit in, suggesting that he was allowed entrance only as a favor. When he began to read, he took off his hat in deference to his sovereign. The governor of Massachusetts Bay kept his on. Randolph asked for a reply. The Governor said the council would consider it. Randolph left the council chamber, trembling from the insult, and then told his story to the discontented, who received him eagerly all the way from Maine to Long Island Sound. When he left in September, there was still no official answer from the council to the King.

Randolph's report burned with the iteration of delinquencies. New England laws suited only the New Englanders' convenience. They were derogatory to the English statutes. In capital cases where no colonial law applied, there was "trial by word of God" and defendants were put to death according to Scriptural interpretation. Ministers were ordained by the people. Magistrates performed the marriage ceremony. Five-year possession of land gave absolute title. There were no oaths of allegiance to the King. The Navigation Acts were ignored. Magistrates habitually disobeyed royal commands. Maine and New Hampshire territory had been annexed to Massachusetts without authority and against the will of the residents. The population of Maine, New Hampshire, and Massachusetts together came (including 200 slaves) to 150,000. Of these, one sixth were voting church members; the other five sixths dissenters from the theocracy. And the rebels were actually coining their own money—from melted-up Spanish silver that had come in from the West Indies trade and other, more dubious sources.[3]

This report, coming after a more than ten-year accumulation of tracts published in England by persecuted Quakers and others, convinced the King that Massachusetts must be completely subjugated. By this time, however, Charles, having become more and more arbitrary at home, was deeply involved with his domestic rebels. He did

[2] Justin Winsor: *Narrative and Critical History of America* (Boston, 1884), III, 319.

[3] Edward Randolph: *Letters and Documents*, etc., 1676–1703, Robert Noxon Toppan, editor (Boston, 1898), II, 216 ff.

command Massachusetts to send agents immediately to England to explain the derelictions. These men parried or denied the accusations, and matters drifted along to the accompaniment of fast days in Massachusetts and sensational publications in London.[4] In 1684 the Massachusetts charter was annulled and the colony lost even the appearance of independence.

What followed united the colonial factions, but it killed the Bible state. It was a gesture as tyrannical, as subversive of the rights of Englishmen as any that ever came from the Crown. The whole of New England was formed into a Dominion. This included Maine, New Hampshire, Massachusetts, Plymouth, Connecticut, and Rhode Island, disregarding the differences in temper of these varied regions. Over the whole Dominion was sent a governor with absolute authority—the hated Edmund Andros. Representative government and all franchise were abolished. Taxation without representation and conformity to English land law were introduced.

These things were done in 1686, the year after Charles II died, by his Catholic successor, James II. Fortunately for New England, the new King was as unwelcome at home as he was in Puritan America. In 1688, in what the English have always called their "Glorious Revolution," they invited William of Orange, husband of James's daughter Mary, to come across from Holland and take the throne. James was forced into exile—a state which by now must have been quite familiar to Stuarts—and Englishmen became "free" Englishmen once more.

The colonies of the Dominion took quick advantage of the upheaval. Andros was arrested and imprisoned in Boston together with such other Dominion officers as the insurgents could lay hands on. The colonies then resumed their old governments.

In 1691 Massachusetts got a new charter which did not recognize the old Massachusetts Bay Company but transformed the church "commonwealth" into a royal province. A House of Representatives was granted. There was a governor appointed by the Crown and given veto power. His salary, however, was to be set by the provincial legislature, giving the people a certain hold over their executive. And the House of Representatives could nominate council

[4] For example, *A Letter from New England*, by "J.W." (1682), reprinted in *Boston in 1682 and 1699*, George Parker Winship, editor (Second Publication of the Club for Colonial Reprints, Providence, R.I., 1905). Also, John Josselyn: *Two Voyages to New England* (London, 1675).

members. Franchise was no longer based on church membership, and religious freedom was guaranteed to all Protestants. Thus was the Bible state legally destroyed.

The old church faction fought the change. Increase Mather, still irreconcilable at fifty, made the hard trip to England to try to get the old charter back. The new privy council knew well enough that only the "faction" wanted it. And in the final stages even the Mathers conceded and accepted the compromise ending the power of church over state.

But although the church's control of the government ceased, the clergy did not relax their vigil over the religious life and observances of the people. Nor was their fanaticism quashed by the tolerant provisions of the new charter. It was simply turned in a new direction. Instead of attacking heretics, they directed their attacks toward Satan himself by purging the community of his agents: the witches, male and female, the sorcerers, and all who were in communication with the diabolic master of the "invisible world." Thus, at the very moment when the people of the Bay were beginning to rejoice at their new liberties, there occurred what has been considered one of the darker episodes in American colonial history. Its temper has returned, more than once, to plague us.

6

The witch trials of New England stand out so prominently in most of our colonial histories that we are inclined to give them undeserved importance. To generations that have outgrown the delusion, the persecution of these alleged devil-worshippers is so fantastic as to arrest us in an orderly following of the sequence of events in seventeenth-century America. Americans, thus startled, sometimes assume that these things are products of a particular society rather than of an age, and the credulous of Boston and Salem are held responsible for some of our later patterns of thought. In reality, the whole of Western civilization suffered outbursts of witchcraft hysteria in which countless thousands died before the first migration of the Pilgrims, and the few dozen accused who came to the gallows in all English America made an infinitesimal incident beside the burnings and tortures in Spain, France, Germany, England, and Scotland that had preceded it.

There was nothing peculiarly American, therefore, about any of the witch hunts on these shores. Nor are the later facsimiles of them which have recurred in our history peculiarly American, however much we may like to think so in the times of our self-abasement. The incidents of our racial discriminations, the anti-Catholic, anti-Semitic, or anti-Negro episodes, the hounding of innocent German Americans in the First World War or of Nisei Japanese in the Second, the "red-baiting" of the 1920's or the far more serious persecution of the so-called "subversives" or "guilty-by-association" of the 1940's and '50's are as nothing compared to the "witch hunts" which have tormented nearly every generation in Europe, Asia, or Africa. In decade after decade we have received in this country refugees from the houndings in the German Palatinate, in Ireland, in Poland, in Austria-Hungary, and Turkey, Jews from the burned-out ghettos of central Europe, escaped victims of Fascist, Nazi, or Communist tyrannies; and we have thought of the conditions from which these folk had fled as more or less normal. But when the mere shadows of such things have darkened America, the American conscience has been quick to condemn, less because of inherent evil than because they were alien to what we remember as American legend.

So it was with the witch mania in the closing years of the century. The truly important event in all that orgy was the rising of the New England conscience after it: the humiliations and confessions of the judges, the juries, Samuel Sewall, and even—forced by the common repentance—of the Mathers themselves.

Perry Miller, who writes with more authority than most historians of the Puritan phase, contends that the witchcraft episodes of 1688 and '92 represent the ultimate effort by the clergy to salvage the "covenant." The laments of the sermons very definitely support this belief. They dwell persistently on New England's "declension" from the standards of the founders: the wickedness of the people, the corruption of society, the infiltration of the debauched, the godless, the "Saducees." The church covenant demanded a propitiation to God for this decay. There must be, in short, a sop to the community conscience—to the "national" conscience, for New England called itself a nation. What better than a truly zealous pursuit of these agents of God's enemies?

God, to be sure, had permitted the operation of the demons. They could have done nothing without this divine permission. But the permission had been given because these declining people needed the punishments. If they had been wicked enough, the Puritan God would not be above allowing the witches to pinch, prick, haunt, poison, and otherwise torment innocent children; to focus especially upon the older boys and girls already tormented by their own adolescence and thus willing enough to let Satan take the blame. It must be remembered that the covenant or national conscience ignored individuals: the innocent must suffer with the guilty if there had been widespread misbehavior in the community. The individual's covenant with his God was a secret and separate affair that could be settled in eternity. Yet when the orgy was over, in the cold dawns of the mornings after, some of the most zealous of the national covenanters found their "hearts high-sorrowful and cloy'd" and their individual consciences so tortured that they almost forgot the wrath of God. Thus the last-stand effort to salvage the church covenant was instrumental in destroying it.

Cotton Mather supplied the first material for the Boston witch hunt. In 1688 he brought a thirteen-year-old girl into his household where he could watch her continuously. This child, immensely flattered by the attention of one of the most famous ministers in the country, did what she could to please him. She threw fits, became rigid, ranted, spoke strange words, coughed up "a Ball as big as a small Egg," looked up the chimney, cried "to the Lord Jesus for help," felt chains on her legs, tried to fly, locked her jaws, mounted an invisible horse and rode it for hours. She made several eloquent speeches (though some of the rhetoric may have been supplied by Mather while the words were getting into his notebook), but perhaps the most inflammatory was one she delivered to a considerable body of "standers by" at the beginning of her alleged victory over the evil forces.[5]

> Well what do you say? [the notebook quotes her as saying—with appropriate capitals] How many Fits more am I to have?—pray can ye tell how long it shall be before you are hang'd for what you

[5] Cotton Mather: "Memorable Providences," in *Narratives of the Witchcraft Cases,* George L. Burr, editor (New York, 1914), pp. 110 ff.

> have done?—You are filthy Witches to my knowledge. . . . You would have killd me; but you can't, I don't fear you.—You would have thrown Mr. Mather down stairs, but you could not. . .[6]

Martha Goodwin must have been a talented actress. She was certainly an emotional young lady with possible epileptic intervals. She was, no doubt, precisely the right age for the experiment, her capacity for frenzied demonstration with the bodily reflections of fever and contortion enhanced by her immediately post-pubic urgency. In any case, the effect on the audience was electric, and they left the Mather household with tales on their tongues that all Boston was thirsting to hear. As a result, an Irish washerwoman—as ignorant and superstitious as her accusers—was convicted and hanged.

But the hysteria reached its peak in 1692 through an exotic factor in a place known as Salem Village—since grown into the thriving town of Danvers. Here Samuel Parris, a minister who was engaged on the side in trade with Barbadoes, had two slaves, John and Tituba, whom he had brought home with him from the West Indies islands. With their rich store of voodoo mythology these Negroes had regaled the children of the community to the point where the older girls, at least, had become expert in the kind of witch lore that such neurotics as Cotton Mather fed on. These girls too, like Martha Goodwin, were ripe in age for the passions of the bewitched.

Mary Walcot, aged seventeen, was bitten on the wrist by an invisible witch; the toothmarks were visible. Abigail Williams, twelve, had "a grievous fit," tried to fly, and cried: "Whish, Whish, Whish!" Three girls from nine to twelve were bitten, pinched, and strangled and, in their fits, saw the cause of their affliction—an elderly woman of the community who held a yellow bird that sucked between her fingers.[7] On testimony of this sort the unhappy woman, Martha Corey, was tried, convicted, and sent to the gallows.

Encouraged and prodded by the zealous ministers, the adolescents remembered the most lurid parts of the voodoo lore and enacted them apparently with considerable skill. The adults of the community soon caught the fever: Mrs. Pope and Goodwife Bibber had "sore fits" in the midst of "Publick Worship," and Mrs. Putnam,

[6] Ibid., p. 117.

[7] Ibid., pp. 153 ff. This "Brief and True Narrative" of the Rev. Deodat Lawson is perhaps the most inflammatory of all the witchcraft tracts.

more discreet, had hers in bed. In addition to the fit, Mrs. Pope complained of "a grievous torment in her Bowels as if they were torn out." All the common ailments deriving perhaps from overeating or undersanitation were ascribed to the witches, and each sufferer picked her favorite enemy as the cause of her trouble. Men as well as women were on both sides—afflicted and afflicting—and presently guilt by association came under the scrutiny of the courts.

It is not a function of our study to dwell on the details. The spread of such waves of panic in which vicious personal hatred is given full scope is a familiar incident in every society and nearly every age. By the autumn of 1692 a hundred and fifty persons had been imprisoned, eleven women and eight men hanged, and one man "pressed to death." The last execution took place on September 22. After that the reaction set in.

By this time the stomachs of some of the ministers who had seen the succession of victims marched to the gallows had turned. When the governor, Sir William Phips (whom the clergy themselves had nominated), turned to the body of the ministers to ask if the trials should continue, they could not give him a direct, clear-cut answer. Finally, in October, Increase Mather, a true believer in witchcraft but with a private conscience more sensitive than that of his son, found a technical defect in the evidence used in the trials and published a tract called *Cases of Conscience* which suggested that innocent persons might have died. Phips acted at once on this advice and closed the courts.

And then came the attack in full flood. There was the letter of Thomas Brattle, a rich Boston merchant and a student of mathematics and astronomy on the side, condemning the trials with fine rhetoric. There were the letters of the Governor to the King's Privy Council, explaining why he stopped the trials. Finally, there was the ridicule of Robert Calef, whose satire of Cotton Mather's *Wonders of the Invisible World* caused Mather to brand him "a very wicked sort of Saducee." [8]

Meanwhile the penitents confessed. Judge Samuel Sewall, once a zealous witchcraft believer, read a paper regretting his errors. The twelve men of the jury that had convicted the witches signed a paper declaring that

[8] Ibid., p. 293.

> we justly fear that we were sadly deluded and mistaken, for which we are much disquieted and distressed in our minds; and do therefore humbly beg forgiveness, first of God for Christ's sake for this our Error. . . .
>
> We do heartily ask forgiveness of you all, whom we have justly offended, and do declare according to our present minds, we would none of us do such things again on such grounds for the whole World. . . .[9]

In all this sequence of afterthought we may sense the change that has come over the world. Calvin's stern God who predestined men and women to good or evil before all worlds could now forgive "for Christ's sake." The merchants who had begun the declension had produced Thomas Brattle, rich, traveled, and understanding enough to bridge the gap between superstition and the age of reason by means of his scientific enlightenment from the Royal Society in England. From now on we see the pale dawn of a new era in modern history and especially in American culture, the era which Franklin was soon to usher in, which Jefferson would bring to full burgeoning.

The witch madness was the last desperate spasm of the first Puritans; through it they stood with their backs to the wall. The echo of their words would continue to be heard in Boston, in New Haven, in Hartford, for another generation or more; with Jonathan Edwards and the revivalists, hellfires would flare up once more, but the power of the church would be, henceforth, over individuals, not over the State.

[9] Ibid., pp. 387, 388.

Chapter VII

Religion, Tobacco, and Negro Slaves

THE SETTLEMENT of the southern and middle colonies was less associated with conscience than that of Puritan New England. There was variation, too, in the economic pressures. It is true that, although the dominant impulse which sent people from East Anglia and other Puritan regions of England to Massachusetts was religious, the problems of poverty were much present. Many letters and journals show suffering among the prospective emigrants from high costs, meager living standards, shortages, taxes, and unemployment as well as from church persecution. But the English who went to Virginia and the Dutch of Hudson's river were agents or employees of commercial companies intent upon gain, not individuals in flight from economic oppression. And in Pennsylvania and the Jerseys, when Penn's "Holy Experiment" was in progress, there were few problems of conscience. Quakers, Lutherans, and Presbyterians lived side by side in the benign climate of tolerance. Profitable farming and milling soon absorbed the energies of all.

As we come into the eighteenth century, however, we find some special moral attitudes arising from diverse regional conditions: circumstances of climate, of agriculture, of coastal geography, and of national origins among the population. Then, as the frontier moved from tidewater into piedmont areas and finally impinged on territory claimed by the French, new Indian problems became acute—ethical conflicts that had their inception with the first landings and that in their later progress have forever harassed the American conscience. Finally came the strong cultural currents from overseas, from upheavals wrought by new scientific discoveries and revolutionary physical formulas, winds of liberated thought channeled by

Franklin into the beginning of a true American culture. In America the eighteenth century brought the people out of the darkness of superstition into the clarity of natural law—from the uncertain terrors of magic into the serenity of rational understanding.

Benjamin Franklin, who lived through all but sixteen years of the century, had probably more influence upon the mores, the moral and political public opinion, and the physical ways of life of Americans than any other individual. He also did more than anyone else to unite the colonies. At his death, which nearly coincided with the ratification of the Constitution of the United States, they were still far from the unity we understand, yet there were certain moral reference points visible from Maine to Georgia. These Franklin, through journalism and postal service, through meteorological observation and the almanac, and, at last, through justification of the political break, had been highly instrumental in establishing. Ethics had been separated from theological dogma. God had turned from his wrath to the benevolence modern Christians believe Jesus meant to convey and was definitely smiling upon American prosperity. Liberty had become a flaming symbol and equality an avatar.

2

The men of the Virginia expeditions found the wealth they sought, but it was neither in gold nor in the fabulous northwest passage. It was in tobacco. When the Virginian colonists began to cultivate the red man's weed with seriousness and with method, it led to two characteristic conditions, both of which posed problems of conscience. One was the size of the plantations, which kept the planters far apart; the other was Negro slavery.

It would be difficult to imagine a sharper contrast in social geography than that between Tidewater Virginia and Massachusetts—or any other New England colony. The town, with its closely adjacent home lots, its tightly knit industrial, mercantile, and church organizations, its crowded, busy waterfront on harbor or river, was virtually unknown south of the Potomac. On the other hand, the multitude of deep indentations of southern coastlines with navigable rivers leading far into the interior made it possible for water transport to reach otherwise isolated plantations. Thus, the planters were able to sell their single staple crop direct to markets abroad without the medium of towns and middlemen. Deep-draft, ocean-going ships could load at the wharves on the individual plantations far from the coast; cargoes could be taken without interruption to European or—as the Navigation Acts finally prescribed—to English markets.

The result was almost a return to the feudal system. Each plantation seat or center became a sort of manor—a self-sufficient unit—either producing what was necessary to its existence or obtaining it direct from England. Between these "manors" lay the vast planted areas. And this isolation, these distances, this wide dispersal of the population set insuperable obstacles to the functions of a church organization—especially those of the Church of England, which, with all its formality and clerical hierarchy, the Virginians had tried to transplant.

The endowments of the established church in England giving comfortable "livings" to the clergy did not extend to the colonies. There local taxation had to do for the poor ministers. Salaries were usually paid in tobacco and corn. But when the price of tobacco fell, the salaries of the clergy became starvation wages indeed.

In 1705 a piece of propaganda entitled "A Plain and Friendly Perswasive to the Inhabitants of Virginia and Maryland for Promoting Towns and Cohabitations," published in London, gives a picture of the "melancholy" religious situation.[1]

> Towns and Cohabitations [the tract declares] would highly advance Religion which flourishes most in Cohabitations: for in remote and scattered settlements we can never enjoy so fully, frequently, and certainly, those Privileges and Opportunities as are to be had in all Christian Towns and Cities; for by reason of bad weather, or other accidents, Ministers are prevented, and people are hindered to attend, and so disappoint one another: But in Towns Congregations are never wanting, and children and servants never are without opportunity of hearing, who cannot travel many miles to hear, and be catechised. . . .

In the beginning, the comfort of religion had been as sorely needed in Virginia as in Massachusetts. The first settlers, racked by disease, tormented by starvation, and harassed by the raids of the "salvages," had been led in daily prayer by the heroic ministers Hunt

[1] *Virginia Magazine of History and Biography,* IV, 264, 265.

and Buck, and we have records of communion being celebrated [2] in the earliest primitive churches at Jamestown. We may imagine the contrast between the administration of this office in "a homely thing like a barne . . . covered with rafts sedge and earth," [3] surrounded by death and pestilential decay, and in the great English churches with their costly altar cloths and silver chalices. But Jamestown was a community with its people huddled for survival: to the hungry, enervated settlers God was constantly present, taking away the tired souls, offering the only hopes by inspiring the rescuers or turning the hearts of the heathen Indians. And in occasional astonishing breaks in their ill-fortune, such as the defense of Captain Smith by the child Pocahontas and the coincidental arrival of Lord Delaware, they must have seen answers to their desperate prayers.

A nostalgia for religious comfort reached into the tobacco prosperity. Tobacco was quite a different kind of wealth from gold. It destroyed communities by the extensiveness of its culture. All through the seventeenth and part of the eighteenth centuries there were sad communications to the Bishop of London, who was in theory the court of ultimate appeal, and there were sporadic efforts at reform. But the economic factor of the staple-crop agriculture won out over the Virginia conscience in the matter of religious exercise, and eventually, because of its vicissitudes, this factor made a more direct contribution to the decay of the Church of England in Tidewater Virginia.

When the price of tobacco dropped, the clergy suffered to the point at which it was nearly impossible to induce ordained priests to come from England. Then the liturgy cracked wide open, vestries attained the power that was expected to belong to the episcopal hierarchy, lay readers appeared in all the parishes, communicants were buried in unconsecrated ground, and, although there was some exaggeration in the stories told, the character of the clergy degenerated, ministers taking to drink and gambling. The result was that, as Bishop Meade explains in his ponderous history, dissent entered and spread through the province; [4] and though this was punished by whipping, the ducking-stool, and all the paraphernalia of persecu-

[2] John Smith: *Generall Historie of Virginia* (London, 1624), pp. 53–65.

[3] Captain John Smith: *Works,* Edward Arber, editor (Birmingham, 1884), p. 957.

[4] William Meade: *Old Churches, Ministers and Families of Virginia* (Philadelphia, 1857), I, 15, 16.

tion in the seventeenth century, the church had not the strength to withstand it.[5]

The records through the period of decline show a poignant contrast between the prevailing lapses among the Virginia clergy and the individual exceptions who heroically strove to keep the flame alive. Near the close of the seventeenth century a test was proposed to be applied to ministers to prove the "signs of Drunkenness." If a clergyman was observed "striking, challenging, threatening to fight . . . staggering, reeling, vomiting, incoherent, impertinent, obscene or rude talking," he was open to criticism.[6] On the other hand, such men as Anthony Gavin and Robert Rose, forever riding through their parishes, ignoring weather and terrain to preach, christen babies, and minister to the ailing, must have brought comfort or renewed faith in the lonely plantations.

> I have three churches [Gavin wrote to the Bishop of London] twenty-three and twenty-four miles from the glebe, in which I officiate every third Sunday, and besides these I have seven places of service up in the mountains. . . . I go twice a year to preach in twelve places, which I reckon better than 400 miles backward and forward and ford nineteen times the North and South Rivers.[7]

In other parts of the South—in the Carolinas and later in Georgia—there was a more varied religious color. The Quakers diluted the Established Church in North Carolina, and Presbyterians, Baptists and Congregationalists in South Carolina. In Georgia the dissenters far outnumbered the Anglicans. Maryland, like Virginia a colony deeply influenced by a tobacco economy, maintained its established church under attack by both Quakers and Catholics.

3

The other ethical consideration which was instrumental in building an ultimate national conscience developed through all the South during the colonial period. This was the attitude toward involuntary servitude, whose point of focus came to be the African Negro.

[5] There was arrest and imprisonment of Baptists as late as the 1770's. *Virginia Magazine of History*, XI, 414 ff.

[6] W. S. Perry, editor, *Historical Collections Relating to the American Colonial Church* (Hartford, 1870–8), I, 341, 342, quoted in T. J. Wertenbaker: *The First Americans* (New York, 1927), p. 129.

[7] Perry: op. cit., I, 360.

This question permeates the whole moral history of the United States. It is peculiarly American. It is interwoven with the political, economic, and military as well as the moral or ethical history. The basic problem has been resolved (as much, perhaps, for economic as for moral reasons), but there is a residue of conflict which even in the mid-twentieth century shades our views of democracy. In this part of our narrative we are concerned only with its origins.

In the seventeenth century there was confusion between slavery and bonded servitude. After the first settlements were established, the majority of the immigrants to all the colonies arrived under some kind of indenture. Either they had voluntarily submitted to a term of labor without pay in order to cover the cost of their passage or they had been kidnapped and sent across under an involuntary bond. As they could then be sold by the ship's captain, the indenture system was a source of profit. The purchaser bought the bond along with the servant, and the servant was obliged to serve out his time for whoever "owned" him, after which he became as free as anyone else. Meanwhile, he could be resold again and again. No disgrace attached to this kind of servitude. Often the service was far from menial; many boys learned a trade under indenture or acquired such skill at farming that they prospered after their release. In the heyday of southern prosperity, many a planter aristocrat, owning thousands of acres and dozens of slaves, had bonded servants in his American ancestry.

In the beginning even Negroes had the status of servants in Virginia. The twenty Negroes whom a Dutch ship landed at Jamestown in 1619, thereby assigning to Holland the legendary credit of providing the "cradle" of American slavery, had a peculiar status. According to James Ballagh, the Dutch ship was a privateer and the Negroes had been captured from a Spanish ship taken as a prize of piracy. As this capture gave no legal rights of ownership, "the negroes were persons of undetermined status."

> If the term slavery [says Ballagh] can be used at all to describe their condition it is only in the sense of political as distinguished from domestic slavery; that is, dependence upon the state similar to the plebian at Rome and the helot at Sparta. . . .[8]

[8] James Curtis Ballagh: *A History of Slavery in Virginia* (Johns Hopkins University Studies in Historical and Political Science, Extra Volume XXIV, Baltimore, 1902), p. 29.

Apparently they were regarded by the Jamestown people as "colony servants." They had been bought with government funds and they worked for the governor and government officers. There was no term of servitude, however, attached to them.

The progress of the Negro from this vague position into legal chattel slavery is of the greatest significance to an estimate of the problems of conscience involved. As far as the seventeenth-century colonists were concerned, the almost imperceptible evolution from uncertainty through custom into law scarcely involves conscience at all. From New England to Georgia, servants were merging into slaves even while others were gaining their freedom.

The operation of moral public opinion, as so often in American history, followed economic compulsions. Negroes in the north, where diversified farming and skilled trades were the rule, did not adapt themselves so as to benefit the economy as a whole. They could not be used in large gangs under an overseer in these occupations and must be trained individually to each special art. A slave-owner having but one or two slaves found their feeding and shelter costly. They did not always fit successfully into city life; on the farms, with their short seasons and bitter winters, they were more care than profit. In the northern activities the servants, looking forward to eventual freedom and thus ambitious to learn, were far more useful and no more costly.

To the tobacco colonies, on the other hand, slaves brought real prosperity—at least in colonial times. Not disturbed by the hot sun in their field work, knowing only a routine that was easy to learn, working rhythmically under a gang boss (usually depicted by northerners as wielding a whip), living together in concentrated quarters, consuming a large common food supply, bringing profit not only in their work but in their sale, they changed an arduous business into an enriching one for the large planters, created a genuine aristocracy and a leisure class of considerable cultural attainment.

Because of this difference it was easier for the people of the North to listen to murmurs of conscience on the slavery question than for the Maryland, Virginia, and Carolina planters whose entire economy was based on Negro labor. It is true that, as slavery increased, many sincere northerners came to preach abolition on strictly moral grounds. Yet it may be doubted that emancipation could have become law in New England, New York, New Jersey, and Pennsylvania if slavery had benefited their people. But all this interplay of conscience and economy was a later phenomenon, as were the infinitely curious wink that Puritan New England gave to its enriching slave trade and the far-fetched southern "alibi" about christianizing the poor heathen blacks.

Even in the South slavery was slow to catch on, and the transition to it from indentured servitude was so gradual that its moral aspects seemed not to differ from those applying to the bonded servants. In thirty years from the first shipment of Negroes there were not more than 300 Negroes in Virginia. As late as 1671, ten years after the colony had given legal sanction to slavery, there were only 2,000 slaves as opposed to 6,000 servants. In another ten years the number of servants had doubled, but the slaves had increased by only one third. After this, however, "servitude gave way before slavery, which was forced on the colony in the large importation of negroes by the Royal African Company under its exclusive charter" [9]

This English monopoly caused the gravest moral count against the mother country in the whole of American colonial history. That New England merchants shared the blame with those of the parent land and even stepped up the unspeakable horrors of the notorious "middle passage" did not modify Virginia's Anglophobia when, in the last half of the eighteenth century, she became frightened by the rising inundation of Africans.

Until well on in the 1700's we find very little conscience in any of the colonies about slavery. The earliest known protest, according to Professor Commager, came from the Mennonites of Germantown, Pennsylvania, in 1688.

> There is a saying, [they resolved in their February monthly meeting] that we should do to all men like as we will be done ourselves; making no difference of what generation, descent, or colour they are. And those who steal or rob men, and those who buy or purchase them, are they not all alike? [1]

In their native country, these disciples of Menno Simons added, "it is a terror or fearful thing that men should be handled so in Pennsylvania." [2]

[9] Ballagh: op. cit., p. 10.

[1] Henry S. Commager: *Documents of American History* (New York, 1947), p. 37.

[2] Ibid., p. 38.

Even in pious New England there was no disapproval by the clergy in the seventeenth century, although an occasional word was said about the highly impractical enslavement of the Indians. Massachusetts, indeed, gave legal sanction to slavery before Virginia—as early as 1641. Connecticut did the same in 1650, while it was not until the 1660's that the Negro entered the Virginia statutes as a chattel slave. Arthur Calhoun tells us that "raising slaves for market" [3] was practiced to a limited extent in Massachusetts until it was proved unprofitable.

> Negro children were, indeed, sold by the pound but the market was sadly sluggish, for negro babies were advertised in Boston to be given away like puppies and sometimes money was offered to anyone that would take them. Thus economic interest hoodwinked the Calvinist conscience. . . .[4]

Nevertheless, the institution continued legal throughout New England until the time of the Revolution, when Connecticut and Massachusetts had 5,000 slaves each, Rhode Island 4,000, and New Hampshire 700. In New York at this time the number had risen to 25,000 and New Jersey and Pennsylvania had 6,000 each.[5] Then, as we shall see, conscience developed apace among thinking people, due to the apparent inconsistency between the ringing words about liberty and equality in the Declaration of Independence and the denial of both of these abstractions to a very considerable part of the American people.

4

Our concentration on Virginia in the early colonial period has for its reason the fact that the moral questions posed by the tobacco economy were more acute there than elsewhere in the South. The Carolinas shared some of them. The Georgia experiment—transplanting to that fair country part of the population of the overcrowded London prisons—was in itself an open declaration of moral principle and one far more creditable to its projectors than

[3] George Moore: *Notes on the History of Slavery in Massachusetts* (New York, 1866), p. 69.

[4] Arthur W. Calhoun: *A Social History of the American Family* (Cleveland, 1917–19), I, 81. Moore: op. cit., p. 57.

[5] Ralph B. Flanders: "Slavery," in *Dictionary of American History,* V, 94.

the clandestine exportation of criminals by English governments which so roused the ire of Franklin. But the events in Georgia must come in a later phase of our study, at the time when a mechanical invention by a Yankee changed the whole of the southern economy and helped prepare the way to the Civil War.

By the second decade of the eighteenth century, moral estimates, especially of New England and the middle colonies, seemed to show many lapses in the century since hopeful Englishmen had first invaded the Indians' vast preserve. It was these estimates that gave rise to the welcome given, north and south, to the emotional religious revivals of Edwards and Whitefield that historians have called the "Great Awakening."

Chapter VIII

First Revival

THE DAWN OF the Great Awakening was preceded by an interval of moral darkness deeper, perhaps, and more pervasive than any other in the colonial period. Never was corruption more blatant or more cynical; never was lawbreaking so generally condoned in high places. All this was brought into sharp focus, beginning at the turn of the century, by an epidemic of piracy on the high seas.

The first decade of the new century was a time of disheartening business depression all through the colonies. War with the French (nearly a chronic condition in the colonial period), with the disastrous failures by the colonists in attacks on Montreal and Quebec, had been as costly in some ways as the Indian raids—by-products of the same conflict. The bungled treaty of Ryswick, which had brought an interval of peace, had made concessions to the French that nearly ruined the New England cod fisheries. In the South, as we have seen, the price of tobacco fell because of the enforcement of the Navigation Acts—a series of statutes which weighted the balance of trade heavily against the colonies. In the middle colonies the price of wheat fell because of competition from England in the West Indies trade.

The uneasy peace of Ryswick lasted only five years. King William's War ended in 1697 and Queen Anne's War began in 1702. In both there was sea fighting. But naval warfare in those days was not the exclusive province of inadequate navies operating under government direction and at government expense. The navies were ably assisted by private enterprise. The ships and their owners were both known as "privateers," and beyond the legalizing "letters of marque" given these adventurers and certain regulations about the prizes they captured, there was little restraint on their activities. There could not be. The seas were too wide, too empty. Once over the horizon, a ship was out of range of communication. The duties of a privateer were to raid and loot enemy vessels—if possible, to bring them into port and, after the judgment of a prize court, to receive most of the profit.

Men grew rich from this practice and, in the sale of the loot, became intimate with the merchants of the seaports. But when the war was over, they were out of legitimate employment. The life of wild, free adventure with its peculiar fascination for the necessarily hardy and reckless men chosen for the patriotic work was theoretically finished. The temptation to find one's way back into some sort of predatory sailing was hard to resist. It was easy to move across the vague lines set by a treaty; to plunder what were no longer enemy vessels; to move, in short, from privateering to piracy. In England this progress had been practiced since the days of Francis Drake; it was hardly surprising that it appeared in the American colonies in that brief interval between English wars as the century turned.

Colonial piracy, however, had peculiarly American aspects. In them we see forecasts of moral delinquencies that have plagued us ever since. Since the establishment of the Board of Trade or "Lords of Trade" in England in 1675, the undirected but growing desires of the English merchants had crystallized into the beginnings of a colonial policy. In a quarter-century the march of England toward economic leadership of the world had acquired its rhythm. It was natural for the colonies to fall into a subservient position. What, after all, were colonies for? At vast expense of life and treasure the American settlements had been established—or so the Englishmen in England said—and the mother country now expected a return. Parliament had made this expectation more certain by passing laws binding the colonies to a fulfillment of the obligation. In the staple products that England needed, they must sell only to England. The manufactures so desperately needed by the colonists must be imported only from England. England must set the prices for both.

The policy worked in the West Indies and in the southern colonies of North America. The planters of sugar, tobacco, rice, and indigo were already under a burden of debt. They had no choice but to obey the law. To some extent, the middle colonies, dedicated to agriculture, were under similar limitations, though New York and Philadelphia were becoming important mercantile centers. But north of Maryland there were other factors in the struggle for survival. The middle colonies had insufficient agricultural products to pay for the imported goods they needed from England. In New York, the Jerseys, and Pennsylvania, ships were built and men went down to the sea in them to trade in foreign lands. Finally, neither king nor Parliament could mold the Yankees to fit a colonial policy. With such meager products from the soil, New Englanders must either fish and trade or go bankrupt. So they evaded the Navigation Acts from the beginning. From the beginning of England's colonial policy they had smuggled.

They and, in a lesser degree, the middle colonies had been forced to smuggle. England had imposed that necessity upon them, and they turned the act from moral obliquity to a patriotic defense of their rights. Some two and a half centuries later Britons forgot this, and between 1920 and 1933 they caricatured the hypocritical Americans who wrapped their bottles of gin in American flags before they drank the contents. By then, however, the techniques of bootlegging developed under English pressure in the seventeenth and eighteenth centuries were working smoothly enough.

Skill in smuggling, ruthlessness learned in privateering, and a growing desire for quick riches combined with the exceptionally convenient features of the coastline to make piracy a natural American sport. Sometimes the privateers—furnished so liberally with letters of marque and reprisal by the provincial governors—graduated into piracy before the war was over. By no means all of the pirates were colonials.[1] The notorious William Kidd, for instance, was a native of Greenock in Scotland and died at Execution Dock in London. But, like most of them, he made his fortune in an American port and used the inlets, coves, and empty harbors of Long Island for his clandestine operations.[2]

The greatest stimulus to this predatory business at the century's turn came from an institution deeply entrenched among our mores. In later days we have come to name this "racket." It has usually consisted in an alliance of wealthy promoters of illegal activity with the agents of government. During King William's War the loot of the privateers putting into New York harbor had brought rapid

[1] Exploits of the most famous colonial pirates are told in *Pirates of the New England Coast*, by George F. Dow and John Henry Edmonds (Salem, 1923).

[2] "Kidd, William," in *Dictionary of American Biography*. Captain Kidd began his career under a commission to chase and capture pirates. How, in the process, he turned pirate himself is one of the more dramatic stories in buccaneering history.

profit to the New York merchants. At war's end these gentlemen were as reluctant to give up the trade as the privateers were to stop looting. Technically, therefore, they went underground but in practice not very far. They did not have to. The merchants and pirates together had bought the government. The pirates, often drunk and disorderly, swaggered through the streets boasting of their triumphs. When the Earl of Bellomont arrived to take over the governorship, he found it had been the custom for the pirates to present fabulous gifts to the governor in return for protection.

New York in 1700 had already acquired its reputation for greed, cynicism, and corruption. Established by the Dutch avowedly as a trading depot, it had continued under the English with business the main preoccupation. To it had gone people from all parts of Europe: its polyglot population even at this early time recognized no common religious compulsion. The Calvinist Dutch Reformed Church was neighbor to the Lutheran, the Huguenot, and the Anglican. The Church of England, after several attempts to become the established church, had become nearly as diluted as in the tobacco country.

Politically there had been chaos. The stupid, drunken, or arrogant Dutch governors had been followed by a succession of weak or corrupt Englishmen. In 1691 the insurgent Jacob Leisler [3] had almost brought the colony to civil war. Later Benjamin Fletcher had accepted silver and jewels from the pirate Robert Coats—worth, it was reported, some eighteen hundred pounds—and had protected him in return.

On the whole, then, the beautiful little community at the mouth of Hudson's river might be said to have had much on its conscience, providing, of course, that there had been such a thing as a community conscience there. The merchants, enriched by illegal operations despite the general colonial depression, could hardly feel any pricks of remorse through the Oriental luxuries heaped upon them by the pirates plying between Madagascar and Oyster Bay or other Long Island havens. The "aristocrats," presented with magnificent land grants by prodigal governors, naturally had no regrets. It was only the little people whose individual consciences had kept the Dutch churches alive, and many of them had moved away across the rivers and were working out their salvation in the backwoods.

[3] "Leisler, Jacob," ibid.

It was the Virginians who ended the pirate terror in 1718. By that time it had become a menace to colonial prosperity. Between 1697 and 1702 it had flourished with the assistance of the merchants, and it had brought wealth of a sort in a time of small pickings by honest commerce. But after the Peace of Utrecht in 1713, which put a period to French commercial competition, colonial fortunes took a swift upturn. It was during the waxing of this prosperity that piracy, renewing its activity in the Caribbean and along the Atlantic coast of America, become intolerable. Legitimate trade was then more profitable and far less risky than high-seas robbery. Furthermore, the pirates hiding in the innumerable inlets of the Carolinas, Virginia, and Pennsylvania or the hospitable Bahamas were no respecters of persons or nationalities, and now it was colonial cargoes that were being looted. It was in these years that the raids of Avery, Bonnet, Hornigold, Low, Williams, and Teach kept coastwise shipping and coastal communities in continual terror. Low and Williams were from Massachusetts.

There are so many picaresque yarns about Edward Teach,[4] the most notorious pirate in colonial history, that it is impossible completely to unravel the twisted threads of romance and fact. Known as "Blackbeard," Teach hid in and operated from various North Carolina coves, where it was suspected that he enjoyed government protection for which various officials had been heavily rewarded.[5] Governor Spotswood of Virginia, however, angry at such corruption, sent two armed sloops to capture the pirate who had done such damage to Virginia shipping. The fight took place off North Carolina territory, and when it was over with a loss of twelve Virginians killed and twenty wounded, Spotswood had another fight on his hands in which he was expected to explain why he had trespassed on his neighbor's province! In any case, the villain and nine of his crew were killed,[6] and Blackbeard's darkly whiskered head was stuck on a pole and carried triumphantly back to Virginia with nine of his crew's survivors. The scene of this grisly triumph still raises gooseflesh on the visitors to Hampton.[7]

[4] Or Thatch, which more probably was his real name.

[5] *The Colonial Records of North Carolina*, W. L. Saunders, editor (Raleigh, 1886–90), II, 327. "Letters of Alexander Spotswood," in Virginia Historical Society Collections, New Series, II, 319.

[6] Ibid., pp. 273–5.

[7] *Virginia* (American Guide Series, W.P.A., New York, 1940), p. 230.

With the death of Stede Bonnet in the same year, piracy faded out. It had made as colorful a contribution to American history as any episode of the colonial period, and its color has mellowed the more criminal and sanguinary details. While the most notorious of its characters came from England, Rhode Island with Thomas Tew and Massachusetts with Hawkins, Johnston, Halsey, Bradish, Low, and Paul Williams certainly played their parts. Though Massachusetts stood aloof from notoriety and pointed accusing fingers at Newport [8] and New York, it is hardly surprising that a provincial conscience that winked at the triangle trade in rum and slaves could have been deeply pricked by piracy on remote sealanes. Furthermore, the old-style Calvinist ministers kept their flocks too busy with jeremiads about the decline of religion for much thought to stray seaward after the Jolly Roger.

But religion in the 1700's was due for a drastic housecleaning not only in New England but throughout the colonies. It was the sort of periodical renovation that is known as "revival." In it many old formal routines and dogmas are swept away, the individual conscience replaces that of the congregation or church community, and at the same time there occur emotional excesses—spasms of artificial conversion—which are deplored by the more sober and serene devout. Yet this phase, even in its orgiastic extremes, is deeply embedded in the history of the American conscience; and it is the curious blend of this frantic evangelism with the religion of reason or "Deism" that formed the moral temper with which we faced the formation of the United States. For all their antagonism and contradiction, neither element killed the other: both still persist.

2

In America the Great Awakening, according to Charles Maxson, had four separate and largely independent origins.[9] These sporadic risings present a curious phenomenon. In every case they seem to have emerged out of a decaying church: they were insurgencies in-

[8] Samuel Eliot Morison, Massachusetts's strongest champion, is still pointing, at least as far as the slave trade is concerned. See *The Maritime History of Massachusetts, 1783–1860* (Boston, 1921), p. 19.

[9] Charles H. Maxson: *The Great Awakening in the Middle Colonies* (Chicago, 1920), *passim.*

spired by a sense of religious declension or at least a failure of religion to satisfy persistent needs of conscience. Whether we can trace them to moral lapses—to seasons of misbehavior—is doubtful. Rather they seem to be attributable to nostalgia for a recent but departed sense of security due to the presence of God. People seem to have gone out of their churches with their faith sterilized by formality, by organization; restless, they went about searching—"thirsting," as Whitefield said—for some new invigorating awareness of a divine presence. Actually religion was, of course, declining: partly because of the fading-out of superstition, partly because a promised land was being so prodigal in fulfilling its promises that heaven was coming down to earth and fasting and humiliation were no longer necessary.

But the American scene was becoming one of endless repetition of the same function: refuge for the poor, the oppressed, the persecuted of Europe, and prosperity was forever being leavened by new influxes of the destitute. This was the kind of folk that brought German pietism to Pennsylvania. More or less the same sort were the Dutch who abandoned dissolute and expensive Manhattan for the Jersey wilds and got eventually to places where their formalized Amsterdam "Classis" or headquarters of the Reformed Church could no longer reach them. And the hounded Scotch-Irish, the bitterly oppressed and persecuted Ulster exiles who invaded Bucks County and various Pennsylvania frontier tracts, had most certainly bypassed prosperity in any form.

The first to come were the Mennonites in 1683. They founded Germantown, now part of Philadelphia. Next, in 1694, came that group of forty mystics called the "Order of the Woman in the Wilderness" because they thought of themselves as carried to America like the woman in Revelation [1] by the "two wings of the great eagle" to a place God had prepared for them. Finally, in 1709, there began that painful flight from the German Palatine miseries which eventually brought more than thirty thousand immigrants.[2] These people, coming to Pennsylvania because it was the province of William Penn's "Holy Experiment"—the "free colony" where "all mankind" was guaranteed civil and religious freedom and economic opportunity—formed a nucleus of pietism which prepared the way for Pennsylvania revival.

[1] Rev. 12:14. [2] Maxson: op. cit., p. 7.

Theodorus Frelinghuysen was the Dutch-bred German pastor who was sent by the Amsterdam Classis to minister to the back-country Hollanders in the Raritan valley. No sooner had he arrived than he horrified half the Dutch Reformed ministers in America. The other half came close to worshipping him. The resulting split in the Dutch Reformed Church went very deep. It is interesting to observe here the same division between rich and poor, between educated and ignorant, that was a constant accompaniment of the revival.

The third focus—that of the Presbyterians—was the so-called Log College of William Tennent in Neshaminy. This Irish preacher founded his school to educate ministers for the Presbyterian ministry, in which he was assisted by his four sons, all of whom became pastors. From the view with which most of us regard religious belief and exercise in the mid-twentieth century, the methods of Gilbert Tennent, frightening his congregations literally into fits by his graphic word pictures of hell, are scarcely appealing. But if we can envisage the dreary aspects of the communities in which such men preached in the 1730's and '40's, we know that any real excitement was welcome. And the convulsed conversions of sinners in the revival seemed to have held a real and novel glamour.

Meanwhile, as these various *foyers* for the Awakening were being prepared, a true intellectual giant was operating in New England in much the same direction. The son of a Connecticut minister of ordinary "pedestrian" [3] talents, Jonathan Edwards became one of the key figures in the history of the American conscience.

Entering Yale at thirteen (when Yale itself was only two years older), he became an intense and tireless student of philosophy and natural science. When he was graduated he went through a long development of religious conviction. These things came to flower in his preaching in a church at Northampton, Massachusetts, in 1734, when he was thirty-one. Here he brought throngs of "sinners" to their knees in prostrated conversion and others, it is said, to suicide. His doctrine was, like that of Calvin himself, that only by a total consciousness of his own depravity can man be brought into a realization of the contrasting glory of God.

[3] Ola Elizabeth Winslow: *Jonathan Edwards* (New York, 1940), p. 22. This brilliant biography is one of the finest contributions to the literature of the Great Awakening.

> O sinner! [he would exhort them] Consider the fearful danger you are in: It is a great furnace of wrath, a wide and bottomless pit, full of the fire of wrath that you are held over in the hand of that God whose wrath is provoked and incensed as much against you, as against many of the damned in hell: You hang by a slender thread, with the flames of divine wrath flashing about it, and ready every moment to singe it, and burn it asunder. . . .[4]

While some of the sinners came, on hearing such sermons, to the conclusion that life was scarcely worth its struggle, others experienced that ecstasy known as conversion and came at last to the certainty that they had been saved. How Edwards conciliated these revelations which he had inspired with Calvin's old doctrine—that man can in no way influence the predetermined divine election—was one of those theological permutations which appeared logical enough to the devout of the 1730's but seem stark inconsistencies two centuries later. Actually, by this time New England, what with its Half-Way Covenant and other compromises, had moved so far from Calvin that Edwards often shocked the new orthodox ministers by relaying from his pulpit echoes from a forgotten Geneva.

3

These four separate revivals might well have died in their locales without ever joining in the huge religious awakening which united the colonies in the 1740's but for a unifying force from outside. The pietists—Moravians, Mennonites, Dunkers, and others—now moving southward through the Valley of Virginia, were out of contact with the Tenents of Pennsylvania; between the Log College and Frelinghuysen of the Raritan was the barrier of language, and they were all far away from the hard-bitten Yankees. But while Edwards was assisting his God in holding the human spiders over the pit and the Germans were seeking theirs in the serenity of silent meditation, there came across the sea the overtones of a young man's voice so vibrant, so thrilling, and so convincing that people from Saco to Savannah were stopping their work and their worship to listen.

By this time there were more newspapers. Franklin had founded

[4] "Sinners in the Hands of an Angry God," in *Sermons by Jonathan Edwards* (Boston, 1785), p. 350.

his *Pennsylvania Gazette* in Philadelphia and Bradford his *Mercury*, and there were organs of news in Boston, New York, Newport, Charleston, and Williamsburg. All of them contained quotations from articles in papers published in England, and this was one of the few sources of information common to all the colonies. In the late 1730's every American paper carried stories of this inspired pastor to whose preachings people all over England swarmed by the tens of thousands. He spoke not only in the churches but to vast gatherings in the open air; not only to respectable congregations but to the rude colliers of Bristol. And he had participated in Oglethorpe's more or less holy experiment in Georgia. He had spent months in Savannah, where he had founded an orphans' home. His voice was said to have such carrying quality that twenty thousand could hear him easily.

George Whitefield had emerged from the Church of England after a "new birth" during which he had gone through a series of agonies and visions, coming at last, as he believed, into the convincing Presence. Since then he had consorted with Wesley and the embryonic Methodists. Since then, too, the respectable, orthodox, established-church clergy had quivered in their lace surplices with indignation at this vulgar impostor, and while the colonial newspapers were printing their awesome stories, London wags and rhymesters were abusing him with ridicule.

The wave of response and expectation that swept the colonies in 1739 was testimony to the universal readiness for a religious awakening. It was the first "wave" of any sort which had been felt throughout the Atlantic community. Even the common fear of the Indians had been sporadic. Now the "thirst," as Whitefield called it, for "God's salvation and a sense of divine love" was almost universal among the colonial masses. This was most certainly one of the events which built American union and, because it was a mass movement, helped build the ideal of equality.

He came to the middle colonies in the winter of 1739–40. Even the free-thinking Franklin was stirred by him to the point that he emptied his pockets into the collection—a rare act for the thrifty printer.

> It was wonderful [Franklin wrote] to see the change soon made in the manners of our inhabitants. From being thoughtless or indifferent about religion, it seemed as if all the world were growing

> religious, so that one could not walk thro' the town in an evening without hearing psalms sung in different families of every street.[5]

By the time Whitefield arrived in New England the accounts of his preaching in the other colonies, together with his published sermons, had raised the popular excitement to the point of hysteria. When finally, in September, he came to Massachusetts he was greeted like a Messiah. Even the moanings and groanings which had filled the Edwards church at Northampton were exceeded by the huge throngs listening to Whitefield. His impact on what we call the "common man" is poignantly set forth in a manuscript account by Nathan Cole, a Connecticut farmer:

> Sudden, in the morning about 8 or 9 of the Clock there came a message and said Mr. Whitefield . . . is to preach at Middletown this morning at ten of the Clock, I was in my field at Work, I dropt my tool that I had in my hand and ran home to my wife telling her to make ready quickly . . . then run to the pasture for my horse with all my might; fearing that I should be too late; . . . I with my wife soon mounted the horse and went forward as fast as I thought the horse could bear, and when my horse got much out of breath I would get down and put my wife on the Saddle . . . and so I would run untill I was much out of breath . . . all the while fearing we should be too late to hear the Sermon . . . and when we came within about half a mile or a mile of the Road that came down from Hartford . . . to Middletown; on high land I saw before me a Cloud or fogg rising . . . but as I came nearer the Road, I heard a noise something like a low rumbling thunder and presently found it was the noise of Horses feet coming down the Road and this Cloud was a Cloud of dust made by the Horses feet . . . and when I came within about 20 rods of the Road, I could see men and horses Sliping along in the Cloud like shadows . . . a steady Stream . . . scarcely a horse more than his length behind another, all of a Lather and foam with sweat . . . every horse seemed to go with all his might to carry his rider to hear news from heaven for the saving of Souls. . . .

The Coles, bedraggled and breathless, got there along with the other "3 or 4000 of people" just in time.

> When I saw Mr. Whitefield come upon the Scaffold he lookt almost Angelical; a young, Slim, slender youth . . . and my hearing how God was with him every where as he came along it Solemnized

[5] *The Writings of Benjamin Franklin,* I, 354, 355.

> my mind; and put me in a trembling fear before he began to preach. . . .[6]

Whitefield's preaching was gentler than that of Edwards or Gilbert Tennent. He was tolerant of all sects—even of the Quakers. But his influence seems only partly to have come from his words. As we read them in print, they seem indeed, as Miss Winslow says, scaled to the twelve-year-old mind. But his voice and his manner were truly hypnotic.

> His personal triumph [writes Miss Winslow] was unparalleled in American pulpit history. . . . Colossally egotistical, intellectually shallow and lazy, he was unimpeachably sincere. He believed what he preached. Therein lay his power. . . . As he proceeded from meetinghouse to meetinghouse, his glory mounted higher and higher until those who followed him lost all sense of rational discrimination. The story of his amazing pilgrimage through New England in 1740 reads like fictionized biography of the age of the Crusades, not solid history of eighteenth-century America.[7]

Powerful as it was in terms of emotional response, the Great Awakening was short-lived. Whitefield was followed—as all such men are—by imitative itinerant preachers of far less magnetism and sincerity. The converts of a Sunday would wake with a sort of spiritual hangover on Monday and soon lapse out of salvation. Also, a far more rational religion was making deep inroads along with the new science. Franklin was the exponent of both, and those who followed him were more steadfast than the hysterical followers of the soul-savers.

Yet, short-lived as it was, the revival had far more consequences than any other evangelical event before or since. It bred tolerance of the various faiths. It was exceedingly democratic. The memory of it was carried on into frontier after frontier, and it had an effect on moral behavior which the free life of the churchless backwoods was likely to oppose. Though its last performances were ended by mid-century, it is impossible to think of anything like a continuous moral core in American life without it.

[6] Quoted by Leonard W. Labaree in *William and Mary Quarterly* (Williamsburg, Va.), 3rd Series, Vol. VII (October 1950), pp. 590, 591.
[7] Winslow: op. cit., pp. 176, 177.

Chapter IX

"*Nature's God*"

Boston, the center of seventeenth-century intolerance and Puritan conservatism, became the cradle of eighteenth-century revolutionary thought in both religion and politics. It is a curious fact that this city—ancient, as American communities go—has achieved the reputation of backwater reaction, of the rigidity, the inviolate principles and reluctance to change of a George Apley stolidly resident upon the bulwark of Beacon Hill when, in fact, the fire of revolt has usually burned hotter in its streets than elsewhere; when, in the novelty of its ideas, the violence of its action, and the dubious morality of its behavior, Boston has frequently shocked the rest of the nation.

That its ministers felt obliged to banish Anne Hutchinson and Roger Williams is testimony to these "heretics' " immense followings even at a time when theocracy was at the peak of its power. From the start of the eighteenth century, the refusal to conform by Harvard College, the radical religious sallies into Arminianism, the growing belief in free will and doubts of the validity of revelation that so shocked the Mathers, and the acrid satires of politics and the clergy that landed James Franklin in jail—all these things were portents not of a society complacent in its static acceptance of prescribed form but of subterranean combustion always dangerously near the surface.

In later years Boston nursed the political firebrand Sam Adams, the instigators of the Tea Party, the first revolutionary committees of correspondence, the fiercest of the abolitionists, the religious innovations of Unitarianism and Christian Science, and, from being the angriest persecutor of papists, acquired the second-largest Roman Catholic population of any city in the United States, regardless of size.[1] Boston, also, for several years held the national record for magnitude of bank robberies and had the unique distinction of being administered by a mayor resident in jail. The communistic and socialistic experiments of Brook Farm and the Fourier phalanxes were instigated by Boston intellectuals, and from them, too, came the bulk of support for Emersonian transcendentalism.

Yet, in the early 1700's, side by side with phenomena quite alien to the inflexible dogmas held by the Winthrops, the Endecotts, the Cottons, the Davenports, the Mathers, and the Edwardses, the deep Puritan core survived. In a sense, however different in tenets and outlook, the liberal—the "enlightened"—churches were built on the old rock. The fact that New England—but especially Massachusetts—had a more firmly established religious and moral tradition than the other colonies, bigoted as it was, seemed to attract and stimulate the new religious and moral thought. For all its limited concept of revelation, its dark certainty of predestination, its curious reversal (as it seems to us) of the order of good works and salvation, and its inherent incapacity for incorporation with a civil government, the tradition was one on which almost any sound Christian structure might be erected. After all, Puritanism had been the very heart and soul of the Reformation, and no Protestant faith could ever be wholly cut off from the Puritan stem.

We see in Boston, in these years, the origins of many concepts and convictions that later took form in the preamble to the Declaration of Independence. In the preaching that often drowned out the echoes of the Calvinist sermons, man achieved a new dignity in a beautiful and rational universe. The old abasement of fallen mankind before an accusing, wrathful God gave way to a sense of benign fatherhood. Into the new words from the pulpits crept concepts of "the Laws of Nature," "Nature's God," "equality," and even "the pursuit of Happiness."

As early as 1699, when the Puritans were still recovering from the shocks of the new Massachusetts charter and the witch hysteria, the Brattle Street Church made the first radical change. It shattered the theological snobbery of the orthodox churches by allowing "persons of visible sanctity" to be baptized and even to attend the Lord's Supper without proof of "regenerative" experience. Also, in the

[1] Number one, Chicago, 1,743,936; two, Boston, 1,360,732; three, New York, 1,302,306.

"manifesto" of the church there was a definite pronouncement of the theory of government with the consent of the governed. Thus, the Brattle Street Church had made one of the first contributions to that democracy which was to become one of the ideals of our republic. In soil so wide and free, where the conditions of men changed so rapidly, there would be less and less room for aristocracy in religion.

It is significant that Thomas Brattle, who sponsored the Brattle Street Church, and his brother William, who introduced the same innovations as pastor of a church across the river in Cambridge, were sons of a merchant said to be the wealthiest in all New England. A merchant's son also was Boston-born Solomon Stoddard, who spread the democratic worship all down the valley of the Connecticut from the frontier town of Northampton, Massachusetts. So, too, were the Colmans, John and Benjamin, of the Brattle group, and John Mico of that church was a merchant in his own right. Such men, as Perry Miller points out, "would no longer subject themselves to the indignity of a public relation of their sins." [2]

The seeds of faiths borne across the Atlantic by new winds of doctrine found an early welcome in the decomposing soil of Massachusetts theocracy. But they took root, too, in other places. In Connecticut they were soon undermining the theological foundations of that bastion of Congregational orthodoxy, Yale College. In New York, Pennsylvania, and the South, their effect was less shocking, as they had been preceded by the happier beliefs of Anglicans, Quakers, and Catholics. The Great Awakening, itself a sort of emotional spasm of little lasting substance, gave sharp clarification to that wave of rational thinking we call the Enlightenment. Superstitious, frightening, putting Satan on a personal level with God, the revivals so roused the contempt of those who had tasted the new science that their "religion of nature" was given a new impetus.

What, then, was this "Enlightenment"? Whence did it stem and why was it important to American morality as well as to American culture? The answer is a prologue to 1776.

[2] Miller: *The New England Mind: From Colony to Province,* p. 255.

2

All through the seventeenth century in Western civilization there were flickers of light on the horizon signaling the imminence of a new dawn. In England there was an almost constant struggle for liberty—for political liberty and liberty of conscience. By the end of the century a people who had beheaded one king and sent another into exile was in no mood to temporize over the tradition of divine right. But their liberation from the tyranny of sovereigns who had once been sacred as God's own appointees was only the beginning of revolutionary thought. If they could dispense with kings, why not with a dictated religion bound within the covers of a book —a religion which had fettered them to beliefs against reason and had dwelt with constant, morbid reiteration on the loathsomeness of man? Was this man who had overthrown kings, conquered perilous seas, and established new societies in strange wildernesses so utterly vile, so beyond redemption, simply because it had been "revealed" that he was tied to a first Adam by bonds of sin?

This was the mood—the "climate of opinion," as Professor Whitehead called it—which was growing parallel with the wonderful events in the realm of science that had happened all over Europe. The church's persecution of Galileo had not dimmed the bright illumination of his discoveries but rather enhanced it. Inquiring minds, wrenching themselves out of age-long theological chains, saw in this time a light over Italy that gave them courage. In France, René Descartes was finding, along with a novel explanation of God, a mathematical vista that would lead to future green pastures of physical understanding. But most stirring of all, as the century wore on, was the upheaval in all the old views and concepts of nature wrought by Isaac Newton. It was from Newton that the true Enlightenment sprang: in all the writings of English philosophers and through the schools of the French *philosophes*—in the free world of the optimist Locke, the mechanistic universe of Hume and Diderot, Helvetius and Holbach—Newton's star is forever visible.

Newton opened God's "inscrutable" workings to the naked eye of man. He dissolved the mysteries that had held man and even whole societies in subject fear. It had been sacrilege to probe the interrelations of the stars. These were the machinery of portents, the signs of heaven. God sent the comets and the eclipses to warn men of his catastrophic punishments. Storm, earthquake, tidal wave, lightning —implements of God's will; it was sin to investigate them. You must not look behind the Great Magician's black curtain to see how he did his tricks. But Newton looked. With a telescope and some mathematics he worked out the scheme of gravity holding the worlds to their orbits. With a prism—a toy—he analyzed light. And to thinking and partially liberated men the apparent ease of his operations and the simplicity of his instruments were stunning realities. The illusions dissolved. Corrupt man achieved a halo. The philosophers constructed a new cosmos. In it natural forces were at man's disposal. Pragmatists like Franklin proposed to make them useful. Thus nature's human victims became her conquerors and man moved from the remote fringe to the center of the universe.

The German philosopher Immanuel Kant, looking back at the great era from its peak, wrote:

> Enlightenment is the liberation of man from his self-caused state of minority. Minority is the incapacity of using one's understanding without the assistance of another. This state of minority is self-caused when its source lies not in a lack of understanding, but in a lack of determination and courage to use it without the assistance of another. *Sapere aude!* Dare to use your own understanding! is therefore the motto of the enlightenment.[3]

This was easy to say—*sapere aude*—in 1784! It was far harder to do a century earlier. When philosophers first "dared to know," God had been the central focus of the thought and action of Christians for more than a thousand years. It was an authoritarian, an inscrutable, but a personal God behaving under amplified human impulses such as love or vengeance. Under this concept men had lived in fear, but it had given them, also, consolation in the certainty that death, sickness, hardship, and poverty came from God's will and must therefore somehow be right.

Because of the hold this concept had on that part of the human race they lived among and knew best, the philosophers were wary even when they "dared" to use their own intelligences. Most of their

[3] *Beantwortung der Frage: Was ist Aufklärung* (1784), opening sentence. The translation here given is that of Ernst Cassirer in his article "Enlightenment," in *Encyclopædia of the Social Sciences.* A more literal rendering is that of Carl J. Friedrich in *The Philosophy of Kant,* Modern Library edition (New York, 1949), p. 132.

published writings affirm their steadfast belief in a "Supreme Being." Inflated with enthusiasm about the wonders of nature, they often glorified the Creator with glowing words, but always he was a glorious abstraction, never a person sitting in heaven on a throne, watching sparrows fall or counting lost sheep. At the same time, in the very reflection of this glory, they undermined all the tenets of the established Christian churches. To us, with our beliefs nourished by science of which even Newton scarcely dreamed, the results of the Enlightenment seem healthy enough. So perhaps they were, but at the moment of their impact they swept away the ground beneath the feet of countless thousands of people.

The first target was Original Sin. The Almighty was scarcely almighty if he could allow the serpent such an easy victory as that of Eden as reported in Genesis. He was hardly benevolent if he could put a curse on the whole of the human race because the first man disobeyed him. And how could one man (Jesus) atone for the sins of all men in the sacrifice of his life and then, by securing their faith, lift them up from the fall into which Adam had plunged them? Following these attacks, there was scrutiny of the virgin birth, the divinity of Christ, and the creation of man in God's image. All these ideas seemed to the philosophers anthropomorphic, and they regarded most of them as petty compared with the sublimity revealed by natural phenomena. Yet—quite inconsistently, it seems to us—the most rational of them clung to faith in the immortality of the individual soul!

Professor Becker finds much that is naïve in the thought of these rebels. To him their cynicism or skepticism was superficial. It was as if they had turned in delight to a new worship. As the eighteenth century came in, although

> God had been withdrawing from immediate contact with men, and had become, in proportion as he had receded into the dim distance, no more than the Final Cause, or Great Contriver, or Prime Mover of the universe,[4]

nevertheless there was a passionate faith among those who had discovered in stars, planets, and the spectrum a more direct and comprehensible revelation than that in the books of the prophets. Thus the eighteenth-century state of mind,

[4] Carl Becker: *The Declaration of Independence* (New York, 1942), pp. 36, 37.

> with uplifted eyes contemplating and admiring the Universal Order, . . . was excited and animated to correspond with the general harmony.[5]

3

Of all those who preached the new religion—if such it may be called—none stands as enduringly in the record of the American conscience as the frail English physician—friend of Newton and the *philosophes*—John Locke. With a clean sweep, in his *Essay Concerning the Human Understanding* he demolished the possibility of original sin and the certainty of God innate in the mind of man. At birth, he said, the human mind is a clean slate, and the fact that he took some thirty thousand words to prove this shows to what length the Christian churches had carried the contrary notion and what pressure of logic Locke felt must be brought to combat it.

> It is an established opinion amongst men [he wrote] that there are in the *understanding* certain *innate principles,* some primary notions . . . which the soul receives in its very first being, and brings into the world with it. . . . It would be sufficient to convince unprejudiced minds of the falseness of this supposition, if I should only show . . . how men, barely by the use of their natural faculties, may attain to all the knowledge they have, without the help of any innate impressions.[6]

Here was immediate appeal to common sense, that quality which America was daily developing in Americans who had to cope with raw nature. Perhaps the frontier woman, for example, found perennial comfort in the thought that God had taken away the long succession of her babies to use as instruments of his will in another world: yet the thought of those little dead hopes having sin innate in their souls could never have been congruous. And when at last one lived and grew, did she not see the clean slate, the white paper behind the wide astonished eyes, being continuously written upon, not with a series of messages from some supernatural source but by the sure pen of experience—sounds, colors, forms—and from sensations the mind's own creations by reflection—the understanding of growth, decay, change, of cause and effect—and, finally, with

[5] Ibid., p. 52.

[6] *Essay Concerning Human Understanding,* Book I, Chap. 2, Sec. 1.

teaching and prodding, punishment, recompense, and pragmatic evaluation, the distinction between right and wrong?

So conscience, too, was not innate! Conscience, that mysterious gift of God, a developed thing growing as the body grew, as new muscular power came to arms and legs and the heat of ideas turned to energy in the mind! Well, that was what all the outward signs of life had shown; that was the scheme life's practice had followed; it was sensible. But on knees in the dark while the wolves called and the wind whispered of fear, many a penitent asked God's pardon for such notions, rational and self-evident as they might be.

Thus Locke's "science of man" entered America—sensible but frightening, liberating but offering no reinforcements from outside oneself. In the cities it was more largely welcome than on the frontiers. Instructed, aware of another world outside, reading more and more, sick of the sense of sin, tired of the preaching of "grace," and wanting to enjoy without twinges the abundance all about them, the top layers of civilized society accepted the optimism the new philosophers offered about humanity, the dignity of man, and the kingdom of earth more immediate than that of heaven.

Along with Locke's science of man, his political ideas inspired Americans. Life, liberty, property—the words rang through the streets with more insistence as the century advanced. The natural rights of man, inalienable, "mankind . . . all equal and independent," "power and jurisdiction . . . reciprocal" were phrases heard with varying shades of response by the Morrises, the Coldens, and the Dutch Schuylers of New York; received with a smile and a nod by Franklin and David Rittenhouse in Philadelphia, interpreted earnestly if ungrammatically to the tough backwoodsman in Vermont by Ethan Allen, and becoming part of the education of a Virginia boy named Jefferson. It was not that everyone read Locke's long, slow-moving treatises. Only a few read them. But almost everyone came to know what they said. Ideas—sometimes only half-clad in words—have always seeped out thus from books and erudite tracts and long, involved speeches into the common stream. It has been said that certain words live forever, even when they have lost their first meaning. In America ideas found by Locke in his own troubled conscience were translated into "pursuit of happiness" or "consent of the governed." Such ideas are now imbedded in the American conscience, and will not die even when we doubt them. They are part of our eternal book along with such still more dubious phrases as "manifest destiny," a "world safe for democracy," and "freedom from want."

4

To get in simple terms the ideas philosophers and scientists were explaining with long words and long books was the crying need of Americans in the eighteenth century. Words had come from pulpits: words built upon Biblical texts, which had been intelligible to the preacher only after long contemplation in the quiet of his study, had for many decades merely benumbed the listeners. They had been kept awake by the hardness of the pews, the coldness of the meetinghouse, and the shuddering of their consciences. To most of them the words were without meaning or held meanings God had not yet given the common man understanding enough to grasp. Thus, their ears had closed and their minds strayed.

Printed words in the seventeenth century were expected to be dignified. The duller they were, the more admirable. Those who read were superior folk: it tickled their vanity that their inferiors could not understand. Even the Bible came to common men secondhand: there was a rule in the Puritan churches that Scripture must not be read without interpretation by the minister. Newspapers were erudite and dull—the property of the upper class. Even the elaborate satires on public conditions that shocked Boston in James Franklin's *Courant* shocked only top-level Bostonians until James's rapscallion brother devised ways to make the vulgar laugh.

It was that boy, grown up, who first answered this great eighteenth-century need in the colonies. In his middle teens in Boston he rebelled against the long words, the involved theology, the endless dialectic of the "revealed" divine inspiration. Why must the Word of God be such a long word—so disputed? The boy, hungry for print, read by firelight through the night all the books on polemic divinity in his father's library and was disgusted at the waste of his time. But he also, at sixteen, read Locke's *Essay Concerning the Understanding* and several scientific and mathematical works; he read books on the shocking new religion of Deism and became, perversely, an ardent Deist as a result. All this time he was literally holding words in his hand, setting them in metal in a composing stick; but he was learning, too, to compose them not for the sake of any æsthetic or pompous effect but as implements of democratic understanding.

Benjamin Franklin was still in his twenties when he brought the Enlightenment to lowly Americans. He vulgarized science until Galileo, Newton, and the other revolutionaries were admired, if not wholly understood, in the very cabins of the frontier. In the animated pages of *Poor Richard* he compelled men to look at the stars, to understand storms, and to laugh at the superstitions of astrology and the fear of God's hand in earthquakes and thunder. But—most important, perhaps, of all to the development of the American conscience—he introduced a practical morality that was wholly alien to American preaching but wholly necessary to American life.

The values of incessant industry, of thrift, of integral honesty, of humility, of generosity, of temperance—not for the glory of God but as means of happiness and success—were stated in the proverbial or "slogan" form which became so dear to Americans. "Time is money," said Poor Richard. Poverty is usually the result of indolence—truer in an abundant than in a scarce era—but it is hard for the poor man to be moral, for "an empty bag cannot stand upright." The pragmatic ethics spiced by humor were infinitely refreshing to the ambitious, hard-working colonist. The man of limited means discovered that virtue did not necessarily go with wealth in such exceedingly graphic pictures as "Pride gets into the coach, and Shame mounts behind"; yet he was instructed, in "Ways to Wealth," of wholly virtuous practices for getting rich. Franklin left out the abstractions of the preacher. He began with the concrete and carried it into principle and law in morality, just as he formed one of the greatest physical theories in the history of science out of the sparks from rods and kite strings in a thunderstorm.

Franklin tried to practice his preaching in his private life. He did it in a practical way by keeping a "little book" of his sins, but the effort was too much; actually it was too petty for so dynamic a mind, and one of the things that endears him to us is his failure in the face of momentary diversion or passion. That he carried his morality into intercourse with kings, diplomats, and sages is, of course, one of the basic facts of American history.

Franklin's methods are easy to criticize. He began traditions that have developed into every sort of vulgarization. The self-help books, columns, and correspondence courses are based on his concepts. Business clubs such as Rotary grew out of his Junto. He was a master of advertising techniques. His humor was often coarse; his advice sometimes seems mercenary. Yet he reached the people; he reached all the people of all the colonies, and he was the first American who did. And, as he embodied in himself everything that we have come to know as American, there was much that was earthy and crude and "vulgar," if you like, along with the true dissent, the rebel fervor, the moral and religious tolerance, and the uncompromising democracy that make us think of him as the first American, perhaps, in the modern sense.

5

The effects of the Enlightenment in America were different from those in other lands. In France, Deism moved into skepticism, materialism, and, in the revolution of the 1790's, militant atheism. The French church, formulated and precise in dogma, had become an institution that was taken for granted—not deeply entrenched in the personal conscience. In England, too, many thought that an established church was all that was necessary for the maintenance of faith; as long as it was there, supported by the state in all its cathedrals, altars, and robes, individuals could think as they liked. But in America, where the fringe bristled with dangers and the memory of privation was still imminent, a church, for all its laying down of law, was less important than the presence of God just outside the cabin door. Ministers were confused; Scripture was receding further into fog the more it was read; there was no one solid set of principles to be accepted and then forgotten. All formalization was in flux, the splinter sects were breaking off like radiation from some theological uranium, the "Awakeners" were shouting hellfire to groaning and twitching crowds uneasy about their souls, but God in some form was essential to nearly everyone.

Thus the Enlightenment was a mellower, a leveler, rather than a destroyer. It became closely involved with the conscience of democracy, the conscience of independence, the conscience, in short, of revolution. It was not a substitute for other faiths; in a sense it was absorbed by other faiths which changed their color when it entered them. The Puritan moral core was never seriously weakened by it. The old Puritan gods were called back at critical intervals all through American history: to justify expansion, to combat liquor and gambling, to "revive" the evangel when cities or mining camps began to look like Sodom, or to assist some Bryan in his attacks on some Darwinian Scopes.

One of the most concise and convincing comments on the transition we have just explored was made by G. Adolf Koch in his book on the history of the Enlightenment in America.[7]

> The philosophy and religion of a people [he wrote] do not exist in the mind apart from the world in which this life is lived, and it follows as an inevitable corollary that where life changes religion cannot remain the same. . . .
>
> The stern way of life associated with the word Puritanism which has become synonymous with negation was admirably suited to the needs of the settlers of New England. As the struggle for subsistence became less keen, denial of pleasures became less necessary. . . . Gradually even some of the clergy recognized the change in times. The founding of the Brattle Street Church in Boston is evidence of the fact that the incoming tides of civilization which had already inundated the town had reached the sanctuary.[8]

Thus, first, the religious conscience of the Puritan stronghold reflected the change. But when, after that, the Enlightenment reached the political conscience, "cradles of liberty" appeared everywhere up and down the coast and especially in the West, where rifles were daily shooting farther and with greater accuracy.

[7] G. Adolph Koch: *Republican Religion* (New York, 1933).
[8] Ibid., p. 285.

PART III

THE Revolutionary Conscience

Chapter X

The Fact *of* Independence

THROUGH most of the eighteenth century we see, in the colonies, a growing split in loyalties. On one side there was traditional devotion to the person of the king; on the other, distrust of his government. But revolution against the Crown, political separation, dissolution of the Empire were unthinkable thoughts for three quarters of the century. Americans were proud of the British Empire. They wanted to continue to be Englishmen; their distrust of the English government centered in the fact that Parliament apparently refused to regard them as Englishmen with all of an Englishman's rights and liberties, and exploited them as "colonials"—a lesser breed.

Fact, however, as often happens, had moved faster than theory. The British colonies in North America had become truly independent long before they realized it. Distance, slowness of communication, diversity of climate and interests had played their part. Thus, while Franklin was proclaiming that the "foundations of the future grandeur and stability" of the Empire lay in America [1] and, later, while he pleaded in England for a total union of the two countries with the colonial concept dissolved, the point of no return had probably, in fact, been passed. The Empire, as it then existed, could have been preserved only by the later commonwealth design. As this was far from the parliamentary pattern of thought in eighteenth-century London, the rift widened. And, as it widened, the colonial conscience grew increasingly confused.

At the height of this confusion there came a wave of disloyalty

[1] Letter to Lord Kames, Jan. 3, 1760, in *The Writings of Benjamin Franklin*, IV, 4.

toward the motherland that was in sharp contrast with colonial professions of devotion to the Crown. Conventional textbooks of American history have either omitted this remarkable misbehavior or condoned it as a normal consequence of British oppression.

There were "extenuating circumstances," and we shall try to explore them in a brief historical review. Yet when all is said, there remains an element of avarice or greed too cynical to be palliated by any consideration of historical stresses. Throughout the American story, when the public conscience has been confused, conscienceless men have had their most fruitful seasons.

2

From the late years of the seventeenth century, war between the traditional enemies, England and France, had extended to North America, where the colonists of the hostile nations sat side by side asserting conflicting colonial claims. The English colonists had always—though sometimes without great zeal—fought the French or, more commonly, their Indian allies. Occasionally we hear echoes of eloquent rhetoric about the colonials pouring out their "blood and treasure" in the service of their "gracious sovereign," but such thoughts were usually given expression in appeals for help from England or in protests against British efforts to exact pay for British aid. In general, what blood and treasure were expended went in self-defense against the devastating Indian raids. Except in the northern provinces, where provincial troops had come into frequent direct contact with French forces, the antagonism toward the French as French—the King's cause, in short—seems not to have preoccupied the majority of the colonists.

The wars culminated in the American branch of the Seven Years' War in Europe. This was known as the French and Indian War until Lawrence H. Gipson substituted the happier title of the "Great War for the Empire." The significance of that war to the Anglo-American crisis cannot be overestimated. From it stemmed the immediate causes of grievance. Though the powder kegs had long been set, the war lighted the fuse.

Late in 1754, after Major Washington had met defeat from the French and Indians near the forks of the Ohio and the French had erected their formidable Duquesne on the site of Pittsburgh, Governor Dinwiddie of Virginia appealed for English aid. It is instructive to look closely at the reception given General Edward Braddock when he arrived with two regiments of redcoats. It is also useful to inquire into the attitude of this arrogant general himself when he met the people he had been sent to protect. The extent of the rift even at mid-century then becomes acutely evident.

One would expect the red carpet to have been unrolled for such a commander of reinforcements. One would expect, also, an effort by the General to co-operate with those colonial natives who were to supply him and guide him in the unknown country. The opposite of these things happened. Braddock was met by indifference in the backwoods of Virginia, Maryland, and Pennsylvania. There seemed to be a bristling at his very presence, as if the farmers and frontiersmen resented the intrusion of aliens into their domain. The wiser of them saw at once that these soldiers meticulously trained in close-order attack were inadequate to cope with the widely deployed Indian tactics—with shooting from behind unsuspected shelters in a strange wilderness.

On the other hand, Braddock, hero of conventional campaigns and steeped in traditional army ritual, looked with infinite contempt at the rawboned, unlettered Americans with their easygoing manners who, nevertheless, knew their way in the woods and the ways of the Indians there. The demonstrations of his scorn merely compounded the antagonism, and but for the assistance of the wisest Pennsylvanian of all, the Braddock expedition might have been abandoned. But Franklin, in the king's service and still deeply loyal, knew also the mood of the Pennsylvania farmers. By threats and cajolery he secured for General Braddock one hundred and fifty wagons driven by farmers who had suddenly become "good and loyal subjects to his majesty" at fifteen shillings a day.[2]

Braddock had large plans.

"After taking Fort Duquesne," he told Franklin. "I am to proceed to Niagara; and, having taken that, to Frontenac, if the season will allow time; and I suppose it will, for Duquesne can hardly detain me above three or four days. . . ."

In his slow, quiet way Franklin warned of Indian ambuscades, surprises on the flanks of the "slender line, near four miles long," of

[2] Ibid., I, 395, 397.

Braddock's army. To which Braddock replied, according to Franklin:

"These savages may, indeed, be a formidable enemy to your raw American militia, but upon the king's regular and disciplin'd troops, sir, it is impossible they should make any impression." [3]

It is not in our province to describe the catastrophe which has occupied so important a place in the American schoolbooks. We note it not only as one of the earliest demonstrations of *de facto* independence, but as a first cause of the numbing of the American conscience toward England. Braddock's defeat had wide repercussions through the colonies. The apparent cowardice of his officers in their headlong flight; the ruthlessness of the King's troops in plundering and pillaging the inhabitants along their line of march, "totally ruining some poor families, besides insulting, abusing, and confining the people if they remonstrated"—these things "gave us Americans the first suspicion that our exalted ideas of the prowess of British regulars had not been well founded" and were "enough to put us out of conceit of such defenders, if we had really wanted any." [4]

Once people begin to doubt the prowess of a king's army, the step toward doubting that of the king himself is not a long one. That the judgment was unfair; that British troops could not be expected to fight successfully in a theater which the French dared not enter except behind a wedge of their savage allies; and that the harrassments accompanying such a campaign were enough to drive the King's officers to almost any extremity made no difference in the consequence to the American mentality and conscience. The affair, the propaganda effect of its wide and exaggerated report, and the events consequent upon it all went to give a moral buttressing to the factual separation that had been progressing over a century.

Were these demonstrations of the proposition that colonials were no longer English subjects justification for the astonishing lapse of patriotic conscience that followed it? Or was this lapse merely the continuation of a custom so long established that it could not be broken even when the survival of the Empire was at stake? Was there not a lapse in moral practice away back in colonial history—

[3] Ibid., I, 400, 401.

[4] Ibid., I, 403. Franklin, to be sure, was writing from memory long after the event and the whole of the Revolution had intervened. Nevertheless, it is hardly possible to believe he was wrong in this estimate.

a lapse essential, perhaps, at the beginning, to survival but later too enticing in its benign effects to permit reform?

3

We have seen how the early New England merchants ignored those Navigation Acts that interdicted free trade with foreign nations. We have seen the protests about this that came, occasionally, from the lords and boards of trade in England during the seventeenth century. In general, however, it was felt that the acts were good for colonial commerce, and the better merchants frowned on those who engaged in contraband trade. And we have seen, over the long sweep, what a fine prosperity was built in the northern colonies on industrious, intelligent, and legitimate business within the framework of that mercantile age.

Through three decades of the eighteenth century the West Indian trade made money for the middle colonies as well as for New England. Flour milled in New York, Delaware, and Pennsylvania found large markets in French, Danish, Spanish, as well as British islands. New England sold fish and lumber and brought back molasses. All over New England, distilleries sprang up, making the molasses into rum. Rum became the national drink, replacing cider. Massachusetts and Rhode Island exported it to the other colonies, in which it was consumed in such prodigious volume that we are led to wonder how our ancestors survived at all, rugged as they were. And in addition to this, of course, rum became of prime importance to the triangle trade.

Then, in 1733, something happened whose effects on the American conscience were so far-reaching that we may not yet have come to the end of them. The planters of the British sugar islands had long been watching with jealous eyes the operations of ships among the French and other West Indies. These planters had built a powerful lobby in the Parliament at London. It was shameful, the lobby told the members, that British colonials should buy sugar from the despised French (among others) simply because it was cheaper. Of course the French could sell cheaper because they had suffered less hurricane damage. It was only right, the Barbadoes planters said, and in accord with British colonial policy, that the British West Indies should have a monopoly of the intercolonial trade.

Had Parliament then made a cursory examination of the facts, they would have discovered that even under perfect climatic conditions the British planters could never have met the American demand. Having found this, being honorable and intelligent men, they would hardly have passed a law calculated to wreck the entire economy of their northern provinces. But group pressures even then tended to subdue intelligence and scruples. Thus, in 1733 there was passed one of the most subversive acts in the history of British commercial legislation. It was known as the Molasses Act, sometimes called a "sugar act." It placed a prohibitive duty on non-British molasses.

From the beginning it was disregarded. That was why it was subversive. Its demoralizing effect was probably unparalleled in American history until 1920, when the eighteenth amendment to the Constitution of the United States was ratified. As Professor Schlesinger has written,

> Although of decided economic advantage to the commercial provinces, the non-enforcement of the Molasses Act proved a serious political blunder for the home government. As British statesmanship should have foreseen, it gave to colonial smuggling every aspect of respectability.[5]

A colonial letter to a newspaper late in the life of the Molasses Act stated there was "no error so fruitful of mischief as making acts and regulations oppressive to trade" that must remain unenforced.

> This [the letter continued] opens a door to corruption. This introduces a looseness in morals. This destroys the reverence and regard for oaths, on which government depends. This entirely destroys the distinction which ought invariably to be preserved in all trading communities between a merchant and a smuggler. But the sugar act has thrown down all distinction: Before this was published, a merchant disdain'd to associate with an unfair trader.[6]

That the law was unenforceable was soon evident to the British. They had only limited facilities for patrolling the coastal sealanes

[5] Arthur M. Schlesinger: *The Colonial Merchants and the American Revolution 1763–1776* (New York, 1917), p. 44.

[6] *Boston Evening Post*, November 21, 1763, Quoted in Schlesinger: op. cit., p. 45.

and manning the customs depots. The expense of watching the long irregular coastline which, as we have seen, was so useful to the pirates was prohibitive. Yet the statute remained on the books. The duties were occasionally collected, and punitive measures were sometimes applied for the sake of appearances; but in general the customs officials had well-greased palms, the fortunes of the merchants accumulated, and the rift widened between the independent children and the neglectful mother. Then, suddenly, the neglect began to cost the parent country heavily in blood and treasure, and on the storm winds that blew across the Atlantic came the first whispers of treason.

4

Apparently the merchants did not in their minds connect the warm, friendly, and profitable French in the Caribbean with the cold and hostile French in Canada and the Ohio valley. Or, at least, if they did see a connection, they did not let it interrupt business. Thus, while Major Washington's troops were turned back by the Ohio French at Great Meadows and Braddock's army was cut to pieces on the Monongahela, while Abercrombie and Howe and Jeffrey Amherst were spending blood and treasure in the Lake Champlain and Louisburg theaters, and while Wolfe and Montcalm lost their lives on the Plains of Abraham, trade was merrily continuing with Guadeloupe, Martinique, and the French end of Hispaniola to the enormous profit, as it turned out, of the hostile as well as the Caribbean French!

The trade now, in wartime, was not merely a carrying of lumber, fish, and bread to the French islands and bringing molasses back. The American merchants had become so cynical in disobeying British law that the step to actually supplying the enemies of Britain with the provisions of war came easily to them. Thus, ships would sail out of New York or Philadelphia laden with food and, though officially bound for British Newfoundland, would anchor and unload in the French harbor of Louisburg. In March 1755 news came to General Braddock, about to march to his defeat, that no less than forty ships from colonial ports were there at that moment.[7] Naturally

[7] *Pennsylvania Archives,* compiled by Samuel Hazard *et al.* (Philadelphia, 1852–1907), 4th Series, II, 373, 374.

rally the French were willing to pay dearly, as it helped them continue the war against the merchants' countrymen. Another trick was to carry the provisions to a neutral port, thence to be transferred to the enemy. In 1757 a ship carrying out such an operation with thirteen hundred barrels of flour loaded at Philadelphia was captured off Jamaica.[8] There was a notorious trade between Rhode Island and French settlements on Hispaniola by means of which shiploads of vital war goods reached the enemy. In 1760 an English investigation revealed the presence of a hundred ships flying the British flag, and with their cargoes insured at great cost, at the Spanish port of Monti Cristi carrying on this lucrative commerce.

Out of the profits the merchants were able to buy protection in high places, making the task of Britain in running down the culprits peculiarly difficult. According to Professor Schlesinger,

> The experience of the British government during the war sharply revealed the strength, sordidness and energy of the forces supporting the contraband trade. Provincial governors had been bought out by the smugglers in one or two instances; and from Massachusetts to South Carolina, the Americans managed pretty successfully to control the vice-admiralty courts in their favor. Governor Hamilton, of Pennsylvania, reported in 1760 that the most eminent lawyers of that province were retained by the smugglers.[9]

Here again we see the same sort of "racket" that we found earlier operated by the pirates. As we look into the details as revealed by contemporary documents and letters, we find all the tricks of intimidation, punishment of informers by subsidized mobs, tar-and-feathering, and boycott that later became characteristic of gangs led by Al Capone and Dutch Schultz.

With the coming of the government of William Pitt in England, the fortunes of the war changed. The early incompetence of the British armed forces was overcome, and the full resources of the Empire, under the firm and efficient direction of the new minister, were concentrated on victory over the French. In 1760 Pitt sent a circular letter to all the colonial governors which read:

> The Commanders of His Majesty's Forces, and Fleets, in North America, and the West Indies, having transmitted repeated and certain Intelligence of an illegal and most pernicious Trade, car-

[8] London Papers, No. 2686, in Huntington Library. Lawrence H. Gipson: *The Coming of the Revolution, 1763–1775* (New York, 1954), p. 30.

[9] Schlesinger: op. cit., p. 46.

> ried on by the King's Subjects, in North America, and the West Indies . . . by which the Enemy is, to the greatest Reproach & Detriment, of Government, supplyed with Provisions, and other Necessaries, whereby they are, principally, if not alone, enabled to sustain, and protract, this long and expensive War. . . . It is His Majesty's express will . . . that you do take every Step, authorized by Law, to bring all such heinous Offenders to the most exemplary and condign Punishment. . . .[1]

In the same year Parliament authorized the use of the navy against smugglers. Yet even these measures had little effect, and in 1762 Governor de Lancey issued a warrant to arrest Frenchmen in New York who had been sent to negotiate a large new project for supplying the enemy. It seems hardly surprising, then, that an old device known as "Writs of Assistance" should have been used by customs officials to help carry out "His Majesty's Will and Pleasure." These writs, authorizing general search of vessels or buildings for contraband goods without the requirement of an oath of suspicion, are listed among the classic causes of the War of Independence.

Actually the writs merely detonated a bomb which had long lain ready to explode. Massachusetts merchants and their lawyers seized upon this dubious legal implement as a rationalization of their independence of English "tyranny." An Englishman's house, they said (still calling themselves Englishmen), is his castle and free from the threat of invasion by forces of the law except by special warrant issued separately for each suspected area and then only when the suspicion is sworn to. But these writs specified nothing, they permitted intrusion upon all privacy, they were against nature, against the Constitution, and no act of Parliament could validate them. In a flaming speech at Boston, James Otis declared that

> by this writ not only deputies &c but even their menial servants are allowed to lord it over us. Now one of the most essential branches of English liberty is the freedom of one's house. . . . This writ, if it should be declared legal, would totally annihilate this privilege. Custom-house officers may enter our houses, when they please; we are commanded to permit their entry. Their menial servants may enter, may break locks, bars, and every thing in their way; and whether they break through malice or revenge, no man, no court, can inquire. Bare suspicion without oath is sufficient. . . . What a scene does this open! Every man, prompted by revenge, ill humor

[1] *Correspondence of William Pitt . . . with Colonial Governors . . .*, Gertrude S. Kimball, editor (New York, 1906), II, 320, 321.

or wantonness, to inspect the inside of his neighbor's house, may get a writ of assistance. Others will ask it from self-defence; one arbitrary exertion will provoke another, until society be involved in tumult and in blood.[2]

The fact that the writs had been in use in England for a hundred years made no difference to these champions of liberty. Such use gave no license for their use in the unrepresented "plantations." We see, then, in American logic a real departure in the direction of increased liberty, specious as some of the heated arguments may have been. But we see also, in the words of Otis, the sense of a long-understood conviction of factual independence any impingement upon which by a British king or legislature would be "tyranny and oppression."

But how quieting to the consciences of the colonial merchants the reports of such righteous indignation must have been! It is said that the actual words of Otis's speech were not widely heard or read. But the substance of it spread abroad or was assiduously spread by champions of liberty springing up in various parts of the provinces. The abstraction "liberty" was interpreted in many concrete forms: would not liberty of person or property mean also liberty to buy and sell where one liked, to defy unreasonable laws, to ignore a war that was not of one's own making? And if the parent country should practice oppression, need we be so sensitive about obstructing her imperial movements?

5

From this point a tide seems to have started on which logic could impose no ebb. Steadily it rose, more and more as the opposing forces rose to meet and confine it. The British government, irate, rankling over recent injuries, exploited its case often with similar illogic until with a series of stern measures it sought at last to recover a hold on its western empire lost through half a century of neglect and dead, unworkable laws. Here, then, was the blame on England, as the consciences of the great English champions of the American

[2] Henry S. Commager: *Documents of American History,* No. 32, I, 46, 47. See also Joseph Hawley: *Commonplace Book*, in manuscript division of the New York Public Library; *American History Leaflets,* A. B. Hart and Edward Channing, editors, No. 33 (1902); and, *passim,* Josiah Quincy: *Massachusetts Reports* (Boston, 1865). There was no official stenographic report of Otis's speech, and we must rely on notes taken in the audience.

cause were aware—Pitt, Fox, Burke—and not in the details of the inflammatory statutes. She had let the horse run with loose rein; when finally he chose his own direction, she pulled up the controls: from then on he leaned upon the bit.

Yet independence was not mentioned. In all the destruction, the burnings in effigy, the dances round the liberty poles, the tarring and feathering and beating of innocent men, few seem to have thought of a final political separation. With Franklin, the wiser champions of home rule hoped by these protests to reform the parent government, to persuade the Parliament and the ministers to relax the tensions.

Even Otis, the firebrand, wrote in 1765:

> God forbid these colonies should ever prove undutiful to the mother country! Whenever such a day shall come, it will be the beginning of a terrible scene. Were the colonies left to themselves, to-morrow, America would be a mere shambles of blood and confusion, before little petty states could be settled. How many millions must perish in building up great empires? How many more must be ruined by their fall? Let any man reflect on the revolutions in government, ancient and modern, and he will think himself happy in being born here in the infancy of these settlements, and from his soul deprecate their once entertaining any sentiments but those of loyalty, patience, meekness and forbearance, under any hardships that in the course of time they may be subjected to. . . .[3]

Again and again petitions went across the ocean addressed to His Most Gracious Majesty, pleading for repeal of the oppressive statutes. And, indeed, there was sporadic relaxation, though in the 1770's things had gone too far for makeshift mending. Yet even when the tea was dumped into Boston harbor, even when at last the muskets of the minutemen spoke at Lexington, the King was still a sacred symbol and the appeal was to Magna Charta.

Thus was the American conscience moved to and fro in the troubled years between wilderness freedom and Empire security. Thus it winked at the contraband trade that was, after all, an outgrowth of the proud, defiant counter to laws against nature and custom as well as against the manifest destiny of American prosperity. And in the end, when all was said and done, the transmuted Englishmen were Englishmen still, carrying an ancient English conscience into an un-English world.

[3] James Otis: *A Vindication of the British Colonies against the Aspersions of the Halifax Gentleman* (Boston, 1765), pp. 16, 17.

Chapter XI

Loyalties

THEY WERE ENGLISHMEN indeed, those colonists in America who rejected the imperial domination of England. In some aspects, they seemed even more English than the people of the homeland who tried to restrain them as they carried the torch of Magna Charta to extremes that often flagrantly defied the British Constitution. They seemed Englishmen certainly to those English statesmen who called themselves Whigs: the great Earl of Chatham, who, as William Pitt, had brought the war against the French in America to victory for Britain; Edmund Burke, that master of rhetoric and oratory in the House of Commons; Lord Camden, Lord Shelburne, Isaac Barre, Richard Price, the passionate young firebrand Charles James Fox, and thousands of disciples of these men. It was the continued, ardent support by the Whigs in England, defying both the King and the parliamentary majority, that weakened the ultimate English effort against the American colonies and helped change the face of our War of Independence from revolution to true civil war.

But this tragic aspect of the conflict was far darker in America than in England. In England the division merely produced a kind of apathy that benumbed enthusiasm for a remote and dubious cause, but on the Atlantic fringe from the north of Maine to the south of Georgia it caused a degree of mental or spiritual suffering only once surpassed in our history. For more than a century American historians confused the bitter truth of this split loyalty with star-spangled propaganda; and even today the American child in his grammar school is likely to be led rapidly past the darker shadows clustering round the first "Glorious Fourth." But no story of the American conscience can ignore the birth pains of our independence, for they are of the very essence of conscience itself. Nor can it omit the record of brutalities, of intolerances, of hatreds, of moral perversions that must balance the glories in the ledger. The true extent of this somber area may never be known, but enough has been found to show the very widespread conscientious reluctance to recognize independence.

It has been estimated that one third of the population—about a million persons—was opposed to the Revolution.[1] Other writers hold that this guess is necessarily conservative, as it is based on what was known of the Loyalists or so-called "Tories." But countless thousands dared not declare themselves; they maintained a passive resistance, avoiding, wherever possible, any aid to the patriot cause. The Loyalists themselves thought the total much higher. The usually objective historian W. E. H. Lecky writes:

> It is probably below the truth to say that a full half of the honorable and respected Americans were either openly or secretly hostile to the Revolution.[2]

In another place Lecky goes so far as to assert:

> The American Revolution, like most others, was the work of an energetic minority, who succeeded in committing an undecided and fluctuating majority to courses for which they had little love, and leading them step by step to a position from which it was impossible to recede.[3]

This was also the contemporary opinion of Governor Thomas Hutchinson of Massachusetts, a fourth-generation American and the direct descendant of the exiled Anne, though he, perhaps the most bitter of all Loyalists, saw wickedness in the motives of the propagandists:

> Many thousands of people [he wrote] who were before good and loyal subjects, have been deluded, and by degrees induced to rebel against the best of Princes, and the mildest of Governments.[4]

[1] John Adams: *Works*, Charles Francis Adams, editor (Boston, 1850–6), X, 63, 87, 110.

[2] W. E. H. Lecky: *England in the Eighteenth Century* (London, 1918–25), V, 47. See also Justin Winsor: *Narrative and Critical History of America*, VII, 187, and Moses Coit Tyler: *The Literary History of the American Revolution, 1763–1783* (New York, 1897), I, 299, 300.

[3] Lecky: op. cit., IV, 224.

[4] *Strictures upon the Declaration of the Congress at Philadelphia: In a Letter to a Noble Lord* (London, 1776), p. 8.

Lecky, it will be noted, merely states a fact; Hutchinson interprets it according to his own bias. But the fact, if true, by no means reflects on the justice and morality of the propaganda motives, however few the propagandists may have been. As Lecky explains, such is the sequence in most revolutions. Granting then, as it seems we must when all the evidence is examined, that the propagandists worked for the most part in sincerity and with the conviction that they saw further into an inevitable future than the mass could possibly see, the evils appear incidental to the end achieved. Whether that end was a great moral achievement, as most people in and out of the United States believe, it certainly appears to us today as a historical necessity.

The evils, nevertheless, left scars which were a long time healing, and the forced flight of that huge body of Americans whose consciences kept them loyal to their king is said to have altered the quality of our population.[5] Perhaps, if these good folk could have been let remain (as many wanted) and forgiven (as of late years enemies have often been), there might have been another hue to the American people in the twentieth century. But their misfortune was of the kind that is a camp-follower of all war—especially of fratricidal war, for brothers are usually harder to forgive than aliens. "With malice toward none," advised a president at the end of a later civil war, "with charity for all"—but to bind up the brothers' wounds then took more than a generation, and some doubt that they are yet healed. After the Revolution, oratory, brass bands, and firecrackers each new year served to drown the whispers of the American conscience about those "brothers" who had lost their homes and their hopes in an America they had supposed was a part of Britain.

2

As we review the story in these uncertain years of the mid-twentieth century, we do so with cooler, maturer, and more selective minds. The world has so altered that that remote age scarcely seems to belong to us, and we look at it as we might regard the passage of republic into empire of ancient Rome. Looking closely at the sequence—with this detached view—we see one instant at which the

[5] Tyler: op. cit., I, 303.

wheel of destiny seems to have come to dead center: when a touch might have reversed its turning, and the whole of American history become a phase of British evolution. The examination of that pendant moment shows, more clearly than anything else can, the deep yearning of the common people of America for conciliation, forgiveness, and peace. As a sudden cooling of hot fever, a sweat of relief, a waking from nightmare, it is perhaps unique in our story.

Colonial discontent over attempts by Parliament to regulate commerce—in particular the Sugar Act of 1764 introduced by George Grenville, minister of the exchequer—came to its climax with the celebrated Stamp Act. This was frankly designed to raise revenue. The British treasury had been drastically depleted by the French war. An expensive part of that war had been fought in America. Presumably, Britain had leaped to the defense of the colonists and with little co-operation from them had removed the French menace from their borders. The Indian menace continued, however, and required, the minister thought, new protection by English troops. Should the cost of this plus the old war costs be borne by the British treasury? Should the colonists contribute no money toward their own defense? With emphatic negative answers to these questions, the members of Parliament passed the bill with little opposition.

The act provided for a tax of from three pence to four pounds on all colonial bills of lading, licenses, wills, bonds, deeds, indentures, leases, contracts, newspapers, advertisements, playing-cards, and dice, and it provided also for penalties for defaults. The device was a stamp to be bought and affixed to the papers. The agents—the stamp-salesmen—were to be Americans and the revenue was to be spent in America. On the face of it, the thing looked reasonable in England, and even Franklin in London, though as colonial agent he had opposed the plan, was not greatly disturbed by its passage until he heard the American reaction.

Unfortunately for Grenville, the Stamp Act hurt precisely the wrong people in America, the merchants, the newspaper editors, and the lawyers. Here were the powerful, here the articulate, forces. The lawyers, particularly, with whom the colonies teemed—men skilled in expedient tactics, eloquent and quick to exploit popular abstractions, but with vague understanding of basic constitutional law—could be counted on to find high-sounding words to keep the stamps off their documents.

These men uttered the battle cry: "Taxation without representation is tyranny," and the people took it up. No wildfire ever spread like the fury from the Kennebec to St. Mary's and back to the vague forest lines called the frontier. In this year there was greater unity in the colonies than at any later time in the course of the Revolution. The poor stamp-distributors were hounded, beaten, burned in effigy, and forced to resign; a drunken mob destroyed the beautiful Boston house—one of the masterpieces of colonial architecture—of Lieutenant Governor Hutchinson, burning his precious books and manuscripts. The forces of law and order in all the colonies were helpless before the mobs. Finally the first united colonial congress met at New York and sent protests and petitions to the House of Commons and to the King.

The unprecedented and unexampled vandalism, however, was balanced before the year was out when the people gave evidence of a true national conscience by an interval of self-sacrifice that perhaps only Englishmen could have maintained. However specious the arguments, however materialistic some of the motives in this turbulent year, that negation by the common folk must stand as one of the moral peaks in American history. The women turned to their spinning-wheels and hand looms to avoid buying English cloth. All the cherished English commodities—tools, ceramics, linen, and India tea—were refused. Some four million pounds owed by Americans to British merchants were held up. It was owing to these bold and difficult acts of resistance that the parliamentary conscience underwent what might be called a sea change.

When the repercussions got to England, the Whig members took up the American cry, but they might indeed have gone on shouting themselves hoarse but for the presence outside the halls of a powerful lobby of merchants which gave wings to their words. The fact was that the profitable colonial trade had come to a standstill. As a result, thousands of people in the manufacturing districts of England had been thrown out of work, and their pitiful letters were effective lobby material.

The astute, pragmatic Franklin quickly saw into the core of the matter and, without wasting words on theoretical principles, connived with this lobby to press on those legislators who had been deaf to Pitt, Burke, and Camden. When he was examined by the House of Commons, he dwelt so convincingly on the mercantile catastrophe that enough members were won over to bring about repeal. It was then, in mid-May 1766, when the news got to America along with Franklin's letter to his Deborah that she could now have a dress not made of homespun, that the pregnant moment came—followed by the most moving and the most sadly abortive scene in the entire tragedy.

3

> We should find it hard [writes Moses Coit Tyler] to overestimate the happiness which, for a few weeks, filled the hearts of the American people at the news that the detested Stamp Act had been repealed. As, in 1765, through the bond of a common fear, the thirteen colonies had been brought for the first time into some sort of union, so in 1766, that union was for a while prolonged through the bond of a common joy. Certainly never before had all these American communities been so swept by one mighty wave of grateful enthusiasm and delight. As the news passed up and down the land, business was suspended, bells were set a-ringing, bonfires were lighted, the imperial colors were unfurled; and thus . . . they gave themselves up . . . to their own spontaneous manifestations of pleasure at having been delivered from a humiliating political stigma, from an appalling political peril.[6]

The news of the American interval of good feeling reached England and there were reports in the English periodicals:

> At Philadelphia [one of them read], the principal inhabitants gave a grand entertainment . . . at the conclusion of which they entered into the following resolutions:
>
> "That to demonstrate our zeal to *Great* Britain, and our gratitude for the repeal of the stamp-act, each of us will, on the 4th of June next, being the birth-day of our most gracious sovereign George III, dress ourselves in a new suit of the manufactures of *England* and give what *home* spun we have to the poor." [7]

At the same time, effusive expressions of gratitude were forwarded to the King. Now, these rhapsodies seemed to say, all is forgiven, let us forget, let things be as they were—for God's sake don't force us now to break the old ties! But by the time these appeals had blown across the Atlantic, George and the Parliament had prepared a sterile ground for them to fall upon.

At the very moment of repeal, parallel with it in the same Parlia-

[6] Ibid., I, 223. [7] *Gentleman's Magazine,* XXXVI, 341.

ment, the Tory members had sought to cover their shame at conceding to the merchants and their fear of a growing insubordination in the colonies. Lest the ringing words of Pitt and Burke and their supporters be allowed to convince Englishmen in England and America that the principle of colonial taxation was wrong, they passed a Declaratory Act [8] which said, in effect, that the Parliament of England had the complete and final right to do what it damn well pleased with the colonies "in all cases whatsoever."

> This flat assertion of Parliamentary sovereignty [state Samuel E. Morison and Henry S. Commager] was couched in the very phraseology of the odious Irish Declaratory Act of 1719, and so indicated the British government's intention to assimilate the American colonies to the same subordinate position in the empire as Ireland long occupied.[9]

The news of this fatal blunder bred of shame, vindictiveness, and fear at first made little immediate impression on the celebrations or the wave of loyalty. But, like the counterpoint in a fugue, it pursued the joyful theme and caught it while the echo of the celebrant church bells still hung over Boston, New York, Philadelphia, and Charleston, bringing with it the bitter aftermath of disappointed hopes.

So the moment passed: it would not come back. From now on, for all the arguments of Franklin and Burke, of Dickinson and Fox, for all the prayers in the churches up to and beyond the bloodshed of Bunker's Hill, the antiphonal transatlantic rage grew louder, almost hour by hour.

4

In resistance to the Stamp Act many of those who were in every other respect loyal to the government of the mother country took common cause with the resentful colonists. When the act was repealed, there was greater unity than ever before among the whole colonial people. From this point, however, the Loyalists began to drop away from the "patriot" party. They were turned away from the cause of resistance to the so-called British tyranny very largely by the violence of the patriot hotheads and by what they considered the sophistry of the propagandists.

[8] 6 George III, c. 12.

[9] Samuel E. Morison and Henry S. Commager: *The Growth of the American Republic* (New York, 1937), I, 31.

As soon as the offensive Declaratory Act was implemented by the heavy-handed though short-lived Townshend Acts, the radicals, temporarily lulled by the recall of the stamp tax, seized on the opportunity to continue their agitation. The Townshend Acts were particularly galling because they provided not only for the revenue the Stamp Act failed to get but also for the costly quartering of British troops at provincial expense. One of the statutes actually dissolved the provincial assembly of New York until this cost was met. At this point there appeared perhaps the most astonishing attempt to rationalize the colonial resistance that we can find anywhere in our legal history.

It was unconstitutional, the advanced thinkers said, for Parliament to exercise any authority whatever outside the "realm." No colony, in short, need obey any statute of any kind except it be passed by its own provincial assembly! The reasoning behind this theory was that the colonies had received their original charters from the Crown and not from Parliament. It was to the Crown, therefore, and to the Crown only that they were accountable! In this logic they went back to the very tyrannies they had fled from and put halos on the heads of the hated James and Charles!

In vain the English lawyers explained that the intervening years had seen a progress away from despotism toward government with the consent of the people. The Constitution, they said, was a growing instrument; it was made up of parliamentary acts and judicial interpretation of those acts; this had come about because of the long struggle to wrest the power away from the Crown and give it to the people's representatives. And even the great English sympathizers with the colonial cause—even Edmund Burke and Conway and Chatham—took this view.

Was this a lapse of conscience? Was it mere sophistry, a cynical juggling of words to cover an inconvenient truth? It has puzzled historians that a political thinker of such high morality as Benjamin Franklin should have so ardently embraced the theory of these colonial lawyers. Yet was not Franklin thinking, as he so often did, a century and a half ahead of his time? As we look at the world today, is not Franklin's view precisely that which Britain adopted when Canada, Australia, South Africa, New Zealand, and Newfoundland became autonomous states in the "Commonwealth of Nations"—immune to the acts of an English Parliament and held to Great Britain only by their common allegiance to the British monarch? [1]

To the English and to the American Loyalists of the late 1760's, however, this opinion represented insubordination if not treason. The Loyalist pamphleteers built their most cogent arguments out of the radical "sophistry," and many thousands of those native Americans who had been in doubt before went over wholeheartedly to the Tory side in these years and split the American conscience wide apart.

The sequence from here on into battle was the result of an irresistible momentum. The radicals had gone too far to turn back. Even the lull following the repeal of the more drastic Townshend Acts was merely the hush before the storm. The propagandists were now thoroughly addicted to their propaganda, and the mobs were more and more ready to wreak their fury at any hint from the leaders of the Sons of Liberty. In 1770 the agitators inflated a small street skirmish into the "Boston Massacre." In 1772 they made their gospel more effective through the intercolonial Committees of Correspondence; in 1773 they instigated the destruction, at night by a band of citizens thinly disguised as Mohawk Indians, of a cargo of tea in Boston harbor. The more moderate and statesmanlike of them tried to bring order and discipline in a Continental Congress in 1774; and finally the improvised militia, defending its property at Concord, was followed by the Continental Army and General Washington in '75. Yet even in this late time the very Continental officers in their new blue coats and tricorns sat in the mess with Washington, raising their glasses: "To the King, God bless him!" [2]

5

Whatever the diluting influx of the Enlightenment and the religion of reason or nature or whatever it was called, the churches were still a potent factor in American society. With the exception of certain southern provinces, the cleavage of the times ran generally along sectarian lines. The clergy and congregations of the Church of England clung to their overseas ties; the Puritan dissenters were—as they had always been—insurgent. In New England the Congregational was the established church; the Anglicans had only

[1] Ibid., I, 72. [2] Ibid., I, 77.

a toehold. In New York, New Jersey, and Maryland the Church of England was stronger; in Pennsylvania the Presbyterians dominated, but the Quakers, because of their pacifist belief, tended to the Anglican side as the conflict warmed. In Virginia, where the Anglican was the established church and where nearly everyone professed that faith, the cleavage disappeared and under the heavy pressures of Virginia's grievances they forgot their loyalty to England. The church there in any case was, as we have seen, in sad decay, and services were conducted by men who had never seen a bishop.

As usual under gathering war clouds, the churches (except the Quakers) were militant. They were not precisely fighting for Christ. Rather they were contending for king and country: the Anglicans for king, the Puritans for country. They dressed up these symbols, to be sure, in the garments of faith: the country was the "Zion wilderness" to the Puritan faithful, the only king in their churches was the Almighty, before whom all men were equal; whereas to the Anglicans, George was divinely guided, and their prayerbook was full of supplications about him and his forebears.

> Most heartily we beseech thee [one such ran] with thy favour to behold our most gracious Sovereign Lord King GEORGE and so replenish him with the grace of thy Holy Spirit, that he may alway incline to thy will, and walk in thy way . . . strengthen him that he may *vanquish all his enemies*. . . .[3]

This the Puritans could not wholly condemn until America had turned its anger away from Parliament to the monarch, but other passages were anathema to them. For example, there was

> A Form of Prayer with Fasting to be used upon the thirtieth day of January Being the Day of the Martyrdom of the Blessed King CHARLES the First; to implore the mercy of God, that neither the Guilt of that sacred and innocent Blood, nor those other Sins by which God was provoked to deliver up both us and our King into the hands of cruel and unreasonable men, may at any time be visited upon us, or our posterity.[4]

The King, indeed, who had sanctioned the persecution of Laud, from whom the Puritans had fled to America! And there was also a special service of Thanksgiving on the anniversary of the Restoration of Charles II.

[3] Morning Prayer in *The Book of Common Prayer* (Oxford, 1770). Italics added.

[4] Special Occasions, ibid.

This church became the special target of the insurgents when it attempted to get bishops from England to be resident in America. Immediately the other Protestant churches foresaw such bishops tightening the bond with England and securing secular power in the colonies, and there was an outcry throughout the northern provinces. As the war clouds grew darker, the Anglican clergy were cruelly persecuted. A moving account of this sort of abuse is given in the memoirs of Jonathan Boucher, rector of an Anglican church at Annapolis, Maryland.

> In the usual and regular course of preaching [he wrote] I happened one Sunday to recommend peaceableness. . . . This was a signal . . . to consider every sermon of mine as hostile to the views and interests of America. . . . I received sundry messages and letters threatening me with the most fatal consequences if I did not . . . preach what should be agreeable to the friends of America. All the answer I gave to these threats was in my sermons, in which I uniformly and resolutely declared that I never could suffer any merely human authority to intimidate me from performing what in my conscience I believed and knew to be my duty to God and His Church. And for more than six months I preached . . . with a pair of loaded pistols lying on the cushion; having given notice that if any man, or body of men, could possibly be so lost to all sense of decency . . . as to attempt really to do what had long been threatened, that is, to drag me out of my own pulpit, I should think myself justified before God and man in repelling violence by violence.[5]

Once, when two hundred armed men came to his church to stop his preaching, Boucher's friends prevented him by force from ascending his pulpit because they said they had positive knowledge of orders given to twenty of the mob to shoot him when he began to preach. Yet even as he left the church on this occasion, the fearless minister forced the leader of the men to go out with him, holding him by the collar and covering him with his pistol.

One passage of Boucher's journal, however, shows that even in the extreme tension of 1775 there was still in the highest quarters of the revolutionists an undercurrent of moderation and deep distaste for full separation. Boucher met General Washington, who had been his friend, at a Potomac crossing. Washington was on his way north to assume his command.

[5] Jonathan Boucher: *Reminiscences of an American Loyalist,* J. Boucher, editor (Boston, 1925), p. 113.

From his going on the errand he was [the *Reminiscences* record], I foresaw and apprised him . . . that there would certainly then be a civil war, and that the Americans would soon declare for independency. With more earnestness than was usual with his great reserve he scouted my apprehensions, adding (and I believe with perfect sincerity) that if ever I heard of his joining in any such measures I had his leave to set him down for everything wicked.[6]

Thus, then, in the very event and heat of war, sat the great man's conscience!

In New England there were other occasions of brutality and courage. There was one Reverend John Beach of Newtown and Reading,[7] Connecticut, who at eighty stuck to his guns while the other Anglican churches in the province were closed and suffered some anxious moments.

While officiating one day in Reading, a shot was fired into the church, and the ball struck above him and lodged in the sounding board. Pausing for a moment, he uttered the words: "Fear not them which kill the body, but are not able to kill the soul: but rather fear him which is able to destroy both soul and body in hell." He then proceeded with the service without further interruption.[8]

Another story of this indomitable octogenarian shows that, even in the feverish days after independence, true religious passion still had power to awe violent men. It seems that

at one time a band of ruffians seized him, carried him to a secluded spot, and told him to say his prayers for he was about to die. He knelt and prayed so earnestly, not for himself but for his captors, that they were ashamed to go on with their murderous plan and let him go home.[9]

The anger and persecutions were not, however, all on one side. In 1774 letters from Loyalists to friends in England were intercepted and came into the hands of the New York Committee of Correspondence.

Believe me [one of these read] the Presbyterians have been the chief and principal instruments in all these flaming measures, and they always do and ever will act against Government, from that restless

[6] Ibid., p. 109.
[7] Now Redding.
[8] Epaphroditus Peck: *The Loyalists of Connecticut* (New Haven, 1934), pp. 16, 17.
[9] Ibid., p. 17.

and turbulent anti-monarchical spirit which has always distinguished them every where. . . .[1]

Another letter attacks the Presbyterians in terms as abusive as any Protestants ever applied to Catholics. In most of these letters and, indeed, in most of the contemporary Loyalist writing of all kinds, the existence of independence is accepted—often three or four years before Americans were ready to recognize it. And this is true, further, of pamphlets published in England and even of speeches in Parliament.

Where the British came into control, as in Long Island in 1776, they committed the same sort of vandalism against the Presbyterians. The steeple of one church was sawed off. The pews were torn out of another and the church was used as a guardhouse. Here the pulpit pillar was turned into a hitching-post. A Whig editor recorded these depredations and asked: "Because we refuse to worship your idol king, will you prevent us worshipping the King of Kings?" [2]

6

What, then, brought the slow, reluctant change to the American conscience?

It seems to have been an accumulation of subconscious conviction that was detonated by one of the two great literary *tours de force* of American ideological history. Governments go to war—or did in former times—for economic or political or, perhaps, predatory motives. These are not enough for peoples. In the wars that were fought by professional soldiers they were enough. But in a civil war which must be fought by amateur troops—volunteers, militia—and supported by popular civil establishments in the rear, there must be moral rationalizations. These are usually furnished by intellectual or emotional writers. Thus, in the second civil war the northerners had their patriotism heated by a highly sensational fictional tract on the evils of slavery called *Uncle Tom's Cabin.* In the first civil war—the Revolution—the percussion cap was a skillfully reasoned, adroitly executed diatribe which achieved its emo-

[1] *American Archives*, Peter Force, editor (Washington 1837–53), 4th Series, I, 301 n.

[2] Claude Halstead Van Tyne: *The Loyalists in the American Revolution* (New York, 1902), pp. 113, 114, and documented sources.

tional effect by its drum-like repetition of short, simple, and shocking statements. It was written by a disgruntled Englishman who had begun his career as a corset-maker and later gone into petty officialdom, but who was nevertheless one of the truly bright geniuses of propagandist literature. It had the exceedingly appealing title—in that era of tragic confusion—of *Common Sense*, and within a few months it wore out the presses, type, and printers of several provinces.

Tom Paine struck directly into the core of American resistance to separation from Britain. Already the pamphleteers had disposed of Parliament. But when Parliament was gone, there still remained the symbol that the colonial conscience could not persuade itself to relinquish. Indeed, the more Parliament was attacked, the more the people clung to that one remaining straw that many thought was all that could hold them up. The fear of letting it go was desperate and widespread. There was something sacred about it, something of the heart rather than the mind, something that appealed, like the concept of God itself, to unreasoning intuition. There was, indeed, an age-old connection between that symbol and God—something that because of its ancient authority was exceedingly difficult to destroy. Yet Tom Paine knew it must be destroyed; he knew, also, that many thousands of people unconsciously wished to be rid of it. He therefore set as his first target the monarchical institution and, as the second, the person of the third George Hanover himself.

The accuracy of this writer's aim at the deep popular prejudice is proof of his understanding of the insurgent American mood. Again and again he quotes Scripture to dispel the hauntings of conscience. He knew, Deist as he was, that the great body of Puritans—or those infected with puritanism—would not move without Scriptural sanction. With an almost diabolical cunning he linked monarchy with Catholic Rome:

> In the early ages of the world, according to the scripture chronology there were no kings; the consequence of which was, there were no wars; it is the pride of kings which throws mankind into confusion. . . .
>
> These portions of scripture are direct and positive. They admit of no equivocal construction. That the Almighty hath here entered His protest against monarchical government, is true, or the scripture is false. And a man hath good reason to believe that there is as much of kingcraft, as priestcraft in withholding the scripture

> from the public in popish countries. For monarchy in every instance is the popery of government.[3]

Again, on fire with his theme, he skimmed the Bible—especially the Book of Samuel—to carry his points to the uninstructed:

> Government by kings was first introduced into the world by heathens, from whom the children of Israel copied the custom. It was the most prosperous invention the devil ever set on foot for the promotion of idolatry. . . . Monarchy is ranked in Scripture as one of the sins of the Jews, for which a curse in reserve is denounced against them.[4]

Finally, in sharp clarity, he drives home, pinpointing the immediate decision, telling Americans that they owe allegiance to only one sovereign:

> But where; say some, is the King of America? I'll tell you, friend, he reigns above, and doth not make havoc of mankind, like the royal brute of Great Britain.[5]

That, thought one American after another as the winter of '75 turned into the spring of '76, is precisely what I have wanted to say and what I dared not say—God forgive me if I say it now!—but Paine has said it, spoken for me, called this German prince a royal brute! So the trappings dropped away before the eyes of the readers, the scepter fell, the tawdry crown toppled, and the sacred George was suddenly a naked, vulgar, and brutal man!

Then, putting in the place of what he had taken away a vista of green pastures for the future, Tom Paine rose to the peak of his eloquence:

> O! ye that love mankind! Ye that dare oppose not only the tyranny but the tyrant, stand forth! Every spot of the old world is overrun with oppression. Freedom hath been hunted round the globe. Asia and Africa have long expelled her, Europe regards her like a stranger, and England hath given her warning to depart. O! receive the fugitive; and prepare in time an asylum for mankind.[6]

Now, he wrote, we can "begin the world over again. . . . The birthday of a new world is at hand." The "free and independent

[3] Thomas Paine: *Common Sense*, with Preface by William M. Van Weiden (New York, 1928), pp. 15, 24.
[4] Ibid., pp. 17, 18, 19.
[5] Ibid., p. 69.
[6] Ibid., p. 73.

states of America" would be that new world. So the word was said at last, spelled out, crystal clear; the most unlettered could not miss it.

In three months 120,000 copies of *Common Sense* had been sold in a population of scarce three million.[7] We may imagine the little pamphlet passing from hand to hand out to the farthest frontier cabin and read aloud to those who could not read.

In vain the Loyalists and moderates published their pamphlets and made their speeches taking *Common Sense* apart, as, of course, it was easy to do. But it could be done only by the erudite, the instructed in dialectics and metaphysics, and their complex arguments were helpless against the ringing phrases that hung in the mind of the common man. Thus the curtain fell; men swarmed to the Loyalist side; others justified mob outrages in the cause of liberty. There was no longer any room for doubt; the consciences on both sides had at long last come clear.

The formation of an American national conscience at this point may be profitably reviewed again and again by every student of our historic political morality. The English in England were far more disposed than the American colonists to forecast independence. As early at 1769 it was prophesied in a letter attributed to the Earl of Shelburne.[8] In 1773 an Englishman whom Josiah Quincy Jr., met on a sea voyage told him that separation was regarded in England as inevitable, although the British government would prevent it as long as possible.[9] In 1774 Josiah Tucker, Dean of Gloucester, wrote a pamphlet [1] positively advocating separation on the grounds that the colonies were such an intolerable burden to Britain that no amount of trade benefits could compensate. In the same year the King's solicitor general accused Franklin of advocating a "Great American Republic" [2] at the very moment when Franklin, in England, was still desperately trying to find a way to maintain the connection with a land he so deeply loved. To him, as to Adams, Jefferson, and Washington, the bare suggestion was an insult. But, as

[7] Ibid., Preface.

[8] *The Letters of Junius,* C. W. Everett, editor (London, 1927), p. 142.

[9] "Journal," 1773. In Massachusetts Historical Society Proceedings, XLIX, 433.

[1] *Tract V. The Respective Pleas and Arguments of the Mother Country, and of the Colonies distinctly set forth* (Gloucester and London, 1775).

[2] James Parton: *Life and Times of Benjamin Franklin* (Boston, 1867), I, 590. See also Lecky: op. cit., IV, 185.

Carl Van Doren writes, "The English by prophesying phantoms were creating realities." [3]

The final reality crystallized in July in the Second Continental Congress at Philadelphia. Even then it was only after long debate, after frightened hesitation, after weeks of backing and filling and changes of mind, with one province entirely abstaining, with Dickinson and Galloway declaiming to the last their impassioned opposition, that the vote was cast. By it the colonies were turned into states, said to be united, and a declaration was presented to a "candid world": a statement which time has shown to be one of the great guideposts in the history of human society.

[3] Carl Van Doren: *Secret History of the American Revolution* (New York, 1941), p. 8.

Chapter XII

The Theory of Independence

As a guidepost pointing toward the future and as a sort of beacon on a hill for the American conscience in the growing nation, the Declaration of Independence has far more significance than as a statement of circumstances existing at the time of its framing. It was intended, it states, to present "facts" to a candid world. But its statements were not facts when the Declaration was signed. Even the "truths" set forth in the preamble were by no means "self-evident." On the contrary, the created equality of all men was impossible of acceptance by anyone who looked about him to see the congenitally deformed, diseased, and insane. In Jefferson's own colony, as in the others in the South, a good half of the population was alienated, despite the self-evidence, from the divinely endowed rights of liberty and the pursuit of happiness—a fact which, all his later life, was disturbing to Jefferson's conscience.

The persecuted and hounded former governor of Massachusetts, Thomas Hutchinson, at once saw the motives of expediency behind the Declaration. In a letter to an anonymous "noble lord" three months after the historic 4th of July, he explained that

> though the professed reason for publishing the Declaration was a decent respect to the opinions of mankind, yet the real design was to reconcile the people of America to that Independence, which always before they had been made to believe was not intended.[1]

We cannot doubt that this was a reason (though not the only one) for publishing the statement. Nor can we fail, at this distance, to detect the fallacy beneath the Declaration's implicit assumption that an undivided people had with one voice insisted upon a disso-

[1] *Strictures upon the Declaration, etc.*, pp. 31, 32.

lution of the "political bands." Jefferson and the others knew well enough that only a part—perhaps even a minority—of the people had been convinced by the reasoning and rhetoric of Tom Paine. But they found it expedient to tell the world that unanimity was a fact, and to tell the people at home that, in defense of their liberties, they had reached the point of no return. To retreat, after this publication, would be an impossibly shameful thing. In short, Jefferson and his collaborators were putting as bold a front upon the enterprise as they could design; they were taking a gigantic step in the dark and they were whistling, so to speak, to keep up their spirits. If they were to rally Americans in rebellion; if, especially, they were to enlist a foreign power in their cause, their first move must display a talent for which Americans have always been celebrated: it must be, largely, a play of bluff.

The complaints against the King in the second part of the Declaration were, taken one at a time, specious, inflated, or out of the imperial context—as Hutchinson's careful reasoning showed. The angry allegations—that the King had refused his assent to wholesome laws, that he had "repeatedly" dissolved colonial legislatures, that he had left provinces "exposed to all the dangers of invasion without and convulsions within," that he had tried to limit the colonial population—suggest a long-continued and wholesale performance, whereas in reality the incidents had been sporadic or occasional. The accusations that the King had obstructed the administration of justice, erected a "multitude" of new offices which he had filled with "swarms" of officers, and that he had deprived the people of the benefits of trial by jury were exaggerations based on a few instances. The courts of admiralty, "standing armies," the "mock trials," and the general condition of martial law that the document mentioned were measures taken by Parliament when it had seemed necessary to put down total insubordination by colonies that were accepted parts of an empire.

But, as Carl Becker points out, these "facts"

> were not submitted as being, in themselves, a justification for rebellion; they were submitted to prove that the deliberate and persistent purpose of the king was to establish an "absolute tyranny" over the colonies.[2]

[2] Becker: *Declaration of Independence,* p. 14.

Thus, the list as a whole was far more than the sum of its parts. The inaccuracies in detail were unimportant, therefore, as long as they made evident the malevolent intent.

2

In this light the Declaration seems to shrink from its stature as a manifesto of immortal truth into an extremely adroit piece of political propaganda. It is only when we see it—as Hutchinson or Dickinson or the carping and jealous John Adams could not possibly have seen it—as a creed, a body of doctrine on which much of the social and political philosophy of a nation has been built, that we may know its true significance. Going back, now, with the parchment in our hands and all the experience of the intervening years in our minds—back to 1776—we see the Declaration as a forecast of circumstances to come and buttressed by some of the noblest wishful thinking on political record. As Becker says, "the framers of the Declaration were not writing history, but making it." [3] They were setting standards—reference points—for the public conscience in the lifetime of the nation they envisaged. Independence—the break from Britain—was merely a first step, necessary, they thought, before the creative work could begin.

Looking at the preamble with its philosophy of the new government, no one could or can take the statement that all men are created equal quite literally. The concept is most certainly not original with Jefferson: indeed, it had been current in America since the words of Locke had first blown across the ocean to their most congenial soil. For two centuries men have denied it or they have tried to rationalize it, to explain it: to say, for instance, that it means equal opportunity or equal rights, or that it implies the Creator's design rather than his achievement in the face of human perversity or social distortion. But the thing will not let us alone; however false we denote it, we cannot forget it; however often, in misanthropic moments, we may call it a fraud and a deceit, it keeps coming back to wake us at night, to shame us into reforming legislation, to stir us, indeed, to war against those who exploit the ine-

[3] Ibid., p. 6.

qualities of man. The equality concept is, in short, of the very substance of the American conscience.

Locke seems to set the concept up as a theorem like the "as if's" the physicists and mathematicians are forever using to accomplish their real and solid ends. We can find neither an absolute zero nor an absolute infinity, yet we see long progressions forever approaching these imagined goals, and if we refused to imagine them, there could be no progressions. The state in which Locke finds all men free, equal, and independent is something that never existed in fact; it is a fictional state, but on it is built the whole argument for democratic government and the proof of that government's legitimacy. We cannot prove a Creator's intent, but by assuming it to be equality we may come forever nearer and nearer to a desirable end. To others the end may not be desirable; but to us it must be inevitably so because we have, engrossed on parchment, the assertion that the Creator intended it, and the Creator does not intend undesirable things.

Keeping our eyes on the avatars of the unalienable rights has caused us a great deal of bloodshed and bitter grief. The struggles against slavery, racial discrimination, and the police state seemed to us necessary because we could never bring ourselves to erase those lines from the parchment. "It was the preamble of the Declaration of Independence," Moses Coit Tyler believes, "which elected Lincoln, which sent forth the Emancipation Proclamation, which gave victory to Grant, which ratified the Thirteenth Amendment." [4] We might add that it also brought about the fair-practices acts in the twentieth century and the decision of the Supreme Court about segregation in the public schools.

There have been intervals in which the words grew dim when greed or vindictiveness gave us myopia. We forgot the unalienable rights of Mexicans when we wanted certain territory; we forgot those of southerners because they had once refused to concede the natural rights of Negroes. We found it expedient, at various times, to alienate the divinely endowed rights of American Indians. Yet these lapses have always been accompanied by loud whispers of conscience and followed by such virulent conscientious fevers that we have passed apologetic legislation and devoted years to the repair of our mistakes.

[4] Tyler: op. cit., I, 517.

Finally, because of a thesis, an abstraction—a fictional concept, if you like—we have moved from a pattern of social hierarchy to one of social equality or classlessness, leveling out at last even the plutocracy which so long distinguished us. As a device to implement this progress we invented mass production and mass communication. In our country the masses have become predominant; we are leading and instructing the "mass world" so deprecated by Ortega y Gasset and feared by Walter Lippmann, and the extremes to which the equality ideal has carried us seem to some to have caused individual anonymity and social mechanization. But are not these things the result of a momentum started by a relentless conscience fortified in our antiquity by a Puritan tradition?

Our other fundamental documents, the federal and state constitutions, are on a wholly different plane from that of the Declaration. To put the thing into the fashionable words of the mid-twentieth century, the Declaration may be called a "directive" which the constitutions "implement." Or it might be said that the Declaration is on a policy, the constitutions on an operational, "level." To us, in this study, the Declaration more than constitutions seems an instrument of conscience: the "still small voice" speaking before the constitutional policeman comes along.

3

Passing now to the second part—the statement of grievances—we seem to lose the guidepost aspect. Here, rather, is an adroit distortion of superficial truths. It appears to be a statement of what the colonial Whigs thought the colonies were; the recapitulation of a long series of proofs of *de facto* independence. They had declared the colonial independence of Parliament at the time of the Townshend Acts. They had stated their sole allegiance to be to the king. However absurd this assumption, they had made it and must abide by it in any public assertion. A king, not a parliament, had given them their original charters; every new king must respect the autonomy these charters provided. Now this king, George III, had let them down. He had treated them not as chartered but as conquered people—as he might treat the French Canadians in a conquered Quebec. It would be an anomaly for the injured colonists to attack a parliament they had divorced. They owed it no allegiance. But as a king of England had once given them freedom, now no king of England could enslave them! Thus, Parliament is not mentioned by name in the Declaration and is only twice obliquely referred to.

For home consumption this concentration against the tyrant was excellent propaganda. It followed harmoniously on Tom Paine's diatribe. It would go far to convince those Americans who still cherished their symbol, of the villainy of the "royal brute." But also for the world outside England—especially for the French, who did not know the facts and who were themselves feeling the pricks of a despotic (if decaying) monarchical regime—the attack on George carried weight. That it was incomprehensible in England—even to some of the Whigs who had defended the colonists and now thought the attack would better have been aimed at the Parliament—did not matter to those who had declared independence. If it angered Britons, so much the better. If Englishmen called it false, that was what you must expect.

But was it altogether false? Was there not, even here, something of that forward-looking, that guidepost quality we saw in the preamble? To Edmund Burke the whole of the revolutionary thought from the start had been more in the future than in the present. It was not a particular act that troubled them in each case, it was what that act portended.

> In other countries [Burke said], the people, more simple, and of a less mercurial cast, judge of an ill principle in government only by an actual grievance; here [in America] they anticipate the evil, and judge of the pressure of the grievance by the badness of the principle. They augur misgovernment at a distance; and snuff the approach of tyranny in every tainted breeze.[5]

The list of grievances, then, which seems intended to prove the King's tyranny, becomes in this light an augury rather than a record. And although it was so harshly criticized at the time and for more than a century afterward by both Americans and Englishmen, yet many later historians have shown that in 1776 George III was aiming precisely at despotic rule and that some of his conduct in other fields was exceedingly shocking to liberty-loving Englishmen.

[5] "Speech on . . . Conciliation with the Colonies," March 22, 1775, in *Works of the Right Honorable Edmund Burke,* 4th edition (Boston, 1871), II, 125.

Lecky, for example, writes of "that system of personal government which he had so laboriously built up," [6] and John R. Green says:

> George was in fact the [prime] minister through the twelve years . . . from 1770 . . . and the shame of the darkest hour of English history lies wholly at his door.[7]

In his extraordinary *History of Civilization in England*, Henry Thomas Buckle delivers a diatribe against George III beside which the Declaration seems almost restrained. He calls him despotic, superstitious, narrow, reactionary, and ignorant, regarding "every liberal sentiment" as an abomination. The American Revolution, Buckle says, was known in England as "the king's war." [8] The King was heartily in favor of every oppressive act against the Americans and believed that such oppression strengthened his personal power. All of this proved a boomerang, according to Buckle, and endangered English freedom.

> The opinions which it was necessary to advocate in order to justify this barbarous war, recoiled upon ourselves. In order to defend the attempt to destroy the liberties of America, principles were laid down which, if carried into effect, would have subverted the liberties of England.[9]

They were not carried into effect simply because the Americans won the war!

> From that risk we were saved by the Americans, who with heroic spirit resisted the royal armies, defeated them at every point. . . .[1]

This evidence (and there is a great deal more) shows that Americans were not alone in fearing the menace of this King's increasing tyranny. But what was the future effect, if any, of this list of grievances—this second part of our Declaration? Did it not absolve the *people* of England, "our British brethren," for posterity—the people whom we should hold "as we hold the rest of mankind, enemies in war, in peace friends"? It was true we had "warned"

[6] Lecky: op. cit., IV, 457, 458.

[7] John R. Green: *A Short History of the English People* (New York, 1894), p. 1696.

[8] Henry Thomas Buckle: *History of Civilization in England* (New York, 1924), I, 319, 333.

[9] Ibid., I, 345.

[1] Ibid., I, 346. In view of his fervor, Buckle's slight exaggeration here is easy to forgive.

them, "appealed to their native justice and magnanimity," and "conjured them by the ties of our common kindred to *disavow* these usurpations." They had been "deaf" but only *temporarily* deaf; once the separation was complete, we could do business with them again. It was only the tyrant King who could not be forgiven, but he would soon be dead. We had, in short, given succeeding generations what, in our slang, we call an alibi. They could read the Declaration without rancor: George had long since been gathered to his fathers, and all tyranny along with him was forever dead.

In all this perspective the whole of the document appears as a living force, recurrently inspiring new growth. As such it will probably be cherished in every part of the free world. But the first five or six years of its existence were so precarious that only the stoutest hearts could hope for its survival. These were indeed the times, as Tom Paine said, that tried men's souls.

4

The star-spangled patriots have always had difficulty in explaining to foreigners how so glorious a war with its succession of overwhelming American victories and the constant superintendence of the Almighty could have lasted so long.

Here, presumably, was a united people of three million in arms in the defense of their land. The fighters were presumably hardy, determined, and patriotic men, many of them proficient in the use of the world's deadliest rifle, fighting on terrain they knew intimately, ideal for defensive shelter and sniping, all commanded by one of the great strategists of all time and assisted by a strong European military power. Yet it took them nearly seven years to defeat a slow, disgruntled professional army totally uninstructed in open fighting, operating three thousand miles from its base, getting only half-hearted support from home, and assisted only by spiritless German mercenaries who, outside their pay and subsistence, had no interest whatever in the war.

The answer, worked out by conscientious historians behind the oratory and flag-waving, is probably not yet complete. It includes apathy, native American hatred of war, innocence of discipline in an agricultural people, slow communications, inadequate service of supply, the malfunctioning of an experimental and amateur government, shortage of manpower due to seasonal exigencies, an absence of manufacturing industries, and moral and material sabotage by an enormous dissident minority. All of these things are revealed in the letters of Washington to the Continental Congress—a more or less impotent body trying to work with a loose league of sovereign nations that called itself (after 1776) the United States of America. (Many twentieth-century patriots have forgotten, for example, the private war, continuing after the beginning of the Revolution, between Connecticut and Pennsylvania.)

As we study all these things, we are not surprised at the extent of the struggle. We are more astonished that victory came at all to the Americans. There were several critical moments at which, with a little more skill on the part of the enemy or a little less cunning and resolution on the part of Washington, the war might well have been lost. It is undoubtedly true that, but for the aid given by France to the American armies, victory would have gone to Britain and the thirteen states would have become British colonies again. Thus, historians are generally agreed that there were two saving factors: Washington and France.

We are interested in the moral elements in this great struggle. Beyond question Washington's influence was moral as well as military; at times his control of troop morale was far more important than any strategy. But the alliance with France presented a dilemma that split the American conscience and kept it split for many years after the war was over. It seemed at times, indeed, as if the French military aid, strong as it was, could hardly compensate for the division in sentiment.

We have learned to accept the expedient necessities of war even when they disturb our consciences. In the World War of 1914–18 the alliance with Japan that resulted in such dangerous concessions in the Pacific was exceedingly discomforting to many westerners. Many Americans were even more uneasy in 1942 when we were aiding Russia with lend-lease and at the later settlement at Yalta. Franklin Roosevelt was criticized for making a deal with the "wrong" French in Africa. Yet at the time our disagreements were suppressed in the interest of "total" victory. Open criticism of our war policy was thought more immoral than the failure to defend our deeper convictions.

The case of the French alliance in the War of Independence is peculiarly interesting to us because of its impact on that hard Puritan core whose development we have so extensively considered. But it is also important to our story because it shows what a change had come over another part of the people in the lapse of religious compulsions that accompanied the Enlightenment. These two facets come into sharp clarity in the Continental Congress in the brief period between the fall of 1774 and the summer of 1776—that critical interval in which independence became an accepted fact.

5

In 1774, at the very moment when the Continental Congress was first assembling in Philadelphia, the Parliament in England passed a bill which became the Quebec Act. As we look back on that statute, coming as it did in the midst of all the oppressive legislation, it appears as one of the most humane and tolerant laws in British colonial history. It was typical of the sort of administration which made Britain the world's most successful colonizer—of the technique, indeed, which had built the original power of the thirteen colonies.

But when the news of it got to Philadelphia, the members of the Continental Congress were overcome with horror. Whether, as a whole, they were thus horrified or whether the news merely offered a new opportunity for protest, it is probable that the New England delegates were sincerely troubled.

The Quebec Act provided that the French Canadians, who had passed into British control in 1763, might retain their old French legal code and their cherished Catholic religion. But the act went beyond mere religious tolerance. It decreed that the Roman Catholic church should become the established church of Canada, to be supported by the compulsory taxation of the inhabitants, and that this system be extended to the Ohio River.

Through Puritan New England the ghosts of John Cotton and the Mathers walked again. So, their sepulchral voices seemed to say, Britain removed the menace of the papist French and their Indian converts from our borders only to restore, in the next decade, the awful power of Rome! What would happen now to the "ancient free Protestant colonies" with the antichrist on their borders, with Canada inundated with hordes of Catholic immigrants from Europe, with thousands of priests infiltrating our very Puritan strongholds and the church extending its wicked power across our frontiers?

In October 1774, therefore, the Continental Congress composed an "Address to the People of Great Britain" reflecting the Puritan conscience. It excoriated first the legal provisions of the act; then added:

> Nor can we suppress our astonishment, that a British Parliament should ever consent to establish in that country a religion that has deluged your island in blood, and dispersed impiety, bigotry, persecution, murder and rebellion through every part of the world.[2]

In October 1774 the Continental Congress could not suppress its astonishment at Britain's kindness to the French Catholics of Canada. By the spring of 1775, however, it had suppressed its astonishment to the point of trying to induce the French Catholics of Canada to join the American insurgents against Britain—an invitation the French Catholics, embittered by the Puritan bigotry, emphatically declined. By March 1776 the Continental Congress, composed of virtually the same delegates who had voted their horror in 1774, had completely forgotten the Puritan conscience. By the spring and summer of 1776, however, several more important things had intervened.

In March 1776, already largely convinced of the need for declaring independence, and alarmed at the turn the war was taking, the Congress sent Silas Deane secretly to France to feel out the possibility that her Catholic King might back the American cause. In the summer, after the Declaration, the Congress, now fully awake to the desperate need of foreign aid, sent Benjamin Franklin to Paris with full powers to negotiate with the Catholic King of France a commercial and military alliance.

In France, of course, there was a very different feeling about England from that prevailing among the ignorant French peasants of Canada. The French were still smarting from their defeat by Britain in the Seven Years' War. Furthermore, the people were

[2] "Address to the People of Great Britain," approved October 21, 1774, in *Journals of the Continental Congress,* W. C. Ford, editor (Washington, 1904–37), I, 87, 88.

suffering an oppression of their own and eagerly embraced any cause of "liberty." And they were enchanted with the enlightened Franklin, who knew well enough that in the country of Voltaire, Rousseau, Diderot, and Condorcet there was no Catholic "menace." Franklin, of course, from his childhood had loathed the Puritan prejudices and the New England bigotry and was, therefore, an ideal choice for the mission.

In the autumn of 1777, after the victorious Battle of Saratoga, Franklin achieved his success. The Continental Congress and the patriots who had lost their religious scruples welcomed the treaty and were eager for the arrival of the French forces. In Paris there was dancing in the streets. But the old rock-ribbed Puritans had not forgotten their traditional hate. There was no dancing in the streets of the solemn New England towns. And when, eager, almost hysterical in the great cause of liberty, the French soldiers who had fallen over themselves to volunteer for Lafayette's forces arrived in America they were chilled by their reception in many places.

When the news of the alliance arrived, new hordes of conscientious Americans flocked to the Loyalist banner. For the Loyalist pamphleteers there was a new field day.

> Tell me, ye sons and daughters of Old England, [ran one *Letter to the People of America* who were trying to forget their ancestry], whether your hearts do not revolt at the idea of an union with France? Whether French manners, French politicks, French perfidy, French fashions, do not inspire you with detestation? Whether the very sight of a Frenchman in your streets, is not an object of ridicule, disgust and contempt? . . . Now, lay your hands upon your hearts; give me honest answers to these questions, and the dispute is ended.[3]

At the same time that fears were stirred in Yankee hearts by such pamphlets, and while prayers were undoubtedly going up to John Calvin's God for protection against the papist invasion, the feeling in the South and to some extent in the middle colonies was quite different. In provinces where the Church of England (that "halfway house" on the road to Rome) held its dubious sway, there was no opposition to the French on religious grounds. We see now, in this first division caused by the alliance, portents of that later post-war

[3] *A Letter to the People of America, Lately Printed at New York; Now Republished, etc.* (London, 1778), p. 31.

split when the new nation nearly fell apart from its divided sympathies and the great conflict between Federalists and Republicans began.

When the French armies began to arrive, there were difficulties. Families of the American soldiers did not want their kin to mix with the sinful, loose-living Romanists. Where the association had taken place, it was said that the corruption was visible. The French were often blamed for the normal relaxation of morals incident to military life. In Newport and other places where French soldiers were in transit or in training, mothers kept their daughters off the streets. There were riots in Boston and even in southern Charleston between townspeople and French sailors, with resulting casualties. After the retirement of the Count d'Estaing from Rhode Island, anti-French feeling was so bitter that "it needed all the tact and unvarying moderation of Washington to prevent . . . an open outbreak."[4]

6

It was the tact, moderation, patience, and humanity of this great man that had as much—perhaps more—to do with saving the Revolution from disaster as his military genius. From the point of view of morals and morale, he seems to have had as difficult a time as he had with supplies, transportation, and finance. It is impossible to prove that no one else could have done what he did because no one knows to what heights a man may rise in an extremity, but as we look over his generals and other officers we fail to find his combination of qualities: total integrity, infinite forbearance, understanding of men under emotional pressures, and an almost miraculous insight into an enemy's intent and capacity.

Perhaps nowhere in the civilized world was there a less warlike people than in the thirteen colonies in the eighteenth century. This did not mean that Americans were unwilling to fight when the occasion was near at hand. As we have seen, they had fought the Indians in many bloody engagements. A militia organized for a particular task—such as those in Pennsylvania and Virginia in the French and Indian War—had performed well. But the tradition was that fighting men would be assembled for a particular job, usually in de-

[4] Lecky: op. cit., IV, 480.

fense of their land; when the immediate danger had passed they would go home.

Now, for the first time, there was a real war involving all the people and depending, for the first years at least, on the people's unassisted efforts. It was a very different matter from the old sporadic fights against the French when the continuity of the war was maintained by England. Now came all the unaccustomed burdens incident to keeping a large body of men continuously under arms: the long periods of boredom between battles; the forced marches toward objectives of which the common soldier was ignorant; the long absences from home with no news of household and family; and the stern discipline that is routine for the trained soldier but completely foreign to the proud, independent farmer.

The Congress knew at the start that they could not depend on militia alone, yet the regular army core organized under the command of Washington could never be truly professional, composed as it was of volunteers from every sector of society. The result was that even Washington could not keep his units together for more than a few months at a time. When the harvest came, men needed on the farms would desert in droves. Others would go home at the end of their brief enlistments. One example of this demoralization was in the campaigns of 1776 when the eighteen thousand men under Washington's command in the summer dwindled to five thousand by year's end. Such a condition is almost inconceivable to the twentieth-century mind, accustomed to the movements of vast armies in methodically planned and perfectly executed campaigns over immense spaces of land and sea.

Another difficulty came from the old sense of distinction among the colonies. New Englanders who fought well in Massachusetts or Connecticut felt that they were moving to foreign soil when they were ordered to New York or Pennsylvania, and many simply refused to go. We see here that the parochial conscience had not yet expanded to the point at which a cause seemed more important than local concerns. Men might talk about the common struggle against tyranny and toward freedom, but when it came to a fight, the heart stayed near the hearth. What was an abstraction such as "liberty" when your family was hungry?

Unfortunately, no regular provision was made for soldiers' families. Sometimes a state legislature would vote help, though we have some melancholy records of procrastination or of failure to implement a vote for subsidy. A series of agonized letters, for example, was written by Ebenezer Huntington, an officer in command of Connecticut troops, to his father, Jabez, a member of the Connecticut Council of Safety. In 1778 he wrote:

> You resolved in your Last Sessions, that the Soldiers family should be Supplied, whether they sent the Money or not, but it is not done, nor will it be done. Not a Day Passes . . . but some Soldier with Tears in his Eyes, hands me a letter from his Wife Painting forth the Distresses of his family in such strains as these, "I am without bread, and Cannot get any, the Committee will not Supply me, my Children will Starve, or if they do not they must freeze, we have no wood, neither can we get any. *Pray Come home.*" These Applications Affect me, my Ears *are not,* neither *shall* they be shutt to such Complaints, they are Injurious, they wound my feelings. . . . Don't drive us to Despair, we are now on the Brink. Depend upon it we cannot put up with such treatment any Longer. Spare yourselves by rewarding the brave.[5]

We have learned how to prevent these attacks upon the soldier's conscience. But in the Revolution, when there was a national army but no national government—except the Continental Congress, which could not control the provincial legislatures—the poor soldier must often have felt that he was fighting alone, with no support from the country he was fighting for, with nothing to keep up his will but personal attachment to his leader.

Washington was able to inspire that sort of attachment. Men dedicated themselves to him in a kind of worship. We cannot recapture any adequate sense of the emanation from his spirit that inspired those under his command so that they forgot cold, hunger, nakedness, and disease to follow him on their bleeding feet. His letters, his speeches, the descriptions by his contemporaries fail to make us feel that peculiar magnetism. We can understand the appeal of Morgan, of the "swamp-fox" Marion, of Light-Horse Harry Lee, of a dozen other dashing heroes. But the aloof, austere Washington, the wealthy plantation aristocrat, was something else. What was the compelling quality of his voice? It is forever lost, along with the changing expressions of his face. To us he must always, to some extent, be frozen in marble: his stances, his attitudes, his ges-

[5] *American Historical Review,* V, 721, 722. *Public Records of the State of Connecticut* (Hartford, 1895), II, 134, 135.

tures—noble, heroic, and fixed. With a straining effort of fancy we may see the pale ghost, sleepless, walking at dawn in the snow along the row of patched tents at Valley Forge, but we cannot follow him with the sunken eyes of the men there or know why that detached figure should leave new strength behind him: the will to face one more desperate day. Only, we are sure, independence could not have been won without him.

The most terrible year of all came just before the final British collapse, when an epidemic of mutiny seemed to jump from camp to camp. On this threshold of disaster it was only the insight of the military commanders into the enemy's weaknesses that made possible the final maneuvers. And, of all the enemy weaknesses, the greatest was a moral one. The cause was lost in England. Too many English consciences were asking "Why?"

As the poet Lowell, looking at the graves at Concord of two British soldiers, expressed it,

> *What brought them here they never knew,*
> *They fought as suits the English breed:*
> *They came three thousand miles, and died*
> *To keep the Past upon its throne. . . .*

Chapter XIII

The Two Critical Questions

THE DECLARATION OF INDEPENDENCE raised questions which were to trouble the conscience of the American people for more than a century; perhaps we have not yet wholly emerged from the forest of doubts that so long restricted our view. As we look back at the continuous struggle to realize the basic ideals set forth in the Declaration, we see intervals in which economic and other pressures have blurred a clear interpretation.

In any review of the fluctuations of public conscience we must keep continuously in mind the prodigious process of growth which inevitably affected American behavior. As we are tolerant of the acts of a growing boy, beset and harassed by the formidable physical phenomena of adolescence, so we must control our judgment of American morality in the formative years by constant reference to the facts of huge and fast expansion. As new strength, new energy, new sources of power come almost overnight to the adolescent, outrunning his mental growth, so the space and riches of America, appearing suddenly to Americans, lured them despite the sternest inhibitions of traditional moral codes into wild thought and intemperate conduct.

Yet through all the changes it is possible to see an evolution wrought by a growing national conscience. The goal of that evolution is democracy. This, it seems to us, was the prophecy of the Declaration. It did not seem so to the Founding Fathers. It did not seem so to various regional consciences during the years of American growth. It is only as the regional consciences merged into the national conscience that we have accepted it as the true prophecy of the Declaration for the United States, a prophecy that even transcended the intent of the Declaration's authors. There is still argument as to whether democracy as it has come to exist in America is desirable. But the facts of the evolution can hardly be disputed.

The dilemmas posed by the Declaration have been rationalized again and again under economic pressures. Sometimes this has been done in the effort to keep a balance of political power under a changing economy. Sometimes the rationalization has been inspired by fears of survival, by the ugly compulsions of war or national emergency, by hysteria, or by avarice. But always, as times and tempers cooled, Americans would wake at night in the chilly consciousness that this or that was wrong, that we had somehow lost our way, that we must go back to the guidepost and choose a road more certain in direction.

Except the Bible, no printed object has been so pored over, so thumbed and dog-eared by the people of the United States as the Declaration of Independence. The Constitution we hand over to our lawyers and our courts, and they in turn tell us of something we may stand on. But the Declaration we study ourselves in privacy: it is our revealed religion. And in parts even of that brief, apparently clear, and exceedingly rhythmic text we find almost as great an obscurity as in the vast reaches of Holy Scripture.

2

The questions which came near destroying the United States were two, one political and one social. The first asked: Are we a nation or a league of nations? In other words, is the term "United States of America" singular or plural? This is a political question, but when it appeared that the people were going to answer it by shooting their brothers it became very much a matter of conscience. And as we follow its constant recurrence and its recurrent settlement in favor of preserving union, we feel a strong moral pressure forever moving toward a single end.

The second question asked: Is Negro slavery as a legalized institution compatible with the doctrine of natural rights as expounded in the Declaration? Here the inference is clearer. If you agree that all men are created equal, you must conclude that Negroes are not men. Before the Declaration this had been the unconscious assumption of most slaveholders. The Negroes were obviously, they thought, of so inferior a race that they were nearer to the lower animals than to that creature God had made in his own image. After the Declaration had been circulated and digested, those who felt it necessary to defend the institution were definite in their statements that Negroes were not intended to be included in the natural-rights doctrine of Locke and the other philosophers of the Enlightenment. But the Declaration had an immediate impact on other consciences, and it was the preamble to that document that started the abolition movement. In general, though there were conspicuous exceptions, sentiment divided along economic lines, and, as so often happened, consciences followed the indices of prosperity.

As these two questions were to meet in the greatest crisis in the history of the American conscience, it is important to examine their origins as moral issues. It will be seen then that the seeds of the second American civil war were sown during and immediately after the first. It will be seen also that they fell on exceedingly receptive soil: soil that had been slowly prepared over a century and a half and intensively fertilized in the revolutionary decade.

We seem to see many points at which the growth of the evil seeds might have been stopped before they produced plants of such nightmare proportions. In theory this might indeed have occurred, but the actual, practical conditions of life in this vast land, where the whole story of civilization was rapidly re-enacting itself on one frontier after another, defeated all theory. There were too many factors, too separate, coming from too many directions at once, too diverse in origin and meaning to make an orderly scheme possible. That the whole complex did not explode into fragmented anarchy is the unparalleled miracle of the United States. It is no wonder that the people, seeing the national integrity growing behind them as they moved over the enormous spaces, came to believe in a "manifest destiny"; that a superhuman force was leading them, as a Hebrew God once led the tribes of Israel into their promised land.

3

The first question arose even before the Declaration was signed. It was advanced by conservatives who were still reluctant to separate from Britain. But if, they said in effect to the radicals, you are so determined upon independence, would it not be better before you declare it to decide what sort of a country you want and what sort of government you will need once you are free? Should not a definite plan of union be drawn up now, one with teeth in it, one that will hold us firmly together after we have won our fight and give us strength to stand up against the world? It should be, they said, a national, centralized government with sovereign power over the separate states. After that we may declare our independence with the assurance that we shall be able to continue, perpetually, in a separate and equal station among the powers of the earth.

Merrill Jensen has given a concise description of that projected government:

> In a general way the conservatives knew what kind of government they wanted: a centralized government that would take the place of the British Government—a government that would regulate trade, control the disposition of Western lands, and settle disputes between one state and another; a government having power to act coercively against any citizen who displayed tendencies subversive of the established conservative order.[1]

These tendencies, according to the "right wing" of Congress, were mainly those having a democratic color. The conservatives were terrified of democracy and therefore of New England, which appeared to be the section furthest advanced toward popular government. The British government had kept the vulgar Yankees in line. Now, if we must break away from that wholesome restraining force, we must substitute something equally strong, otherwise New England might well dominate and coerce the other provinces. Thus, in 1775 Edward Biddle had said to Alexander Graydon:

> I . . . sicken at the idea of thirteen, unconnected, petty democracies: if we are to be independent, let us, in the name of GOD, at once have an empire, and place WASHINGTON at the head of it.[2]

[1] Merrill Jensen: *The Articles of Confederation* (Madison, Wis., 1940), p. 111.

[2] Alexander Graydon: *Memoirs of His Own Times* (Philadelphia, 1846), p. 285.

Yet some of the other members were afraid of the central government for the precise reason that it would give New England control! On the very eve of independence Edward Rutledge of South Carolina wrote:

> The Idea of destroying all Provincial Distinctions and making every thing . . . bend to what they call the good of the whole, is in other Terms to say that these Colonies must be subject to the Government of the Eastern Provinces. . . . I dread their overruling influence. . . . I dread their low Cunning, and those levelling Principles . . . which are so captivating to the lower class of Mankind, and which will occasion such a fluctuation of Property as to introduce the greatest disorder. I am resolved to invest the Congress with no more Power than is absolutely necessary. . . .[3]

The New Englanders themselves were firmly against any infringement of provincial sovereignty that might rob them of their precious colonial heritage. And, in the end, the majority of Congress, for one reason or another, came round to the radical view. Every colony, after all, had suffered from the "despotism" the British government had become. Most of the people were heartily sick of *that* "centralized" rule. Why, then, substitute something just like it for the new United States? What guarantee was there that it, too, would not develop into tyranny?

In any case, the majority, in the early summer of 1776, was opposed to delaying the vote for independence and the Declaration. These men had wrestled for many a long night with their doubts and fears; many of them had communed with their God in the devout fashion of the day; they had decided at last, and now they felt they could not wait. They knew that if independence must wait on a decision as to the government of the United States the debates would be endless and meanwhile the armies would not know what they were fighting for. The government formula could come later; the ideological statement must precede it and should, indeed, be the basis of the government.

4

There came about then a yes-and-no pattern which held up the development of a national political conscience for many years. It

[3] Edward Rutledge to John Jay, June 29, 1776, in *Letters of Members of the Continental Congress,* Edmund C. Burnett, editor (Washington, 1921), I, 517, 518.

also left the country in a state so vulnerable to both external and internal forces that it took the constant effort of calm and deep-thinking minds to maintain any integrity in the so-called "united" states.

They were united enough while the war lasted to bring it to a successful conclusion. But even during the war years the question of what sort of uniting government the states could go on with was never adequately answered. Immediately after the Declaration a committee headed by the conservative John Dickinson [4] had composed Articles of Confederation which had teeth in them. The second Article, especially, was so binding that, if it had been retained, it would have made civil war morally impossible.

> The said colonies [it read] unite themselves so as never to be divided by any Act whatever. . . .

For nearly five years the Continental Congress spent what time it could spare from the war extracting the teeth from Dickinson's draft. The state of Maryland, particularly, so feared the power of her big neighbor, Virginia, that she held up the ratification of the confederation articles until the document had become virtually impotent in binding power. As it finally went through in 1781 on the eve of factual independence, it provided for nothing but "a league of friendship" in which "Each state retains its sovereignty, freedom and independence" and only a handful of powers, such as war, treaties, and diplomatic relations with foreign powers, were delegated to the "confederacy" called the United States.

Meanwhile, the Revolution was drawing wearily toward its close. In less than a year after the ratification of the Articles it was over and peace negotiations had begun in Paris. The moment the common cause ceased to unite the states, the confederacy, morally speaking, fell apart.

The jealousies, the hatreds, the distrust, and the fears of the pre-war days returned twofold. The dissensions we find reflected in the letters of those years had been pushed only just below the surface in the continental emergency. As a man will join with a despised neighbor in putting out a fire dangerous to both, so the provinces held their noses, so to speak, and joined hands against the greater evil. The commercial rivalries between Boston and Philadelphia,

[4] Dickinson refused to vote for independence and to sign the Declaration.

the Puritan horror of southern indolence and Sabbath-breaking, and the land-war between Connecticut and Pennsylvania were as acute as international quarrels.

> Philadelphia [wrote John Adams when he first attended the Continental Congress], with all its trade and wealth and regularity, is not Boston. The morals of our people are much better; their manners are more polite and agreeable; they are purer English; our language is better, our taste is better, our persons are handsomer; our spirit is greater, our laws are wiser, our religion is superior, our education is better.[5]

And in 1773 Josiah Quincy, Jr., a dyed-in-the-wool Yankee, spread his Puritan prejudices over the pages of his journal of a southern visit.

> I spent yesterday [he wrote of a Virginia day] chiefly with young men of fortune; they were gamblers and cock-fighters, hound breeders, and horse-jockies. To hear them converse, you would think that the grand point of all science was properly to fix a gaff and touch with dexterity the tail of a cock while in combat. . . . The ingenuity of a Locke or the discoveries of a Newton were considered as infinitely inferior to the accomplishments of him who know when to shoulder a blind cock or start a fleet horse.[6]

Now, cut loose from British rule, law, and order, the states encountered added troubles. As the ban on westward migration was removed, land hunger grew. Some of the older colonies had seventeenth-century charters that extended their grants west to the "South Sea" or Pacific Ocean. Virginia and North Carolina especially were determined to exploit some of this territory. But other states such as Maryland had precise, tight boundaries. Privately, citizens of several "landless" states had moved west of the Appalachians and made deals with the Indians; land companies had grown up, selling these wilderness stretches to individuals. Now it appeared that these infringed on the claims of the land-rich states, and such disputes contributed new venom to the post-war situation. This quarrel did more than anything else to split the United States asunder in its infancy. That it was ever resolved was due to the extraordinary wisdom and statesmanship of the Founding Fathers, acting under perhaps the greatest handicap of our political history.

[5] John Adams: "Diary," 1774, in *Works*, II, 395, quoted in Jensen: op. cit., p. 118.

[6] Josiah Quincy, Jr.: "Journal," in Massachusetts Historical Society Proceedings, XLIX, 467.

5

In all this near-anarchy—which was watched by foreigners with alternate amusement and hope of profitable intrigue—was there any binding moral force? Was there any need, felt by the people of every state, for some philosophical reference point, some common spiritual abstraction that might take the place of a flag or a throne and justify all the bloodshed and agony? To find it we must go back to the guidepost. In the heat of war the people of the states were guided by it or by the long thought behind it in the Enlightenment, and as each new state went about the business of making its separate instrument of government, the principles of Jefferson's preamble became part of every one.

As soon as the Declaration was published, the states began writing their own constitutions.[7] These varied widely in detail: some put more restrictions on the franchise than others; some proclaimed religious liberty. Most were based on original colonial charters. Connecticut and Rhode Island kept their liberal royal charters intact. But all the new constitutions contained bills of rights: statements about the natural, inherent, inalienable rights of man that no law could touch—the substance of a Creator's endowment that was forever beyond the reach of legislatures or courts. Equality, liberty, and property: these were recognized by all as being under God's protection.

The prevalence of these philosophical declarations suggests how completely indoctrinated the provincial statesman had become with the political and even the religious ideas of the Enlightenment. They had come a long way from the subjugation of man in determinist Calvinism and the hellfire terrors of the Great Awakening. We may mark here a very definite stage in our history of the American conscience. There would be plenty of lapses in the years to come. But here, repeated again and again in actual practical instruments of government, was a set of principles which had never before been anything but theory. Apparently these states meant to live by what to Locke and Montesquieu had been a mere philosophical ideal.

[7] New Hampshire, South Carolina, New Jersey, and Virginia slightly anticipated the Declaration.

In 1780, when the last of these constitutions was adopted, the states were not democracies in our understanding of the word. In no state was there a full representation of the people. In every state there was property qualification of the franchise. In some states persons were forbidden to hold office because of their religious affiliations. There were various schemes for electing representatives to the state legislatures. In general the governments were quite individual, retaining much of their traditional patterns. But they all stated principles which were to lead to a democratic future. In addition to lists of the rights of man, there were universal insistence on trial by jury and a unanimous rejection of executive prerogative.

As soon as the constitutions were drawn, certain articles of them affected consciences differently in different states. Northerners were early convinced that the terms "equality" and "inalienable rights" applied to all mankind regardless of race, creed, or color. They were anxious, therefore, to conclude as soon as possible some sort of legislation assuring universal freedom. In the South, custom was too strong for such drastic change; therefore, the problem of conscience was at first postponed and then rationalized. This brings us to our second great ethical question: was Negro slavery compatible with the natural-rights doctrine of the Declaration and of the state constitutions? If this had been decided in the negative by the whole of the new nation, our history might have been very different and we might have avoided the great American tragedy. But could it have been so decided? The only answer the historian can give is that a negative would have been easier in the 1780's than at any later time.

6

When the Revolution began, Negro slavery was legal in every colony. Massachusetts ended it for her 5,000 slaves in 1781, and New Hampshire freed her 700 in 1783. Between 1780 and 1784 plans for gradual emancipation were adopted in Pennsylvania (6,000) and Connecticut (5,000). The state of New York, where there were 25,000 slaves, began the process in 1799 and New Jersey with 6,000 trailed along in 1804, and in neither of these last two was emancipation completed until 1827.[8]

[8] Ralph B. Flanders: "Slavery" in *Dictionary of American History*, V, 94.

In these states the conscience had free rein. No economic strings were tied to it. Slavery had proved an expensive luxury in New England for reasons we have reviewed. Men were glad enough to relieve themselves of the burden, especially when they could do so with a sense of virtue. But even in the middle states, with their larger farms, conscience and economics worked together. In general, except where there were large staple crops, white hands worked better.

But from Maryland on down south any sort of emancipation was exceedingly difficult. The entire economy of the tidewater regions in the tobacco states rested solidly on the tradition of slave labor. So, too, in the vast rice and indigo regions of the Carolinas. The physical arrangement of the plantations and the whole feudal way of life had been adapted to this form. Furthermore, it was believed that only Negroes could stand work in the fields in the southern climate. This need for Negro labor did not, to be sure, necessitate the continuation of bondage, but the problem of wholesale emancipation of ignorant and helpless people was something no planter could face. While an immense amount of sophistical nonsense was talked on this subject in the South, there can be no question that the individual planter would have faced a very special problem of conscience if he had suddenly cut off the subsistence of his workers while he remained unable to pay money wages.

To consider the people of the southern states conscienceless in this matter is, therefore, historically incorrect. In Virginia, particularly, we find strong moral pressure against the institution. Many planters freed their slaves regardless of consequences. It is said that more slaves were freed in Virginia than there were in Massachusetts, Rhode Island, and New Hampshire combined.[9] The outstanding Virginians of the revolutionary and post-war periods were opposed to slavery. Jefferson's attempt to insert a protest against it in the Declaration was defeated, but he succeeded, eleven years later, in getting an anti-slavery provision into the Northwest Ordinance. Washington stated repeatedly that he wished the institution could be ended, "it being among my first wishes to see some plan adopted, by which slavery in this country may be abolished by slow, sure and imperceptible degrees." [1]

[9] Ibid.

[1] George Washington: *Writings*, W. C. Ford, editor (New York, 1891), XI, 62. Washington himself was a large slaveholder and, though he was opposed to slavery

James Madison was consistently against the institution, particularly against the importation of slaves. Personally he wished "to depend as little as possible on the labour of slaves." [2] In his "Notes on the Confederacy," made in 1787, he cites various discrepancies between the attempted union and the theory of government which was the ideal of independence, adding: "Where slavery exists, the republican Theory becomes still more fallacious." [3] In one of his *Federalist* articles he expressed the hope that the "traffic which has so long and so loudly upbraided the barbarism of modern policy" would eventually be "totally abolished." [4] The inconsistency of slavery with the principles of the Declaration and of the various bills of rights never ceased to trouble his conscience, and as late as 1831, after his state had abandoned all thought of emancipation, he wrote about "the slaves who remain such in spite of the declarations that all men are born equally free." [5]

Yet Madison, like the others, saw the great difficulty of discussing the slavery question in any convention in which there were delegates from the extreme South. Writing his reminiscences of the constitutional convention of 1787 to Lafayette in 1830, he stated clearly what he believed to have been the conflict between conscience and economic necessity:

> A sensibility, morbid in the highest degree, was never more awakened among those who have the largest stake [in slavery]. . . . I scarcely express myself too strongly in saying, that any allusion in the Convention to the subject . . . would have been a spark to a mass of gunpowder.[6]

The most outspoken of the Virginians was George Mason, who may be counted among the "Founding Fathers."

> Slavery [he said] discourages arts & manufactures. . . . [Slaves] produce the most pernicious effect on manners. Every master of slaves is born a petty tyrant. They bring the judgment of heaven on a Country. As nations can not be rewarded or punished in the

---

on principle, he felt it impossible to follow Jefferson's example without ruin to his estate and danger to the Negroes.

[2] James Madison: *Letters and Other Writings* (Philadelphia, 1865), I, 161.

[3] Ibid., I, 322.

[4] *The Federalist,* No. 42, Modern Library edition (New York, 1941), p. 273.

[5] Madison: *Letters,* I, 161.

[6] Ibid., IV, 60.

> next world they must be in this. By an inevitable chain of causes & effects providence punishes national sins, by national calamities.[7]

Mason was immediately answered from South Carolina (with Georgia one of the most ardent pro-slavery states) by Charles Pinckney with the world's oldest sop to conscience: "If slavery be wrong, it is justified by the example of all the world." [8] Yet even in South Carolina, where the continuance of slavery and the slave trade was, or seemed to be, most vital to the economy, there were two conspicuous opponents in the Laurens family.

But there the difficulties of acting according to private conscience in this matter were expressed by Henry Laurens to his son, John, who wanted to free slaves for service in the War of Independence:

> I abhor slavery. . . . I found the Christian religion and slavery growing under the same authority. . . . I nevertheless disliked it. . . . Not less than twenty thousand pounds sterling would all my negroes produce if sold at public auction to-morrow. I am not the man who enslaved them; they are indebted to Englishmen for that favor; nevertheless I am devising means for manumitting many of them. . . . Great powers oppose me—the laws and customs of my country. . . . What will my children say if I deprive them of so much estate? These are difficulties but not insuperable. I will do as much as I can in my time; and leave the rest to a better hand.[9]

As a colony, Virginia had wanted to end the importation of slaves, and one of her grievances against the British was the refusal of the Board of Trade to stop the highly profitable British commerce between Africa and the colonies. It is true that there were other motives here besides the purely humanitarian, yet it is equally true that the wiser Virginians—wiser economically as well as morally—saw Negro slavery as a sort of Frankenstein's monster which might well ruin the economy of the state and bring insurrection if the proportion of blacks to whites increased indefinitely. It is probable that, other things being equal, the institution would have declined and perhaps disappeared, at least in the tobacco country.

But other things were not equal, and in the course of a few years various new, compelling factors turned the tide of conscience.

[7] Debates in the Federal Convention of 1787 as reported by James Madison in *Documents Illustrative of the Formation of the Union* (House Doc. No. 398, 69th Congress, 1st session, Washington, 1927), p. 590.

[8] Ibid., p. 591.

[9] *Correspondence of Henry Laurens of South Carolina*, Frank Moore, editor (New York, 1861), pp. 20, 21.

7

From the war which had brought it into being, then, the United States emerged in plural form with two great question marks standing against the future conscience of its people. There is doubt in the minds of many historians as to whether, in the immediate post-war years, either the people or the Founding Fathers seriously believed that secession would be legally or morally defensible.[1] In spite of the extractive operation on Dickinson's Articles of Confederation, the words "Perpetual Union" remained in the title of the document.[2] As long as the Articles, however, were the sole uniting instrument, secession was not likely to occur to anyone as a necessity. Under them the states could act much as they pleased. The Articles never touched on the issue which eventually became the reason for actual secession. There was no great provocation. There was, to be sure, the grievous land question, but as the states argued this, there was a flexibility (interspersed with bitter quarrels) which showed an increasing desire to settle the issue amicably.

But as the years went on, it was evident that the Confederation was not going to work. The Revolution, from which the whole country emerged in great fatigue and deep financial depression, had left too many problems that crossed state boundaries. There was the Continental army, for example, still largely unpaid, for which no state was responsible. There were foreign intrigues which the central government was not strong enough to control. There was need of a power in the federal government able to check quarrels between states. There was need for a more equitable system of representation in the Congress. In short, if the United States were to remain united and safe, they must have a national constitution paramount to state constitutions, providing for a true national government.

Thus arrived those vital two years 1787–89 in which the final union was born. The famous debates, the extraordinary propaganda for the new constitution, which was later collected into that little book called *The Federalist*, and all the pro and con arguments are

[1] See, for example, Andrew C. McLaughlin: *A Constitutional History of the United States* (New York, 1935), I, 216.

[2] The full title was "Articles of Confederation and Perpetual Union."

so well preserved, so studiously annotated and documented, that infinite material is available to the scholar. There is neither room nor reason for including the details of the story here: the result was an instrument new to history, a written statement of the fundamental law on which a nation was to rest—presumably forever. Actually, only one other constitution—only one other prescription for form of government—the British—has lasted longer.

But the story touches ours most particularly at three points. First, the issue of the slavery question was evaded and at best compromised in the Constitution of 1787. Second, secession was not prohibited. Third, the people would have none of it until amendments guaranteeing the "natural rights" were promised.

Slavery was gingerly handled in the debates. Even some of the northern delegates to the constitutional convention—men definitely opposed to slavery—thought the convention ought not to "intermeddle" in what was so obviously an internal affair of certain states.[3] The focus turned away from slavery to the slave trade—the importation of Negroes—to which Virginia was opposed; a business, incidentally, in which righteous New England was replacing Great Britain. The conscience of most Virginians was aided in this opposition by the fact that Virginia already had more slaves than she needed and the fear of insurrection was already present. South Carolina and Georgia, however, frightened the convention into a compromise. The trade was to be prohibited, but not until after ten years.

From the point of view of the 1950's this compromise was a lapse of conscience, particularly of the northern conscience. Perhaps it is fairer to regard it as a conflict of conscience. To such men as Oliver Ellsworth of Connecticut, the loss of the southernmost states would have been a serious matter. Charles Pinckney was threatening the withdrawal of South Carolina and Georgia from the Union. And Edmund Randolph of Virginia echoed Ellsworth's scruples.[4] The unforeseeable result of the compromise was that, with the coming of the cotton gin in 1794, the trade grew so strong and so "necessary" that it could not be stopped even at the year set, in 1808.

The failure to prohibit secession was a result of the old difference of opinion in the era between the Articles of Confederation and the Constitution. The result was that the Constitution remained, like

[3] *Formation of the Union*, pp. 590 ff. [4] Ibid., 594.

the Bible, subject to many interpretations. As Merrill Jensen explains,

> The conflict of interpretation has been continuous ever since the first debates over the Articles of Confederation. . . . Men then differed as to the kind of government which should be created for the new nation. . . . The members of the Convention of 1787 differed as to the need for and the amount of constitutional change. When the Constitution was submitted to the public in October 1787 the controversy rose to new heights.[5]

Some three quarters of a century later, the argument was still going on:

> The Civil War itself was the bloody climax of a social conflict in which the ultimate nature of the Constitution was argued again and again. . . . But even the Civil War did not finally settle the constitutional issue. . . .[6]

Professor Jensen follows the controversy through the financial crash of 1929 and into the New Deal. We need not go with him so far. It is enough for us at this stage that when the Constitution of 1787 was ratified two years later, the question of whether a state might withdraw from the Union still seemed to be an open one, though no issue had arisen critical enough to make it a practical probability.

Finally, from the Anti-federalists and especially from the frontiersman Patrick Henry came protest so violent that a full summary of the "rights of man" had to be included in the first ten amendments. These represented the voice of the people. It is significant that it came loudest from the West because that is where democracy came from. What, then, was the West? To discover that we must explore a document which for a long time was virtually ignored by American historians but which was in some ways as important to the future of the country as the Constitution itself. It set the pattern for the whole physical development of the continental nation. It contained, too, a provision which quieted many a restless conscience. It gave substance, solidity, and wealth to that ambiguous new power, the government of the United States. And it is the best possible introduction to any story of the frontier.

[5] Merrill Jensen: *The New Nation* (New York, 1950), Preface, p. viii.
[6] Ibid., p. ix.

PART IV

Manifest Destiny

Chapter XIV

Land and Morals

LIKE MANY of the instruments that were basic to the expansion of the United States, the great Ordinance of 1787—or Northwest Ordinance, as it was called—evolved in an atmosphere of greed, jealousy, political chicanery, and lawlessness. In this atmosphere we see a foreshadowing of that unscrupulous behavior that seems characteristically American: the ruthless struggle among individuals for the control of great blocs of wealth and power; the impulse among migrant men to take the law into their own hands, superseding courts and statutes; the corruption of legislatures by lobbies or moneyed interests; and the gambling in fanciful promises that brings fraud and ruin in its train.

A lapse of moral standards coming between war and constitution was not unnatural. It was, as we have seen, an uncertain time; in such intervals, when men must guess at the future, they are likely to try to make futures for themselves. The diversity and conflict of these tend toward anarchy and chaos. Any post-war period, furthermore, is pregnant with unhappy emotion. It is a cooling-off time. The fever of the fighting years, of burning patriotism, is over. After the bloodshed and destruction come grief and poverty; after the pouring out of treasure, debt; after the heroism, disillusion. These things were all present in the 1780's.

But there was, along with these, a positive passion that dominated imagination in every state. It possessed men's souls more fully than patriotism or God. It led respectable and high-minded men into reckless gambling. It probably caused more compromises with conscience than any other single American element—and it was uniquely American. But it also turned the little league of parochial communities into an empire.

From the earliest scenes of the American drama, American eyes had focused their hopes on a western horizon. Even before Englishmen and Europeans had become Americans, the sunset was the symbol of their dream. Born and nourished in rebellion and escape, the migrants remained always migrant at heart, forever searching out the new, the empty, the untried—the thing that promised release from every irritating circumstance. Through the colonial years there was constant movement away from law and taxes and other men, south from the north, west from both into forest and foothills. Often enough, too, men were seeking liberty of conscience, freedom to worship their own God in their own fashion away from the scorn of neighbors of other faiths. And among the Puritans the march into new wildernesses was always a means of glorifying the Almighty and thankfully accepting his gifts.

Up to 1763 the Appalachian range had generally marked the limit of settlement. But when the British in that year had said: "Thou shalt not cross it," the barrier became a challenge. It has always been an American impulse, the moment a prohibition is proclaimed, to try to circumvent it. In the years following the Proclamation of 1763, which forbade the Ohio valley to settlers, people had thronged into it, made their own deals with the Indians for whose protection the Proclamation had been made, and acquired claims to large territory. So when independence came at last, it meant, above all, to most Americans freedom to seek a new estate, to gratify to the full the ancient American passion for land, land, land!

The basic individual desire was, of course, to own property, to develop it, to gain from it an independent living, to acquire prestige from the ownership, and to establish new little uninhibited worlds. But where so universal a demand exists, there are certain to be persons who see large sources of profit in cornering as much of the commodity as possible and reselling it to the highest bidders. There was, therefore, in the 1780's a conflict among three elements: the private settlers, the men who envisaged an extended political domain, and the men who wanted to make money as rapidly as possible. Out of this melee of forces there evolved a plan that tried to satisfy them all. This was the Ordinance of 1787; it became what we should call the "blueprint" for the whole development of the American West.

2

The interplay of forces was so complex during that uneasy time that, unless we simplify the sequence and try to find some steady undercurrent, we are likely to lose the thread of our story. Perhaps the steadiest undercurrent in the Congress of the Confederation was the need, intensely felt by the wiser members, of means both of liquidating the war debt and of providing some solid material basis for a strong United States government. This was the continuous theme. Counterpoint (often highly discordant) was provided by the pride, jealousy, fears, and avarice of the different states, the anxiety of the speculators for quick profits, and the wayward flow of emigrants into land to which they had no title, there to set up separate and sovereign government of their own. The task of the Congress to keep a balance among these motifs was almost superhuman, and the record of its patient maneuver through these years is an answer to those who allege its supine weakness in the "critical" period of the Confederation. Eventually, however, the basic theme became fortissimo to the point where a final settlement had to be made, even if it was a concession to avarice.

For our story it is enough to remember that the politicians of the various states came gradually to the conclusion that the only way to settle the conflict among them was to let the Continental Congress absorb all their claims to Western lands as material for future states. Some of these claims were so fanciful that it is surprising that the legislators of certain states—especially Virginia, Massachusetts, Connecticut, and New York—were able to rationalize them. They were based on seventeenth-century charters issued when the English monarchs had only the most shadowy knowledge of American geography. The first James, for example, had granted to Virginia in 1609 a strip running to the "South Sea" or Pacific Ocean, which he had supposed was only a few hundred miles west of the Atlantic coast. Virginians in 1780 dared not claim the whole of this, as Spain stood solidly in the way west of the Mississippi and it was the fashion in the war years to be nice to Spain; but they did insist on territory as far as the Mississippi and north to the Great Lakes.

To Virginia's neighbor Maryland this was not only absurd but it conflicted with the claims of some of her own highly influential citizens. Fortunately, Maryland stuck to her guns (loaded as they were with moneyed interests) and refused to ratify the Articles of Confederation until the states with land claims promised to cede the claimed land to the central government to become, eventually, new states, and meanwhile to provide revenue to pull the whole Confederation out of its grievous debt. The promises were made by 1781, and, although it took more than twenty years of backing and filling to fulfill them all [1]—years spotted with corruption and fraud as cynical as anything in our history—there was by 1785 something that was recognizable as a "Public Domain," the beginning of a continental republic.

It was this concept, grand in its extent, that filled the minds of such leaders as Washington and Jefferson. Washington had seen the West as it stretched down the Ohio from Pittsburgh, and he saw it as a source of infinite power if only we could keep harmony and integrity long enough to develop it. It was this hope that made him feel the need of isolation in those formative years—that freedom from "foreign entanglements" for which he was so speciously quoted by the isolationists of another century when such freedom was anachronism. During his presidency he wrote to a friend the sum of his long thoughts:

> nothing short of self-respect . . . ought to involve us in war; for sure I am, if this country is preserved in tranquillity twenty years longer, it may bid defiance, in a just cause, to any power whatever, such in that time will be its population, wealth, and resource.[2]

The land also was much on Washington's conscience. In the "times that tried men's souls" the Congress had made promises to the officers and men of the Continental army of grants of land in reward for their services. When the war was over and the promises were delayed by the bickerings of the states, the despair of the poverty-stricken unpaid veterans greatly distressed their general.

To Jefferson the Public Domain promised great political achieve-

[1] The cessions were: New York, 1782; Virginia, 1784; North Carolina, 1784; Massachusetts, 1785; Connecticut, 1786; South Carolina, 1787; Georgia, 1802. North Carolina repealed her cession of 1784 and made another in 1789. For the recommendations by Congress in 1780, see *Journals of the Continental Congress*, XVII, 806–7, and XVIII, 915.

[2] *The Writings of George Washington*, John C. Fitzpatrick, editor (Washington, 1931–44), XXXIV, 401.

ment. He saw the prospective new states as carrying the principles of his Declaration into a wide and happy future. Already, in 1784, he had drawn up an ordinance for the making of sixteen new states north of the Ohio, and he had managed to insert in it a clause eternally banning slavery from these states. The following year, however, he was sent to relieve Franklin as minister to France, and his plan went into the congressional hopper to be shaken up and largely scrapped.

But there was no let-up in the agitation. The conscience at the core of Congress was constantly being prodded. The army men were restless in the extreme under the indomitable persistence of their land dream.[3] Meanwhile, throngs of people were floating down the Ohio on flatboats to squat without title on the spots of their own sweet choice, moving south through the Cumberland Gap into the valley of the Tennessee and north up the Muskingum, coming into conflict not only with legal claims of states and land companies but with tribal preserves which the Indians would only cede by treaty to a responsible government.[4] Thus, to the laments of disappointed veterans there were added tales of frontier warfare, of lawless communities existing in a sort of jungle civilization, and of incipient independent republics traitorously hostile to the Confederation. So when Jefferson's plan of 1784 proved unsatisfactory to the Congress, another was quickly substituted.

3

The Ordinance of 1785,[5] which superseded Jefferson's, was a model of disinterested planning for posterity of a kind that had never been seen in the world before, in which an empire was to be automatically turned into a republic as its "colonies" achieved population and an age, so to speak, of discretion.

But this Ordinance was too good to be true. Its design worked too slowly for the government's need of quick cash. Also, it closed the door to speculators. There began, then, two years of intensive lobbying in the Congress in which we see the sort of pressures that have

[3] *Journals of the Continental Congress*, XXXII, 243.
[4] Ibid., XXXII, 327 ff.
[5] Ibid., XXVIII, 375–8.

been so often repeated when fortunes were at stake. Meanwhile, however, the land was as scientifically surveyed as the methods of the time permitted. It was divided into squares called "townships" containing thirty-six square miles each, and these in turn were divided into thirty-six sections, each one mile square and containing 640 acres. As Americans know, the squares are still there, just as they were laid out in the 1780's, but nothing so astonishes the foreigner as this checkerboard country when he first encounters it driving westward into the state of Ohio.

The so-called Northwest Territory, which constituted the first public domain, skirted the Great Lakes on the north and stretched west to the Mississippi. Its southerly boundary was the Ohio River.

The new domain was immensely attractive to thousands of prospective pioneers. But the Ordinance of 1785 bore little relation to the pioneer pocketbook. It asked the purchaser to pay a dollar an acre for his land and required him to buy at least a section. As no one but a plutocrat in 1785 possessed $640, and as plutocrats were not generally the sort that would clear and plow and build and suffer on new land, the wheel of Manifest Destiny came to a dead-center stop.

The plutocrats and those who hoped to become plutocrats were, however, anxious enough to make money without enduring the efforts and hardship of the pioneer. As always, there were two sorts of opportunity open to Americans: the chance to gain possessions by the hard labor of slow acquisition and development, and the chance to exploit the labor of others and acquire a quick fortune without personal discomfort. This latter sort was the one that stepped into the breach created by the Ordinance of 1785 and started empire on its westward course.

The chief agent of the speculators was a Congregational clergyman, heritor of the mantle of John Calvin and bred in the Puritan tradition. Manasseh Cutler was a native of Connecticut and a graduate of Yale College. How, in the press of duties into which his exceptional talents led him, he found time to preach the Gospel of Christ is a forgotten secret of those strenuous times. In addition to his capacities as businessman, persuasive salesman, propagandist, public-relations expert, politician, and lobbyist, he was a practicing physician, an astronomer, a botanist, an electrical experimenter, and a dabbler in archæology. Cutler himself never dodged hard work. On the contrary, he personally visited the territory he was working with, driving 750 miles in a sulky in less than a month. But he was employed by absentee capitalists or gamblers.

The task the Ohio Company of Associates gave the Reverend Manasseh Cutler was to persuade the Congress to sell it a large bloc of territory at a rock-bottom price. The company would then sell this land to individuals at a price they could pay, yet yield a considerable profit to the investors. Cutler was sensible enough not to ask the Congress to tear up the philanthropic Ordinance of 1785. He knew perfectly well that no decent, sound-minded pioneer would venture into this wilderness, pay good money for land there, and then make a farm without a guarantee of government protection. And that guarantee must promise the "natural rights," a measure of home rule, and the chance to bring up children in a proper religious atmosphere, and it must forbid oppression or any suggestion of dictatorship from the rear. So Cutler did not advocate the scrapping of the Ordinance. He merely wanted it rewritten.

It took a year for the Yankee preacher to complete his ticklish mission. There was strong opposition to the commercial taint. In general, the Congress of the time was divided by the line which has divided the entire political history of the United States. On one side of the line were the Jeffersonian [6] advocates of republican democracy, the rights of man, and the private, individual interests of the true pioneer; on the other stood the disciples of Alexander Hamilton, supporters of what we call "big business," believing in a ruling class of merchants and moneyed men. The opposition came from the Jeffersonians. The disciples of Hamilton wanted quick liquidation with immediate governmental profit.

4

Nowadays we are extremely sensitive to the possibility of outside interests in the lives of our legislators and government employees. Cabinet members have been forced to resign and senators have been investigated because they were said to be influenced by their connection with private corporations. Our conscience in this respect has,

[6] Jefferson himself was in France, but his influence in Congress was still strong and the memory of his own plans for the public domain still very much alive.

of course, been stimulated by the wonderful snooping capacities that have been developed by the American press.

But no such delicacy of scruple kept the Founding Fathers awake in their curtained beds. Thus, we find many members of the Congress consistently furthering legislation that accorded with their private interests. From the beginning of the land debates and quarrels, such members as Robert Morris, Samuel Wharton, James Wilson, Charles Carroll of Carrollton, George Morgan, and even Benjamin Franklin were stockholders in land companies, though Franklin, being abroad for ten years from 1776, took little personal part in the dispute. And at the time of Cutler's lobby, William Duer, at the very center of the deal, was secretary of the Board of the Treasury, the body with whom the sale contract should be made.

Cutler's collaboration with William Duer was his first and probably his only misstep. Duer was one of the most extended speculators of the day; indeed, until we come to the gold-bonanza and railroad days, it is hard to find his equal. His office made many of his enterprises possible, for, in addition to his land-company manipulations, he speculated in the domestic and foreign debt, in state debts, treasury warrants, loan-office certificates, notes of hand of firms and individuals, continental certificates, "claims of individuals and firms against the United States, and United States claims against firms and individuals." [7]

At the moment the Reverend Cutler was plotting the Ohio Company deal, Duer was thinking in terms of a much larger tract farther to the west—some five million acres. To carry out his plans, he had formed the Scioto Company with Royal Flint, Andrew Craigie, Richard Platt, and other figures prominent in the financial circles of the time. These men had no intention of investing money. Duer himself had not the slightest interest in settlements or the development of territory. They were all gamblers on the slimmest of margins. Their plan was to purchase from the government not land but an option on land, the mere "right to take up" the millions of acres. Once they had the option, they could then sell the land and pay the government later.

It happened that more members of the Congress held stock in the Scioto than in the Ohio Company. So Duer suggested to Cutler that

[7] Archer Butler Hulbert: "The Methods and Operations of the Scioto Group of Speculators," in *Mississippi Valley Historical Review*, I (March 1915), 508.

they dine together in the suburb of Brooklyn—a safe distance from New York, where the Congress met. There, in Stone House Tavern over a fine oyster dinner [8] provided by the plutocrat Duer, it was decided that in order to secure the votes of members holding Scioto stock, the Scioto option would have to be included in the act of Congress permitting the Ohio purchase. It was a bribe pure and simple, but such things were not out of character with the times.

It was decided at the dinner that the matter must be kept a "profound secret." [9] But, as Hulbert tells us, "secrecy was the very breath of life to the men of high finance" [1] in those times, so it was custom rather than any fear of the public conscience that kept the mouths of these cloak-and-dagger conspirators shut as they ferried back that night across the East River.

5

The Northwest Ordinance was adopted by the Continental Congress on July 13, 1787. It provided for an immediate government of the territory, to be succeeded by other governments becoming more and more democratic—or, as it was then called, "republican"—as the society of the settlers grew. At first there were to be a governor, a secretary, and three judges, all appointed by the Congress. The governor, secretary, and two of the judges were to be resident in the territory and to have large freehold estates. As these officials were to make the laws and execute them, this first government was even more imperial than that of the British Empire in its most tyrannical epoch. The laws, to be sure, must be taken from the legal codes of the thirteen "original" states, but this was a scarcely enforceable provision, as the government would be far away from the Congress. The reason for this dictatorship was that the Congress took an unfavorable view of the moral character of pioneers.

Immediately following this provision in the Ordinance, however, the silver lining appears. As soon as there should be five thousand free male inhabitants of voting age, they could elect members of a house of representatives, and this legislature could send a delegate to Congress. Finally:

[8] Hulbert: op. cit., I, 504.
[9] Ibid., I, 502.
[1] Ibid., I, 503.

> There shall be formed in the said territory, not less than three nor more than five States. . . . And, whenever any of the said States shall have sixty thousand free inhabitants therein, such state shall be admitted, by its delegates, into the Congress of the United States, on an equal footing with the original States in all respects whatever. . . .

Thus, however imperial the first provisions might sound, the document as a whole completely negated the old principle of empire. No colony existed for the material benefit of the "mother country"—that is, the Confederation of the thirteen eastern states—and every colony was an embryo state. The pattern was bitterly resented and fought by the eastern merchants because it shattered their long dream of exploiting the West. But it was a triumph of the congressional conscience which, however it may have compromised with the land speculators, could never get away from the compelling dicta of the Declaration of Independence.

This was particularly true in that part of the Ordinance which might be called its "bill of rights." This even went beyond the Declaration, but on the road down which that guidepost pointed.

No person should ever be molested on account of his mode of worship or religious sentiments. Every person should be entitled to the benefits of habeas corpus, trial by jury, proportionate representation, judicial proceedings according to common law, bail, moderate fines, and the prohibition of cruel and unusual punishments. Life, liberty, property, and contracts were to be inviolable except under due legal process.

> Religion, morality, and knowledge, being necessary to good government and the happiness of mankind, schools and the means of education shall forever be encouraged. The utmost good faith shall always be observed towards the Indians; their lands and property shall never be taken from them without their consent; and in their property, rights, and liberty, they shall never be invaded or disturbed, unless in just and lawful wars authorized by Congress; but laws founded in justice and humanity, shall from time to time be made for preventing wrongs being done to them, and for preserving peace and friendship with them.

Finally, and with the most far-reaching penetration into the future history of the republic, "Article Six" was inserted just before the third reading of the document in Congress. The fact that nine delegates from the southern states voted with their nine northern colleagues for the inclusion of this article and that it was especially promoted by two Virginia delegates shows that the virulence of sentiment on the subject had not yet reached its peak.

> There shall be neither slavery [Article Six read] nor involuntary servitude in the said territory. . . .[2]

So, as Saint Paul so eloquently said of the human body, natural and spiritual, the people of the great Northwest Territory might have said that

> It is sown in corruption; it is raised in incorruption: it is sown in dishonour; it is raised in glory; it is sown in weakness; it is raised in power. . . .[3]

Unfortunately, the moral tonic of the Northwest Ordinance had to be administered by fallible human beings to fallible human beings, and in the rough days of the settlement there were plenty of lapses. But, on the whole, the people who built the new states of Ohio, Indiana, Illinois, Wisconsin, and Michigan were sound and decent folk. The nucleus was composed of Revolutionary veterans —men who had endured the years of poverty and disappointed hopes that we have seen. The pioneer communities of Marietta and Cincinnati were founded almost exclusively of such and their families; most of them were God-fearing, courageous, and energetic.

The contract of the Ohio Company with its Scioto rider went through Congress in July 1787, and was signed in William Duer's office in October without, apparently, so much as the conscientious flicker of an eyelash by this complacent treasury secretary. By this time the cost per acre had sunk from one dollar to about nine cents. And Duer, proud, aristocratic, and luxury-loving, rode on to greater glory until in 1792 his whole fictional pyramid collapsed and he died in a debtor's prison.

6

The Scioto Company, after the contract for its option was signed, went gaily ahead, selling the land it did not own and earning for the

[2] The Ordinance of 1787 is printed entire in *Journals of the Continental Congress*, XXXII, 314–20. The final vote is on p. 343 of the same volume. The text is also included in Henry C. Commager: *Documents of American History*, pp. 128–32, and in F. N. Thorpe: *Federal and State Constitutions* (Washington, 1909), II, 957 ff.

[3] I Cor. 15:42–3.

infant United States its first evil repute in Europe. In the wide over-extension of its speculator-directors there were connections in England and Holland, and to these they added a French company, which they sent Joel Barlow to France to organize. Barlow was a poet, not a businessman, and that doubtless was the reason he was chosen. "Poetic license," Hulbert explains, "was needed on a mission to sell lands which the group did not own." [4] Quite innocent himself and believing in a fictitious map of the territory, he sold to gullible Frenchmen thousands of acres of supposedly cleared and cultivated farmland producing eighty bushels of wheat to the acre, which in reality was virgin forest, swamp, or rocky waste. In this he was assisted by a highly unscrupulous Englishman with the contradictory name of Playfair. When the purchasers, eager as Europeans have always been to emigrate into the Utopia of the new world, discovered that they had been duped, they spread the evil report over France, and the American began his career as what Kipling called "the scandal of the elder earth." Some six hundred of these poor Frenchmen arrived in 1790, and most of them returned in bitter disappointment. Five years later Congress, under the sort of attack of conscience it often suffered in later years, reimbursed the hundred who remained with tracts of good land in what is now Scioto County, Ohio. By that time the company had dissolved into total bankruptcy.

The irresponsibility in the Northwest Territory, however, was mild compared with the loose behavior in other parts of the country in these early years of the first land craze.

In 1784, while North Carolina's cession of her western land claims was pending, the frontiersmen in this territory (later the state of Tennessee) made a declaration of independence of their own and called themselves the sovereign state of Franklin. They elected their own governor, established their own courts, set up their own currency, and wrote a state constitution. For four years, during which Congress refused to recognize the illegal state, it was torn by faction fights which seemed at times to approach civil war; it was in serious trouble with the Indians, and its politicians engaged in what appeared to be treasonable intrigues with the Spaniards across the Mississippi. The unstable government collapsed at

[4] Hulbert: op. cit., in *Mississippi Valley Historical Review*, II (June, 1915), 65, 66.

last, but there remained an atmosphere of restlessness and discontent which lasted until the state of Tennessee was admitted to the Union in 1796.

In Georgia, in 1795, the state legislature was responsible for the greatest fraud ever perpetrated by an American body of lawmakers. Georgia had not yet ceded her western land claims. Twenty-five million acres of these (known as the Yazoo lands) the legislature sold to four land companies at a secret price of a cent and a half an acre —the directors of the company being members of the legislature and having corrupted the other members with large promises of profit. The land was eagerly bought by northerners as well as Georgians at greatly advanced prices until the fraud was discovered. In sudden shame, then, the legislature rescinded the sale and publicly burned the original act in an attempt at expiation. This effervescence of conscience left the unhappy people who had bought and paid for the land in good faith high and dry with neither money nor property. One celebrated victim of this deal was Phineas Miller, partner of Eli Whitney. Miller's Yazoo speculation wiped out the fortune which should have been used for the promotion of Whitney's cotton gin.

Here again, nineteen years later, the United States Congress was obliged to come to the rescue of those defrauded persons who were able to keep alive their claims. In 1814 the Supreme Court declared Georgia's act of conscience unconstitutional and gave the opinion that the rescinding of the sale was a breach of contract. In consequence, the Congress was obliged to pay the claimants the truly colossal sum (for 1814) of $4,282,151.12½.

By the turn of the century, then, we see that Americans in general had put a long distance between themselves and their early righteousness. In the times when enormous opportunities of wealth glittered before their eyes, even the descendants of the strictest Puritans forgot the old standards, and the whole of public opinion seemed to wink at their operations. This, in the century's closing years, was only partly true, as the people were still separated into so many unrelated parts that public opinion did not exist in any sense that we know it.

The dream of fabulous futures was beginning to come to enterprising and energetic men, but they were wrong in their guesses as to the difficulties of attainment. As Merrill Jensen puts it,

> They were men with a Midas touch for whom the object of desire was too often just beyond their reach. In their striving for what they well knew was the golden future of the new nation, they often overreached themselves and ended in crisis, disaster, and bankruptcy. . . . Hence men like Robert Morris, William Duer, and James Wilson went down in one crash after another during the 1790's. If they had had the experience and the means of a later generation of tycoons, they might have enjoyed the riches they so well realized could be gained in the new nation.[5]

We are beginning now to see the westward migration dividing into the three parts that were to characterize it all the way through to the final closing of the frontiers: first, the restless pioneers, the wedge of the movement, never staying long in one spot, moving relentlessly on into the vacuum; second, the settlers, men and women who earnestly wanted to live a secure and abundant life by their own prodigal labor; and, finally, the gamblers, the speculators, the builders of business, who moved into the settlements that had already been made and exploited them for easy profit. This was the scheme and, while it matured, there grew up much of the good that still gratifies and the evil that still plagues us.

[5] Merrill Jensen: *The New Nation* (New York, 1950), p. 233.

Chapter XV

Morality on the Frontier

"THE FRONTIERS," said Thoreau, "are not east or west, north or south, but wherever a man fronts a fact." To Frederick Jackson Turner, the American frontier was "the hither edge of free land." And Turner called the West "a form of society, rather than an area." Perhaps, too, the West was a state of mind as well as a geographical fact—a definition once applied to Boston. Surely it was an urgent dream long before it was a reality, and when men and women were confronted with the stark truth, it turned often enough into nightmare.

Our concern with the moving frontier, whose rapid and irresistible movement began immediately after the Revolution, is in its effect upon that moral core of the American people which we have seen hardening under Puritan and other religious and social influences. At first there is backsliding. In the release into trackless freedom, the old values disappear and new ones are uncertain in the vastness of the promises ahead. In the escape from social discipline, life becomes a free-for-all with a diversity of objectives, and the devil take the hindmost, who is there, perhaps, through no fault of his own. Staid, mature folk become rampant children: we blush for their juvenile delinquencies against the somber savagery of the western scene. Cursing God and man as they push forward in the frenzy of their escape, singing their drunken songs as they girdle and kill the million ancient trees, spitting oaths and tobacco juice into the majestic Ohio, whose bordering forests echo their loud obscenities; boasting, gambling, drinking, stealing, and shooting their way into the silent dignity of the Indian domains, they scarcely present a picture of integrity.

Yet, after a time, a kind of unity emerges. The scattered, syncopated movements meet in a concerted rhythm; there come a kind of common complexion to all the faces, a common cast to the bodies, and a common twang to the speech. In the likeness of the struggle, north and south blend and lose identities, folk forget that they were once English, Scotch-Irish, German, Dutch, French, Virginian, or Pennsylvanian, and the babies born on the flatboats or in the wagons or on the dirt floors of the forest lean-to's will belong to a new race. In time we shall see this western race absorb the dissensions of north and south; in time it will whip the East into line and present to the world the spectacle of a formidable national unit. But in the course of that development we shall see repeated splits, reunions, lapses, recoveries, and relapses in both public conscience and private morality.

From our present pinnacle of survival it may be instructive to look back and inquire what permanent, perhaps ineradicable features of the American character were formed in the massive nineteenth-century migration—the so-called conquest of the continent.

At first glance we see fear of privacy, dependence on group solidarity, rebellion against constituted authority, evasion of law paradoxically combined with a love of legislation for its own sake, the constant compulsion to turn liberty into license, the belief that each man's business is every man's business, insistence on being one's brother's keeper, the deification of woman resulting, perhaps, in an excess of homosexuality and other perversion, large-scale waste, a nearly pathological restlessness or discontent with environment resulting in perpetual migration (now rotary), suspicion of intellectual activity, contempt for the arts, insistence on conformity, cultivation of the social function of the churches as a substitute for religion, the leveling of education, the cult of political mediocrity, and general complacency toward crime. Some of these tendencies evolved most curiously from conditions that seem, as we review them, calculated to produce opposite characteristics. But also, as Turner wrote:

> That coarseness and strength combined with acuteness and inquisitiveness; that practical, inventive turn of mind, quick to find expedients; that masterful grasp of material things, lacking in the artistic but powerful to effect great ends; that restless, nervous energy; that dominant individualism, working for good and for evil,

and withal that buoyancy and exuberance which comes with freedom—these are the traits of the frontier, or traits called out elsewhere because of the existence of the frontier.[1]

To these we may add the generosity for which Americans have become so celebrated abroad, the openness and candor, the friendliness to strangers, the almost instinctive hospitality—traits which sometimes embarrass Englishmen and Europeans—and, above all, the unique humor. The moving frontier molded these things. The abundant literature of the period tells us how: the good and the bad, what quieted and what troubled the American conscience.

2

The post-war migrations, beginning in that nadir of moral standards and behavior that we have seen as a consequence of the long, exhausting struggle, naturally carried with them a quantity of people of violent and dissolute character. In the first waves were criminals fleeing justice, malcontents of every sort, including many men and women who were tired of religious compulsions or social conventions and hoped to find in the backwoods an escape from conscience. These were the "pioneers," the folk we have been taught to revere in what are supposed to be the late, "degenerate" times. It is true that in the first waves there were occasional heroes well deserving of our praise, but most of them found it impossible to settle down: they lived by hunting, lapsing into a primitive barbarity in which only their gun and their speech raised them above the beasts they shot. It was a common thing for these men to corrupt others, so that from all the early communities there was a drifting away into the "high timber," evasion of the stern work of clearing, plowing, and planting; and as the eternal woods drew them on, they deserted and forgot their families.

The worst of these characters sometimes waited to prey on the soldier people of the second and third waves who honestly wanted to settle down on the land and become respectable farmers. We find such people occasionally forming groups such as in Logan County, Kentucky, a hell for honest immigrants until, all law failing, the

[1] Frederick Jackson Turner: *The Frontier in American History*, new edition (New York, 1948), p. 37.

good citizens were obliged to restore and maintain order at gunpoint.

> Logan County [wrote Peter Cartwright] when my father moved to it, was called "Rogues' Harbor." Here many refugees, from almost all parts of the Union, fled to escape justice or punishment; for although there was law, yet it could not be executed, and it was a desperate state of society. Murderers, horse thieves, highway robbers, and counterfeiters fled here until they combined and actually formed a majority. The honest and civil part of the citizens would prosecute these wretched banditti, but they would swear each other clear; and they really put all law at defiance, and carried on such desperate violence and outrage that the honest part of the citizens seemed to be driven to the necessity of uniting and combining together, and taking the law into their own hands, under the name of Regulators.[2]

The Regulators were at first defeated. Then they rallied, "hunted, killed, and lynched many of the rogues, until several of them fled, and left for parts unknown. Many lives were lost on both sides, to the great scandal of civilized people." [3] The Regulators of Logan County were successors to the Regulators of the Carolinas and the predecessors of the Vigilantes and similar organizations.

As Pittsburgh became the great way-station for the river migrants, it was the haunt of every sort of racketeer, confidence man, swindler, and outright robber. Timothy Flint, writing in the vogue of his time, attributed these conditions to the growth of stultifying industry there.

> Accustomed to scenes of parsimony, misery, and beggary, and to transient and unprincipled men, occupied in the hardening pursuits of manufacturers, [Pittsburgh] had been brought to think all men rogues, misery the natural order of things, and of course little entitled to consideration, and every way of getting money fair game.[4]

An English traveler, some years later, found similar conditions in this gateway to the Ohio valley:

> The river Ohio is considered the greatest thoroughfare of banditti in the Union. Here the thief, in addition to the cause of his flight, has only to steal a skiff, and sail down the river in the night. Horse-

[2] Peter Cartwright: *Autobiography*, W. P. Strickland, editor (New York, 1856), pp. 24, 25.

[3] Ibid., p. 25.

[4] Timothy Flint: *Recollections of the Last Ten Years* (Boston, 1826), pp. 17, 18.

> stealing is notorious in the western country, as are also escapes from prison. . . . Runaway apprentices, slaves, and wives are frequently advertised . . . tavern keepers complain of young men going off without paying for their board.[5]

These things are related of times after Jefferson's Louisiana Purchase when the Ohio had become the main artery from the East to the Mississippi, when an occasional steamboat might be seen on the rivers. But in the very earliest post-war period, when the boats, for the most part, drifted downstream and never came back, we see the formative period of those conditions. In the 1780's and 1790's there was a large and steady migration down the river from Pittsburgh. An entire family with its livestock, furniture, and supplies would be loaded on a flatboat or "ark" and float to a chosen spot, then turn the boat into a house. Despite the perils of the river in the form of snags and sandbars and occasional Indian attacks, many of these journeys were gay, with a fiddler playing constantly on the deck, with boys and girls dancing or making love, and with apparently unlimited supplies of raw whisky. At Pittsburgh the men of the family would bargain for days or even weeks for barrels of flour or for hogs and other supplies for their settlements; then, too often the cargo would end at the bottom of the river and the unhappy people be lucky if they escaped with their lives. In such circumstances, many found it easier to sing the coarse Ohio songs than to pray to a distant and uncertain God, or, far from church and parson, to curse rather than worship this apparently hostile Deity.

In 1796 the surveyor Andrew Ellicott, with a considerable company of workers and a military escort, floated down the Ohio from Pittsburgh. Ellicott's boat was forced to stop for repairs at a small town. Immediately his men, seduced by the town's inhabitants, "got intoxicated and behaved extremely ill." Apparently the people of the community were lying in wait for travelers in difficulty, and Ellicott found this a common practice.

> This will generally be found the case in all small, trifling villages, whose inhabitants are principally supported by selling liquor to the indiscreet and dissipated in the neighborhood, and to the independent traveller. . . .[6]

[5] James Flint: "Letters from America," in Reuben G. Thwaites: *Early Western Travels* (Cleveland, 1904–7), IX, 167.

[6] Andrew Ellicott: *Journal, 1796–1800* (Philadelphia, 1814), pp. 7, 8.

The parasitical existence of these pioneers who had moved beyond any restraining government or productive community must have been on a low level. The structures housing these people

> are generally of the poorest kind, and the inhabitants who are commonly sellers of liquor, as dirty as their cabbins, which are equally open to their children, poultry and pigs.[7]

The great Ohio gateway to the West, however, must have led through wholesome as well as degenerate areas. There seems to have been a marked difference between right and left banks. The Northwest Territory, of which we have seen the beginnings, was at first settled by New Englanders. Stout Yankees like Manasseh Cutler and General Rufus Putnam had inspired their respectable countrymen to migrate in an enterprising, expansive spirit, earnestly hoping to carve out new states where they could carry on their religion and education in freedom and at the same time plant profitable farms. Across the river was Kentucky, a slave state, settled, to be sure, by all kinds of people—rich, poor, large planters and small farmers, from Virginia and North Carolina. Here life was easier: the climate was softer and the heaviest labor was performed by Negroes. In Kentucky in the early years religion had lapsed according to Puritan standards: the Sabbath was profaned by games and horse racing. The sons of the wealthy planters disdained any sort of work, and the profligacy of their lives shocked many travelers otherwise charmed by their good manners, their hospitality, and their easy poise.

The picture of the contrast drawn by Thaddeus Harris, writing of the year 1803, must be read remembering that Harris was a confirmed and prejudiced Yankee with the usual Yankee habit of looking down his nose at "foreigners" from other states. To him a Virginian was as alien as a Turk or Russian, and his attitude reflects the tendency of New Englanders to hold themselves aloof from the melting-pot as long as the frontier would let them.

> The industrious habits and neat improvements on the west side of the river, are strikingly contrasted with those on the east.[8] *Here* in Ohio, they are intelligent, industrious, and thriving; *there* on the back skirts of Virginia, ignorant, lazy, and poor. *Here* the buildings are neat, though small, and furnished in many instances with brick

[7] Ibid.

[8] From a glance at the map it will be seen that the Ohio runs roughly north and south through the section Harris was describing.

> chimnies and glass windows; *there* the habitations are miserable cabins. *Here* the grounds are laid out in a regular manner, and inclosed by strong posts and rails; *there* the fields are surrounded by rough zigzag log fence. *Here* are thrifty young apple orchards; *there* the only fruit that is raised is the peach, *from which a good brandy is distilled!* [9]

Harris goes on to dilate on the degradation of all "back-woodsmen," most of whom "are emigrants from foreign countries, [meaning the southern states] but the state of Ohio was settled by people from NEW-ENGLAND, THE REGION OF INDUSTRY, ECONOMY, AND STEADY HABITS." [1]

The steadiness of the Yankee habits, however, did not greatly impress Jacob Burnet, who was in Cincinnati and Fort Harmar a few years earlier. Recent Indian hostilities had required military garrisons. According to Burnet,

> Idleness, drinking and gambling, prevailed in the army. . . . As a natural consequence, the citizens indulged in the same practices, and formed the same habits.[2]

Of nine lawyers in Cincinnati when he first came there, seven "became confirmed sots, and descended to premature graves." [3] Thus, either a total reform took place in the six or seven years between the visits of these gentlemen or else Burnet from New Jersey was able to see phenomena to which the patriotic Bostonian, Harris, was blind. Also, in his "notes," Burnet suggests that the righteous in Ohio, under army influence, occasionally lost the respect for the seventh commandment held by their Puritan forebears.

3

In every part of the frontier it is easy to see the beginnings of what developed into state and eventually national prohibition. The conditions in those days when, in the West, whisky supplanted rum as the prevailing beverage, when it was homemade, untaxed, and es-

[9] Thaddeus Mason Harris: *Journal of a Tour into the Territory Northwest of the Alleghany Mountains* (Boston, 1805), p. 58. Harris's italics.

[1] Ibid., p. 59.

[2] Jacob Burnet: *Notes on the Early Settlement of the Northwest Territory* (Cincinnati, 1847), p. 37.

[3] Ibid.

sential to every celebration—civil, military, and religious—were so entirely without restraint that, in the light of modern researches into alcoholism, the survival of our rugged ancestors and the evidence of their immense achievements are astonishing indeed.

The extensive distilling of whisky began in western Pennsylvania, where large surplus quantities of grain were raised and the farmers found it difficult to dispose of it to merchants obliged to transport it over difficult roads and on upstream craft. Liquor distilled from the grain, however, was easily transportable and highly profitable. It was here that government's first attempt to tax this native beverage met with the opposition in Washington's administration that became celebrated as the "Whisky Rebellion," and even after the federal army had marched, giving one of the first demonstrations of the power of the central government, the tax was long evaded. As late as 1802 the French visitor François André Michaux, journeying to Pittsburgh, was struck by the flood of cheap whisky in the little mountain village of Bedford.

> The day of our arrival was a day of rejoicing for the country people who had assembled . . . to celebrate the suppression of the tax laid upon the whiskey distilleries. . . . The public houses, inns, and more especially the one where we lodged, were filled with the lower class of people, who made the most dreadful riot, and committed such horrible excesses, that is almost impossible to form the least idea of. The rooms, stairs, and yard were strewed with drunken men; and those who still had the power of speech uttered nothing but the accents of rage and fury. A passion for spirituous liquors is one of the features that characterise the country people belonging to the interior of the United States. This passion is so strong that . . . in fact, I do not conceive there are ten out of a hundred who have resolution to desist from it a moment provided they had it by them.[4]

Whisky was served at all social gatherings or to friends who dropped in, as a matter of course; it was an essential part of weddings, baptisms, and funerals. Ministers on these occasions indulged as freely as most members of their congregations. Those who deplore our late cocktail parties and the serving of drinks as a mark of hospitality in the mid-twentieth century, calling it a symptom of modern jitters, will do well to look back at this robust period of

[4] F. A. Michaux: *Travels to the West of the Alleghany Mountains . . . Undertaken in the Year 1802* (London, 1805), pp. 39, 40. Reprinted in Thwaites: op. cit., III.

American growth before they criticize their contemporaries too heartily. William Warren Sweet, the historian of American religion, writes that liquor

> was considered on the frontier almost as much of a necessity as bread and meat. Everybody indulged—men, women, and children, preachers and church members as well as the ungodly. Stores had open kegs of whiskey with cups attached for all to help themselves. It was freely served at all the social gatherings, log rollings, corn huskings and house raisings. At the loading of flatboats there was always a keg of whiskey on the bank with head knocked off and a gourd ready. As a sad consequence of the abundance of the fiery liquid, a large section of frontier society was debauched and whiskey-sodden. Of all the many cases of church discipline to be found in frontier church records, drunkenness was by far the most common single cause.[5]

The dawn of conscience in this respect was observed in the East when in 1808 a physician named Billy J. Clark established the first temperance society. A quarter-century earlier Benjamin Franklin's celebrated friend Benjamin Rush had published his *Inquiry into the Effects of Spirituous Liquors on the Human Mind and Body*, but few had been stirred by it to the extent of altering their habits. One of the first reflections of this dawn appears in 1817, when this dialogue occurred between the circuit-rider Peter Cartwright and a fellow divine.

> When I came to the local preacher [of Nashville, Tennessee] I said "Brother W., do you drink drams?"
>
> "Yes," said he.
>
> "What is your particular reason for drinking drams?" I asked him.
>
> "Because it makes me feel well," he answered.
>
> "You drink till you feel it, do you?" said I.
>
> "Certainly," said he.
>
> "Well how much do you drink at a time?"
>
> He replied gruffly, that he never measured it.
>
> "Brother, how often do you drink in a day?"
>
> "Just when I feel like it, if I can get it."
>
> "Well, brother, there are complaints that you drink too often and too much; and . . . you must meet a committee of local preachers . . . to investigate this matter. . . ."[6]

[5] William Warren Sweet: *Revivalism in America* (New York, 1944), p. 118.
[6] Cartwright: op. cit., pp. 184, 185.

The complaint was not that the preacher, like other preachers, drank but that he drank "too often and too much," so we see that the conscience that insisted on teetotalism in the Methodist clergy was still a good way off. Cartwright "had hard work to get a committee that were not dram-drinkers themselves," but he eventually found enough clergy to expel Brother W. for "immoral conduct."

4

Away from the towns, the prevailing characteristic of the frontiers, north and south, was loneliness. In the isolation in which thousands, eventually millions, of families lived inarticulate, their thoughts forever hid from the civilized world from which all the people came, countless tragedies lie buried. Long sufferings of ill-mated couples, bitter night quarrels, drunken orgies, sickness, the deaths with no minister to bury, and no church to comfort, the hungers of sex, wanderlust and nostalgia, the long succession of infants dead in their first weeks and the relentless necessity to reproduce more and more to do the work of home and homestead will never be told. We have glimpses: the more literate wrote sporadic diaries and sometimes long letters giving precious bits of news to remote relatives and friends—news that would be old and cold, perhaps forgotten by the writers, when it arrived. Fancy must fill the blank spaces, but with the data at hand this is not difficult to do, and armies of story-tellers have done it.

The settlers had little to read. The Bible, of course, was endless exercise, though for those who had always heard it read and interpreted in church, most of its meaning was now vague. It was formally read at family gatherings, the children being forced to listen under the threat of the lash, though the father, reading, gathered little inkling of any significance. There being no meetinghouse, sermons were not heard, and therefore doctrinal discussions no longer provided the pastime they had done back east. If men talked of God at all, it was of his awful presence in the forest silences; it was to pray for his hand on the forces of nature. When, for instance, in the Mississippi valley a fearful series of earthquakes frightened the people out of their wits, religion spread like fire up and down the land and preachers seemed to spring overnight out of the ground.

It was natural, in such loneliness, where meetings were rare, that any gathering should produce great excitement. The new settler putting up his cabin or house drew people from quite distant places to take part in the "log-rolling" or "house-raising." In the intervals of the strenuous work there would be singing, eating, drinking, and long, loud talk. The breaches of the silences were great events. The more noise the better. Any such gathering would last several days. A wedding would bring people twenty miles or more; the drinking, fiddling, dancing, and singing would last all night. Even at the funerals the mourners soon found the invariable "tub" of whisky and for a time grieved no more, remembering the sly wickedness or the human weaknesses of the deceased rather than his godliness.

No stranger was ever allowed to pass unnoticed. The questions: "Whar ya goin'?" "Whar'd ya come from?" "What's your name?" were universal and led to some caustic comments by overseas travelers on the impossibility of privacy. To refuse to answer was ground for a quick fight. But if the stranger did answer, with good will, he was welcome to everything the settler could give him, including a great deal of alarming advice. Even in more populous communities, inquisitiveness was normal. James Flint was greatly incensed when, in a tavern, a stranger openly eavesdropped on his private conversation with a friend.

> Accustomed to mix with a diversity of company at taverns, elections and other places . . . they do not well brook to be excluded from private conversation. On such occasions, they exclaim, *"This is a free country"* or a *"land of liberty,"* adding a profane oath. They do not keep in view that one man has a natural right to hear, *only* what another is willing to tell him.[7]

Reaction from the loneliness created an intensely gregarious desire among the frontier people. In the groups that formed as a result, it was natural enough for each man to regard every other as his equal friend: both were emerging from the same variety of misery and the lot of all was a common one. Why, then, should there be private subjects which all might not discuss? This sense of commonalty was not, therefore, native in the individuals; it was a frontier product.

It is significant that, as the frontier moved, the men who talked about the "free country" applied the term not to Ohio or Indiana but

[7] "Letters from America," in Thwaites: *Early Western Travels,* IX, 167, 168.

to the United States. This was a new departure, and it reflects the dependence of the new West on the federal government from which had come the land and which would bring them into statehood. The migrants forgot the East whence they had come, and presently in the new states the old thirteen were regarded with suspicion. The West was as much "freer" than the East as the early America had been than Europe. Thus, not only European but New England and New York travelers were shown "what a free country really was."

The aggressiveness with which the frontier people proclaimed the equality of all men (in the South of all white men) suggests what modern psychiatrists call "inferiority complex." The traveler met the reiteration wherever he went, spoken as if the speaker expected to be contradicted. Anyone from the East was suspected of anti-democratic views. It was assumed that he would look with disgust upon the crude shelters and clothes of the new settler. The advancing waves carried (particularly in the North) extreme social democracy with them. They had escaped from eastern class-consciousness, and the farther they got away from it the more completely they divested themselves of its taint.

South of the Ohio the existence of slavery created a fear among white workmen of being regarded as inferiors by their employers—in short, of being classed with the blacks. James Flint tells of an incident illustrating this.

> A gentleman, in a State where slaves are kept, engaged some carpenters from a neighboring free State to erect a barn. On the day of their first arrival they eat along with himself. On the second day the family took breakfast a little earlier than usual, and caused the table to be covered anew for the mechanics, previous to their coming in. They were so highly offended with this imaginary insult that they went off without finishing their work.[8]

Here is an early demonstration of the passionate effort to maintain and nurture the equality concept. From the beginnings of the westward movement, servants or any sort of "inferiors" were on the American conscience. For a while the Negroes, always alien, never quite "people" in the nineteenth century, were beyond the pale of conscience as servants; then Irish, then immigrants from southern Europe were legitimate inferiors as servants, common laborers, or factory hands. But we began early in frontier days to stumble over

[8] Ibid., IX, 168.

the word "servant"; to have servants was effete as well as undemocratic, and the term "help" came in as a sop to the republican conscience.

It has been said that the East created the federal government and that the federal government created the West. The new states were formed out of territories which in their pre-state existence were wholly dependent on the central government. Their people responded by supporting and strengthening that government. In the West the central power was recognized and accepted while it was still a vague institution to most of the people in the original states. Westerners felt themselves deeply integrated into the national scene. As soon as they were settled and ordered in their communities they took such an active part in national politics that their ballots were able to balance the eastern vote.

In the meantime, however, while something like a regional public opinion was forming west of the Alleghenies and across the Mississippi, one of the most dramatic and sensational phenomena in the whole of American history began its furious battle with western sin.

Chapter XVI

Frontier Religion

THE EVIL ODOR of the frontier soon drifted back to those eastern ministers whose nostrils were sensitive to the scent. It coincided with alarming emanations from their own environs. From Europe, during and after the War of Independence, dark waves of thought had struck the immaculate shores of the American continent along with the French armies that saved the Americans' war. As we have seen, the desire to welcome these saviors had predisposed certain American minds toward the rationalism expounded by Voltaire and other French philosophers. Then, some six years after the treaty that legally ended the American revolution, a revolution broke out in France and the citizens marched to the sound of those thrilling words *"liberté," "égalité,"* and *"fraternité"* and the sanguinary verses of the *Marseillaise*. The impact of this French struggle for freedom shook the thirteen American states like an earthquake and brought shudders to many in the Protestant clergy, especially when its anti-religious aspects came into view.

In every town and village in the coastal United States there were bonfires as the news was received. People danced round liberty poles, wearing liberty caps, proclaiming themselves Jacobins and *sans-culottes,* calling each other "citizen," singing a medley of *"Ça ira"* and "Yankee Doodle"—a musical and linguistic feat of some complexity—and drinking even more than the usual quantity of rum. Speeches were made claiming the French Revolution as the immediate offspring of the American; vows of eternal friendship with France and devotion to the common cause of liberty were sworn; and the headless effigies of the unhappy Bourbon king and his cake-eating wife were carried through the streets lit by flickering pineknot torches with macabre effect.

In New England these demonstrations offended the mercantile as well as the Puritan conscience. As the godless views of the French *philosophes* were molded into slogans and shouted in the Paris streets, the Congregational ministers drew their flocks back in fear of the atheist contagion. But the merchants were even more disturbed. Ever since the peace treaty with Great Britain, they had known that the only real profit was in trade with England, not with France. And as England was deeply shocked by the French Revolution and, indeed, resorted to her ancient habit of declaring war against France, it did not seem to the merchants that American sympathies with the head-rolling in the Place de la Concorde were helpful. In England so universal was the hostility that even Edmund Burke, that great apostle of liberty, had turned against the *"citoyens."*

The merchants had allies in the American capital. There the Federalists, believing in a powerful mercantile ruling class and an aristocracy of wealth, were severely frowning on the Jacobin demonstrations. Simultaneously they were flirting with the old enemy and older friend Great Britain. To Hamilton and John Jay as well as to the respectable Boston shipping magnates, blood was thicker than water, especially when gold was mingled with it. Jefferson and his Republicans might chafe and fume, the unbreeched street throngs might sing their bloody songs and listen for the echo of Dr. Guillotin's thudding machine, but the steady hand of the American government was guiding the torn infant nation into the even channels of propertied destiny. The Federalists were, of course, profoundly right, as events showed. In the 1790's, when the rapscallion Directoire eventually emerged from the French blood bath, it became evident even to the most fervent American "Jacobins" that friendship with France was dependent on French politics. Thus were the people saved and sobered, and for a while Locke's word "property" took the place of Jefferson's "pursuit of happiness" in the American concept of inalienable rights.

2

But there was a residue of rationalism that, as late as 1800, seemed to be corroding the very foundations of the churches. Not only the old Calvinist, Congregational, and Presbyterian but also the rising Methodist and Baptist sects felt the threat. One deeply shocked

Methodist minister, later remembering the awful corruption, wrote in his reminiscences:

> It was proclaimed over all the land that France—enlightened, scientific, fashionable France—had renounced the gospel, had burned the Bible in the streets of Paris by the hands of the common hangman, and had inscribed in broad characters, over the entrance into the common burying-ground, that "death is an eternal sleep."
>
> And moreover it was confidently asserted by those who had opportunity to know, that Thomas Jefferson, regarded in the west as a great political luminary, had rejected the gospel, and adopted the infidelity of France; that most of our statesmen were following his example.[1]

But Brother Gallaher had not been concerned primarily for the eastern flocks. There, at least, there were churches to bring the wayward into the Presence and preachers to exhort and lash the backsliders. But in the West—already a breeding-ground of every godless impulse—the helpless West, unchurched, with neither minister nor communion table to save the people from hell's flames, such philosophy would be the last word of catastrophe. And it was well known that these heresies had traveled in wagons and on packhorses into the wilds of Kentucky and Tennessee and by 1800 had probably reached the Mississippi.

The principal vehicle of the rationalism was a book. Ironically, it was by an author who had been adored by the Revolutionary generation in America. With his *Common Sense* in 1776 he had detonated the explosion of independence. Thousands whose stammering consciences had rejected separation from England as long as they possibly could had found their last ties broken by this book's devastating exposure of a king's spurious power. Another of this author's books, *The Crisis*, came at the lowest point of army morale, and its opening words, read by Washington's order to the troops in their camps, heartened hundreds of desperate men and brought them back to their duty. Rarely have wartime words carried such impact: they rank with Churchill's great speech in 1940.

> These are the times that try men's souls. The summer soldier and the sunshine patriot will, in this crisis, shrink from the service of their country; but he that stands it *now,* deserves the thanks of man and woman. Tyranny, like hell, is not easily conquered, yet we have

[1] James Gallaher: *The Western Sketch-Book* (Boston, 1850), pp. 28, 29.

this consolation with us, that the harder the conflict, the more glorious the triumph.

But when in 1796 Tom Paine had published *The Age of Reason*, he had become, suddenly, a depraved atheist. It was the circulation of this book in the United States and its evident popularity in the new West that especially distressed the Protestant clergy in the East.

As Hesketh Pearson has pointed out, *The Age of Reason* is likely to strike the modern reader as "a profoundly religious book." [2] It refused, however, to concede that the Bible was the word of God—a doctrine sacrilegious in the eyes of Paine. It attacked the Old Testament in the same scathing tenor as that of Paine's attack on the sham sanctity of George III. Yet, far from being a statement of disbelief in God, it reiterated praise of the Creator whose proper worship had been degraded by faith in a so-called revealed religion. The only true revelation, said the Deist Paine, was in nature. Here in every plant and tree, in every aspect of weather, the Creator was revealed to mankind.

To the disillusioned emigrant moving out of civilization, this sort of religion had an appeal. He felt little gratitude to the God of the churches. He was tired of Protestant doctrine and ethics and, especially, of the Protestant Sabbath. In the forests he felt the presence of Paine's God far more immediately than he had felt that of the Scriptural God in the churches or "meetings."

This was certainly not a universal view, as many emigrants carried their old dogmas with them, but it was prevalent enough to disturb the ministers. One of them said that in the region of Lebanon, Kentucky, nine tenths of the population, men and women, were "avowed disciples of Thomas Paine," [3] and other estimates placed at least half of Kentucky's wilderness people in that category.[4] Gallaher speaks of the "abominable example" [5] set by Jefferson and the other popular statesmen whose Deism was synonymous in the minds of "true believers" with atheism.

It was this backsliding rather than the drunkenness, thievery, murder, and general lawlessness of the frontier that impelled the Presbyterians, the Methodists, and the Baptists toward that vast movement of the opening years of the nineteenth century which was

[2] Hesketh Pearson: *Tom Paine, Friend of Mankind* (New York, 1937), p. 176.
[3] Gallaher: op. cit., p. 33.
[4] Ibid.
[5] Ibid., p. 29.

called the "Great Revival." Bring these wayward people back to God, convert them, give them that deep consciousness of sin which Paine had tried to replace with an exaltation of man's estate, and righteousness would triumph at last! This was the preachers' promise.

3

In the century's closing years the people of the West, without knowing it, were eager for the variety of religious exercise the preachers prepared for them. This was not because they were in a particularly repentant mood. It was not because they wanted to be lifted out of their depravity. Many of them, indeed, did not know that they were depraved until the ministers told them. It was not that they had been preoccupied with the question of their salvation or that they wanted to be told about heaven and hell as Edwards and Whitefield and the Tennents had told their grandfathers. What they wanted was excitement.

It is scarcely possible, in the constantly articulate and constantly entertaining world in which we live, to imagine the dreariness, the monotony, the unrelieved labor of the early frontier life. No American farm is so isolated today that radio or television cannot reach it; scarcely a farmer's family is without a car to take it into the bright lights of urban gaiety. But the relaxation and recreation of seeing new sights, of meeting new people, of art, however crude—music, pictures, drama—were absent from the western settlements, whose people used the poignant word "lonesick" about themselves.

When rumors spread that a circuit-riding preacher was coming to So-and-So's cabin, or to some more advanced settlement where there was a frame courthouse in which people might gather, it was as exciting as the news in later times that the circus was on its way. Backwoods families would travel twenty miles or more by wagon or on horseback to hear the new voice. Scoffers and Deists along with those who were nostalgic for a church would go to hear it. The preaching might not change their views or improve their behavior, but it was something new—it was excitement, change of scene.

Circuit-riding began, in general, with the Presbyterians, though there were a few pioneer Methodists and Baptists. It soon appeared, however, that the Methodists carried far more appeal to the settlers than the Presbyterians—at least than those who insisted on Calvinist orthodoxy and on the intellectual rather than the emotional emphasis. There was, however, a wildcat Presbyterian group calling itself "Cumberland Presbyterians," deprecated by the orthodox, which leaned toward the Methodist approach. To the Methodists, the Baptists, once persecuted by respectable Puritans, made a close second in frontier popularity.

The frontier people had no taste for doctrinal dialectics. They had no leisure for study, no intellectual environment. Even those nurtured in the Presbyterian faith had of necessity broken with its practice, being without church or synod or any organization. To most of them Princeton College, the great intellectual Presbyterian center, carried little prestige. In their hope of a happier future destiny in the West they had moved beyond the predestination doctrine. Their migration, their clearing, building, and planting in the new land, but, above all, the jumping of that barrier which would forever separate them from Europe and the past—as even the Atlantic had not done—were all acts of free will opposed to any conviction that God had separated the sheep from the goats and that nothing man could do by himself could save him. And perhaps it was this very Calvinistic concept of the impotence and low estate of man that had turned westerners toward Tom Paine.

In withering words Paine had written in *The Age of Reason* of the Calvinist debasing of the human creature:

> It is by his being taught to contemplate himself as an out-law, as an out-cast, as a beggar, as a mumper, as one thrown as it were on a dunghill, at an immense distance from his Creator, and who must make his approaches by creeping, and cringing to intermediate beings, that he conceives either a contemptuous disregard for everything under the name of religion, or becomes indifferent, or turns what he calls devout. In the latter case, he consumes his life in grief, or the affectation of it. His prayers are reproaches. His humility is ingratitude. He calls himself a worm, and the fertile earth a dunghill; and all the blessings of life by the thankless name of vanities.[6]

While this is hardly a just appraisal of what nineteenth-century Calvinists really believed, it scared away those who had not the time or leisure to analyze it. On the other hand, the Methodists'

[6] *The Writings of Thomas Paine*, Moncure D. Conway, editor (New York, 1896), IV, 44.

conviction that avowed repentance and a good life could secure for the humblest, the most illiterate of humans the highest estate of heaven was instantly exciting to simple souls with troubled consciences or waning hopes. For men and women who had lived and labored in fear of storm and Indian and wild beast—for whom the wolf was often literally as well as figuratively at the door—this positive approach was satisfying. Especially to the hopeless Negro there was hope in the message of the Methodist and Baptist; its fruit is still with us in the tremendous "spiritual" songs that have become a part of American folklore.

But perhaps most exciting of all was the fact that the circuit-rider was a stranger, far-traveled, usually a person gifted with a flair for histrionic eloquence, and always with the prestige of selflessness, of severe bodily sacrifice. He was rugged, unpolished, often unwashed, but he spoke the language of the moving backwoods, not that of the static churches. His appeal was intensely personal, intimate, distinct to each individual: he seemed to regard his listeners as separate entities, not as a "congregation." What he said mattered not at all. His mere presence, his voice, opened a hundred or a thousand safety valves, and out poured the pent emotions of months of silence: no wonder that the outpourings took forms that are incredible to us today or that are relegated by us to the realm of pathology. In the cries, the "jerks," the prostrations, the barking, the jumping, the dancing, and even the sexual releases that are usually held to be evil results of "revival" exercises we may see the effects of long-suppressed grief at defeated hopes, of long, constant, but constantly conquered fear, of inhibited loves, hates, and urgencies, or the monotony of the same voices, the same sounds, and the same duties.

The first circuit-riders preached in cabins or barns or any village public building. But the preachings soon became so popular as mere diversions that soon no frontier structure could hold the people who traveled twenty or thirty miles to swell a local population. When the especially popular or sensational preachers—men like Peter Cartwright, Lorenzo Dow, or Jesse Lee—would appear, the listeners would spread outdoors and a stentorian voice was required to reach them. Also, in such a gathering there was noise. As there were no baby-sitters (except in the slave states, and there the Negroes were so frantic for religion it was difficult to keep them at home), women brought infants as well as young children, and the families always brought their dogs. In the early days,

> an average congregation would consist of perhaps fifteen families. Each couple had an average of five children, two of whom were infants and a third was too small to keep quiet during services. It would be conservative to estimate five dogs to a family. As one minister facetiously remarked, there were in a congregation "forty-five babies and seventy-five dogs, with only sixty adults to police the mob." [7]

These little indoor gatherings, however, gave way when the preachers set out in earnest to revive religion on the frontiers. In the year 1800, then—the year the federal government moved into the Potomac swamp called Washington and the year before Thomas Jefferson took John Adams's place in the still unfinished executive mansion; when the cotton kingdom was growing by leaps and bounds and slavery with it in the deep South—the mass saving of souls began through an institution known as the "camp meeting."

4

The first genuine western camp meeting was probably that of July 1800 at Gasper River, Logan County, Kentucky. As this was near the state's southern border, people undoubtedly came across from Tennessee as well as from more northern parts of Kentucky. They came in the great, big-wheeled covered wagons that were coming into use at the time, on horseback, and in every sort of carriage. As many came from long distances, requiring days of travel, it was decided to continue the meeting for several days to give these remote visitors a proper recompense for their pains. Tents were pitched, rude huts were built around the central gathering-place—a clearing in the vast virgin forest. The forest furnished a retiring-place for private prayer and other more mundane purposes.

At this first meeting there were exhibited many of the emotional outbursts that later became a familiar feature. Agony and distress seem to have accompanied the preaching as men and women came to feel the crushing burden of their sins. Even the children were caught in the epidemic, and weeping, ranting boys and girls under

[7] Everett Dick: *The Dixie Frontier* (New York, 1948), p. 183.

twelve acquired great prestige in the wide confessional. After these people had awakened, however, to their souls' danger, they would pray in hysterical fervor and would receive the mercy; then they were expected to lapse into exalted calm, and a new beauty would spread over their faces.

> Through every part of the multitude there could be found some awakened souls, struggling in the pangs of the new birth, ready to faint or die for Christ, almost upon the brink of desperation. Others again . . . beginning to tell the sweet wonders which they saw in Christ. Ministers and experienced Christians were everywhere engaged praying, exhorting, conversing, and trying to lead enquiring souls to the Lord Jesus. In this exercise the night was spent till near the break of day.[8]

Many of the experiences were undoubtedly agonizing, as any large, sudden release of emotion is likely to be. Other behavior was probably artificial, a species of exhibitionism for which there was always an eager audience. The greater part of the demonstrations were unconsciously imitative, hysterical reflexes in people nervously conditioned by a special environment. In most cases, however, conscience—real or imaginary—was the motivating cause.

After the first immensely popular Kentucky meetings, the gatherings multiplied all along the frontiers. In all, the so-called "exercises" became epidemic. The most notable and sensational of these was the prostration or sudden falling to the ground of persons presumably rendered unconscious by their awareness of their sins. The victims were known as "the slain of the Lord," and preachers boasted of the number thus affected during their sermons. When a listener fell, he or she was often paralyzed or speechless; sometimes, however, the fallen one received the gift of tongues and uttered involuntary words glorifying God or Christ.

From 1801 to 1804 the meetings became much larger and more elaborate. Preparations were made far in advance, and various structures were built to accommodate the people. According to Peter Cartwright,

> They would erect their camps with logs or frame them, and cover them with clapboards or shingles. They would also erect a shed,

[8] "McGready's Narrative of the Revival in Logan County," *New York Missionary Magazine* (1803), p. 192, quoted in Catharine C. Cleveland: *The Great Revival in the West* (Chicago, 1916), p. 57.

> sufficiently large to protect five thousand people . . . and here they would collect together from forty to fifty miles around, sometimes further than that. Ten, twenty, and sometimes thirty ministers . . . would come together and preach night and day, four or five days together; and, indeed, I have known these camp-meetings to last three or four weeks, and great good resulted from them. I have seen more than a hundred sinners fall like dead men under one powerful sermon, and I have seen and heard more than five hundred Christians all shouting aloud the high praises of God at once. . . . Some sinners mocked . . . some of the old starched Presbyterian preachers preached against these exercises, but still the work went on . . . gathering additional force, until our country seemed all coming home to God.[9]

As each "sinner" fell, the faithful gathered round him, singing hymns and praying for mercy. With many such groups active all over the meeting-ground, it is doubtful if the preaching could be heard widely or in detail. Sometimes the preachers themselves would fall—for everyone, after all, is a sinner—and these collapses would cause special excitement. Cartwright, who was not immune to prejudice, asserts that Presbyterians were particularly subject:

> not being accustomed to much noise and shouting, when they yielded to it went into great extremes and downright wildness.[1]

The joy, which evidently mingled with the agony as the consciences were first tormented, then soothed, is told in a letter from a man who had just returned from a meeting in South Carolina which was typical in 1802.

> The penetrating sighs and excruciating struggles of those under exercise, the grateful exultations of those brought to a sense of guilty condition, and to a knowledge of the way to salvation; mingled with the impressions which are naturally excited by the charms of music and the solemnities of prayer . . . and to all this added the nature of the scenery, the darkness of the night, and the countenances of all the spectators, speaking in terms more expressive than language, the sympathy, the hope and the fear, of their hearts, were sufficient to bow the stubborn neck to infidelity, silence the tongue of profanity, and melt the heart of cold neglect though hard as adamant.[2]

[9] Cartwright: op. cit., pp. 45, 46.
[1] Ibid., p. 46.
[2] Letter from Ebenezer H. Cummings to a friend in Augusta, dated July 7, 1802, printed in *Augusta Herald*, July 28, 1802, reprinted in Cleveland: op. cit., Appendix III, pp. 167, 168.

Another passage of this letter conveys the social impact of the camp meeting on the isolated folk:

> Families who had never seen each other, until they met on the ground would pour forth the tears of sympathy, . . . many friendships were formed and many attachments contracted, which, although the persons may never meet again will never be dissolved.[3]

The dramatic set in which all these actors moved is warmly described in *The Kentucky Revival:*

> The scene at night was peculiarly impressive. Torches, candles, and the blazing campfires among the trees threw a weird light upon the moving crowd, the animated preacher, the agonized sufferer, and the prostrate bodies. Under these circumstances there was something truly awful in the medley of sounds that fell upon the ear.[4]

The most celebrated of the involuntary exercises at the camp meetings was the "jerks," an affliction which seems to have been highly contagious and which, once it was widely advertised, was invariably present. There is considerable difference of opinion about the cause of the jerks: some said it was similar to a possession by devils, while others thought it was sent directly by God to awaken men and women to the need for conversion. There were preachers who believed they could send a sinner into the jerks by an act of will, and these undoubtedly held the threat before the eyes of the recalcitrant or the profane, thus cowing their antagonist. Others maintained with Cartwright that

> No matter whether they were saints or sinners, they would be taken under a warm song or sermon, and seized with a convulsive jerking all over, which they could not by any possibility avoid, and the more they resisted, the more they jerked. If they would not strive against it and pray in good earnest, the jerking would usually abate. I have seen more than five hundred persons jerking at one time. . . .[5]

Cartwright, however, seems to have had occasional flickers of humor over this exercise—for a preacher a rare lapse.

> To see those proud young gentlemen and young ladies, dressed in their silks, jewelry, and prunella, from top to toe, take the *jerks,*

[3] Ibid., p. 168.
[4] Richard McNemar: *The Kentucky Revival* (Cincinnati, 1808), p. 23.
[5] Cartwright: op. cit., p. 48.

> would often excite my risibilities. The first jerk or so, you would see their fine bonnets, caps and combs fly; and so sudden would be the jerking of the head that their long loose hair would crack almost as loud as a wagoner's whip.[6]

The many stories, varying in detail, agree on the appearances of the various phenomena, and there can be little doubt of the fact that very large bodies of people were nervously afflicted and could not help themselves. Catharine Cleveland has made a careful study of the psychology of the camp meeting. The "exercises," she finds, were not unique in the American revivals. She cites cases of similar epidemics in the eleventh, thirteenth, and fifteenth centuries in Europe and two in France early in the eighteenth. There were other instances of mass religious hysteria in the 1700's in England, Scotland, and Ireland. In the American revivals, while epilepsy undoubtedly accounted for some cases, the majority were among perfectly normal people living under abnormal conditions and subjected to extremes of nervous excitement to which they were not accustomed. And the fact that the attendants at the meetings ate and slept virtually not at all was certainly contributory.

The much touted sexual effect of the meetings has probably been exaggerated. It would be inevitable for young people in moments of nervous exaltation to indulge occasionally in acts for which they may have long hungered. Surely the opportunity, in the dark fringes of the meeting-grounds, was always present. Yet the constant warning against sin was an undoubted deterrent, and it is psychologically possible that the sexual urgency was sublimated into other channels of emotional expression. Cases have been cited of young women carried away by the illusion that the sexual act was somehow related to the church as the bride of Christ, but when the passion was spent, the girls came screaming their remorse into the center of the meeting.[7]

The phenomena of the revivals often resemble those of witchcraft days. Some of the demonstrations allegedly the work of God were, in the seventeenth century, thought to be provoked by practitioners of black magic. The performances were precisely the same.

[6] Ibid., p. 49.

[7] Gilbert V. Seldes: *The Stammering Century* (New York, 1928), p. 56. Frances Trollope, in *Domestic Manners of the Americans* (London, 1832), Chapter 15, dwells on the sexual aspects of the camp meeting with probably exaggerated emphasis.

Like all revivals, this one wore itself out in a few years. With the movement of education into the settlements, with the building of churches there, with the rapid growth of the western settlements, the thicker population of communities east of the Mississippi, the opening of a new artery in the Erie Canal, and the prevalence of the steamboat on the great rivers, civilization followed the pioneers and caught up with the settlers. With new prosperity promising treasures on earth, those of heaven were less anxiously sought. Diversions of all kinds—theatrical troupes, "scientific" lectures, greater quantities of books, magazines, and newspapers, new political propaganda, and controversy between merchants and agrarians—gave more sophisticated entertainment than the lurid camp meeting.

Farther west there were always occasional flare-ups of revival movements, but they never again created so general an atmosphere of hysteria. More orderly meetings in the South continued to comfort unhappy Negroes, for whom heaven was seldom found on the plantations. Revivalists of the Moody and Sankey variety preached to vast crowds, and later the Billy Sundays presided over "sawdust trails" to salvation, but the epidemics of jerks and prostrations rarely recurred.

It is difficult to appraise the value of the Great Revival of 1800. Perhaps it was mainly negative—an antidote to unrelieved severity in the conditions of living. It might be proper even to call it a counter-irritant. Though few retained the first exuberant sense of salvation and many "sinned" worse than ever, the revival left a religious residue that mattered a good deal to those who felt the importance or necessity of religion. The rigid creeds were broken down. Scarcely anyone who had been impressed by the revival ever wholly returned to the total-predestination doctrines of the Calvinists. Happiness was becoming more and more possible in this world as Manifest Destiny moved into the golden West, and the dubious journey to heaven grew less alluring.

Chapter XVII

The Paradox of 1812

THE DESTINY of the American people that was daily becoming manifest[1] as the waves moved on to the Mississippi and beyond led the emigrants into avarices and ambitions some of which have troubled the American conscience ever since. In the first fifteen years of the nineteenth century only the New England conscience suffered; perhaps if it had prevailed, our own would be freer today. But the course of empire, once it gets started on a scale like the American, is exceedingly difficult to stop, and when it is on this lavish and orgiastic scale, it breeds the sort of imperialistic thought that the twentieth-century American does not like to associate with his democracy. Yet without it, and without certain lapses of the western conscience, the United States we have today would hardly have been possible.

It might be supposed—as Samuel Eliot Morison and Henry S. Commager in their caustic review of the epoch[2] suggest—that a people which had acquired the enormous Louisiana territory before they had come near settling the vast acreage that had composed the public domain before 1800, would have been satisfied to rest awhile before reaching out for more. But because of American methods of settlement and farming and the American pioneer spirit of restlessness, the land hunger had become insatiable. It did not occur to the pioneer farmer that when the fertility of his soil was exhausted he could restore it by the conservation methods in use in America today and in use in Europe centuries before 1800. He simply sold his

[1] Though the phrase "Manifest Destiny" was not used until 1844, it is obvious that the concept was present from the time of the Revolution if not before.

[2] Morison and Commager: *The Growth of the American Republic*, I, 307.

land and moved on to some other virgin tract. As the tide of migration increased, a farmer always "took up more land than he could possibly cultivate, in the hope of selling at a profit." [3]

In the forming states of the Northwest Territory the land hunger reached across the northern border; its pangs were rendered acute by the vision of British Upper Canada. In Ohio and Indiana Territory the hostility to the British, gentled in New England by the profits of sea trade, was continued by those emigrant Yankees who had put a mountain barrier between themselves and the ameliorating influence of the Atlantic. South of the Ohio migrant Virginians or Carolinians, who had never had a carrying trade to restore friendship with England and who were still chafing from old tobacco debt, were equally hostile to the ex-mother. Moreover, in every part of the frontier the growing nationalist sentiment and the waxing pride in freedom, independence, and equality made the memory of British oppression more and more repugnant. Finally, the Louisiana Purchase had brought confidence to the westerners; in possession now of both banks of the Mississippi, the nation appeared unconquerable, an appearance productive of arrogance and chauvinism.

Across the Atlantic, Europe was in greater peril than it has ever been since until the days of Hitler. By 1807 the colossal shadow of Napoleon darkened the land from Italy to Russia. The Scandinavian countries were in the grip of his "Continental System," and there was fear everywhere—even in the maritime states of New England. There the merchants, the shipowners, the sea traders, cherishing their profitable commercial relations with England, were naturally suspicious of Napoleon and his conquering French. For them destiny was overseas, not westward, and we see, in these years when English and French were pursuing each other over the ocean, the first great conflict which came near destroying the Union.

The Yankees might well fear the West. With terrifying rapidity new states were taking shape and their population increasing. Jefferson's purchase from Napoleon of the Louisiana territory added an acreage, not precisely known but surely fabulous, out of which God knew how many states would presently be carved. As the westerners had like sentiments all along the frontier; as they were attached to Jefferson, to all the Republican principles, and even somewhat to the French; as they loathed the British and were wholly ignorant of

[3] Ibid.

maritime conditions, the Yankees wondered what would happen when these folk got control, through the superior number of their votes, over Congress.

Under the influence of these fears, the behavior of the New England leaders became, in our view, treasonable. Half a century later the Yankees were to call southerners traitors for holding and expressing some of the very sentiments they themselves gave voice and print to in the first fifteen years of the new century. From the time of the Louisiana Purchase, secession was threatened in New England. When Jefferson made that profitable deal with Napoleon, Timothy Pickering, Boston's most violent Federalist radical, hoped a confederation of New England and New York could form a separate republic. For the next ten years Federalists in New England worked continually in peace and war to obstruct the government and divide the nation. To the New England leaders, however, this was not treason. They were still clinging to a belief that national sovereignty was not paramount: to the old certainty that imbued the Puritan theocracy that they were independent of the rest of the world; that their faith in themselves transcended all external obligations; and that the other states were right only if their views accorded with New England's. God was still revealing them to themselves as his chosen people. It was their duty, then, to separate, to declare their independence and form whatever confederate government would maintain their principles and fortify their conscience.

2

The Yankee conscience in the early 1800's did not precisely hang in a vacuum. It would have been difficult even for a Puritan public conscience to detach itself wholly from the fifteen and a half million dollars a year the Massachusetts merchant marine was earning by 1807 in freight revenue alone.[4] This was equal to the total federal income of 1806. It was war profit, most of it; the ships of Boston and Salem and Newburyport conducted nearly forty per cent of the neutral carrying trade to the belligerents, England and France. The bulk of this truly colossal sum was in pounds sterling,

[4] Samuel E. Morison: *The Maritime History of Massachusetts, 1783–1860,* p. 189.

which meant that the bulk of the cargoes went to equip the navy of Lord Nelson and the army of the Duke of Wellington, and Napoleon, becoming daily more and more strapped for money, was making desperate efforts to stop the commerce.

The result was an attempted love affair between New England and her late enemy. Forgotten were Lexington and Concord and Bunker Hill. Forgotten were Lafayette and his liberating army. Napoleon was the new antichrist. The French, after all—except for that brief interlude when they were so necessary—had presented anathema after anathema: first the idolatrous papists, then the corrupting atheists, then the ruthless world conquerors. At heart we are still Englishmen, we of New England, blood and bone; a few years of family quarrel cannot change us! This was the sentiment in 1807, compensating the merchants for a succession of unholy acts committed by *alma mater* upon the high seas.

For England had not forgotten. England, to be sure, was on the paying, not the receiving, end of the affair; England was sore beset by the war; worst of all, English sailors were deserting by the hundreds, perhaps by the thousands, and, lured by high wages, were becoming naturalized Yankees and signing up on Yankee ships. The British government did not recognize foreign naturalization. Aliens could become naturalized Britons, but, once a Briton, always a Briton. Especially no Briton could ever become a citizen of the upstart United States. England was still smarting from her defeat by these bad boys, from the exile of the Loyalists, and from Jefferson's apparently friendly negotiations with Napoleon. So her ships stopped American merchantmen with shots across their bows; her captains, without warrants, searched the captive ships, dragged out the suspected sailors, and removed them—naturalized or not. Many a born Bostonian or Philadelphian went with the others. But the merchants did not care. What was a sailor or two—a thousand sailors or two? Small loss when the gain was fifteen and a half million dollars a year! The merchants cared only when a ship was intercepted by the French blockade or when it went as a prize into a French port.

But Thomas Jefferson cared. By 1807 he had filled for six years that perennially controversial office of president of the United States. He was thought by his enemies to favor the French. In fact, he favored nothing but the nation of which he was chief executive. Rarely has a president acted so wholly at the dictates of his patriotic conscience. As the impressment of sailors and the capture of cargoes increased, he said: "A plague on both your houses." He told the Congress—which, in this second term, he held largely in the hollow of his hand—to clap an embargo on every American port, and Congress obeyed. After the 22nd of December, 1807, American ships must stay in their own harbors. The hulls might rot. The crews might starve. The owners might be driven to the pawnshops. The rich merchants might have to delete Madeira and vintage claret from their diets. The embargo would hold until the fighters overseas should recognize the neutral rights of the United States of America.

From the days of Thomas Jefferson to the days of Franklin Roosevelt, no American president has offended the mercantile conscience without arousing a species of hatred that is peculiarly American. It empurples faces; it raises blood pressure until the instruments break; it takes away the appetite, especially at breakfast when the morning paper arrives; it induces pungent profanity even among the godly, and obscene stories among the ribald. It extends beyond the president to his wife, his children, and his servants. Madam, the First Lady, turns out to be an alcoholic, a sporadic lunatic, or a person of easy virtue. The members of the Cabinet are reprobates or embezzlers; they are awake nights plotting the nation's downfall, engaging in intrigues with alien agents, and giving aid and comfort to the country's true enemies. In later years increased medical knowledge has shown that this venom causes ulcers, jaundice, cerebral lesions, and coronary thromboses.

Jefferson's embargo, with its paralyzing effect on sea trade, produced all the now familiar symptoms in New England. Timothy Pickering, then a senator in the Congress, presented the views of the mercantile group in 1808. In the President's desire to preserve peace he saw precisely the opposite aim.

> The peace and safety of our country [he wrote] are suspended on a thread. The course we have seen pursued leads us on to war—a war with Great-Britain—a war absolutely without necessity—a war which whether disastrous or successful, must bring misery and ruin to the United States; *misery* by the destruction of our navigation and commerce (perhaps also of our fairest seaport towns and cities) the loss of markets for our produce . . . and the other evils incident to a state of war: and *ruin,* by the loss of our liberty and independence. For if with the aid of our arms Great-Britain were

subdued—from that moment, (though flattered perhaps with the name of *allies,*) we should become the *Provinces of France.*[5]

At first Pickering had opponents even in the Puritan stronghold—such Anti-Federalists as James Sullivan, governor of Massachusetts, who wrote him that he was aiming to "disunite, divide and dissolve the nation" and "where will this end but in an overthrow of the national government?" [6] But as the embargo went on forcing Yankee seamen "by thousands to starve or beg," [7] Republicans like Sullivan were eliminated, and the Boston press printed shameless editorials advocating secession.

We know today that Jefferson's embargo was an act of conscience pure and simple. It had little effect on England and seems to have encouraged Napoleon. When in 1809 Jefferson left the White House forever, embittered by the attacks on his good faith and the perversions of his intent, he asked for its repeal.

But, like many hated presidents, Jefferson had strong support away from the commercial areas. In the West he was a sort of god, and his successor, Madison, carried on the western torch.

3

In the West, from 1806, the second war with Great Britain was slowly cooking. Like most western issues of the period, this one was involved with the Indians. And here we come on one of the most poignant and tragic stories in the darker pages of our history—a story that our historical conscience can surely not ignore or forget. Balancing it was the vast, inevitable surge: the manifest destiny that subdued all twinges, and, never for a moment forgotten by the emigrants, the scalpings and burnings of the past. To reinforce the more recent of these memories was the fact that in the Revolution, and in the later northern-border disputes with Britain, Indians had fought with their customary barbarity as British allies. This last fact had

[5] *A Letter from the Hon. Timothy Pickering . . . Exhibiting to his Constituents a View of the Imminent Danger of an Unnecessary and Ruinous War* (Northampton, Mass., 1808), p. 10.

[6] Governor Sullivan to Colonel Pickering, Boston, March 18, 1808, printed by Pickering in a pamphlet entitled *Interesting Correspondence, etc.* (Newburyport, 1808), pp. 4, 5.

[7] Pickering: *A Letter,* cited above, p. 10.

finally vitiated the gentle provisions of the Ordinance of 1787 promising justice to the Indians—provisions the settlers had tried with patience to preserve until at last, exhausted by the intransigence of the aborigines, they had called in Anthony Wayne to end the open conflict with British and Indians alike at the Battle of Fallen Timbers in 1794.

What few white Americans realized was that these alliances—first with French, then with British—were all incidental to the great, basic Indian fear that their land was being invaded, their hunting-grounds—the sole means of their livelihood—being stolen from them to make the white man's farms and cities. To the settlers the hunting-demands were unreasonable. Why should such vast tracts be reserved for a handful of Indians so that they might roam at will and forever through infinite spaces of forest following their game, whereas if they were willing to farm the land as the white man did, there would be room for both to live peaceably side by side?

But here we see the conflict that, historically, has beset the whole human race in the transition from the hunting to the agricultural stage: the primary impact of civilization on savagery. There have been tragic shadows in all the transitory epochs; what made the Indian suffering so acute was the rapidity of the change. Many thoughtful Americans have believed that if the Indians could have been lifted by education into the agricultural stage, they could have been integrated into American civilization. But, under the dynamic urgency, events moved too fast. With the white man's destiny becoming daily more and more manifest there was no time for him to shoulder the "white man's burden."

The focus, in the Northwest Territory, was on two individuals whose influence in the tribes increased steadily through the first decade of the new century. One of these was the great Shawnee chief Tecumseh; the other was his charlatan brother Tenskwatawa,[8] known as the "Prophet."

Perhaps no champion of this unhappy race was ever nobler or wiser than Tecumseh. As we read his speeches, recorded in the official writings of his inferior white opponent, Governor Harrison of

[8] Another version of the Prophet's name was Ellksattawa. This was an adopted name meaning "The Open Door." Originally he had been Lauliwasikau, but as he became aware of his divine powers he changed it—a procedure followed by some of the more powerful Russians following the revolution of October 1917.

Indiana Territory, we are struck by the melancholy beauty of his thought, the astuteness of his reasoning, and the stern control of his slow anger. In his words—and he spoke many—we see both the essence and the detail of the whole Indian tragedy; calling persistently on the Great Spirit, they carry overtones that brought uneasiness to the white conscience. Tecumseh's concepts were simple: they took little account of the complexities of civilization.

> How can we have confidence in the white people? [he asked.] When Jesus Christ came upon the earth you killed and nailed him on a cross; you thought he was dead but you were mistaken. . . .[9]

It was the Chief's brother, however, who first came to the attention of the settlers. In the Prophet we see in Indian form many of the qualities that were common among evangelist preachers. He had magnetism and the power of conjuring quick, vivid images. He had all the tricks of voice and gesture of the true spellbinder. He was exceedingly intelligent and able to turn to account a wide knowledge of happenings in the white as well as the Indian countries. His reasoning—to Indian minds—was irrefutable; he had a thorough understanding of Indian psychology and a familiarity with Indian superstitions. With all this equipment, he was able to work up much the same sort of religious fervor or frenzy that we have seen in the more sensational of the Methodist camp meetings.

In his youth Tenskwatawa had been indolent and alcoholic, with a strong aversion to the hunting, sports, and warfare traditional among the males of his race. Normally such a person would be persecuted in his community. But Tenskwatawa was able, after a boyhood encounter which cost him an eye, to persuade his fellows that he had supernatural powers, that the Master of Life had chosen him for special activity, and that if he withdrew from the customary exercises of his tribe, it was at his master's command. He even convinced them that his habitual drunkenness was divinely ordained.

Certain chiefs, however, doubted his claims; others set up rival ones. These he got rid of indirectly by inducing his followers to kill his critics.

[9] Speech of August 20, 1810, in *Governors Messages and Letters*, Logan Esarey, editor (Indiana Historical Collections, Indianapolis, 1922), I, 467. Harrison's punctuation has been corrected for clarity.

> In this way [writes Henry Schoolcraft] he disposed of Tarhe, the wise and venerable sachem king of the Wyandots, who, being accused of witchcraft was condemned to be burnt at the stake.[1]

The Prophet's most spectacular exploit came after he had attracted the attention of the Governor. Harrison then made to Tenskwatawa's followers a speech he afterward regretted.

> Demand of him [Harrison advised them] some proofs at least of his being the messenger of the Deity. . . . If he is really a prophet, ask of him to cause the sun to stand still, the moon to alter its course, the rivers to cease to flow, or the dead to rise from their graves.[2]

It was at noon of a hot summer's day shortly after this that the Prophet answered the Governor's challenge. He had announced in the morning that when the sun was at the zenith he would darken the earth by raising his hand and calling upon the Master of Life. Sure enough, on the instant, although there was not a cloud in the sky, the face of the sun was obscured and the bright day turned to an uncanny twilight. From then on there could never be a question among his followers of his miraculous powers, and as the story spread, his disciples multiplied. It is evidence of his astuteness that he was able to turn the forecast of an eclipse told him by a white settler to such good account. Thenceforth the Governor had good reason to fear his influence.

4

The Prophet's mystic powers, however, might have had little effect on the lives of the white settlers had not his principal religious revival coincided with the great patriotic crusade of his brother. Tecumseh's long thought, present in his mind since the whites had burned his home when he was twelve, began to crystallize into a program in 1805 when he and his brother were living at Greenville. At this time the Prophet adjusted his exhortations and exercises to the policies of Tecumseh. He seems, then, to have given up drinking (perhaps under his brother's influence) and to have instituted among

[1] Henry R. Schoolcraft: *Archives of Aboriginal Knowledge* (Philadelphia, 1860), p. 353. (For full title see Bibliography *post.*)

[2] Elmore Barce: "Tecumseh's Confederacy," in *Indiana Magazine of History*, XII (1916), 169, 170.

his disciples a regime of abstinence and of stern morality—as the Indian conscience understood that abstraction.

There is abundant evidence that white men had given liquor freely to the Indians from the very earliest times in an effort to bend them to their will. But there is also plenty of proof that, in the Northwest Territory at least, this was done by individuals and not, as is often believed, in systematic government practice. In any case, many Indians had been completely debauched, and this was one of the counts Tecumseh had against the Americans. He connived, then, with his prophet brother to institute the Spartan program of teetotalism and exercise that from 1805 to 1811 was reforming and strengthening the tribesmen who gathered round the two men.

From the spring of 1807 a series of letters from governors, officials, and army officers in the Northwest Territory flowed into the office of the War Department in Washington. In them was reflected the alarm of the settlers at the ever increasing crowd round the Prophet, at the drum beats and rifle shots and all the sounds indicating preparation for war that came from his camp. Rumors and reports were running then along the American spy grapevine. One quoted a sermon preached by the Indian Adam, the first father, who had returned to earth in order to deliver this message:

> I am the father of the English, of the French, of the Spaniards, and of the Indians. . . . *But the Americans I did not make. They are not my children but the children of the evil spirit.* They grew from the scum of the great water when it was troubled by the evil spirit, and the froth was driven into the woods by a strong east wind. They are numerous but I hate them.[3]

From some of the reports it was guessed that the British were having a hand in instigating an uprising. In the following year Harrison warned the secretary of war that the Prophet's revival boded no good to the Americans. In 1809 the letters directly accused the British of inciting, with the aid of "spirituous liquors," Indian hostility toward the territorial governments.

> The powerful influence of the British [wrote the governor of Michigan Territory] has been exerted in a way alluring to the savage character.[4]

[3] *American State Papers.* Edited under the authority of Congress by Walter Lowrie and Walter S. Franklin. Class II, Indian Affairs (Washington, 1834), I, 798.

[4] Ibid., I, 799.

In 1810 Harrison pinpointed the focus of trouble when he wrote to Secretary Eustis:

> There can be no doubt of the designs of the Prophet and the British agent of Indian affairs, to do us injury.[5]

The reasoning was plausible. For many years Englishmen had carried on a highly profitable fur trade with the Indians in the Great Lakes region. We remember that the famous British Proclamation of 1763 was designed to maintain peace west of the Alleghenies by preventing the migrations of the colonists into the hunting-grounds. Although the treaties with the British following the Revolution [6] had established American rights to this territory beyond the shadow of a doubt, still the British in Canada were keeping up a sporadic hostility. This, indeed, was not altogether illogical, as American orators were continually speaking about the conquest of Upper Canada and anticipating Felix Grundy of Tennessee, who, when war finally came, announced: "We shall drive the British from our continent." [7]

5

It was after the Treaty of Fort Wayne in 1809 that Governor Harrison became aware that it was Tecumseh who was to be most feared. The treaty had been disastrous to Indian hopes of keeping their beloved hunting-grounds. Through it approximately three million acres of land claimed by the Indians were ceded to the government of the United States. The terms included annual payments by the United States in money and goods. It was no less legitimate a treaty than any that had been made, and no more morally defensible. If we apply a strict ethical standard or one of absolute moral values, no such treaty is wholly honorable. But this judgment takes into consideration an irreconcilable difference of understanding between the red man and the white because of their different cultural levels.

To the Indian, land could not be sold. It had been a gift from the

[5] Ibid.
[6] Especially John Jay's treaty of 1794.
[7] George Dangerfield: *The Era of Good Feelings* (New York, 1952), p. 37.

Great Spirit. The land "was an integral, inseparable part of nature that sustained the beings that lived upon it." [8]

> Sell a country! [Tecumseh was reported as saying.] Why not sell the air, the clouds, the great sea as well as the land? [9]

When the white man had first arrived, some Indians had told a Moravian missionary from Pennsylvania:

> The land they settled on was ours. We knew not but the Great Spirit had sent them to us for some good purpose, and therefore we thought they must be a good people. We were mistaken. . . .[1]

In earlier days Indians had remained on the land they had sold, not understanding the "impossible" sale and believing the land was still theirs to hunt in; their grievances when the laws forced them off had become cumulative. By Tecumseh's time the chiefs of some tribes had grown cynical and accepted the Americans' propositions for what there was in it for them. The purpose of Tecumseh's crusade was to bring his countrymen back to the ancient faith and stiffen their resistance to the American invasion.

He told Harrison that the Treaty of Fort Wayne had been signed by treacherous chiefs in his absence. Many tribes, he said, had not been consulted, though all the tribes had owned the land in common. Harrison, who had apparently acted in good faith,[2] and who at times had shown kindness and patience toward the Indian tribes, was bewildered by Tecumseh's gentle but insistent, stubborn, relentless arguments. Yet he admitted the Shawnee Chief's extraordinary power.

> The implicit obedience and respect [he wrote the war secretary] which the followers of Tecumseh pay to him is really astonishing and more than any other circumstance bespeaks him one of those uncommon geniuses, which spring up occasionally to produce revolutions and overturn the established order of things. If it were not for the vicinity of the United States, he would perhaps be the founder of an Empire that would rival in glory that of Mexico or Peru. No difficulties deter him. His activity and industry supply the

[8] Randolph C. Downes: "Land, Indian Conception of ownership of," in *Dictionary of American History*, III, 233.

[9] Ibid.

[1] Rev. John Heckewelder: "History, Manners, and Customs of the Indian Nations Who Once Inhabited Pennsylvania . . . ," in Memoirs of the Historical Society of Pennsylvania, XII, 79.

[2] Dangerfield expresses some doubt of this. Op. cit., p. 26.

> want of letters. . . . You see him today on the Wabash and in a short time you hear of him on the shores of Lake Erie or Michigan, or on the banks of the Mississippi and wherever he goes he makes an impression favorable to his purposes.[3]

Tecumseh made his claims crystal clear to the Governor. He used the customary ceremonial language, addressing the Governor as "Brother" and acknowledging Harrison's past favors, but he insisted on nothing less than the repeal of the cessions, adding: "If the land is not restored to us you will soon see when we return to our homes how it will be settled." [4]

Perhaps if the Chief had remained on Tippecanoe Creek, where the so-called Prophet's Town had been established, the Governor would have hesitated. Perhaps, too, if Harrison had struck then, the outcome would have been different. But in August 1811 Tecumseh left the Prophet's Town on one of his long pilgrimages—southward, this time—to rally other tribes to what had become a vast anti-American crusade. He had left orders to all his followers to bide their time, not to move against the people of the territories until the hour was ripe.

In the back of his mind Tecumseh may have been hoping for British aid. Already the British had been watching him and helping him with supplies and ammunition. Harrison, a soldier as well as a politician, knew this. Furthermore, he was besieged by frontiersmen alarmed by the doings in the Prophet's Town. There had been scattered murders, horse thefts, and other crimes. There was fear all through the Indiana river valleys and even in Michigan Territory. From President Madison, Harrison got an assignment of troops from the regular army and the Kentucky militia, and by November he was prepared to strike.

It is not precisely soothing to the American conscience to remember that the battle that followed won fame for Governor (now General) Harrison that eventually brought him to the White House. There were, of course, other factors. The name of the battleground fitted rhythmically into the political slogan "Tippecanoe and Tyler too" that was shouted all over the United States in 1840. In point of fact, the attack on the Prophet's Town was not particularly valorous. It was far from a military *chef d'œuvre*. And the carnage was dreadful.

[3] Harrison: *Messages and Letters*, I, 549. [4] Ibid., I, 466.

Oddly enough, on the eve of battle Harrison seems to have had an attack of conscience and halted the advance. According to Dangerfield:

> Conscience had never been listed among the impedimenta useful for an Indian campaign, and the representations of his officers were so vehement that the governor, unwillingly, consented to move forward again.[5]

The Prophet, having observed this irresolution, sent messengers to meet Harrison with the proposal that he attend a conference in the morning.[6] Harrison agreed: he made camp, and in the dawn the Indians, frightened by the size of the Governor's force, launched a surprise attack. The battle lasted two hours. The Indians retreated at last, leaving thirty-eight dead and carrying many others with them. The American casualties numbered one hundred and eighty-eight, of whom sixty-two were killed or mortally wounded. The dead included a colonel, a major, three captains, and two subalterns.[7] It was hardly a glorious victory.

But it ended forever the hopes of Tecumseh. It decided finally the argument about land cessions. It spelled certain eventual defeat for the natives of America. From then on the Indians were to become part of Manifest Destiny. Their role, like that of the Americans, was to move forever west—with this difference: in their migration the Indians would move backward. Victims of the course of empire and of their subordinate level in the scale of civilization, they had no choice. There was not time for them to change their ways.

Tecumseh died in a last desperate attempt at revenge against the Americans. In the War of 1812 he joined the British and fell in the Battle of the Thames.

6

If we will play for a while that game known as "the if's of history," we shall see how easily the War of 1812 might have been

[5] Dangerfield: op. cit., 30. In the absence of adequate explanation in such primary sources as *American State Papers,* Indian Affairs, I, 775–9, Dangerfield's account seems wholly reasonable.

[6] *American State Papers,* Indian Affairs, I, 776.

[7] Ibid., I, 779.

avoided. If the British had relaxed their stubborn violence on the sea, there might have been no War of 1812. But this presupposes no Napoleon breathing hot down the British neck. If the British had accepted more readily the results of the American Revolution, the border incidents might not have occurred. But here we ignore the rankling over the exiled Loyalists and the American insults hurled across the Canadian border. If the Federalists had stayed in power, the paradoxical anti-war influence of New England might have prevailed. But with the rising power of the democratic West this could not be. Finally, if there had been no certainty in the Northwest Territory that Tecumseh was in league with the British, things might have been quieted down in the Great Lakes region. But the land-hungry frontier folk wanted Canada, and as a preliminary they had to suspect the British of every thinkable malicious act.

The comic aspect (to us) of the war politics that followed Tippecanoe lay in the fact that westerners who had never seen the Atlantic suddenly grew violent over the British seizing of sailors, whereas the Yankees whose sailors were being seized worked with might and main to subdue the western agitation. No one, in short, was acting from pure motives.

The westerners were exploiting the maritime crimes because they wanted inland Canada; the people on the coast were trying to ignore the high-handed British conduct because even under continued British attack the sea trade was so extremely lucrative.

The solution, of course, lay in Washington. Little "Jemmy" Madison was a peace-loving soul. He did not want war with Britain or anyone else. But the Twelfth Congress was packed with angry, articulate westerners. In the end, Manifest Destiny prevailed. War was declared against Britain on the 19th of June 1812.

Looking back over the centuries at harassed England facing one of the strongest tyrants of all time and nearly exhausted in the struggle, the declaration seems like a stab in the back. Even so, the war did not run a smooth course for the Americans. The border fighting began disastrously for them. The Canadian general, Brock, was a brilliant adversary. It was not until Perry finally met the enemy on Lake Erie that the tide turned. The British burned the city of Washington, destroying many precious records. New England was almost lost to the Union, and her citizens did everything they could to obstruct the war's progress. Finally, when the Battle of New Orleans prepared another candidate for the White House, thousands of Americans wondered what it had all been for.

Yet the more thoughtful historians have not seen it as total loss. It convinced Britain that the future would be happier for everyone if she improved her diplomacy and acted, not against, but with her giant fledgling. The westerners accepted the fact that they could not have Canada; they concentrated on the land south of the Great Lakes (finding it indeed a handful) and came to cement a lasting friendship across the border.

The War of 1812 was followed by what has been called the "era of good feelings." In this period the Monroe Doctrine took shape. New England, instead of being crushed by the war, discovered it had been instrumental in building new manufacturing industries.

There had been little progress, to be sure, toward a national conscience. As the era of good feelings advanced, there came to be many bad feelings over the Negro's status.

The question could not be ignored. It could not be forever postponed. It did no good to sweep it under the rug. If it was quashed in one place, it would pop up in another.

At the moment we are concerned with the part Negro slavery played in the movement of Manifest Destiny.

Chapter XVIII

Portents of Conflict

PERHAPS the institution of slavery never weighed more heavily on the private consciences of southerners than in the year 1793. In the 1780's, as we have seen, leading southern voices were raised against it. Jefferson, Washington, and other Virginians foresaw a period of gradual emancipation. They could envisage this, for it looked then as if tobacco, which had exhausted the land, could not go on forever supporting the institution. Farther south, rice and indigo were hardly profitable enough to justify a system which was regarded as a sort of curse or "necessary" evil. The continual, often hysterical, though generally unwarranted fear of insurrection that kept running like fire through the plantations and that both worried and brutalized slaveowners seemed a high price to pay for a system which might or might not be economically sound.

By 1793, then, historians are generally agreed that slavery was on its gradual way out in the South.[1] But in that year there arrived in Savannah, Georgia, a talented Yankee just graduated from Yale on his way to become the tutor for some boys living in the upland country. His sojourn at the plantation of Nathanael Greene's widow resulted in an economic upheaval that effectually blocked the exit of the Negro slave.

This is history. But to return for a moment to our "if's," we shall see that it was the cotton gin—not Eli Whitney—that was the vehicle of destiny. For if the young man had not arrived to relieve the urgent labor pains of Mother Necessity, another midwife would have been just around the corner. As it was, it took much litigation to establish Whitney's priority over Hodgen Holmes and others. Moreover, the need was so great, the machine so easy to construct, and the new federal patent office so weak, that the cotton gin immediately ceased to be Whitney's property.

[1] Dangerfield: op. cit., pp. 202, 203.

Georgia had two kinds of cotton: the sea-island long-staple cotton, difficult to grow and easy to clean, and the upland, short-staple cotton, easy to grow and so hard to clean that it was a commercial failure. The seeds, black in the sea-island cotton and slippery enough to be rolled out, were green in the short-staple variety and sticking to the fiber. Whitney's gin, or "engine," drew the fiber through slots that separated it from the seeds. By the turning of a crank, fifty times as much cotton could be cleaned daily as could emerge from slowly picking slave fingers. This meant that not only in the few islands off the coast but in all the great upland areas of Georgia and South Carolina this short-staple cotton—already growing wild like a weed—could become a crop of far more value than all the others combined.

The long vista of incessant conflict between conscience and prosperity opened by the cotton gin presents the most important phase of our story. The steps of rationalization by which the institution of slavery passed from a necessary evil to a positive Christian benefit under the soft pressure of green-seed cotton established a technique of thinking that has been useful ever since to the American conscience and will perhaps remain so to the end of American time. This general kind of mental process is, of course, primarily Anglo-Saxon, not simply American. But the southern circumstances thrust it into an extreme form. Furthermore, in America it was crystallized and hardened; it achieved its method largely in defense against the virulent northern attack: the attack from a land where conscience was free from economic temptation.

Apart from the ethical consideration of slavery—an institution which scarcely any American today can regard with anything but horror—it is impossible to withhold a measure of sympathy for the cotton-planter in his acute dilemma. Here was a gift of God suddenly offered him in this vast potential harvest. But, for its cultivation in the field, cotton required labor in huge, immediate quantity. This labor was not skilled labor. It was simple labor, needing only simple minds. It could be performed by persons of nearly all ages, male and female. It could be done to the rhythm of simple songs, measured by a savage beat, carrying messages of agony to a God up beyond the burning sky. The cotton labor required only an infinite capacity for sweat—bodies and tempers impervious alike to humid heat and the lashes of an overseer's whip.

The planter would have welcomed some other labor than this for the destiny that in the 1790's was before him. But there was no other adequate labor. The labor against which the northern eagle screamed had fastened itself like an octopus upon his land. It had come slowly, gently, with overtones of drawling talk and lazy laughter subduing the misery. The black people pouring from the ships that had given them weeks of hell had laughed and sung in the momentary relief of the new air, the wide, sunny land. They had been docile then, lazy but docile, inefficient, without incentive, but malleable, fit to work under the hand of discipline. Their scope was exceedingly narrow. Their inability to rise—as slaves—to other occupations than those of the field made their owners wonder (before the gin) if some sort of free wage labor might not produce a better future. Even in the "deep" South free Negroes were already becoming carpenters and mechanics, but they were thought to be troublemakers among the slaves, and there were great efforts to move them out of the states. Those kind gentlemen who had freed their slaves, therefore, had seen the objects of their kindness rewarded with even greater persecution than the poor Negroes had suffered before.

If at this point the South could have turned industrial as the North was doing, the institution would soon have died. But with God (ably assisted by Whitney and the plantation carpenters) suddenly offering this fabulous gift of cotton, what choice was there? Here was the crop of crops, to which the established labor of the land was better adapted than to any other. It would have taken stronger consciences than those gentled for generations by an easy climate and an easier way of life to have resisted the temptation to carry on with what was already there into the golden future. Nor was it merely a matter of wealth. For many, cotton offered a veritable means of existence in lands threatened with poverty. But apart from material considerations, Negro slavery had built and maintained a way of life extremely difficult to abandon. In the caste hierarchy it had constructed, the slave gave his owner prestige. Even the small farmer, the "poor white" who owned no slaves and was often in desperate straits, got solace from the fact that there was a stratum beneath him.

All this seems evil as we look at it from here, but it was nevertheless inexorable fact. Gradual emancipation would have been possible only if the need for unskilled labor had declined. Even then, freedom could have brought comfort to a Negro only if he was separated from his enslaved brothers. For this reason many slaves feared freedom, and certain freed Negroes are said to have sought servitude again. In general, in most parts of the North—however much northern orators berated the slaveholders—immigrating free Negroes, hoping for security and work, were anything but welcome. We have records, for instance, of shocking brutalities in Philadelphia and Cincinnati perpetrated against free black refugees thought to be competing against white labor.[2] It was this situation—the impossibility of a Negro population enduring half-slave and half-free—which gave humanitarians, North and South, the idea of establishing an African colony of free American Negroes. The republic of Liberia was at best but a makeshift sop to tender American consciences, but its existence proved that the consciences were there to be eased.

2

Whatever northern moralists or humanitarians might have thought or said, there were few political repercussions as long as the institution of slavery was confined within the borders of the thirteen original states. The consciences of politicians are often immune to the twinges that afflict ordinary citizens, at least up to the point where party power or personal ambition is menaced. But with the westward movement this happened. As the cotton kingdom spread westward from Georgia and South Carolina into the hospitable lands of Alabama and Mississippi and even across the great river into Louisiana, where it vied with sugar, political power followed it. Beyond the Mississippi, land-hungry eyes were already looking across the Arkansas country into Mexican Texas, into which many Americans had already poured. Toward the end of the second decade of the century the political spotlights of North and South came to a common focus on the territory that called itself Missouri.

Northerners thought Missouri too far north for slavery to be

[2] Edward Raymond Turner: *The Negro in Pennsylvania* (Washington, 1911), p. 145. This book is carefully documented from contemporary sources. See also, *passim,* Carter G. Woodson: "The Negroes of Cincinnati Prior to the Civil War," in *Journal of Negro History,* I (January 1916), 1–22.

necessary or comfortable. Along most of its eastern border was Illinois, one of the states carved out of the Old Northwest Territory and dominated by New England settlers and influences. Should not Missouri adopt, therefore, the principle embodied in the Ordinance of 1787 and prohibit involuntary servitude? On the other hand, both Kentucky and Tennessee had gateways into Missouri in its southeastern corner. It was, indeed, at the junction of Kentucky and the Missouri Territory that the Ohio River, down which so many Kentuckians had migrated, joined the Mississippi. Into the Missouri Territory a quantity of southerners had already traveled with their slaves. Even at the time of the Louisiana Purchase there were between two and three thousand slaves within the present limits of the state.[3] By 1820 there were nearly ten thousand to fifty-four thousand whites.[4]

The conditions in Missouri, however, were different from those in the original slave states. Here diversified farms replaced plantations. Except for the southern part, Missouri had no place in the cotton kingdom. Slavery was, therefore, not a "necessity." The Negroes were farmhands or domestic servants. Their main function was to maintain the way of life of the slaveholder. The fight to make Missouri a slave state—when it should become a state—was, therefore, a political fight in which economics played a minor part. The agitation was not to keep the land from ruin, but to maintain a balance of power in Congress between the slave and free regions. For the first time, then, we see a definite political division based on the institution. The states of the cotton kingdom would lose the political power they held in Washington if Congress should be dominated by free-state representation. So the aspect of slavery as a political weapon further diverted consciences from its moral color.

This is not to say that the slaveholders of Missouri did not want to keep their slaves.[5] It merely says that they could not reasonably plead economic necessity. Actually, as soon as the agitation began, immigrants from Virginia, Kentucky, and Tennessee poured into the territory with their slaves. These immigrants wanted Missouri to

[3] Harrison A. Trexler: *Slavery in Missouri, 1804–1865* (Baltimore, 1914), p. 9.

[4] Ibid., p. 10.

[5] Trexler emphasizes this in opposition to what he calls the "orthodox view." Op. cit., Chapter 4.

become a slave state as much as the cotton-planters wanted it to add to their political power, but here, too, as well as in Congress, there were strong political overtones. Why not let us decide the question ourselves? [6] the Missourians asked. What constitutional right has Congress, which represents not our territory but the states already in the Union, to make decrees that affect only us? But to northern consciences the question was beginning to affect the nation as a whole. Northerners clung to the pattern of the Ordinance of 1787. Until a territory became a state, it belonged, so to speak, to the national government.

Here the cloud of civil war becomes considerably bigger than a man's hand. The provincial consciences are merging, under the movement of Manifest Destiny, into regional consciences covering wide areas. The politicians of both regions are seizing on constitutional ambiguities to accelerate their rationalizations.

The debates on the Missouri question, long and hot, are of course forever famous as presenting the crisis from which disunion must eventually emerge. To the constitutional student they must be intensely instructive, showing the honest effort at true interpretation that lay beneath the superficial bickering. To the student of the history of a national conscience, however, these legalities are subordinate to the basic issues of slavery and civil war. The outcome of the debates—the celebrated compromise of 1820—is too well known to require pages here. We need not occupy ourselves with the abortive attempt to link Missouri with Maine or the efforts to sugar-coat the restrictive amendments. But it is important to note that the intransigent House of Representatives was finally brought to terms by the passionate speech of Representative Kinsey of New Jersey, who favored the compromise on the ground that if it was rejected, the Union would break. That menace, he said, could no longer be laughed off.

> Gentlemen of the majority have treated the idea of disunion with ridicule; but, to my mind, it presents itself in all the horrid, gloomy features of reality. . . . Opinions from which every gentleman, a few months past, would have recoiled back with horror, as treason to imagine, are now unhesitatingly threatened; that which had no ideal existence, engendering as this discussion progresses, assumes a positive shape, and . . . presents itself in all the dreadful ap-

[6] Ibid., pp. 105, 106.

> pearances of reality. May God, in mercy, inspire us with a conciliatory spirit, to disperse its fury and dispel its terrible consequences.[7]

Was Charles Kinsey in March 1820 already hearing the rumble of the guns, the cries of the wounded, at Gettysburg?

The Missouri Compromise [8] set the geography of a nation half-slave and half-free. It let in Missouri with no restriction on slavery, but it ran a line across the Louisiana Purchase on the parallel 36° 30′ north of which slavery should never be permitted. The compromise was a desperate effort to sweep the whole ugly question under the rug. But a group of ardent, sometimes fanatical northerners calling themselves abolitionists would not let it stay there. Again and again they rolled back the rug, pointed to the evil thing, and called God to witness that slavery was an abomination. This goaded the southerners to call God to witness that slavery was a blessing, that history and Scripture proved it, and that emancipation was a brutal and inhuman act. Thus, as many times before and since, was the Almighty placed by the fighting consciences of his children upon the horns of their dilemma.

3

The first rolling back of the rug occurred immediately. When Missouri submitted for the approval of Congress its state constitution, an article of that instrument roused the ire of northern members to a new explosive point. The article ordered the state legislature to "pass such laws as may be necessary to prevent free negroes or mulattoes from coming to or settling in this State under any pretext whatever." This insult to men who were citizens in the free states was declared a violation of the federal Constitution, which expressly stipulated that "the citizens of each State shall be entitled to all the privileges and immunities of citizens of the several States." [9] To this Charles Cotesworth Pinckney, who had written this clause in the federal Constitution in 1787, replied that

[7] *Abridgment of the Debates of Congress*, T. H. Benton, editor (New York, 1858), VI, 568, 569.

[8] A clear, compact history of the compromise is given in 46 pages by James Albert Woodburn in American Historical Association, *Annual Report, 1893*, pp. 251–297.

[9] Article IV, Section 2.

"at the time I drew that constitution, I perfectly knew that there did not then exist such a thing in the Union as a black or colored citizen, nor could I have conceived it possible such a thing could ever have existed in it." [1]

Perhaps it had taken thirty-four years for this concept to become credible even in the free states, but in 1821 northern members of Congress leaped to their feet to confirm its reality. John Quincy Adams of Massachusetts, then secretary of state, was so stirred by the debate that he made a confession to his diary which a decade earlier would surely have been regarded as treasonable. Referring to the offensive article in the Missouri constitution, he wrote:

That article was in itself a dissolution of the Union. If acquiesced in, it would change the terms of the federal compact—change its terms by robbing thousands of citizens of their rights. And what citizens? The poor, the unfortunate, the helpless. Already cursed by the mere color of their skin, already doomed by their complexion to drudge in the lowest offices of society . . . this barbarous article deprives them of the little remnant of right yet left them—their rights as citizens and as men. . . . I would defend them should the dissolution of the Union be the consequence. . . . If slavery be the destined sword in the hand of the destroying angel which is to sever the ties of this Union, the same sword will cut in sunder the bonds of slavery itself. . . . It seems to me that its result must be the extirpation of slavery from this whole continent; and, calamitous and desolating as this course of events in its progress must be, so glorious would be its final issue, that, as God shall judge me, I dare not say that it is not to be desired.[2]

Thus the whole question was reopened and many thousands of words were spoken—both humanitarian and political—and no one any longer hesitated to mention the sword that hung over the nation in its forty-sixth year. The political digressions included a powerful argument against the constitutional provision for representation in the House which permitted slave states to compute each slave as three fifths of a man in the apportionment.[3]

[1] *Annals of Congress*, 16th Congress: Second Session, column 1134 (February 13, 1821).

[2] John Quincy Adams: Diary, November 29, 1820, in *Memoirs*, C. F. Adams, editor (Philadelphia, 1875), V, 209, 210.

[3] For discussion on this in the Constitutional Convention of 1787, see *Formation of the Union*, pp. 352–62.

The debate was ended—after weeks of dangerous heat—by some of the most innocuous "weasel words" ever contained in a resolution. The words "negro" and "mulatto" were omitted and the state was merely required to declare by a "solemn public act" its assent to the constitutional provision entitling citizens of any state to the privileges, etc., thus leaving to Missourians their own southern definition of "citizen"—the adjective "white" being inherent. In this way the rug was readjusted and war deferred. The "solemn public act" was passed, nullified until 1847, when it was wiped out entirely by a new act providing that "No free negro nor mulatto shall under any pretext emigrate into this State from any State or Territory," thus precisely obeying the original state constitution's demand. Missouri thus declared her independence of the Union which had admitted her on the basis of equality with the other states.

The regional fight that ensued and was carried on with occasional interruptions for the next forty years belongs to other chapters in the sequences of the regional conscience rather than in the part of our story that is dedicated to the westward movement. There was, however, one circumstance resulting from the spread of the cotton kingdom along the Gulf states and beyond the Mississippi that had a more profound effect upon the Virginian conscience and provided more ammunition for the northern moralists than any other in the history of American Negro slavery.

4

As we have seen, the need for slaves in Virginia had steadily declined. Virginia was not part of the cotton kingdom. The Tidewater was dedicated to tobacco, and as the land became progressively exhausted by this exigent crop, its culture became more expensive and less profitable. The slaves, however, in the normal course had increased, and thoughtful Virginians as they contemplated the census figures grew alarmed.

In 1790 the whites in Virginia had outnumbered the blacks by 25,000. Ten years later the Negro population had increased until it was 3,000 in excess of the white. From this point the proportion grew steadily in favor of the blacks. In 1810 they led by 48,000;

in 1820 by 65,000; in 1830 by 81,000. The 1830 census showed that fifty-six per cent of the Tidewater population was black.[4]

The apprehension caused by the growing black figures, however, was nothing to the wave of fear that in 1831 not only paralyzed Virginia but swept over the entire South. The cause of this was what became known as the Southampton Insurrection in August of that year when a fanatic slave led a massacre which in brutality and horror rivaled some of the Indian orgies of slaughter in earlier days.

The slave, Nat Turner, whose mind was steeped in superstition and his reason confused by the ignorant evangelism of Negro preachers, believed himself a prophet. In a delusion of grandeur he felt called upon to lead his fellows in a crusade ordained by the Lord. It was said that he had been inflamed by abolitionist propaganda, but there seems to have been no evidence of this. That his conceit had been stimulated by free Negroes is more probable. It is still more likely, however, that his belief in a true call from God was sincere and that, like many another fanatic who had been exposed to bloody chapters of such books as Isaiah, he was sure God's wrath was devastating and that he was the instrument of that wrath against the white man.

Having the kind of power over his fellows that the Indian "Prophet" Tenskwatawa possessed, he assembled and armed a body of slaves, and on a sultry August night in the neighborhood of Southampton, Virginia, they killed sixty-one whites without regard to age or sex. It was one of the few genuine insurrections in the United States, and it was quickly put down, but it seemed an echo of the successful rebellion in Haiti and a portent of race war. Reports of it terrified people throughout the deep South, and measures of great severity were taken against the slaves of the cotton kingdom. In Virginia, however, it had the effect of turning consciences toward the basic moral values of the institution. This, of course, was not unnatural in view of the tradition established by Washington, Jefferson, Madison, and the others whose views on slavery we have observed.

The Virginian conscience on Negro servitude was divided into

[4] Joseph Clarke Robert: *The Road from Monticello, A Study of the Virginia Slavery Debate of 1832* (Historical Papers of the Trinity College Historical Society, Series 24, Durham, N.C., 1941), pp. 8, 9.

two parts, and the division was both geographical and economic. Moving westward, we have in the first part the Tidewater and the Piedmont; in the second, the Valley of Virginia and the trans-Appalachian country. The census figures of 1830 are a key to opinion in the various sections. In the Tidewater, 56 per cent of the population was black; in the Piedmont, 54 per cent; in the Valley west of the Blue Ridge, 23 per cent; and in the trans-Allegheny section (now West Virginia) only 10 per cent.[5] Thus, in the Tidewater and the Piedmont, slavery was the traditional labor on the great plantations, and the planters in general made heroic efforts to justify it; but in the mountains and westward the diversity of the farming, the chill of the climate, the Moravian and other religious elements in the Pennsylvania "Dutch" population that had migrated there, were all prejudicial to slave labor. The western sentiment, then, was bitterly anti-slavery.

The eastern opinion was not quite solid; individual consciences even in the oldest, the most conservative, sections were heavily burdened with the sense of evil in the institution. But politically the weight was in the East because there the black population—mere "property" as it was—counted in the representation. Western Virginia could send far fewer delegates to the legislature than Tidewater and Piedmont. It was therefore outvoted on public questions. Westerners were especially bitter because easterners were constantly voting for legislation that benefited the East and ignoring the farmers' appeals for appropriations for western improvements.

To the student who approaches this history for the first time, a puzzling question now arises. Why, if slavery had ceased to be profitable in eastern Virginia and in Maryland—when it was, indeed, a burden and a menace—did any pro-slavery sentiment persist? The answer gave the abolitionists their most powerful ammunition.

The African slave trade ended as the cotton kingdom moved into its tremendous stride. In 1808, the year of the constitutional provision closing the trade, cotton production came to 157,000 bales. But as far back as 1802, when production had risen, due to the cotton gin, to 116,000 bales from the 6,000 bales of ten years before,[6] planters in the cotton states had anticipated the coming slave short-

[5] Ibid.

[6] U.S. Department of Commerce, Bureau of Statistics: *Historical Statistics of the United States, 1789–1945* (Washington, 1949).

age by searching for new reservoirs of labor. They and their agents found them on declining plantations of Maryland and Virginia. At this early date, then, the domestic slave trade began to replace the foreign. A new class of men—the traders—operated between Virginia and South Carolina, and it was a common sight to see "coffles" of slaves in the streets "exposed to view, loaded with chains as though they had committed some heinous offense." Parents were "being wrested from their offspring and children from their parents without respect to the ties of nature." [7]

For years the more sensitive of the Virginia and Maryland planters tried to resist so loathsome a commerce, but year by year the demand in the cotton kingdom grew and the prices offered for slaves rose to unprecedented heights. When sums as large as a thousand dollars were paid by traders for "prime field hands," it took a stout conscience to say no. This was especially true if the slaveowner, by keeping his superfluous slaves, faced poverty and the perpetual fear of insurrection.

By 1816 the slave trade was becoming a major industry. Much of its activity had centered in the District of Columbia, which, with its Potomac outlet, was a convenient headquarters. In the national capital, then, the ugly scenes were played continually before the eyes of northern legislators, and it is hardly surprising that Washington became a theater of instruction for the abolitionists. That Virginians as well, however, were horrified by the abuses is evident from a speech in the House on March 1, 1816, by John Randolph, who said that by comparison with the domestic trade "the traffic from Africa to Charleston or Jamaica was mercy, was virtue." In one case, the Negro was taken from savage wilds and barbarous conditions; in the other, from civilization, "habituated to cultivated life, from his master, his friends, his wife, his children, his parents." [8] He said that the District had been made

> a depot for a systematic slave market—an assemblage of prisons where the unfortunate beings, reluctant, no doubt, to be torn from their connexions and the affections of their lives, were incarcerated and chained down, and thence driven in fetters like beasts, to be paid for like cattle.[9]

[7] Frederic Bancroft: *Slave-Trading in the Old South* (Baltimore, 1931), pp. 23, 24.

[8] *Annals of Congress, 1815–1816* (Washington, 1854), Col. 1116.

[9] Ibid.

He struck a note to which southern consciences in Washington were especially sensitive when he said that he had been told by a foreigner of "high rank":

> "You call this the land of liberty, and every day that passes things are done in it at which the despotisms of Europe would be horror-struck and disgusted." [1]

To show the extent to which the domestic trade had already gone, he quoted a sentence from an advertisement of a Negro sale:

> *"No objection to* TRADERS *bidding."* The increase in the price was the temptation for which their base, hard-hearted masters sold out of their families the negroes who had been raised among them.[2]

In the following fifteen years large firms grew up whose agents traveled through the border states picking up lots of slaves, who were then assembled in headquarters prisons until the time came to send a large cargo south by water or overland on foot to markets in St. Louis or New Orleans. The transported slaves were always chained, and as the groups or "coffles" clanked their way through the towns driven by a white agent armed with a whip, even the most hardened advocates of the institution would turn their faces away from the repulsive sight. The fact that so many of these driven creatures had lived happy lives on their home plantations—often as domestic servants or children's nurses in the great cool houses of the Old Dominion—made their lot especially poignant.

Such firms as Woolfolk, Sanders and Overley; Franklin and Armfield; Purvis and Company; and Joseph W. Neal and Company grew wealthy on these operations, but they were regarded much as the bootleggers of the 1920's were looked upon by their patrons—necessary but contemptible businesses. There was, however, the difference that the operations of the slave-traders were wholly legal and carried on in the open. Some of them, paradoxically, seem to have been men of good character and integrity. Austin Woolfolk, for example, one of the most successful among them, was said to be

> a most mild and indulgent master, and an upright and scrupulously honest man. . . . When he makes his appearance among his slaves, they gather around him with every demonstration of affec-

[1] Ibid., 1117. [2] Ibid.

tion; and even the little children manifest the most eager solicitude to share in his attentions.[3]

As this concession and the statement that Mr. Armfield "is a man of fine personal appearance, and of engaging and graceful manners" come from a bitter abolitionist, we can scarcely doubt their truth. But the same writer tells a harrowing story in the report of a conversation with a trader on board a steamboat carrying some fifty Negroes down the Potomac. The trader told him:

"Children, from one year to eighteen months old, are now worth about one hundred dollars. That little fellow there," pointing to a boy about seven or eight years old, "I gave seven hundred and fifty for last night. . . ." [4]

Professor Andrews goes on to draw this picture of the cargo:

Husbands are here whose wives remain in the District, and wives are now looking back upon the dome of the Capitol, which is still in sight, and near which their husbands reside, whom they are never more to meet.[5]

5

The accumulated torment, remorse, aggressive rationalization, sectional bitterness, and panic fear of insurrection poured out in the session of the Virginia House of Delegates following Nat Turner's exploit in the winter of 1831–2. This was the last public debate on the institution of slavery as such ever to take place in the South. Many Virginians were astounded that a question that had presumably been swept under the rug a decade before should now be so freely aired in all its ugliest aspects.

The novelty [says Robert] of publicly discussing slavery in the assembly hall was acknowledged on all sides, by those favoring as well as by those condemning the policy of open doors and full newspaper accounts. Conservatives prophesied dire effects from bandying wild schemes of abolition; they feared, at best, a serious decline in the price of slaves, at worst a train of new Southamptons. Lib-

[3] Ethan Allen Andrews: *Slavery and the Slave Trade* (Boston, 1836), p. 81.
[4] Ibid., pp. 146, 147.
[5] Ibid.

> erals, breathing the air of a new age of reform, rejoiced that the subject had come from under the old taboo. . . .[6]

A consideration of the topics discussed at this remarkable session reveals the dedication of conscience in this difficult period to the ideals of free speech. No aspect of the "evil" escaped scrutiny. Even the recent practice of breeding Negroes for the market became the material of speeches.

> It is a practice [said Jefferson's grandson Thomas Jefferson Randolph] in parts of Virginia to rear slaves for market. How can an honorable mind, a patriot, and a lover of his country, bear to see this ancient dominion, rendered illustrious by the noble devotion and patriotism of her sons in the cause of liberty, converted into one grand menagerie where men are to be reared for market like oxen for the shambles? [7]

John Marshall's son Thomas said that slavery was

> ruinous to the whites—retards improvement—roots out an industrious population—banishes the yoemanry of the country—deprives the spinner, the weaver, the smith, the shoemaker, the carpenter, of employment and support.[8]

Other speakers said slavery was a cancer, that the best Virginians were emigrating from the state to escape from it, that it promoted civil dissension—some even went so far as to predict civil war within the state: not a wholly fantastic suggestion in view of the separation of West Virginia three decades later.

Many remedies were suggested. One was to emancipate gradually and ship the Negroes out of the country as soon as they were freed. Others wanted immediate total abolition. Conservatives said emancipation was impossible. Some advanced the new argument that slavery was a positive good approved in history and Scripture. The debate ended in January 1832 with a vote that decided nothing. Summing up the debate and vote, a newspaper announced:

> 1. That it is not expedient at this session, to legislate on abolition.
> 2. That the coloured population of Virginia is a great evil.
> 3. That humanity and policy in the *first place,* demand the removal of the free, and those who will become free (looking to an extensive voluntary manumission).
> 4. That this will absorb our present means.

[6] J. C. Robert: op. cit., p. 20. [7] Ibid., p. 97. [8] Ibid., p. 22.

5. (Undeniable implication) That when public opinion is more developed; when the people have spoken more explicitly, and the *means* are better devised, that it is expedient to commence a system of abolition. The House of Delegates have gone this far, and in our opinion, it had no right to go farther.[9]

The people of Virginia never spoke again. It is true that many Virginians went north to continue their agitation. But from now on the principal anti-slavery voice that was heard in Virginia was the insistent shrill scream of the northern abolitionist. From now on the abolitionist conscience adopted the slogan, erroneously attributed to the Society of Jesus, that "the end justifies the means." By incessant pricks and prods the fanatics goaded even the southern anti-slavery conscience into aggressive defense. As we examine the history, read of the incitements of the slaves to rebellion, the lies and slander, the underhand indirect dealings of Puritan descendants in the slave business, and the cynical behavior of financiers and stock jobbers in New York, the impartial student must conclude that if there should come a Day of Judgement, the North as well as the South would have much explaining to do.

[9] *Constitutional Whig,* January 28, 1832, cited in Robert: op. cit., p. 36.

PART V

THE
Regional Conscience

Chapter XIX

The Moral Issue of Abolition

BY 1840 the concept of Manifest Destiny was complete in the American mind, though the felicitous phrase was not invented until five years later.[1] But it had different colors in different imaginations. Minds inured to regional traditions saw those traditions carried to far outposts in the irresistible continental sweep. The result was the maturing of regional consciences into forces of great and conflicting strength. Although the territorial conquest as far as the Pacific was generally regarded as foreordained, the sectional minds differed as to the methods God had prescribed for its achievement. To the southerner, Manifest Destiny could be fulfilled only with the aid of slaves; to the northerner, slavery would defeat the Almighty's purpose.

There were certain specific obstacles in the transcontinental path. Texas had broken from Mexico and declared itself an independent republic in 1835, but Mexico had never accepted the break and her shadow hung so fearfully over the Lone Star nation that Texans appealed continuously for annexation to the United States. They were, after all, American immigrants, these Texans: the Spanish-speaking natives were unimportant in influence. A distant parallel—still disputed—bounded the territory of Oregon on the north, and Great Britain was the powerful antagonist in that debate. California, the

[1] The phrase was first used in an article by John L. Sullivan in *United States Magazine and Democratic Review*, July 1845. Albert K. Weinberg: *Manifest Destiny, A Study of Nationalist Expansion in American History* (Baltimore, 1935), p. 112.

great avatar of so many destinarians, was still Mexican, but so thinly defended in its upper portion that its annexation would not be difficult. Harder would be the taming of the intervening Great Plains, stronghold of the ruthless, wild-riding, and fighting Comanche Indians. But the greatest obstacle of all was one of conscience, and here we are brought back to our tormenting topic. We must, therefore, approach the great western question mark through a further exploration of that crescendo of moral conflict following the events of 1831. For a time it halted the march of Manifest Destiny itself.

American consciences in this period were caught in the fringe of a wide European humanitarian movement. Britons, troubled by the writings of Dickens and Carlyle, were taking stock of the human damage wrought by the "dark Satanic mills" of the Industrial Revolution and using political instruments to reform shocking conditions in English penology. In France and Germany there was agitation to revise oppressive laws. England had abolished slavery in her colonies for humanitarian reasons, and it was disappearing in the Latin-American states. New movements were springing up in several parts of Europe to reform methods of care for paupers and the insane. Here and there temperance societies were forming.

When this tide washed the shores of New England, her people, who had always stood on the brink of a crusade, plunged into reform with a more frantic zeal than had been seen anywhere overseas. Temperance movements, based partly on fear because of new medical "discoveries" showing the ravages of alcohol in body and mind, tried to impose themselves on what were perhaps the freest-drinking communities in the Western world, and thousands of people quieted both appetite and conscience with patent medicines whose alcoholic content was concealed. Reform expressed itself in parades and mass meetings, in floods of oratory as tediously flowery as any in the overstuffed Victorian era. It was natural for this spirit to pervade an area whose people had always been zealous in discovering the mote in their brother's eye.

But New York soon caught it—not the Sodom at the mouth of the Hudson, but the western part of the state—and some of those most ardent in using religion as a springboard into reform operated in Rochester, Utica, and the towns of Oneida County. Here were the earnest if fanatical evangelist Charles G. Finney; the more thoughtful Theodore Dwight Weld and the gentle bachelor who exercised a somewhat abnormal protectorate over Weld's youth, Charles Stuart; Arthur and Lewis Tappan; John Leavitt; and others whose names have faded from the pages of history. Of these Finney's was the most dynamic personality; he drew the others into what was known as "Finney's Holy Band," which made a persistent "inroad . . . into the dominions of Satan." [2]

One of these dominions was, of course, the liquor traffic. In those days before prohibition legislation had destroyed temperance, men sometimes listened with troubled consciences to the barbed words of such reformers as Weld. By this time drinking had become a corrupting practice in many places. In the growing and more crowded cities, where the effects of alcohol were no longer absorbed by cold and hardship, men were misbehaving to their families and in their communities in ways adverse to the advancing civilization. Weld's eloquence was so sobering "that, more than once, liquor dealers who heard him went home and emptied their barrels into the gutter." [3] Gilbert H. Barnes tells us:

> Upon occasion, Weld's eloquence impelled liquor dealers to collective action. At Rochester, where he spoke on temperance at the close of 1830, eight or ten liquor dealers pledged themselves to abandon the business.[4]

"Collective action" was, indeed, becoming characteristic of the time. We see precisely here the origins of the spirit and technique of organization, so uniquely American, which in the twentieth century have added such burdens to our society. In the 1830's the countless new reform societies were beginning to federate. The varied objects of these groups

> were promoting home and foreign missionary enterprise, distributing Bibles and religious tracts, financing Sunday schools, promoting temperance, and saving the sailors. There were innumerable lesser societies, to promote peace among nations, to reform prisons and abolish imprisonment for debt, to stop the carrying of mails on the Sabbath, and the wearing of corsets.[5]

[2] Gilbert H. Barnes: *The Antislavery Impulse, 1830–1844* (New York, 1933), p. 15, citing Weld MSS., 1828–31.
[3] Ibid.
[4] Ibid., Chapter 1, note 28, p. 206.
[5] Ibid., p. 17.

Once a year, as Barnes explains, New York City, customarily a Babylon, became a Zion when in May the convention of the national benevolent societies met there to report the year's progress and "lay their plans for next year's assault upon the wicked." [6] As most of the societies had evangelistic origins, the conventions were accompanied by prayer and hymn-singing. But there was one curious psychological phenomenon connected with all this association, noted by that uncommonly astute observer Calvin Colton. The churches, deprived of the alliance between church and state, had become political in organization and activity! [7]

> The separation of Church and State, and other causes, have given rise to a new species of social organization, before unknown in history; and one of a very important and formidable character. . . . Within the space of about thirty years it has entirely changed the character and aspects of the American religious world, and set up a gigantic religious power, systematized, compact in its organization, with a polity and government entirely its own, and independent of all control.[8]

We may see here the beginnings of that zeal for organization for its own sake which has come to submerge the objectives of many of today's charities, societies, committees, and "leagues" for reform. This excessive, sometimes frenzied zeal, activating political pressure, created a force terrifying to the unorganized. Under the dominance of pressure groups the power of the individual, so dear to Americans of early days, began to disappear except, of course, on the frontier. Most important to our study, the collective impulse was a vital factor in crystallizing the regional consciences. Collective pressure in the North, when it focused on the abolition of slavery as a reform measure, created a "solid South" out of a diverse and individualistic region in which that wholesome conflict that is so essential to the health of a republic had been rife.

[6] Ibid.

[7] *A Voice from America to England,* published anonymously in London in 1839 as the work of "an American Gentleman" later disclosed as Calvin Colton of Massachusetts, is one of the most lucid, direct, and penetrating descriptions of the United States in the 1830's that can be found. It ranks with Tocqueville and Martineau.

[8] Ibid., p. 87.

2

The abolitionists were far more successful in uniting the South than they were in creating a homogeneous northern climate of opinion. Wise northerners understood that the Constitution sanctioned slavery, and that behind the Constitution lay the theory of the compact between sovereign states out of which the Union developed. The belief that it was entirely within a state's province to decide whether or not its Negro population should be in bondage was a wholly legitimate one.

But a still more powerful factor than constitutional consideration operated among northerners, wise and unwise alike. This was the concept of property that went back to the philosophy of Locke. Jefferson's substitution of the phrase "the pursuit of happiness" for the word "property" in the popular trio had not altered American minds in their view of inalienable rights. Slaves were property. If government or revolution could remove that property, might not all the rest go the same way?

These two arguments operated against abolition. In addition, there were more selfish and cynical reasons. Along with every other sort of speculator in New York City, there were those who were engaged in artful ways in the slave trade. There were others who were heavy investors in cotton, cotton agents for both Old and New England importation. In the North, where the American Industrial Revolution, coming late after England's, was making headway with long strides, manufacturers felt dependence on southern markets, for in this era both the planting South and the agrarian West were in all but name colonies of the Northeast. Finally, there were those who foresaw civil war and feared it as sober and thoughtful men must always fear that most terrible of all combat.

Many churches, even in Boston, followed the conservative lead. The clerical conscience may have reprobated slavery in private, but the organized clergy was reluctant to put road blocks in the path of mercantile trends. Thus, when the anti-slavery movement first came into New England on the coattails of temperance, prison reform, peace propaganda, and female rights and drew the true Puritans into its fold, the respectable churches closed their doors against abolitionist preaching. This was thoroughly in the tradition of the old theocracy: the higher echelons fought to maintain a *status quo* at any cost. If a wink at chattel slavery would help preserve the kind of aristocracy that both Hebraic Scripture and John Calvin ordained, it would be heresy for conscience to interfere. It mattered not that, in the crushing defeat of the Federalist party, the voice of the people had said that in this democracy a ruling class of merchants was obsolete. Boston, held in a vise between the jaws of State Street and Beacon Hill, must keep to the old form—or so, at least, thought the orthodox ministers.

Yet Boston, as we have seen again and again, was the battlefield of the great Puritan conflict. That conflict, from the remotest beginnings in little English villages, has always been between church and conscience. True puritanism, contrary to much popular belief, has never been static. Yet, through all its changes—through the rise and fall of theocratic power, congregational covenants, dogmas of "grace" and "works," thanksgivings, humiliations, bleak Sabbaths, whipping-posts, and witchcraft—one impulse has kept it alive: the incessant search for the "still small voice," the absolute partition between right and wrong. The greatest dissenters were no less puritan than the orthodox from whom they departed: William Bradford, Roger Williams, Jonathan Edwards, Solomon Stoddard, the evangelists, even the Unitarians and transcendentalists—all were in the same restless search. If Williams found it in the "filthy smoke holes" of the Indians or Jesse Lee in Methodist revivals, Thoreau in the woods round Walden Pond, or the followers of Joseph Smith and Brigham Young on the border of the Great Salt Lake, it made little difference. All of these New England Puritans were refugees first, in flight from the static and stuffy confinement of respectable churches. Perhaps the final definition of a Puritan is a trite and simple truism: he is one who knows no compromise with conscience.

Thus, despite State and Beacon, silk-hatted mob violence, and jabot-breasted ministers passing by with averted eyes on the other side, Boston became the hotbed of militant abolitionism. In approaching that movement, it might be instructive to consider an extreme case—a kind of flaming symbol of the relentless puritan conscience.

3

In the sea-trading and shipbuilding town of Newburyport, Massachusetts, in December 1805 a boy was born to a desperate mother and a drunken father. The parents were immigrants of English and Irish stock—the very antithesis, one supposes, of New England Puritans. Yet in the baby's first breaths the puritan infection seems to have entered his soul. In every look and act of the boy, the growing youth, it was evident that he had made a pact with conscience as inflexible as that of the most dedicated of the Christian martyrs.

Perhaps a psychiatrist of the new school would say that William Lloyd Garrison had a martyr "complex" or "fixation"; that he was an incurable masochist; that he was happy only under the lash or nailed to the crucifix of his obsession; that he sought persecution in the unlikeliest places and induced hatred in his best friends that he might revel in an ecstasy of suffering. Yet this judgment would be inadequate. Garrison's behavior was neither wholly neurotic, the result of glandular malfunction, nor the product of unhappy youth. He was simply one whose sensitiveness to oppression and sin was so acute that it transcended control and often submerged intelligence. He lived in a time when militant reform was in the air; when man's inhumanity to man was at one of its peaks. Few sensitive consciences could resist the movement to rescue the persecuted and relieve the oppressed. Garrison's trouble was that he shut the door to knowledge of his enemy. He refused to seek reasons. He was not interested in the causes of the sins he loathed. Nor was he willing to employ rational remedies. Thus, along with the incidence of good that accompanied his crusades there was incalculable harm.

At thirteen Garrison was apprenticed to a printer; in seven years of apprenticeship he acquired skill and, from working for several reforming editors, a passion for reform. He began quite naturally with temperance—a persistent obsession which diluted some of his later propaganda. He then agitated for world peace—a curious preoccupation for a temperament so prone to violence, and ironic in view of his later promotion of civil war. At last, under the influence of the Quaker Benjamin Lundy, publisher of a paper called *Genius of Universal Emancipation*, he entered his life work. He became Lundy's assistant, began his anti-slavery propaganda, and when

Lundy moved his paper from the West into the slave center of Baltimore, Garrison promptly got himself into jail for libeling a coastal slave-trader from his birthplace, Newburyport, who was doing business in Chesapeake Bay. When he got out, elated by this first "persecution," he went to Boston convinced that he could do more good north than south; and there, on that battleground of conservative and radical, he started the paper which in time would earn him the hatred or criticism of nearly every white man in the nation.

In the first issue of the *Liberator*, Garrison made it clear that he would countenance no dalliance with the rights and wrongs of Negro slavery. He would tolerate no "gradual emancipation," no piecemeal manumission, no constitutional or political consideration.

> I shall strenuously contend for the immediate enfranchisement of our slave population. . . . I *will* be as harsh as truth, and as uncompromising as justice. . . . I am in earnest—I will not equivocate—I will not excuse—I will not retreat a single inch—AND I WILL BE HEARD.[9]

From then on, he kept his word, to the consternation of those who sympathized with his anti-slavery views, and to the unmitigated loathing of those who did not. If the churches were lukewarm, he attacked the churches until he was called an atheist. If moderates talked about constitutional sanctions, he attacked the Constitution until he was labeled traitor. When wise abolitionists advocated political action, he attacked them because that was too slow. He attacked the kindred anti-slavery societies that counseled less violent language.

> How then [he said in 1834], ought I to feel, and speak, and write, in view of a system which is red with innocent blood, drawn from the bodies of millions of my countrymen by the scourge of brutal drivers;—which is full of all uncleanness and licentiousness; which destroys the life of the soul;—and which is too horrible for the mind to imagine or the pen to declare? How ought I to feel and speak? As a man! As a patriot! As a philanthropist! As a christian! My soul should be, as it is, on fire. I should thunder—I should lighten. I should blow the trumpet of alarm, long and loud. I should use just such language as is most descriptive of the crime. I should imitate the example of Christ, who, when he had to do with people of like manners called them sharply by their proper names—such as, an adulterous and perverse generation, a brood of

[9] The *Liberator*, Vol. I, No. 1, January 1, 1831.

> vipers, hypocrites, children of the devil who could not escape the damnation of hell. Moderation, under such circumstances, is deliberate barbarity, both to the oppressor and the oppressed—calmness is marble indifference.[1]

Southerners read this report of one of Garrison's speeches with anything but marble indifference—as, indeed, they had read his diatribes since his bitter attack had begun. To brand the institution of slavery an evil or a cancer was one thing; to accuse as a sinner every slaveholder to whom slave labor was the only means of life he knew, was very different. Gentle southerners, religious people with consciences, humane slaveholders who often felt love or affection for their black servants, men and women who in childhood had adored their "mammies" and played with slave children: such people were deeply hurt by Garrison's "blasphemous" imitation of Christ. Through the proud South the hurt bred anger, and as the Garrison fanaticism persisted, there was a renewal of the old fear. Having held him responsible for the Nat Turner insurrection, slaveholders expected him to stir further trouble among the Negroes. And while it is unlikely that Nat Turner's crusade was Garrison-inspired, the *Liberator* followed it by printing passionate letters from free Negroes urging their southern brothers to rebellion. It was soon discovered that strenuous efforts were made by Garrison's followers to distribute his paper among the slaves, the result of which was a concerted practice among southern postmasters of destroying all incendiary propaganda.

To focus upon Garrison to the exclusion of his fellow abolitionists may seem to give to our story a historical unbalance. But our story is concerned, at the moment, with the southern conscience. Garrison was the first to unite southern opinion to the point at which it could dictate to individual consciences. It is probable that southern politicians were more disturbed by the abolitionists in Congress. But among the people Garrison was the spearhead of the moral attack. His language spared no one south of Mason-Dixon. Even those who had never owned a slave felt that he was attacking their morality as well as that of the wealthiest planter. His diatribes seemed to cover every province of society, and although the vast proportion of the white population even in the cotton kingdom had no concern whatever with slave labor, yet upland farmers and poor

[1] The *Liberator*, March 8, 1834, p. 39.

whites alike—folk who had themselves despised the institution—came to feel that they, too, were included in the "brood of vipers" simply because they lived in a lost and degenerate land.

It was at the height of the Garrison aggression that the tide of southern conscience turned. Pastors preached sermons, pamphleteers crowded the presses, and professors lectured to prove that American Negro slavery was one of the great benevolent institutions of all time. The Negroes had been rescued from the hell of their native Africa where for countless generations they had been enslaved by savage Negro masters; they had been brought into civilization among gentle people and instructed in the Christian religion. They had continued to be enslaved, to be sure, but they had known nothing else in all history: what cruelty it was, in fact, to free such people and let them flounder in an atmosphere utterly unknown to the race! And the slave—unlike the white wage-slaves of northern factories—was cared for and protected by his master from the cradle to the grave, even in those years of infancy and senility when he could not earn his keep.

The institution was the "ladder of civilization." The great civilizations of Greece and Rome were founded upon it. It was possible for true culture to be achieved only if the unthinking manual labor was performed by slaves. But how much more benevolent was the American institution! In Greece and Rome slaves were the currency of war. They were the captives. In an enemy's army they might have been men of high rank. When cities were sacked, gentle men and women were often enslaved. But the Negro had been *born* a slave. He belonged to an inferior race—a race destined by God to serve his superior white masters. Not to accept this divine ordination was to fly in the face of Providence.

> Do they not blaspheme the providence of God who denounce as wickedness and outrage, that which is rendered indispensable to his purposes in the government of the world? [2]

So asked Governor James H. Hammond of South Carolina, and two learned doctors, John H. Van Evrie and Joseph Clark Nott, rushed to support the "inferior race" theory with ethnological testimony. And the southern churches were not far behind. By literal ac-

[2] "Harper's Memoir on Slavery," in *Pro-Slavery Argument* (Philadelphia, 1853), p. 4.

ceptance of Scripture the ministers were able to contend that both Hebrew prophets and Christian disciples approved slavery. Did not slaves build the temples of Solomon? Did not Jesus and Saint Paul enjoin the obedience of "servants"? Did not the tenth commandment forbid the coveting of one's neighbor's servant? Did not the word "servant" obviously always mean "slave" in the Bible? Here the good preachers in their zeal seem to have approached an exegesis at variance with their fundamentalism. But their "evidence" spurred Governor Hammond to new eloquence.

> I may safely conclude [he wrote after citing much of God's word], and I firmly believe, that American Slavery is not only not a sin but especially commanded by God through Moses and approved by Christ through his apostles. And here I might close its defence; for what God ordains and Christ sanctifies, should surely command the respect and toleration of man.[3]

Many of these arguments, artificially engendered as they may have been, were characteristic of the South. Isolated from the dynamism that industrial revolution was bringing to the rest of the world, untouched in their agrarian way of life by great scientific discoveries or technological inventions, immune to enlightenment in philosophy and religion, their defense when dialectics became necessary went back thousands of years to the classical antiquity in which, in their secluded libraries, the aristocratic planters were immersed. Or, to convince lower strata, they expounded the most Hebraic of Calvinist dogma, long abandoned in Puritan New England—the ordained hierarchy of mankind which the earliest Puritans had thought it blasphemy to supersede by social democracy. Perhaps the arguments helped strengthen already accepted southern convictions; in the North, however, it was believed that civilization had advanced somewhat since the building of Solomon's temples, and all the tragic, forced sophistry only deepened the abolitionist certainty of degenerate obsolescence in the South.

[3] Ibid., p. 108. The volume *Pro-Slavery Argument* is a collection of essays. It contains, in addition to the Hammond article, similar arguments by Chancellor William Harper, Professor Thomas R. Dew, and author William Gilmore Simms —all important to this history. See also Benjamin Stringfellow: *Negro Slavery No Evil* (St. Louis, 1854), pp. 9–35. Several pro-slavery arguments are reprinted in A. B. Hart: *American History Told by Contemporaries* (New York, 1897–1901), Secs. 25–9. Good Secondary sources are William S. Jenkins: *Pro-Slavery Thought in the Old South* (Chapel Hill, 1935), and John H. Franklin: *From Slavery to Freedom* (New York, 1947).

4

One by one, even in New England, Garrison's supporters dropped away. The Quakers Lundy and Whittier were shocked by his violent language. Others could not stomach his violent condemnation of the Constitution. Also, the quieter and wiser abolitionists knew that the only way to accomplish results was by politics and the ballot. The most effective anti-slavery men of all were those who built up the Free Soil and eventually the Republican parties, and the political victory came only when northern labor and western farmers became convinced that their salvation lay in opposition to the encroachment of slavery on free territory. This may have been an empty threat, but in those emotional times such chimeras had easy access to overheated and propagandized minds.

Meanwhile, as the southern states nullified what laws they disliked, in the North it became a dictate of conscience to disobey all laws favorable to slavery. The celebrated "Underground Railroad" became the nullification of the Fugitive Slave Act. No clandestine operation in the Second World War was more elaborate or more effective than this system of routing escaped slaves to Canada and freedom. To southerners, to whom slaves were wealth, this was sheer robbery. If an Underground Railroad agent or "conductor" was captured in the South, "lynch law" was held to be justified. By the late 1850's the Constitution seemed in danger of being scrapped, orderly process of law largely ceased to function, and what passed everywhere for conscience began to supersede government. It seemed evident that only dissolution could avoid anarchy.

To the end many—perhaps most—southerners believed that peaceful dissolution was possible. The best southern minds thought that the Union was a mere agreement among sovereigns. The overwhelming majority felt no twinge of conscience at secession. To them it was neither treason nor revolution. The act seemed hardly more criminally rebellious than it seemed later when the delegates from certain nations walked out of the League of Nations or the U.N. organization. It is true that there were many strong unionists in the South, but their convictions were not motivated by conscience. And, as evidence that the constitutional matter was not an issue of regional conscience, many thousands of northern constitutionalists agreed with the prevailing southern point of view—indeed, William Lloyd Garrison, the very symbol and embodiment of pure conscience, was strenuously advocating a secession of the free states!

The terrible war from which the American people have never wholly recovered is part of our story only in the moral aspects of its causes and in the moral lapse which was largely its consequence. It took four years to convince Americans, north and south, that Union was a basic physical fact, not a mere paper agreement. The last two unspeakably tragic years in the South proved inexorably that the southern states could not exist as a separate nation. Whether slavery or the staple-crop plantation system or debt or sparse settlement or lack of industry had brought the seceding states into their hopelessly colonial status was not important. Their gallant fight was doomed from the start.

The abolitionist conscience was quieted for a time by the victory. As we trace all their arguments—the lurid pictures of the bleeding slaves, the exposure of the stinking horror of the middle passage, the tears of Little Eva and the prayers of Uncle Tom—back through the philosophy of such English and European anti-slavery writers as Tocqueville and Harriet Martineau, it all comes down to an abstraction—a positive moral conviction, awakened by awareness of natural law and the inherent rights of man.

"Perhaps," says Avery Craven in his able defense of southern views, "the idea was always worse than the fact." [4] The puzzle of this sentence lies in the word "perhaps." Surely if he will review again the abolitionist literature and oratory from Jefferson to Sumner, from Crèvecœur to Garrison, and then reread all that he himself has written, Professor Craven will erase that speculative and doubting word. No fact in American history has ever fired a puritan soul as ideas have always done. And the people of the free-soil states, in the first half of the nineteenth century, despite all the mixtures and circumstances, were still predominantly Puritan in their moral judgment.

[4] Avery Craven: *The Repressible Conflict* (Baton Rouge, 1939), p. 38.

Chapter XX

Eagle Against the Western Sun

WHILE THE war clouds gathered through the '40's and '50's several events which confirmed Manifest Destiny had a profound effect upon regional consciences and, indeed, upon the future behavior and moral attitude of Americans in general. It was in these years that the curtain rose on that era of ruthless nationalism developed from the exploitation of natural wealth by boundless American energy. So powerful were the portents disclosed as the new scenes appeared that for a time attention was distracted even from the bitter sectional struggle. It is not surprising that Americans saw the hand of God beckoning them across the land, but in their rush to obey the signal they followed it in many an ungodly way. And their belief in the doctrine of natural right came in those years to have what Albert Weinberg calls the "bulk which comes with elephantiasis." [1]

On the eve of the Mexican War there was, according to legend, a sign in the western sky.

> Early in the spring of 1846, the story ran, a prairie thunderstorm overtook a party of traders who were returning to Independence, Missouri, from Santa Fé. When it passed over, the red sun had sunk to the prairie's edge, and the traders cried out with one voice. For the image of an eagle was spread across the sun.[2]

According to John T. Hughes, from whom Bernard De Voto got the story, the traders knew that

> in less than twelve months the eagle of liberty would spread his broad pinions over the plains of the west, and that the flag of our country would wave over the cities of New Mexico and Chihuahua.[3]

[1] Weinberg: Manifest Destiny, p. 41.
[2] Bernard De Voto: *The Year of Decision: 1846* (Boston, 1943), p. 3.
[3] John T. Hughes: *Doniphan's Expedition* (Cincinnati, 1848), p. 19.

Already the American flag was on the Pacific coast. In a month or so a large part of the vague "Oregon country," a land jointly held by Britain and the United States, would become a territory of the Union. Thousands of emigrants from all the states had already driven their covered wagons over the celebrated Oregon Trail from Independence, so that at least the area below the forty-ninth parallel was more American than British. Fanatic expansionists had reached greedily for a more northern parallel with the slogan "fifty-four-forty or fight" and had voted for President Polk in the hope that he would frighten the British out of their share of Oregon.

South of this magnificent possession lay California, loveliest "jewel" of all, still lazily held by Mexico and thinly peopled by life-loving equestrian Mexicans, gentle but proud, and a scattering of Yankee settlers who had sailed round South America on trading ships and sometimes married Mexican girls. Richard H. Dana, who made the journey "before the mast" in 1834, tells of these expatriates who had left bleak New England in search of a lotus-eating paradise where they might forget all of their Puritan inheritance. Forced by Mexican law to become Catholics before they could take up land, these men explained that "a man must leave his conscience at Cape Horn," [4] and surely their Calvinist ancestors must have turned many times in their graves at this ultimate apostasy.

That Providence fully expected the United States to acquire this newest Canaan from shiftless papists who could never properly exploit its milk and honey was obvious to many American citizens even in 1846—two years before the final proof appeared in the Sacramento valley. Thus, at the very moment that the traders saw the eagle across the sun, Commodore John Sloat of the United States Navy was waiting anxiously for news of war with Mexico before he should raise the star-spangled banner over Monterey and announce that Upper California was a territory of the United States.

But what was this "war with Mexico"? Was it a mere ruthless aggression with no other purpose than the acquisition of territory? Was it trumped up on the flimsiest of excuses? Was it, like a later war with Spain, a consequence of propaganda in a yellow press or forced by the oratory of demagogues? Or, as James Russell Lowell

[4] Richard Henry Dana, Jr.: *Two Years Before the Mast, A Personal Narrative* (Boston, 1911), p. 99.

wrote, "Thet the war is a war for the spreadin' o' slavery"? [5] Why was it that so many generations of American students squirmed with twinges of conscience when their history books opened to the Mexican War?

Few episodes have so harassed the consciences of historians. According to the revisionists, we need squirm no more. These scholars of new schools can usually be counted on to reverse traditional judgments. Their claim is that previously undiscovered material has disclosed new aspects. In this case the disclosures reveal that the contemporary criticisms of Lincoln, Calhoun, Giddings, Corwin, Theodore Parker, and a host of others were biased and untrustworthy and that the Mexican War was "an inescapable and a not inglorious step in the historical process by which the United States of America was brought to its present place in the world." [6]

One recent apologist writes:

> It has long been our national habit to deplore the War with Mexico as an act of unprovoked aggression, to belittle the victorious campaigns of Taylor and Scott, and while enjoying to the full the fruits of conquest to shed crocodile tears over the means by which they were won.[7]

It is curious that in this pure and magnanimous age of the mid-twentieth century when from our pinnacle we are so eager to condemn our selfishness of the past, we should suddenly be asked to regard as "glorious" the invasion of a weak neighbor and the acquisition of 850,000 square miles of what she regarded as her territory. It is particularly at odds with the normal course of historical conscience that in an era when we were normally disposed to regard any manifestation of Destiny as glorious, a good half of public opinion as expressed in press, pulpit, and forum should have been so bitterly and, indeed, treasonably critical of this war.

It is this opinion with which we must concern ourselves here. What we think or are told to think today about the events of more than a century ago does not properly belong in this history. But the conscience of the 1840's—which persisted for some three generations—is exceedingly germane. Our story is, after all, rather about

[5] *The Biglow Papers,* No. 4.

[6] Robert Selph Henry: *The Story of the Mexican War* (Indianapolis, 1950), p. 37.

[7] Alfred Hoyt Bill: *Rehearsal for Conflict* (New York, 1947), Preface, p. vii.

the moral judgments on our behavior as it occurred than about our mellowed reflection on events long past.

Before we explore the public response in the 1840's to the war with Mexico, it will be helpful, perhaps, to review briefly the bare facts of that conflict.

2

In March 1836, after Texas had declared itself an independent republic forever divorced from Mexico, Antonio López de Santa Anna, the current Mexican military dictator, thought he could teach the rebels a lesson and restore Mexico's power. Accordingly, he laid siege to a Texan stronghold in the Alamo mission, a group of buildings in the outskirts of San Antonio. The Alamo was held by 145 Texans (later reinforced to 187) while Santa Anna's attacking army numbered between 6,000 and 7,000. The tiny force held out for thirteen days until their food and ammunition were gone. Even then, when the attacking army broke through, the men fought with their backs to the wall, with clubs and rifle butts, until every one was killed—one of the last to die being the eccentric hero Davy Crockett. The defense of the Alamo was one of the great lost causes of history, comparable to Balaclava, and no Texan was ever allowed to forget it or the barbarities of the Mexican general. Soon after, Sam Houston led a Texan army to victory against Santa Anna at San Jacinto, and from then on, though the Mexican government never admitted it, Texas enjoyed a *de facto* independence.

For nine years following these events Texas perennially asked the government of the United States to annex it to the Union. Although her population was largely American and there seemed every reason for her admission, the government kept postponing action. There was every reason, that is, but one. Texas presented rich opportunities for the growing of cotton. Her people therefore wanted (and had) slaves. So Texas became another Missouri. All through the cotton kingdom the determination that Texas must be a slave state was universal. But the growing anti-slavery forces in Congress pushed the question back under the rug, and there it stayed until James Polk defeated Henry Clay in 1844.

In the meantime the expansionist fever had mounted to such a pitch that even the slavery question was temporarily shelved. Especially in the West, in the Mississippi valley, up the Missouri River, in the broad prairie lands, the restless people were preoccupied with thoughts of continental conquest. The impulse seemed almost mystic, as if, indeed, some supernatural force were sucking Americans into the vacuum. Men did not plan what to do when they got there, wherever they were going; there was just the inarticulate urgency to go, go—to sweep away every obstacle in the path until the final ocean barrier was reached. Every sight and sound, from the smoke and flame pouring from the tall stacks of the racing riverboats to the whistle of the wood-burning locomotives, seemed to have the single meaning.

Polk was elected on the expansionist platform, and expansionists crowded his Congress. The pressure was so strong, indeed, that even before his inauguration Congress voted the admission of Texas, slaves and all. This vote was partly, to be sure, because the English were carrying on an intrigue with Sam Houston which seemed to threaten American destinies in the Southwest. But Polk in 1845 approved it because it was an answer to the screaming of the hungry eagle throughout his campaign. Then, after a plebiscite in Texas had voted to accept the annexation, Mexico in protest broke off diplomatic relations with the United States. It was the Mexican government's claim that Texas was still Mexican notwithstanding the fact that it had flown its own "lone star" flag without interference for nine years.

Polk immediately sent General Zachary Taylor with a regular army detachment to protect the new state. Taylor's orders were to cross the Nueces River and to occupy the north bank of the Rio Grande. On this move hung the controversy. Only the most mythical claims included the territory between the Nueces and the Rio Grande for Texas. Polk then, despite the breaking off of relations, sent a "minister plenipotentiary" to Mexico with a bagful of gold. His instructions were to offer a liberal adjustment of the American government's extensive and legitimate financial claims against Mexico, plus many millions of dollars in cash for New Mexico and California. How many millions is not definitely known, as the minister, John Slidell, was instructed that "money was no object." President Herrera refused to receive Slidell. But a revolutionary party—which in Mexico City always stands just outside the palace gates—took this opportunity of suspecting Herrera of making a "treasonable" bargain with the United States, overthrew his government, and seized power. This party was hotly anti-American, and the news disquieted Polk and increased the chauvinistic pressure of the militant expansionists. As the distraught President sat, pen in hand, repeating, like Hamlet, the question "to fight or not to fight," from south of the Nueces the answer came.

No president likes—or ever liked—to ask Congress for war unless he is sure true provocation has come from the potential enemy. But when a Mexican force attacked General Taylor in the disputed sector, Polk's conscience was cleared. He did not stop to debate the boundary question. He assumed that it was "American soil" on which American blood had been spilled. Even the revisionists concede that the assumption was wrong, but Polk's apologists insist he acted in good faith, believing what the Texans told him. He wrote to Congress then that "war exists, and notwithstanding all our efforts to avoid it, exists by act of Mexico herself" [8]—words he was never permitted to forget.

The war lasted something over a year and brought glory to Alexander Doniphan, Winfield Scott, Jefferson Davis, John Wool, Samuel Colt, and others, and carried Zachary Taylor into the White House. No one can detract from this glory. The United States forces were generally outnumbered, and, as usual, thousands died from disease in the hostile climate.

In September 1847 Mexico City fell to American arms and United States marines entered "the halls of Montezuma," an event they have been singing about ever since. With the capture of the capital it remained only to execute the treaty of Guadalupe Hidalgo, by which Mexico ceded Texas, New Mexico, and Upper California to the victor. Out of the ceded territory the states of Utah, Arizona, and Nevada were later carved, along with the western half of Colorado.

With the treaty had come an apparent show of conscience of which Polk's apologists keep reminding us. With the army Polk had sent what Samuel Eliot Morison and Henry S. Commager call "an

[8] Henry S. Commager: *Documents of American History,* I, 310, 311. Professor Commager's comments in his introductions to Polk's war message suggest that the controversy between the traditional historians and the revisionists is not wholly ended. I, 310.

absurd little gentleman named Trist" [9] as commissioner to negotiate peace terms when and as they should be negotiable. Annoyed by some of Trist's acts, Polk recalled him, and there occurred what Allan Nevins calls "the most curious negotiation in the history of the United States." [1] Trist refused to be recalled. He may have been "absurd," but he was exceedingly stubborn. He liked the treaty he was negotiating, and he foresaw endless delays unless he concluded it. He could not ask questions or protest by telegraph or long-distance telephone: the telegraph was still trying to answer Morse's question "What hath God wrought?"; the telephone was still undreamed of.

Polk raged and fumed until the still, small voice spoke. Or was it the voice of New England and the furious abolitionist North? In any case, he forgot Trist, turned a deaf ear to the expansionists who were prodding him to annex the whole of Mexico, and sent the treaty of Guadalupe Hidalgo to the Senate, which, after hot debate, ratified it. This, minus many a long parenthesis, was the sequence of events.

3

From the moment Congress had voted to annex Texas, conscience had prodded the anti-slavery men of the North to unbridled fury. There will always be question as to whether this was a pure sense of right and wrong or fear of political power and lessening of economic security. There were a lot of what aviators call "gremlins" crawling about under congressional seats as well as in the great exchanges of Wall and State streets. There was one, for instance, named Tariff, spawned of the new northern industrialists—a terrifying monster to the agrarian South. The slavery gremlin and the disunion gremlin were often in audible conflict, but, more ominously, they were often in silent accord. And there were the gremlins of party—Whig and Democrat—that kept biting senators and representatives while they were speaking.

Yet it is impossible to dismiss all the resounding, still memorable words as factional or the pure, hot passion as synthetic. Why should John C. Calhoun of South Carolina, one of the stoutest defenders

[9] Morison and Commager: *The Growth of the American Republic,* I, 492.
[1] Allan Nevins: *Ordeal of the Union* (New York, 1947), I, 19.

of slavery and the nullifier of tariff, join the northern chorus unless conscience had been overwhelming? For no one could suspect his somber words in the Senate of any other inspiration:

> Every Senator knows that I was opposed to the war; but none knows but myself the depth of that opposition. . . . On the passage of the act recognizing the war, I said to many of my friends, that a deed had been done from which the country would not be able to recover for a long time if ever; and added, it has dropped a curtain between the present and the future, which to me is impenetrable; and for the first time since I have been in public life, I am unable to see the future.[2]

And it would be far-fetched to impugn the sincerity of the young representative from Illinois in the House who was so emphatic in his certainty that Polk had been wrong from the start in instigating (as he believed) the Mexican War. In 1848 Lincoln wrote W. H. Herndon that

> the war was unnecessarily and unconstitutionally commenced by the President,[3]

and to the Reverend J. M. Peck later in the same year:

> It is a fact that the United States Army in marching to the Rio Grande, marched into a peaceful Mexican settlement, and frightened the inhabitants away from their homes and their growing crops.[4]

Lincoln never changed this view, yet he did, as he insistently repeated, vote for supplies for the armies, once war had begun. Here was the rational Lincoln, so different from the uncompromising Puritans of New England. Once Taylor and Scott had marched, he could not countenance the disaster of cutting off their supplies—however much he had disapproved their marching. In contrast was the stand taken by Joshua Giddings, representative from Ohio, descended from a long line of Yankees.

> This war [he said when the first resolution for war appropriations was before the House] is waged against an unoffending people, without just or adequate cause, for the purpose of conquest. . . .

[2] *The Works of John C. Calhoun,* Richard K. Crallé, editor (New York, 1856), IV, 371.

[3] *Complete Works of Abraham Lincoln,* J. G. Nicolay and John Hay, editors, Gettysburg Edition (New York, 1905), I, 351.

[4] Ibid., II, 25.

> I will not bathe my hands in the blood of the people of Mexico, nor will I participate in the guilt of those murders which have been, and which will hereafter be committed by our army there.[5]

It is interesting to consider the difference between the patriotic conscience of those times and that of 1917 or 1942. As in the War of 1812, New Englanders freely committed what would be treason in the twentieth century. In the Mexican War were added the voices of many anti-slavery zealots from other parts of the North. To obstruct a fighting army, to call the "brave boys" criminals, would have been prison offenses in the World Wars. Yet Giddings, some seven months after his first speech, had worked himself up to an even higher peak of conscientious objection.

> Can we expect Christians [he asked the House in December 1846] to remain silent, while reading the dark list of damning crimes which have been committed upon a weak and distracted people by those armed ruffians and murderers who have been commissioned by this government to make war upon our fellow beings on the other side of the Rio Grande? [6]

And into what discord must this, in the Senate by Thomas Corwin, have thrown the martial music at Buena Vista:

> If I were a Mexican I would tell you, "Have you not room in your own country to bury your dead men? If you come into mine we will greet you with bloody hands, and welcome you to hospitable graves." [7]

As treasonable to our view was the bitter satire of the Cambridge poet James Russell Lowell, whose Yankee dialect verse in the *Biglow Papers* "exposed" the war as a southern conspiracy to extend slavery. Ezekiel Biglow said, for example, of the star-spangled banner: "Thet air flag's a leetle rotten," [8] and Hosea Biglow openly encouraged the soldiers in the United States Army to desert.[9] Ezekiel said: "Ez fer war, I call it murder" and:

[5] Joshua R. Giddings: *Speeches in Congress* (Boston and Cleveland, 1853), p. 201.

[6] Ibid., p. 283.

[7] Speech of Thomas Corwin of Ohio delivered in the Senate of the United States, February 11, 1847 (Washington, 1847), p. 19.

[8] *The Biglow Papers*, No. 1, second stanza.

[9] Ibid., No. 2, last stanza.

Ef you take a sword an' dror it,
An' go stick a feller thru,
Guv'ment aint to answer for it,
God'll send the bill to you.[1]

And it would have been a brave minister, during the First or Second World War, who would have proclaimed from his pulpit, as Theodore Parker did in Boston:

> I maintain that war is a Sin; that it is national infidelity, a denial of Christianity and of God. . . . The political authors of a war on this continent, and at this day, are either utterly incapable of a statesman's work, or else guilty of that sin. Fools they are or traitors they must be.[2]

The question arises: was there greater freedom of speech in the mid-1840's than, for example, in the mid-1940's? An affirmative answer to that question would be inadequate. The true explanation seems to be that between the two dates a civil war took place and wrought, out of two regional consciences, a national conscience. Patriotism in the 1840's was either to the North or to the South. The Union, it must be remembered, was still insecure. Garrison favored secession by the North. John Quincy Adams preferred division to slavery. Yancey and other "fire-eaters" wanted a separate southern republic. Only such profound realists as Lincoln knew that through all the bombast and name-calling, through all the conflict of Whig and Democrat, of planter South and factory North and migrant West, Union was an irrevocable fact. The embryo of the national conscience was in Lincoln's mind.

It is inevitable that we should think of the war of 1846 as a prelude to the war of 1861. On it there was a split of conscience along the same lines. In it Ulysses Simpson Grant and Robert Edward Lee earned their first laurels and for the last time fought together under the same flag. It ended with the great question unanswered; indeed, less answerable than ever. But in the very year it ended, news swept the country that made Americans east, west, north, and south forget everything else—even, for the moment, slavery. For in that westernmost land of all, the final proof of Man-

[1] Ibid., No. 1, fifth and sixth stanzas.
[2] Theodore Parker: *A Sermon of War* (Boston, 1846), p. 7.

ifest Destiny had sparkled and glittered; California, the lotus-eater's paradise only just wrested from feeble Mexican hands, had become, overnight, El Dorado.

4

No part of that ultimate earthly paradise was more lush than the Sacramento valley. At the junction of the Sacramento River and the American River, which flows into it from the east, stood "Sutter's Fort." This was the headquarters of John Augustus Sutter, a Swiss who had established a sort of feudal ranch on a grant from the Mexican government. It had been the first happy gate of welcome to the tired overland immigrants who had been trickling in from the East. Sutter, in his great prosperity, with his herds and flocks of four thousand oxen, twelve hundred cows, fifteen hundred horses and mules, and twelve thousand sheep, could afford hospitality.[3]

A millrace from the American River ran through Sutter's Fort, and there, on the 24th of January 1848 Sutter's foreman saw gold. The Mexicans, it turned out, had many a time seen gold in many a stream, and it had amused them but seldom inspired them to separate it from the sand. This was the sort of thing the Americans could not understand in their Latin brothers. As with so many "backward" peoples, the California Mexicans' philosophy was to work only for a sufficiency: once their wants were satisfied, they sat down to enjoy them rather than look for more. That was why—the forever restless, forever migrant Americans thought—they were halting progress; that it was God's design that their land should fall into more energetic hands. It was the same attitude that they held toward the Indians, and the people of both these "inferior races" would have been enslaved had they been amenable to slavery.

The news of Sutter's gold spread slowly. It was too good to be true. Too many a tall tale in the American collection of fables had turned out to be a fancy of the boundless American imagination. Americans had not yet learned that all the dreams would come true, given time; that even Paul Bunyan and Mike Fink were only symbols of incredible truth. But when credulous men took a chance

[3] Carl L. Cannon: "Sutter's Fort," in *Dictionary of American History*, V, 212.

and tried and brought back nuggets and dust they had gleaned by merely swishing river water in a washbowl, men from San Diego to Bangor, from Kennebunk to Savannah, Australians, Chinese, Frenchmen, and Britons forgot wives and children, packed up and left for the goldfields—sometimes forever, sometimes to return poorer than they left.

The mushroom growth of California was a singular phenomenon. Half of the gold-mad immigrants had come by sea round the Horn, bringing the great clipper-ship era to its peak; some had defied yellow fever and crossed Panama, others had left the Oregon Trail at Fort Bridger. But California was isolated from all the rest of the United States (except Oregon), yet its growth was such that it was ready for statehood less than two years after the Treaty of Guadalupe Hidalgo. From a population of 10,000 (only 4,000 of whom were Americans) in 1846, it had grown to 92,500 by 1850.

The wealth, sudden and easy, brought corruption. Gold was new to the American character. There had been dreams of it, to be sure, and men had died for the dream in John Smith's Virginia, but wealth came only when the dream faded and the reality of tobacco replaced it. Gold had never been the goal of the westward advance, and the slow, solid facts of chopping, stump-pulling, clearing, and plowing, of building roads and then canals and at last railroads—these things had kept the advance even and the work hard. But now the glittering seducer seemed to tell us the sweat and privation were over: in the newest Canaan you dipped your hand in the cool stream and brought it up filled with the means of ease and luxury forever, for you, your heirs and assigns and children's children. So the steady march changed to leap-frog jumps or circlings round the land, leaving the vast western plains empty.

And then it was not so easy after all. You had left your wife and kids in Boston, and after a hundred and fifty days of tough going you found your stream and, sure enough, someone was there before you. You found another stream and washed all day and there was five dollars in dust, the price of half a dozen month-old eggs in San Francisco. Or you struck it so rich the first day it seemed a shame to save it all when in town the glaring saloons, the faro tables, the haunts of the gay, painted Mexican whores promised a night of fun. Tomorrow your pockets were empty, and you struck it rich no more. Yet even in the maddest days sensible men invested their gold in solid things, generous men shared their new wealth with the luckless, and there was a vigor and freshness, a naïve optimism, as counterpoise for the most abandoned dissipation.

In California in '49 and '50 we see assembled all things American as the years had formed them. Distilled from the mass of greedy, generous, drunk, healthy, reckless, sensible humanity was that essence which by the end of this decade had become unique in all the world. California was the crucible, gold the catalyst that brought it forth. In California, sectionalism, the prejudices of North and South and East, were forgotten. In such an atmosphere there could be no preponderance of evil. The orgies were momentary and regretted. The victims were usually beaten in a fair fight. Beneath everything the foundation was too solid; on the surface the air was too invigorating for decay to flourish. As Stephen Benét in his great poem wrote of all the good and bad ingredients of the American frontier,

> *Receive them all—and should you choose to touch them*
> *With one slant ray of quick American light,*
> *Even the dust will have no power to smutch them,*
> *Even the worst will glitter in the night.*[4]

The residue of evil after the first brief gold rush was over was a product, not of the placer miners, but of large operators behind the scenes. Much of it was in evidence after the gold got East and found its way into the large-scale gambling incidental to the capitalization of new business and industry. We shall encounter this more directly in the post-bellum Sierra bonanzas to which the early gold fever led. But the corruption that caused the most extensive lapse in the American conscience came not with the fact but with the idea of gold, when the forward-looking imagination turned from the concept of land wealth to that of money wealth. This mutation brought the worm through to the puritan core.

5

By 1850 the California fable had crystallized into hard fact, and the hundred thousand residents were clamoring for statehood. But

[4] From *John Brown's Body,* Rinehart & Co. Copyright 1927, 1928, by Stephen Vincent Benét; copyright renewed 1955, 1956, by Rosemary Carr Benét.

they would have no slavery. A majority wanted the state constitution to forbid it.

The attitude of California brought into sharp focus a scene of the irrepressible conflict that had developed in Washington. The celebrated "Wilmot Proviso" hung threatening southern ambition. If passed, it would forbid slavery in the land acquired by the treaty with Mexico. Across the northern path stood the new drastic Fugitive Slave bill aimed to wreck the Underground Railroad. How to resolve these problems and yet admit California as a free state taxed the most astute strategic minds.

Fortunately, there were wise men in Washington from both sides of Mason-Dixon who dreaded split more than any peril. With the Compromise of 1850 they were able to keep the peace for one more decade. The Fugitive Slave law passed. The slave trade was prohibited in the District of Columbia. New Mexico and Utah territories were to be free of restriction as to slavery. And California, the gargantuan infant, was to be admitted as a free state in which, by its people's own wish, involuntary servitude should be forever banned. It was an uneasy bargain made to the obbligato of bitter laments on both sides, but it was a last, despairing hope.

Chapter XXI

Urban Morality

At mid-century the American scene presented a set of paradoxes and contrasts more curious, more striking, than ever before or since. It was a time of transition in morals and mores such as can occur only to a people that has come suddenly upon something too big for it. The new wealth, the new space, the new speed, the new inpouring of a vast human stream—these things were overwhelming; they split the people in two—into those who could meet the impact and those who could not, the triumphant and the defeated.

The industrial revolution had hit the East with full force and the stream of gold had come from the far West to meet it. Whether the gold was real metal or only promise, it supplied fluid capital for the industries coming up like mushrooms in the night in the old northern states, and for the railroads that were already planting new industries in what was now the "middle" West. The news of new building, new growth, came crowding over the wires, and fortunes rose and fell at the click of a telegraph key. A thousand schemes died every day in the hatching; another thousand grew into giants between dawn and nightfall.

Gold, new inventions, new methods of production, the huge wheat yield and its mechanized harvest that forced railroads and lake transport beyond capacity, and the rocket rises of land values—swamp or wood lot—brought an orgy of gambling. The axis of the nation's roulette wheel was now in Illinois: the most prodigal players sat in New York watching its periphery, stacking their chips against fictional futures that miraculously turned into money. Old, simple methods of exchange had disappeared; the romantic mysteries of high finance had replaced them. In that city without a conscience men were fascinated by the new toy—stock turned malleable by the magic of the telegraph—and the temptation to mold it to a heart's desire was like the lure to a child of a lump of clay coming suddenly into its hands. In such exciting times God and religion were postponed, and moral scruples were no longer allowed to blunt "smartness"—the new ideal.

Out in the swamp of Chicago a rugged population was kept alive, in conditions that would quickly kill their effete descendants, by the mere promise of riches.

> In Chicago the drains in the streets, the alleys, and the vacant lots were "reeking with every description of filth"; "all the slops of the houses, and the filth of every kind whatsoever, incident to cities, are emptied in the gutters, and offend the nostrils of every traveler . . ." complained a zealous advocate of clean streets. Michigan avenue was decorated with manure heaps while the contents of stables and pigsties were deposited upon the lake shore, a horrible stench arising from that "Gehenna of abominations." The rain washed this filth into the lake to be mixed with the drinking water supply of the city. . . .[1]

Hard metal did not change hands as the hopeful visualized massive buildings where the manure heaps now stood; indeed, already by 1850, braving the stench from the lake, "large warehouses and stores . . . splendid hotels, . . . public schools and dwellings, frequently magnificent churches"[2] had been erected largely on credit, and a man's note was usually final and no questions asked. Here, in the midst of aromatic realities, men tended to be more honest than in the cleaner countinghouses of New York. The Midwest with all its sinkholes and dumps was daily promising real, not paper, wealth, and for wealth that could be seen and touched and felt, paper was an adequate symbol. It was not worth while to cheat. When men could see business going on at the rate of thirty million dollars a year in a place that had been a nearly empty morass a decade before; when they saw twenty million bushels of grain passing through the lake port annually; when they saw the McCormick factory working with a production line annually turning out some two thousand reapers and knew that six and a half million dollars' worth of farm implements and machinery were sold per year in Chicago; when they saw houses that had cost five hundred dollars to build renting for four hundred a year,[3] they knew that they could trust

[1] Arthur Charles Cole: *The Era of the Civil War, 1848–1870,* Vol. III of *The Centennial History of Illinois* (Springfield, 1919), pp. 3, 4. For his quotations, Professor Cole cites *Chicago Democrat,* March 30, May 7, 1849; August 7, 1851.

[2] Ibid., p. 6.

[3] Ibid., p. 2.

one another's signatures—for the time being, at least. For the time being, the notes of individuals or notes on the so-called "wildcat banks" were accepted, though sometimes with caution; the entrepreneurs determined to turn the paper into goods before the inflation caught up with them. There was a robust conviction that, whatever happened, some good would result.

> On this kind of worthless currency . . . [a Chicagoan told a visiting Virginian in 1848] we are creating a great city, building up all kind of industrial establishments, and covering the lake with vessels—so that suffer who may when the inevitable hour of reckoning arrives, the country will be the gainer.[4]

It turned out, however, that the sufferers from "worthless currency" were few enough compared with the number of men who used it to make legitimate fortunes from Chicago's growth.[5]

But while the "American dream" was in full career in the West, a new menace was growing in the older northeastern cities which presented a darker contrast to prosperity than any other in all the vivid chiaroscuro of the period and gave southerners, harassed by northern attacks on their peculiar institution, a chance to point an accusing finger northward and to display the slave as living in a comparative paradise. To see this menace in full clarity, we will do well, for the moment, to focus on the city of New York.

2

Perhaps nowhere in the United States in this dawn of the Gilded Age was there a gayer show of wealth and fashion than on Broadway in New York. The street was crowded with the smartest carriages; on the sidewalks there was an incessant parade of richly dressed women and bewhiskered men with tall silk hats, embroidered waistcoats, and gold-headed canes. Facing the street were the ornate fronts of the great hotels of which New Yorkers were so proud, the opulent stores, the theaters and opera houses, the offices of commercial firms and international merchants, and counting-houses bright with the glitter of new gold. At night the brilliant sa-

[4] John Lewis Peyton: *Over the Alleghanies*, 2nd edition (London, 1870), p. 336.

[5] Ibid., p. 337 n.

loons were filled with the young "sporting" men engaged in continuous celebration, and on the darker side streets edging the broad artery hundreds of prostitutes stood ready for an easy meeting.

But if you should leave Broadway and walk east along Anthony Street,[6] you would come in precisely one minute to a center of destitution as depraved and desperate as any in the world. This was the "Five Points" immortalized by Dickens in one of the most unctuous of his horror passages in 1842 and grown steadily worse ever since. That this sinkhole of lost humanity truly "beggared description" is evident from the strained overreaching for words even by talented writers.

> Debauchery [wrote Dickens] has made the very houses prematurely old. See how the rotten beams are tumbling down, and how the patched and broken windows seem to scowl dimly, like eyes that have been hurt in drunken frays. . . .
>
> From every corner, as you glance about you in these dark retreats, some figure crawls half awakened, as if the judgment hour were near at hand, and every obscene grave were giving up its dead. Where dogs would howl to lie, women, and men, and boys slink off to sleep, forcing the dislodged rats to move away in quest of better lodgings.[7]

And so on for some five pages.

Dickens went to the Five Points under heavy police escort. Evidently it was, and for many years remained, one of the sights of the city, pandering to the morbid curiosity of hundreds of visitors. For a consideration police would guard these horror-chilled persons from attack and take them even into the houses so that the unhappy inmates could be seen in their private degradation. Ten years after Dickens's visit, a South Carolinian—eager to expose northern delinquencies—was taken into one of the dwellings

> and up a flight of rickety stairs. There lies a drunken female, screaming and yelling—only a fit of delirium tremens. . . . The next flight brings us upon a drunken beast in the shape of a man, rolling and pitching about upon the floor like a catfish in mud. Near by you see a poor little boy *pulling* at a piece of meat, the only meal he has had probably for twenty-four hours. Another flight. We enter an eight by ten room; . . . five or six bloated and

[6] Now Worth.

[7] *American Notes*, Chap. 6, in *Works*, Autograph Edition, Richard Garnett, editor (London, 1899), II, 101–3.

> haggard-looking brutes in human form are sitting or lying around the room. . . . Not two shillings worth of furniture in the room, including the clothes upon *the bodies* of the inmates.[8]

Such exhibits were not peculiar to New York; that great metropolis simply amplified similar contrasts in Boston or Philadelphia. In the 1850's no city of the northern sector of the eastern seaboard was without a scourge of poverty, crime, and drunkenness unlike anything seen or dreamed of in the New World since the first landings. There had, as we have seen, been "starving times" before and bitter hardship, sporadic crime, Indian massacres, and other troubles—relieved, always, by migration or by robust resistances, religious revivals, and reform movements—but this was different. It had a static sordidness like the foul air of a windowless room. There was no movement, no purpose, no energy, no will to resist in the slum areas of the newly crowded cities. A new smell had come into the Northeast. It was familiar enough to Europeans but alien to America: the stench of final despair, of immobility, of a poor that no longer cared, that looked only to the almshouse and the prison for salvation.

The answer was, of course, that the United States had opened her gates wide to the oppressed of all the world and the oppressed had poured in. In many parts of Europe the oppression or the hunger had been acute in the 1840's. The years preceding the great revolutionary upheavals of 1848 were heavy ones. Germans, pressed into military service, harshly regimented in civil life, taxed and crowded, were escaping in wholesale quantity. Marx and Engels had found in England residues of the industrial revolution that made excellent material for their Communist Manifesto. But, worst of all, the Irish famine of 1847 had reduced that unhappy people to a state of starvation hardly paralleled in modern civilization. Could there have been any other answer when the gates of the promised land stood so wide open that from Cork and Liverpool and Bremen you could almost see the gold paving in the streets?

The gates, however, were seen not only by the oppressed, but also by their government officials, who had another motive. Taking care of paupers and housing criminals in prison had entailed a huge perennial cost to British and continental governments. What means of

[8] William M. Bobo: *Glimpses of New York by a South Carolinian* (Charleston, 1852), pp. 95, 96.

relief was more obvious than the paying of passage money for these folk to the land of liberty? Perhaps the extent of organized movements to flood the United States with such characters [9] has been exaggerated. That it was widespread can hardly be doubted from contemporary testimony in public investigations.

> Our country [stated a report of the House of Representatives in 1856] has been converted into a sort of penal colony, to which foreign governments ship their criminals. It is not only the thriftless poor who come hither, spending their last cent in crossing the Atlantic to add to the burden of our poor laws . . . but inmates of the prisons of Europe are sent hither by their governments to prey upon society and to contaminate our people with their vices.[1]

Only since 1840 had immigration grown into monstrous figures. In the decade of the '30's the total from all countries had been less than 600,000. In the '40's this had jumped to nearly 1,750,000; in the '50's more than 2,500,000 came to the United States. By far the largest proportion came from Germany and Ireland: from 1840 to 1860, there were something less than 1,500,000 Germans and above 1,500,000 Irish. Most of the immigrants entered northern ports—Boston, New York, and Philadelphia, with New York taking the largest share.

The Germans tended to move west and added their numbers to the populations of Cincinnati, St. Louis, Chicago, and Milwaukee. The Irish remained where they landed. Perhaps the Germans were more enterprising and possessed more skills. Certain it is that most of the Irish were at the end of their rope when they arrived. Many were unemployable. Many had been wards of charity at home. They were generally unpopular among native Americans. There was still a strong prejudice against their religion. Except in domestic service, they fitted uneasily into the available jobs. It is true that Irish women helped solve the "servant problem"—the poor girls being ruthlessly exploited by families who could well afford a decent wage—but this function took only a few from the street. The rest found solace in liquor and soon filled the jails, the hospitals, the asylums

[9] This was not, of course, unprecedented. In colonial days such a quantity of felons was sent over from England that Franklin suggested that the colonists return the kindness by sending back shiploads of American rattlesnakes.

[1] House Report No. 359, 34th Congress, 1st Session, 1856, p. 1. The report contains affidavits and other testimony to support its contention.

for lunatics and imbeciles, the children's reformatories, and the poorhouses.

By the middle of the decade New York had nearly as many foreign as native citizens, Boston and Philadelphia half as many. In 1855 in Philadelphia, out of 30,000 arrests for drunkenness and breaches of the peace, 26,000 were of foreigners. In the same year in New York 32,703 were picked up for drunkenness and crowded into the city prisons: of these, 27,338 were foreigners. The proportion is suggested by the record of a single week in midsummer of that year when 252 foreigners were arrested for drunkenness in New York: of these 211 were Irish, 16 Scotch, 12 English, 7 German, 3 French, and 3 Welsh. For the whole country, census returns from 1830 to 1850 showed a population increase of 61 per cent and a simultaneous increase of pauperism of 706 per cent. In New York State in 1855 one out of every seventeen persons was a pauper.[2]

Juvenile delinquency seems to have been as much a problem as that of a later day. In 1849 in Boston there were 1,066 arrests of children between six and sixteen for vagrancy. The parents of 103 of these were Americans; of 963, foreigners. In the same year in New York, two thirds of the 2,955 vagrant children picked up were females between eight and sixteen. That this condition worsened rapidly is evident from a sentence of the same report describing juvenile delinquency three years later.

> It has been stated in the public journals, that of 16,000 commitments for crimes in New York City, during 1852, *at least one-fourth* were minors, and that no less *than 10,000 children are daily suffering all the evils of vagrancy.*[3]

Even the zealous reformers, in the time they could spare from abolition, could not cope with the rising tide. A group of heroic women and clergymen braved the stench and obscenity of the Five Points and established a mission in its center in 1854, yet, as the autobiography of Jacob Riis shows, conditions there twenty years later were not greatly improved.[4] The Association for Improving the Condition of the Poor in 1852 issued a disheartened report of efforts in New York to ameliorate the diseases of poverty.

[2] Ibid., pp. 4, 5.
[3] Ibid., p. 16.
[4] Jacob Riis: *The Making of an American* (New York, 1902), pp. 235 ff.

During the past year [it stated], nearly 80,000 persons of this class, exclusive of those in the Alms-house and Emigration Hospitals, were gratuitously attended and prescribed for by three of our City Dispensaries.[5]

Misdemeanors soon grew into crimes, and in every seaboard city large areas were unsafe for respectable people. Robberies and burglaries increased in size and daring; murder and arson became commonplace; the police, unable to meet the crime wave, often grew corrupt and protected only those who could pay for protection.

Behind all of this maladjustment stood a background of man's inhumanity to man that nearly parallels that of the slave trade. And ahead of it, too, stood circumstances that gave the southerner material for another of his irrelevant protests.

3

The mass emigration from Europe provided a succession of field days for the shipowners and their agents. The business was divided between British and American firms. There were Grimshaw of Liverpool and the affiliated Thompsons of New York. In New York also were W. & J. Tapscott, Douglas Robinson & Company, Rawson and McMurray, and Roche Brothers & Company. "A conspicuous American was William F. Harnden . . . who is said to have brought 100,000 immigrants to the country." [6]

As in the slave trade, the more passengers that could be crowded into a ship the more profitable the voyage. As the traffic would not bear a higher fare than twenty or twenty-five dollars a passenger, crowding to the point of indecency was necessary.

> The ordinary ship of the period [Robert G. Albion tells us] had two decks; and the immigrants were normally carried in the " 'tween decks" between the upper and the lower. . . . Frequently there was less than six feet between decks, so that a tall man could not stand erect. Seldom were there any port holes: the only ventilation came through the hatchways which were generally fastened down in bad weather. A few hanging lamps gave a fitful light in an

[5] New York Association for Improving the Condition of the Poor, *Annual Report, 1852*, p. 33.

[6] Robert G. Albion: *The Rise of New York Port* (New York, 1939), p. 340.

> atmosphere which grew every hour more foul. Eager to make the most of the space which they had chartered, the shippers erected tiers of wooden benches so close together that there was hardly room to pass between them and that scant space was inevitably cluttered with luggage. Naturally the number of immigrants who could be crowded into the bunks was not as great as the number of slaves, who, chained together and lying "spoon fashion" had been jammed into Liverpool vessels of similar size. Nevertheless, the steerage shippers got extremely effective results. . . .[7]

Disease bred on shipboard, and it was not surprising that when the immigrants landed, epidemics started in the port cities; hospitals and welfare agencies—such as existed—were heavily burdened. Sometimes when a ship was blown off its course the food would give out and the passengers, required to bring their own supplies, would starve. In the indecent crowding, women were often raped or easily seduced and arrived pregnant with a bastard child to add to the communities' burdens. Several shocking disasters occurred in which captain, officers, crew, and cabin passengers would take to the boats, leaving the immigrants to drown or burn. In one such case some four hundred steerage passengers were left to die in a burning ship.[8] In 1853 cholera afflicted the passengers of forty-seven ships, and nearly two thousand immigrants died at sea.[9] Perhaps these people were fortunate to escape the multiple miseries that so many others suffered in the land of promise, but the tragedies cast a heavy shadow over the boom period that followed the discovery of Sacramento gold.

Once he had landed, the immigrant's experiences usually robbed him of what resources, courage, or energy remained to him. In the 1840's and early 1850's every port was infested with a species of human vermin—the "runners" and the boardinghouse-keepers. Runners would accost an immigrant, persuade him to go to a certain boardinghouse, sometimes even seizing his luggage. Others were employed by hotels, railroads, river-transportation companies, or promoters of western land. The runners were former immigrants themselves who spoke the language of the newcomers and thus won their confidence.

[7] Ibid., pp. 341, 342. In general, conditions on American and German ships were better than those on British packets, but they were bad enough.

[8] Ibid., p. 345.

[9] Ibid., p. 348.

For an exorbitant price an unsuspecting immigrant would be given a neatly-printed ticket, with a picture of a steamboat, railway train, and canal packet on it, and assured that he was getting rapid first-class passage to a western destination. Actually he was being given the cheapest and slowest passage. He would be taken to a lodging-house which rooked him; he would be overcharged for every article he bought; he would be deluded with false offers of employment. The Commissioners of Emigration estimated that in 1854 these swindlers plundered immigrants in New York of two and a half millions in money and property; with the result that thousands of the newcomers fell upon charity.[1]

This explanation of why the immigrants remained in the ports they landed in stirred New York authorities at last to action. Here conscience was prodded by economic considerations, for the cost of keeping the aliens alive was raising the taxes of prosperous citizens. The Commissioners of Emigration [2] in 1854 decreed two reforms: they opened the famous Castle Garden to the newly arrived, compelled them to go there direct from the ship, and drew a cordon of police round the building to fight off the runners. They then imposed a tax of $1.50 on each entering immigrant. This was a local improvement, as the federal government had not yet assumed the immigration burden, but as the tide ebbed in the depression of 1857 and later during the Civil War, conditions in most of the ports grew slightly better.

In all this period there was constant propaganda to persuade the immigrants to go west. In the New York commission the slogan was "Keep them moving." When Castle Garden opened, the commissioners arranged for cheap, convenient transportation out of the city. The press kept up a steady pressure.

Westward Ho [exhorted the New York *Citizen*]! The great mistake that emigrants, particularly Irish emigrants make, on arriving in this country is, that they remain in New York, and other Atlantic cities, till they are ruined, instead of proceeding at once to the Western country, where a virgin soil, teeming with plenty, invites them to its bosom.[3]

Many accepted the invitation. Nor can there be doubt that many of the best American citizens and the heads of many great American

[1] Nevins: *Ordeal,* II, 285.

[2] The words "emigrant" and "emigration" were generally used in the period both for incoming migrants and for those going west.

[3] February 3, 1855.

dynasties arrived among the very dregs of the great influx after suffering the worst ills of the passage across. But perhaps the best answer to the "mistake" the *Citizen* emphasized was given by the New York Association for Improving the Condition of the Poor.

> Our city [stated its report], operating like a sieve, lets through the enterprising and industrious, while it retains the indolent, the aged, and infirm, who can earn their subsistence nowhere.[4]

4

As the industrial revolution matured in America, work in the new factories involved much drudgery, monotony, and repetition. From the earliest days of the republic, when there was a shortage of skilled labor in the East, there had been recurrent effort to build the human skills into machines so that manufacturing could be done by unskilled workers. In the textile factories, with their thousands of power-operated spindles and looms, the work could be done by young girls and children. In the '20's and '30's in Providence, Lawrence, Lowell, and other textile centers, mills were owned by men with stern consciences and deep religious feelings. There was then an idyllic interval for labor, reversing the notorious treatment of English workers. Hours were long, to be sure, but time was set aside for schooling and the girls were given quarters for rest and recreation and were comfortably housed. In other Yankee factories, wages were high and there were genial, democratic relations between the boss and his labor.

But as processes became more standardized and skill was no longer needed, many Americans grew bored, insubordinate, and impatient to get out and use their initiative and energy in other fields. It was at this point that immigration came to fill the gaps. New American bosses with less religious backgrounds welcomed the "inferior races"—men and women who were docile, subservient, and content with long hours and low pay. The result was that many of the people who escaped from the ports of entry were caught up in the industrial network and became what southerners called "wage slaves." This worked hardship on those Americans who had continued as workers, for the whole wage scale was forced down by

[4] *Annual Report, 1858*, p. 36.

the flood of foreigners. It was natural, then, for labor movements to begin in the '40's and '50's, but their fight was long and bitter, and in the years of the great industrial development of the country it was one of the important indices of the American conscience. The general belief among Americans that labor agitation was instigated by foreigners is the reverse of fact. Europeans at mid-century wanted steady work. They hated strikes or resistance that interrupted it. It was the Americans who fought to keep the United States from falling to a European level.[5]

Apart from the hardships caused by this lowering of standards, the conscience of the American worker was troubled by the degradation that surrounded him. With the mass of immigrants so amenable to exploitation, the land of liberty seemed to be dissolving. The chains the immigrants brought from abroad were being fastened on free Americans. As foreign docility and the low living standards of immigrants hardened employers, the chances for all of shortened hours, higher wages, decent working conditions, and the abolition of child labor dwindled.

Hours were normally twelve or thirteen, occasionally as much as sixteen a day. Child labor was universal. The normal income for a worker was between two and three hundred dollars a year. As no man could support a wife and four or five children on such pay, it was necessary for the whole family, including the twelve-year-old children, to work. After the depression of 1857 daily wages fell to seventy-five cents for an able-bodied man, twenty-five and thirty cents for a woman, while young girls, paid $1.50 a week, sought the easier way of the prostitute.[6]

These conditions were exploited in the South, and many sermons were based on statistics of "white slavery" in the industrial communities. If such capitulations eased the planter conscience, they could hardly evade the fact that, along with the "happy and contented" Negro slaves, the southern economy was steadily sinking while prosperity was steadily marching across western New York, Indiana, Illinois, Michigan, and Wisconsin.

[5] Marcus Lee Hansen: *The Immigrant in American History* (Cambridge, Mass., 1940), pp. 86–8, cited in Nevins: op. cit., II, 287.

[6] Nevins: op. cit., II, 291.

5

Of all the divergencies in this sharply divided period, the contrast between North and South was most menacing. In the South in these years the clock had stopped. It had not only stopped in relation to the North, but the whole of world civilization had passed it by. For industry, science, discovery, invention, philosophy, literature, and the arts had steadily advanced in Western Europe, in spite of political upheavals.

Inextricably bound to the soil by the plantation system, held to old semi-feudal forms of life, unable from the exclusion of skilled labor to develop any but occasional or sporadic manufacturing industry, tied to northern and English markets which it often glutted by vast cotton production, generally deep in debt to the factors of the textile interests on both sides of the ocean, and harassed by the ever increasing prices of manufactured necessities forced by northern protective tariffs, the South had achieved a more dismal colonial status than that of the thirteen British colonies before 1776.

That southern awareness of these discrepancies should have been incessantly aggravated by the fanatical utterances of the abolitionists on the main cause of their troubles is something for our historical conscience to meditate upon. These attacks were analogous to the abuse of an individual because he was suffering from a congenital disease. If the abolitionist had held to the basic theme that the theory and the system of slavery were immoral, that along with the Negroes the whites were also suffering from it in conscience as well as in economy; if they had offered the southerners a helping hand to find means of ridding themselves of the encumbrance—as if it had become everyone's problem—we might have been spared a conflict that has never quite ended. But by 1860 the ways had diverged too far.

Curiously enough, Harriet Beecher Stowe in her detonating story had considered these things. The opening chapters of *Uncle Tom's Cabin* show the true southern dilemma. But the only part of the novel that impressed southerners and northerners alike was the lurid portrayal of white brutality to the Negro. The southerner knew well enough that she had chosen isolated cases to bolster the cause, but northerners were convinced, not simply that brutality was always a potential in such a system, but that it was universal in concrete fact.

Thus, by 1860 the regional consciences had achieved their ultimate divergence, and the conflict that followed was probably truly "irrepressible."

Chapter XXII

The Victor's Conscience

IT IS THE CONSCIENCE of the victor, not the conscience of the defeated, that has become increasingly troubled since the Civil War. Remorse over secession has seldom brought a sleepless night to any descendant of a secessionist. No true southerner living today in any part of what was once the Confederacy will ever allow the word "rebellion" to be attached to the war, and, although the euphemism "the war between the states" is probably a product of the northern conscience, any suggestion that it was treason to fire upon the flag of the United States is and probably always will be deeply resented. Even slavery, the defense of which southerners contend was not the war aim of the South, does not becloud the southern retrospect. No one wants slavery back, but, once the shrill abolitionist voice was stilled, there came a general admission that, though it had been an evil, it was a disease rather than a fault.

Northerners, on the other hand, have tumbled over one another in their eagerness to propitiate the onetime enemy. They have wept over book after book reflecting the plantation way of life and its destruction, gorged themselves on literary spoonbread and juleps, mourned the leisure, the hospitality, the gentleness, and the nobility that have "gone with the wind," and dwelt with bitter meditation on the wickedness of such one-time heroes as Sherman and Sheridan. Northern historians have combed and recombed the archives in the search for northern guilt in war and reconstruction; they have outdone the southerners themselves in execration of carpetbaggers, scalawags, the Union League, the Thaddeus Stevenses, Benjamin Wades, and Charles Sumners of the Radical Republicans. Lately they have even occasionally re-examined the behavior of Abraham

Lincoln and uncovered aspects of tyranny which earlier generations would hardly have admitted about so sacred a figure.

It is the North that has extended the sympathetic hand, that has invited reunions of blue and gray, that has steadily urged everyone to "let bygones be bygones" while at the same time flagellating itself back into old memories. It is a southern pose, on the other hand, to remain belligerent, to bolster its own memories with pride, to wave the stars and bars on every occasion, and to hear no evil of Lee, Jeff Davis, or Stonewall Jackson. In view of northern exploitation of their own "guilt," this pose is hardly surprising. Without it the chauvinistic pretense might well have died out long ago.

In only one realm of social behavior, northerners in general seem to assert their moral superiority. This is in the treatment of the Negro. But there has been increasing evidence that this is no longer wholly a matter of regional conscience. In the 1950's when the question of segregation in the schools was brought into the open, a very considerable body of southern opinion, extending even into the deep South, has shown itself opposed to tradition. Such courageous citizens as Hodding Carter, editor of the Greenville (Mississippi) *Delta Democrat-Times*, have come out in definite opposition to the segregation dogma, and such powerful southern writers as Lillian Smith have reinforced this position with tragic emphasis in regional fiction. At the same time, as large, though less articulate, a body of northern opinion favors discrimination and shows it in occasional race riots disgraceful enough to build up new northern remorse in the future.

What is the answer to this curious aftermath of the most terrible struggle in the history of modern democracy? Is it the indomitable American love for the underdog? Is it a haunting memory of foul play? Is it a well-justified sense of guilt at having kicked a man when he was down? Or is it the almost pathological habit of self-criticism that has its roots in the puritan conscience? The southern regional conscience, to be sure, was critical enough in the past. But the South has escaped the full pressure that has turned a custom into a disease.

These are the questions we must try to answer if we are to make a scrupulous study of the American conscience. For never in our history have ethical guesses and moral judgments been put to so severe a test as in the fifteen or so years following 1861.

2

In the war it is difficult to find great evil apart from the overwhelming evil of war itself. It can never be quite just to pronounce sentence on acts committed in such an epidemic of passion as swept the country when the unhappy people stood on the brink of wholesale fratricide. We may isolate facts in the lying decade that preceded and judge them wrong. We may find many perilous blunders of judgment in the last months before the catastrophe. Perhaps the southern states could have gained their points by staying in the Union; perhaps their aims were defeated not at Appomattox but at the moment of secession. Perhaps, with patience even greater than that of the supremely patient Lincoln, negotiation could have been carried on even after Sumter. But these are afterthoughts conceived in cool intervals and at a time when we have learned much more about war than any American knew in April 1861.

And after the guns had fired, cheered by the gay crowds in their beaver hats and their crinolines along the Charleston waterfront, there were shameful moments. We know how Lincoln had to steel himself to suspend the most sacred civil rights, including habeas corpus. We know of the treason honeycombing the country behind the lines on both sides; of the useless slaughter in a dozen battles, due to the ineptness of generals; of the hideous devastation of property in the Shenandoah valley and on the line of Sherman's Georgia march; of shocking conditions in the prisons. But is not every one of these things inherent in war; is not all of it covered by one blanket indictment which at once makes all guilty and none guilty? And, after all, even in war there are balances. Even today it is difficult for a sensitive person to read without tears of the desperate heroism of the Irish units before Fredericksburg—a sort of compensation for the Irish draft riots in New York. And above all the horror still stand the dominant figures of Lincoln and Lee, examples of integrity scarcely paralleled in the world's recorded history.

In nearly a century we have never tired of retelling the stories of valor and disaster, of pomp and despair, of the secret conflicts between love and conscience, of the split families, the wasting disease, the feverish swamps, the fetid prisons, the bare, bleeding feet, and the long starving times. These are folklore now, but behind them stand the questions we can never stop asking. Many of them are the same questions that men asked in '60 and '61 and that the war did not answer. The questions that Virginians asked as they walked the painful tightrope of 1860, looking first at their southern cousins, then longingly north to the flag and the old republic, until the guns at Charleston shook them off. The questions of right and wrong asked at a thousand firesides in Maryland and Kentucky, in Missouri and Kansas and Tennessee, men praying to God at night for guidance and fathers and sons marching separate ways in the morning.

These are all part and parcel of war, especially the war we call "civil," and we can recite them to the end of the book and get nowhere. If we are to discover anything on which to base moral judgments, we must turn away from the armies, fascinating as that view will always remain; we must stop thinking about scorched fields and the lonely chimneys of burned houses and find backgrounds remote from the sound of guns. These there were in '60 and '70 aplenty, and some of them were not pretty. They have no color of glory and they inspire no thrill of patriotism. There is—still hanging over them—the stink of sordid greed, of cynical disregard for God and man. It is these of which we may well be ashamed.

But are there not always such backgrounds to war? Yes, but these in both kind and degree were peculiarly American. They were the joint product of new wealth and new politics. The wealth first and then the politics numbed even sensitive consciences. The moral disaster areas were not produced by the war. The parallel heroism and sacrifice simply made them more macabre. And the war gave to the cynical operators the power of appeal to the ideals of innocent men, duping them into dishonorable behavior.

3

We are able after the many years in which such wholly transmuting events have occurred to see the national scene in the Civil War period without distortion. To look only through the glass of regional conscience is archaic. That conscience has been superseded in three American wars by a national conscience of remarkable uniformity.

There may be strong regional consciences today in various sections, but they are vastly different from those of the 1860's and '70's, and in national crises they are subordinated. Sometimes the crisis must stand in extremely high visibility, as that of Pearl Harbor stood in December 1941, when the loud isolationist voice of the month before was suddenly muted. But to try to preserve either remorse or glory from 1865 reminds one of the attitude of Miss Havisham in *Great Expectations*, who kept everything in her house precisely as it had been on her disastrous wedding day, including her faded bridal dress, the decomposed wedding cake, and with all the clocks stopped at the moment of calamity.

In point of fact, by 1861 the nation as a whole had slid away from the high moral standards the earlier days of the republic had promised. This took different forms, north and south. The flood of wealth had not gone to the South, but that is not to say that southerners did not want it, nor that many of them would not scruple to get what they could by whatever means. Also, in the South, with its large proportion of mulattoes, it was impossible to deny that sexual intercourse between white and black had flourished, with the inevitable inference that it was often the duty of a female slave to entertain her master. The prevalence of dueling to uphold fictitious standards of "honor" may have been immature rather than immoral, but its results were no less tragic. There was, too, as appeared in the reconstruction period, an increasing body of businessmen eager for an industrial South who were far more interested in profits than in the war and who consistently engaged in trade with their opposite numbers in the enemy.

That there was more northern than southern corruption was natural because the means were greater. Beginning in state capitals, graft soon spread to Washington. Here the first inroads were made by the growing railway corporations, which issued passes freely to executive and legislative officials. From this mild lapse, which was seldom held unscrupulous in the lush '50's and '60's, there was rapid progress into the sale and purchase of votes. In the national capital, lobbyists were working like termites, subverting senators and congressmen. Businessmen who wanted favors made use of such go-betweens as a matter of course. Individual consciences were no longer guided by the absolute standards of puritan or religious-revival eras. The criterion was what was or was not "done." The group conscience was replacing the individual consciences. This was happening mainly in the cities, where business competition was keener than ever before and where one must either be "smart" or be left forever behind.

Western delinquency was more robust, more openly criminal. The sneaking hypocrisy of the eastern cities, where rich church vestrymen owned acres of rotting tenements and charged high rents to operators of whorehouses and gambling "hells," was unpalatable in the open spaces. The bloody butcheries in Kansas in '58 and '59 were frankly brutal, and one of the heroes of this drama—the mad John Brown of Osawatomie, whose soul "marched on" through the war—became a symbol. The conflicts of "bleeding Kansas," however, were in the fringe of war and were thus more normal than the blood-chilling Mountain Meadows massacre, in which Mormons collaborated with Indians in the killing of some hundred and fifty emigrant men and women in southern Utah.[1] That men calling themselves "saints" should participate in such an atrocity as a gesture of mass revenge seems to us a departure from proper Christian behavior, but to the "gentile" or non-Mormon conscience of the period any religion that permitted polygamy was not of Jesus Christ.

Farther west the gold had given out in California, leaving desolation and disillusion in the wake of its exhaustion. It would be difficult to expect sensitive consciences among the thousands who had braved or sacrificed everything on the path of their ruin. For years Californians had taken the law into informal hands, creating "vigilantes" to exterminate the natural criminals as well as those whom despair had turned to crime. This was a wholly American performance, this impromptu justice: we may find precedents as far back as records go. The process through which it went was routine: gangs of outlaws, gangs of makeshift "regulators" in default of police, then the regulators turned outlaw, and the period of uncertainty until orthodox police arrived. The courts were drumhead tribunals, horse-stealing was equivalent to murder, and the miner who, as the saying went, shot his man for breakfast was excused. But there was something about this kind of lawlessness, this quick settlement at

[1] This most shocking episode of the pioneer period was, like several earlier incidents, a product largely of neurotic fanaticism.

the muzzle point of Sam Colt's shooting-iron, that was more wholesome than the slow decay at the core of the body politic, and its scars were easier to heal.

Then, on the eve of war, a mountain shepherd, "loud-mouthed, haggard, slothful, braggart," [2] named Henry Thomas Paige Comstock found substances in the Nevada Territory Sierras that were to turn Californians east and set a little group of San Francisco bankers thinking so hard that when war came they could scarcely attend to it. The substances were gold and silver, and the discovery started the long dream of the Comstock Lode, a punctuation mark in American history that altered the whole sense of the frontier story. For now came two-way migration, the east-west marches that were to meet a decade later at Promontory Point.

Men shot and stole and claim-jumped at Virginia City, Nevada, and the men in San Francisco played checkers with the mining gangs. Gold and the war got to New York about the same time, but New York was equal to the combination. Gold became a bright toy in Wall Street. The men who bought and sold it profited heavily from the first northern war disasters. While men died by thousands at Bull Run and Shiloh and Fredericksburg, other men cheered in the New York Stock Exchange. For many merchants who had lost southern markets and southern cotton, patriotism was in the discard. Others were glad of secession because it removed those who had put obstacles in the way of railroad expansion. The fact that the war left the protective tariff in the hands of northern industrialists was welcome to the new tycoons, and they cared little whether or not the seceded states were ever brought to terms.

And these tycoons were waxing rich with remarkable acceleration due to war contracts. As always, technology advanced rapidly—a progress which benefited North, not South. Machinery was invented that put the productivity of shoe manufacturing on a scarcely believable level. The ready-made clothing industry got its first impetus from machine manufacture of uniforms. Not the least of the inventions was that of condensed milk. The making of steel on the English Bessemer model was perfected. New systems of finance came into being. These things combined to create a wave of prosperity that was certain to dim consciousness of the war's hor-

[2] George D. Lyman: *The Saga of the Comstock Lode* (New York, 1937), p. 12.

rors. Finally, after prodigious losses on the field of battle and imponderable suffering in battle's aftermath, occurred the scandal of the draft.

That the Union conscience could have remained quiet under the flagrant injustices and the mercenary aspects of the first military conscription is an index of the depth to which the nation's moral standards had sunk in 1863. No priority was ordered for youth. Married men took the same chance as bachelors. Exemption could be bought. Three hundred dollars got a man out of one draft. If a draftee could induce (by bribery) a substitute to enlist, he was immune to service for the war's duration. If the substitute died, it was not necessary to procure another.[3]

In New York the first drawings threw the switch for a three-day riot of devastating proportions. It was led by the Irish, whose love for the Negro had never been excessive, and whose worst sadistic impulses were released by the draft news. Negroes were not only killed but tortured wherever they were found. Eventually troops had to be withdrawn from the Union army and sent to New York, thus contributing to the success of Confederate fighting forces.

There were similar injustices in the southern draft system, inducing the poor whites to say that it was "a rich man's war and a poor man's fight." Exemption followed the aristocratic pattern, although substitution was stopped late in 1863.[4] There was a somewhat ludicrous conflict between the rights of "sovereign" states and the Confederate Congress, and South Carolina even nullified some of the draft provisions—a practice in which under Calhoun she had been well trained. This disagreement as to whether the Confederacy was a nation or a league of separate sovereign states, still persisting in the throes of war, suggests that even with victory the southern republic might not have long endured. For the North the Civil War ended that long difference.

In the field there were about two hundred thousand desertions from the northern armies and half that number from the southern. This meant one deserter for every seven enlistments in Union forces; one in every nine for the Confederate.[5] Under all the circumstances these numbers are not surprising.

[3] For an excellent brief summary of the conscription provisions, see Morison and Commager: op. cit., I, 601 and 601 n.

[4] Ibid., I, 603, 604.

[5] Ibid., I, 603 n.

5

The words that today come alive for every American child as soon as he is able to read or understand words were soon erased in the years that followed Lee's surrender. But they were words that needed to be put into force by him who spoke them, and when the time came to crystallize into deeds that rare mood of forgiveness, he was dead. When the echo of the pistol shot reached the South, many southerners remembered the words and knew that the jig was up.

It was not a conventional wartime speech, though the war was still in progress as it was spoken.

> With malice toward none, with charity for all, with firmness in the right as God gives us to see the right, let us strive to finish the work we are in, to bind up the nation's wounds, to care for him who shall have borne the battle and for his widow and his orphan, to do all which may achieve and cherish a just and lasting peace among ourselves and with all nations.

Of all the if's of our history this one has the most tragic implication. If Booth's hand had been stayed, the national conscience would be happier today. They might have called Lincoln traitor—Thad Stevens and Ben Wade and the others who hated him—but Lincoln was immune to vilification, and the same strength that had carried him through all the hate and intrigue of the four years could have taken him through the reconstruction as well. Our dominant thought of Lincoln comes from his gentle moods—to most of us he is a sort of saint—but his will was of steel, and nothing but death could have diverted him from his intent for the time of peace. He had, after all, more than any soldier, "borne the battle."

Occasionally a president rises above his party. Even the Republican "radicals" were afraid of Lincoln. But when Lincoln was dead they were not afraid of the poor "drunkard" Johnson. It has taken years of "revisionist" writing to show that Johnson was not really a drunkard, that his intentions were good, that he meant to follow Lincoln's lead in restoring the southern states mercifully to the Union, and that, despite his Carolinian birth, he was at no time traitor to the Union cause. The point is that the radicals were not afraid of him; they even dared impeach him on the flimsiest of grounds and, but for one vote, the impeachment would have dethroned him.

Lincoln's plan for reconstruction rested on the power of pardon which constitutionally belonged to the executive. In his speech delivered in Washington the week before his death he took no side on the current theoretical controversy on the status of the seceded states. Whether the states were in fact separate from the Union, or, though they had tried to separate themselves, they had failed and therefore had never in fact been out of the Union, was a question which did not agitate his practical mind.

> We all agree that the seceded States, so called, are out of their proper practical relation with the Union, and that the sole object of the government . . . is to again get them into their proper practical relation. I believe that it is not only possible, but in fact easier, to do this without deciding or even considering whether these States have ever been out of the Union, than with it. Finding themselves safely at home, it would be utterly immaterial whether they had ever been abroad.[6]

So, with certain exceptions, he would pardon the "rebel" citizens, and as soon as ten per cent of the voters of 1860 in each state should take an oath of allegiance to the Union, then that state might, on forming a new state government, be readmitted. The new state constitutions must, of course, contain provisions for the emancipation of slaves. The plan was without hate and without vengeance.[7]

But there were professional haters in the Congress. They hated the South with deep abolitionist hatred, and some of them, though of the President's party, hated him too. From the moment in 1863 that he first proclaimed his plan, they fought it. To them it was ludicrously lenient. It contained no punitive provisons. It gave no "civil rights, no suffrage to the Negro, for whose salvation the war had been fought. In a short time, under it, the South would resume its old arrogance, the Democratic party would regain its control. Finally, reconstruction was the function of Congress, not of the executive, and Lincoln was usurping it.

Lincoln did not accuse the haters (as some historians have since done) of insincerity. He simply disagreed. But his disagreement was

[6] Lincoln: op. cit., XI, 88.
[7] Commager: *Documents of American History*, No. 230.

powerful. After the surrender of Lee's army Lincoln not only had most of the people behind him but they were in an attitude almost of adoration. Generals who had scourged the southland—Grant, Sherman, Sheridan—wanted what he wanted, for combat troops are always gentler to a vanquished army than armchair fighters.

By the time Wilkes Booth came into Ford's Theatre on that Good Friday night in 1865 some of the states had already complied with Lincoln's requirements. But after that it did not matter. The radicals reversed his policy. Their frightened distaste for Lincoln turned to savage hate of Johnson. It is true that Johnson, the half-educated tailor from Tennessee, did little to make his enemies love him. Perhaps he did his best, but could anyone have filled Father Abraham's giant shoes?

We all know—too well—the bitter sequel. Again and again in lurid colors the scenes have been painted: the long military occupation; the march of the carpetbaggers from the North, becoming citizens of southern states, manipulating their politics, conspiring with renegade Confederates to pack the legislatures with illiterate Negroes, buying and selling votes for their private power and profit, raising taxes on the impoverished people and recklessly spending the money, inviting the lawless retaliation of such underground groups as the Ku-Klux Klan, and engendering a race hatred that has endured ever since.

There were good things, as the newest revisionists keep insisting, along with the bad—there usually are. There were honest men, south and north, among the crooks. Some of the state constitutions evolved under the provisional governments were excellent—in part, at least. Education for the colored people greatly improved, and much was done to aid material recovery. These things are all, no doubt, true. It is also true that conservative southerners—or "Bourbons," as they were called—manipulated the Negro vote to their own advantage and, under the new impulse of industrialization, to the hurt of the poor whites who clung to their agrarianism.[8] And it is further true that when the vengeful pressure was finally relaxed and the southern Democratic party came back into power, it used devices of surpassing ingenuity to nullify the fifteenth amendment and suppress the Negro vote. Thus, while in the reconstruction years

[8] Howard K. Beale: "On Rewriting Reconstruction History," in *American Historical Review*, XLV (July 1940), 822.

from 1868 to 1877 the North subverted the Constitution, the South has subverted it ever since.

It is still difficult to strike a balance. But the first step is to try to sweep away the cobwebs of sentimentality that keep beclouding the issues. For instance:

> Many of the severest critics of Reconstruction governments [says Howard K. Beale] hold up the ante-bellum South as America's nearest approach to Utopia. We need to remind ourselves constantly that it was this ante-bellum life that had fastened ignorance or inexperience upon millions of whites as well as negroes and that it was this ignorance and inexperience that caused trouble when the Radicals were in power.[9]

And he says further:

> We must cease considering Reconstruction as a heart-rending story of oppressed and oppressing personalities isolated in time and space. . . . Radical corruption will not be understood by those who insist that it was a peculiar Radical phenomenon of the period 1868–1877. . . . Similarly, the extravagance of radical legislatures can be understood only as part of a national era of expansion that affected Western and Northern states, Northern cities, and the Federal government. All of these were using public funds to further "progress."[1]

In other words, northerners would do well to stop making their repentant gesture to the South, saying: "We acknowledge and bewail our manifold sins and wickedness" and begging forgiveness from a victimized people who, until we maltreated them, dwelt forever in sweetness and light. Our conscience is still troubled, to be sure, but it is a national conscience, a conscience aware that evil forces were sweeping the entire country and that, despite a few great leaders, we were sinking rapidly in those years into our moral nadir of all time.

That Lincoln, if he had lived, could have alleviated the aftermath of the Civil War is almost certain; but even he could scarcely have held in check the full tide of national corruption.

[9] Ibid., XLV, 812.

[1] Ibid., XLV, 811.

PART VI

THE National Conscience

Chapter XXIII

Moral Paralysis in the Gilded Age

BEFORE THE WAR was two years old, Lincoln saw Union as a fact, not as a theory. It made no difference what view one might take of the federal "compact." Whether or not parts of the Union might have a "right" to separate from the rest, the physical facts forbade it. As we had settled the country, certain inexorable forces had followed the settlement with a definite pattern, so that, for instance, "outlets [to the sea] east west and south are indispensable." Lincoln saw the economic factors.

> That portion of the earth's surface which is owned and inhabited by the people of the United States is well adapted to be the home of one national family, and it is not well adapted for two or more. Its vast extent and variety of climate and productions are of advantage *in this age* for one people, *whatever they might have been in former ages.*[1]

Modern civilization, in which man created his own environment wherever he might be, demanded the movement of foodstuffs and raw materials from the places of their best production to the centers of their large consumption. We no longer lived on subsistence farms. The life forces of such a nation as this involved surpluses in Kansas, scarcities in Connecticut. Georgia cotton must go to Massachusetts mills to be exchanged for shoes for the Georgia planter and his workers. These things the people of the Confederacy would have to learn, but Lincoln saw them clearly beyond the fighting that went day after day against him. But, perhaps most conclusive of all, he

[1] Annual Message to Congress, Dec. 1, 1862, in *Complete Works*, Gettysburg Edition, VIII, 111. Italics added.

saw the inevitable cohesion of the states under the new forces of technology that made "climate and productions" accessible to all.

> Steam, telegraphs and intelligence have brought these to be an advantageous combination for one united people.[2]

The interdependence of the sections, indeed, was so strong that, even if a temporary split should be possible,

> It would, ere long force reunion, however much of blood and treasure the separation might have cost.[3]

Yet what Lincoln saw was difficult for others to see, even in the North, where the integrating forces were so strong and had operated so rapidly. The nation, it seemed, was forming itself, apparently without human agency: East and West, suddenly powerful with gold and steam, squeezing the middle into a national mold. No wonder so many astonished Americans saw the hand of God in this work! But there were others who saw the Devil there too.

2

As soon as the southern votes were eliminated from the Congress, the vast dream they had thwarted so long became palpable reality. The dream was a railroad. It would connect the Atlantic with the Pacific. Already there was a great sprawling network of rails reaching westward beyond Chicago. Much of it was waste: spurs, furiously competing lines, lines built of nothing but hope or graft or politics. Some were only on paper though many thousands of taxpayers' money had gone into their planning. State and even municipal governments had sunk vast sums in useless branch tracks with the promise of new development of piddling towns and newly smoking factories. But out of the tangle a central thread could be isolated, the encumbering mass of lines could be erased, and then, if the thing could be stretched farther and another iron band be pushed from the West to meet it, the dream would come true. And already, before the war's end, the erasing process had begun; a ruthless consolidator with limitless vision named Cornelius Vanderbilt and a smart trio of bandits, Gould, Fisk, and Drew, would complete it, with wholesale ruin to both competitors and innocent bystanders.

[2] Ibid. [3] Ibid., VIII, 115.

But the trans-Mississippi span—the crux of the system—had been stalemated by the South. This must have federal sanction and support, moving, as it would, through so many states. But whenever the question rose, the old ghost stalked in the Congress. Would the span enrich slave or free states? Would it give power to Arkansas, Texas, and New Mexico or to Iowa, Nebraska, Colorado, and Utah? Then, after Sumter, the ghost was gone; northerners could vote the railroad where they pleased. Even the grim reverses of the first war year did not divert the planners from their plan. Thus on July 1, 1862, as the Peninsular campaign was falling apart and two months before the second disaster at Bull Run, Lincoln, with one eye on the sinister dispatches from the field, signed "An Act to aid in the Construction of a Railroad and Telegraph Line from the Missouri River to the Pacific Ocean. . . ."

Even in the tallest American tales, the wildest American fable, there is scarcely a parallel to the reckless prodigality of this statute and the ones that followed it. Indeed, the crescendo of government outpouring of gifts upon the private entrepreneurs of the American railroad era seems to have been unprecedented in world history. It is hardly surprising, therefore, that there were many eager hands reaching for the booty, and that as time went on and no end to the golden future was visible, the hands were less and less guided or restrained by conscience.

The act created a corporation called The Union Pacific Railroad Company, which was to build from the one hundredth meridian between the Platte and the Republican river valleys to the western boundary of Nevada. It was to have a right of way two hundred feet wide each side of the track. It was to be granted five alternate "sections" of the public domain per mile on each side—an outright gift of 6,400 acres per mile. Finally, the government would underwrite construction costs: $16,000 per mile for level country, $48,000 per mile for mountains, and $32,000 per mile for intermediate terrain. This was to be covered by an issue of six-per-cent bonds payable in thirty years, and these were to be a first mortgage on the railroad.[4]

This was *"laissez faire." Laissez faire* meant that government should not interfere with business. It might subsidize business to any extent and this was still *"laissez faire."* If *laissez faire* had been interpreted to mean that government should have nothing to do with

[4] *U.S. Statutes at Large,* George P. Sanger, editor (Boston, 1863), XII, 489 ff.

private business, there would have been no transcontinental span. American "free enterprise" has always meant that government should be free to supply capital for enterprise providing it should promise not to "go into business" and realize profits. If it should go into business and make money, that would be socialism, and Americans were nearly as frightened of socialism in 1862 as they were in, say, 1956.

But the fabulous bounties of the Railroad Act could not be socialism, as there were no strings attached and little opportunity for the community in general to have a direct share in the enterprise unless they bought bonds. It was expected that the public would stampede to buy such gilt-edged securities. This, however, they did not do. Perhaps Americans were too intent on the war. Perhaps they wanted to give all they had to help finance the war.[5] Thus, for the general public the Railroad Act was a less exciting wartime *divertissement* than it was for the promoters and for the hundreds of lobbyists who crowded the Capitol hoping for some place on the band wagon.

Unable to sell bonds, Congress increased the appeal. It doubled the land grants. It removed a dubious clause which at first had restrained the railroads from going into the mining business (as well as the lumber and real-estate businesses) on their lands. Government now took second-mortgage bonds for its loans, giving a prior lien to the bonds of the companies.

It took two years for this new philanthropy to develop. The war was still on. By this time the insiders in the Union Pacific had decided that it was not good for the public to own the bonds. They therefore established a holding company to buy up all outstanding securities and thus concentrate the profits in a few hands. These men had very little to lose.

3

The Railroad Act of 1862 and its later upward revisions had created the Union Pacific corporation. They also gave power to a California corporation, The Central Pacific Company, to build eastward on precisely the same terms that it offered Union Pacific

[5] Federal War Bonds were sold for the first time by Jay Cooke and Co. of Philadelphia.

until the twain should meet. The acts did not, however, create the holding company. That was a device invented by a small group in a probably smoke-filled room in the dark of the moon.

In some ways the American financial conscience has come a long way since 1864. Or perhaps more people are watching the operators. In any case, we are less naïve. Such obvious trickery as that of "Credit Mobilier" [6] would surely be attacked in the 1950's, and its inventors would end in some sort of jail instead of having monuments erected to them.

The Credit Mobilier was a construction as well as a finance company. No one seems to have called public attention to the curious coincidence that the stockholders of the Credit Mobilier had the same names as the directors of the Union Pacific Company, or if anyone did, the news was probably accepted with a wink and the remark that such businessmen were "smart" indeed. The ingenious scheme made it possible for these gentlemen to vote as much of the public funds as they wished into their own pockets under the heading of "construction costs"—always providing, of course, that the road was built.

Very little seems to have been said about this until three years after the last silver and gold spikes had been driven at Promontory Point in Utah and the eastern locomotive had met the western locomotive in a shower of champagne. Probably even then nothing would have been said but that, 1872 being an election year, a properly aromatic scandal was politically useful. The public in general had been so happy about the railroad—so many speeches had been made, flags waved, toasts drunk, and national boasts broadcast—that it would have seemed unpatriotic to challenge small business details. Also, after the frauds of the Tweed ring in New York, the gold corner and "Black Friday," the sale of the courts to Erie, and shadowy dealings even involving the presidency, the public conscience was calloused.

But in 1872 the campaign ending in the re-election of Grant was hot. On September 4 the New York *Sun* broke the story of the Credit Mobilier and disclosed that important members of Congress were implicated. In the forefront stood Oakes Ames, Representative from

[6] This grand and, to Americans, mysterious title was borrowed, of course, from France, and as few Americans could pronounce it in the French manner, the accent on "Crédit" was dropped.

Massachusetts, who had acquired a certain picturesque aspect from the fact that in private life he was the nation's largest manufacturer of shovels. Oakes had supplied the controlling force of the Credit Mobilier, while his brother Oliver was president of Union Pacific. In an excess of zeal but, as he explained, with no evil intent, he had distributed large quantities of Credit Mobilier stock among senators and congressmen. When these gentlemen could not afford to buy the stock outright he agreed to let them pay for it with the dividends the stock should earn. In a private letter he had written that the shares had been placed "where they will do the most good to us." As a result, "I don't fear," he wrote from Washington, "any investigation here." [7]

In the election year, however, the *Sun*'s disclosure spread panic in the Capitol. The story, written in the exaggerated and sensational fashion of the day under the heading "The King of Frauds," was calculated to inflame—momentarily at least—even a public long calloused to immorality in high places. In an election year, then as now, the public conscience was inflammable. The heat was quickly felt in Washington, and the guilty legislators squirmed and fell over each other in their efforts to rid themselves of the tainted stock and all evidence of their acceptance of it. And, although the general pandemonium seems to have had little effect on the outcome of the election, it was obvious when the new congress met that an investigation could not be avoided.

The committees were reluctant to proceed. They knew the scandal would besmirch some of the most respected characters. Along with Ames, James Brooks of New York, James Garfield of Ohio, Senator Patterson of New Hampshire, and Vice-President Schuyler Colfax among others were involved.

Under examination both Colfax and Garfield swore falsely about their stock, though Garfield was excused on the ground of fallible memory. Ames admitted everything, but saw no harm in what he had done. He said his deals with members of Congress were the

> "same thing as going into a business community and interesting the leading business men by giving them shares." [8]

[7] H.R. 42:3 Report No. 77, p. 5.

[8] Poland's speech, Feb. 25, 1873. J. F. Rhodes: *History of the United States* (New York, 1906), VII, 11.

After summing up all the examinations and questionings, one of the committees reported on the whole Credit Mobilier affair, stating:

> The men who controlled the Union Pacific . . . resorted to the device of contracting with themselves to build the road, and fix a price high enough to require the issue of bonds to the full extent, and then divide the bonds or the proceeds of them under the name of profits, on the contract. . . . Any undue and unreasonable profits thus made by themselves were as much a fraud upon the government as if they had sold their bonds and divided the money.[9]

The "unreasonable" profits, according to another report, had amounted to more than twenty-three million dollars in cash value.[1]

Oakes Ames, Brooks, and Patterson were recommended for expulsion. On this the Senate refused to take any action on Patterson; the House changed expulsion to censure and voted to "absolutely condemn" the behavior of Ames and Brooks. That the vote was completely cynical was evidenced by a rush of many of the voters to apologize to both men, shake their hands, and say they "had to do it" but against their will.

Ames was immediately dined and wined in his home town, and after his death (said to have been hastened by the congressional action) was eulogized by such pillars of integrity as Edward Everett Hale, Samuel Tilden, and William Evarts and was "vindicated" by vote of the Massachusetts legislature. He then had a memorial hall dedicated to him, and both he and Oliver had monuments built to their memory on the line of the Union Pacific in Wyoming. Colfax became a popular lecturer. Patterson was elected to his state legislature and appointed to the faculty of Dartmouth College. Garfield was elevated to the presidency. Thus, quickly, the public flames had died down. Meanwhile,

> Grant's second term had commenced amid the idle show, the luxurious vulgarity and the free extravagance which were characteristic of the age.[2]

[9] H.R. 42:3 Report No. 77, p. ix.

[1] Report No. 78, p. xiv, xv.

[2] Ellis P. Oberholtzer: *History of the United States Since the Civil War* (New York, 1937), II, 75.

4

As usual, there has been controversy among historians as to the enormity of the Union Pacific profits. They were not, says Ellis P. Oberholtzer,

> much larger than was justified by the labor and risk which attended this important national service.[3]

J. F. Rhodes speaks of the "gross exaggeration" of the charges.[4] But to the student of the national conscience it is evident that public opinion in general accepted the postulate that the end justifies the means. The road, after all, had been completed. It was the greatest single feat in the nation's history. Its potential for future good and happiness was incalculable. What right had government to challenge the methods of the great promoters? Was that *laissez faire*? Was it *laissez faire* to investigate such picayune details? Was it not crass ingratitude to require these brilliant entrepreneurs to account for their expenditures?

In this vein wrote J. B. Crawford, the contemporary historian of the Credit Mobilier.

> Have any of the conditions which the government required been unfulfilled? The road was completed as required. . . . Was it the duty of the company to build the road by using as little of the loan of government as possible, or had the road the right to use all of the loan? . . . And if the company, in building the road, let the contracts to themselves, did they thereby stand in such a relation to the government that they must account for all the profits they received? [5]

That the device of the Credit Mobilier was not original or unique appears in the fact that almost precisely the same game was played at the Pacific end of the span by the swashbuckling California operators Leland Stanford, Charles Crocker, Mark Hopkins, and Collis Huntington. The construction company of the Central Pacific was less grandiloquently named the "Contract and Finance Company." It was admitted that this company realized at least $54,000,000 net profit on construction costing about $36,000,000,

[3] Ibid., II, 608.
[4] Rhodes: op. cit., VII, 2.
[5] J. B. Crawford: *The Credit Mobilier of America* (Boston, 1880), pp. 80, 81.

but, as the company's books got conveniently lost as soon as investigation threatened, it was never proved how much more was gained.[6] Here, however, at least one voice of conscience (or political acumen) was heard when Governor Newton Booth of California said, in his inaugural address:

> The organization of corporations within corporations is a refinement of subtlety and fraud which should be positively prevented by law.[7]

5

The lapse of the public conscience in America in the score of years following the Civil War applied to many things besides railroads, but railroads led the way. Rail communication was the backbone of the nation's growth. It was the *sine qua non* of continental conquest. It maintained the national integrity through the temptations to break off pieces from the American stem; it prevented the map of the United States from looking like the map of Europe or like the map of South America—crisscrossed with border lines between nations that often hovered on the brink of hostility. It brought the wealth of the Far West quickly to the industries of the East and stretched them westward. The sense of these things gripped the mind and will of every thinking American. Without articulating it, he knew the necessity of speed in this time: the imperative need of organization, of consolidating every acre of ground gained and attaching it firmly to the central spine.

The first continental system, in its physical building, its physical performance, and its psychological inspiration, created a new world of opportunity. In the Union Pacific construction it employed veterans of the Civil War who in an ordinary post-war slump would have been out of jobs. It called on and developed the highest engineering talent and built much of the "Yankee ingenuity" we celebrate today. When the trains ran they carried hundreds of thousands of new immigrants to settle the empty lands of Minnesota, the Dakotas, and

[6] Harry J. Carman and Charles H. Mueller: "The Contract and Finance Company and the Central Pacific Railroad," in *Mississippi Valley Historical Review*, XIV (December, 1927), 326–41, gives all sources.

[7] Quoted in Gustavus Myers: *History of the Great American Fortunes* (New York, 1936), p. 525.

part of the Great Plains. They brought other thousands to the western mines, they built huge lumbering enterprises, they exploited the ore of the Mesabi range, and they created the American steel industry that soon led the world's production. They altered the nation's food pattern by centralizing the packing industry, and they remade the nation's geography by creating cities apart from waterways. In the railroad's trail followed innumerable manufactures, large and small, from coal for the locomotives to blankets for the sleeping cars.

Under the impulse, greed, cutthroat competition, lawlessness, corruption, violence were inevitable. To the transcontinentals that followed Union Pacific, government became more and more bountiful. The land grants that had been unprecedented in 1864 seemed small parcels, for instance, beside the entire counties that passed to the Northern Pacific a few years later. By 1873 Congress had either granted or pledged to the railroad corporations nearly two hundred million acres of the public domain.[8] The use of this land and its sale enriched the railroad promoters to the point where they became, in effect, feudal barons, and their example led millions to emulate them in whatever way they could. We have no accurate record of the fringe of ruin that edged the great railroad domains. We know that thousands of settlers were driven off their legitimate claims because government had granted their land to the corporations. And we know that many prosperous communities were turned into ghost towns overnight when the railroads bypassed them. These effects were to deepen the trend toward constant mobility which has increased ever since as a basic American trait.

An interesting variety of bribery and blackmail accompanied the laying out of certain lines, especially at the Pacific end. Towns were asked for contributions to the construction company, the money to be raised by taxes. Those raising the largest sums were placed on the line of the projected road; those that failed in their quota were bypassed and ruined. In this way the California financiers were able to add appreciably to the enormous wealth the federal government had already granted.

An easy device for using the railroads to build a monopoly and stifle competition in the new oil industry was invented by the ingenious John D. Rockefeller when he set out to construct the

[8] *Annual Report, Secretary of the Interior*, 1873, p. 288.

Standard Oil Company. Rockefeller paid a road the current freight rate—that is, the rate other companies were paying—to transport his petroleum. Secretly, however, he arranged with the road to rebate a portion of this money. As there was hot competition among the railroads, agreement was forced. With the resulting low cost of his product he captured the markets, and competing enterprises were forced to the wall. Rockefeller's exploitation of such methods, however, was merely an extreme example of what could and did happen in the atmosphere of unrestrained *laissez faire* in the gilded age.

The questions of business ethics raised in this frenzied period are often moot indeed. In the long view that comes from nearly a century of perspective, historians have reduced many of them to a choice of evils. The abuses of free competition were manifold and destructive. To defeat one another entrepreneurs resorted to nearly every crime, including murder. The duplication resulting from hundreds of small companies making and selling identical products resulted in low quality and in that ambience of "buyer beware" which in the days when people understood Latin was known as *caveat emptor*. Lying, deceit, fraud, and robbery were nearly universal in business. As no laws whatever covered business dealings, a chaotic free-for-all foreshadowed industrial and mercantile suicide. Finally, as we see it now, that greatest of all material American institutions, mass production, could never have developed under such conditions.

It was at the point, nearly, of dead center in "free enterprise" that the "robber barons" stepped in. Out of their ruthless, cold-blooded programs order eventually came. As we shall see, the American conscience, returning in a sort of backwash flood after the frontiers closed, held up to the public view the horrid details of the trust-building, and Americans beat their breasts in shame. But in that time of condemnation when big business was placed in what we call the doghouse, no one seems to have remembered what preceded the monopolistic trend. Today we are finding out. As we view the long sweep of history, then, the robber barons appear as instruments of destiny. With all their wickedness they seem to form a historical necessity. Without the sequence of Vanderbilt, Huntington, Hill, and Harriman we might have lost our national integrity; without Rockefeller, Carnegie, McCormick, Morgan, and a host of others capped by Ford, we should have no mass production, and without mass production we should not have our kind of economic and social democracy.

Nothing, however, is more curious than the shibboleth to which the businessman of the mid-twentieth century so stubbornly clings. Leapfrogging over the order that through long, strenuous efforts of consolidation and organization has finally brought the United States into the van of world production, he returns to the dark chaos and sings the praises of "free enterprise." For it was precisely the restraint of freedom in enterprise, partly by business itself and partly by government regulation of interstate commerce, that made possible the degree of output, the high standard of quality, and the relatively integrated business ethics that we have today.

We live, however, by "slogans"; our guideposts are abstractions. That so many of them have lost their validity is irrelevant. We still boast of "rugged individualism" in a society of group dominance and in the same breath praise "team play," organization, solidarity, *esprit de corps*, and even the new anonymity in management and technology. Perhaps the echoes from a long-dead past are a stimulant in the present flux. In any case, they seem to be necessary to a still romantic people of whom by far the most incorrigible romanticists are the "hard-headed" men of business.

6

The most striking characteristic of the "gilded age" to the student of the American conscience is the complacency of public opinion toward the epidemic of misbehavior. In the press, in oratory, in the halls of Congress, in the state legislatures, and in the churches there were occasional criticisms, but they were relatively few and far between. In a democracy these media of articulation are supposed to reflect the views of the "man in the street." What, then, did this symbolic person think about the corruption that poisoned the air he breathed? Was he enraged when men who had acquired their wealth by fraud, chicanery, or piracy displayed their gains at the peak of vulgarity? Did he resent the coach-and-fours, the marble mansions, the exotic balls, the liveried servants belonging to men whose fathers had earned their livelihood with a pick and shovel? Or did he—unlike any other man-in-the-street in the world—put himself in fancy into the mansions and coaches and so forbear to condemn? Did he say to himself: "If it happened to him yesterday, why not to me tomorrow? If I throw the stone at him today, shall I not myself be stoned next year?" It was the attitude of the men standing round the roulette wheel in a casino. To each there was the chance.

This seems to be a more than plausible explanation of the quiescent public opinion—an explanation supported by the fact that when the "unlimited" opportunity came to an end the conscience returned. But in this twenty-year interval of the "gilded age" the wealth potential seems to have warped the moral judgment of a cross-section of the American people from the president down. Grant often showed either a moral ignorance or a moral cynicism. He seems, for instance, to have been charmed by the extravagances of the notorious bandit and lecher Jim Fisk. He would accept the resignations of public officials who were forced out of office by scandals "with regret." [9] He made the most dubious and sometimes shocking appointments, such as those of William Simmons, Caleb Cushing, Casey of New Orleans, "Boss Shepherd," and Ambassadors Schenk and Webb. His administration ignored or condoned the scandalous "Whisky Ring" of tax-dodgers in St. Louis and systematic frauds perpetrated on Negroes and Indians.

Perhaps the most naïve outrage of all to which Grant lent his signature was the "salary grab" of 1873. The day before his second administration began, Congress voted to double the president's salary, to raise the pay of senators and representatives by fifty per cent, and to make other increases for the justices of the Supreme Court, the members of the Cabinet, the vice-president, and the speaker of the House. Even to this the public might have shown its usual complacency but for the fact that the members of Congress added the insult of voting themselves the raise retroactively for two years. Without a murmur the President signed the bill. A year later the national conscience forced repeal of nearly all the increases, at which time there was one of the most disgusting exhibitions of congressional breast-beating in all our history.

As we scan this somber scene, we cannot help wondering what had happened to that tough "moral core" that we saw hardening

[9] As, for example, those of Thomas Murphy, Collector of that "sink of political corruption," the New York Custom House, and Secretary of War W. W. Belknap. Morison and Commager: *Growth of the American Republic*, II, 73; Rhodes: op. cit., VII, 23 ff.

under the Puritan influence. Had Americans lost their attachment to religion, to a stern Deity, to the hope of immortality? Or had they transformed their God into a golden calf and found heaven in the here and now? Had they lost their faith in hard work, in frugality, in sacrifice, in the diligent following of a calling—in all those virtues that Franklin preached? Or had the original American Calvinism, which even in the days of colonial puritanism had considered the accumulation of a fortune the normal result of the virtuous pursuit of a "calling"—had this rugged philosophy been so perverted that easy riches too had come within the frame of virtue? To answer these important questions we must look behind the "visible" American people and discover that still greater part that, while the huge cities were taking shape, lived along the frontiers or in rural realms and were, for a while, unseen and unheard.

7

Parallel with the corruption in industry and government in the East the conquest of the continent was still going on. Indeed, the migration to the new states and territories had never before reached such proportions. Families were taking advantage of the Homestead Act of 1862, which offered a quarter-section of free land to citizens who could prove that they were bona-fide settlers. Between 1870 and 1872, 6,000 homesteads were taken up; in the following year more than 10,000, and in the fiscal year 1875–6, 22,500.[1] In addition to the homesteads, quantities of cheap land were bought from the railroads or from perennially restless pioneers moving away to new wildernesses or to the mines and cities. Most of this migration was still in great caravans of covered wagons, and the migrants met the same hazards of Indians, wild animals, flood, and drought encountered by the earliest settlers.

And, established on their farms, many of these folk met prairie fires, blizzards, droughts, and locust plagues. In Kansas, for instance, in 1874 there was a procession of wagons moving eastward; on their white covers, unhappy defeated pioneers had scrawled: "In

[1] Allan Nevins: *Emergence of Modern America, 1865–1878* (New York, 1927), p. 118. Reference to Thomas Donaldson: *The Public Domain* (Washington, 1884), p. 208.

God we trusted, in Kansas we busted." [2] The great majority, however, endured the suffering and brought their farms to the national rural standard. In the more remote regions there were still subsistence farms on which, in the first years, food and clothing were meager and hard work for every member of the family was incessant.

But even in the rural Midwest, where there were more towns reached by railroads and therefore supplied with more comforts, farm life was strenuous and lonely. To drive the wagon to the nearest community was a difficult "chore," particularly in early spring when the roads were deep in mud. The trip to the "depot" or village was an event; a day was given to it; it involved buying supplies for long weeks ahead and reunions with other lonely farm families. Recreation came only with occasional fairs, religious camp meetings or "revivals," and that great institution that delighted so many generations of rural children, the traveling circus. More and more, as industry crept closer to the rural community, salesmen or "agents" came to the farms, bringing cheer and gossip along with their samples. There is a persistent legend that these persons with their store clothes and urban manners often tempted the lonely farm girls away from the cows and the corn to their ruin, but against this stands the equally persistent legend of rustic female chastity. In any case, the arrival of one of these polished "gentlemen" was an event for all the family, and in the case of the book agent he was a herald of culture.

The rural folk, millions of them of New England stock, were the custodians of the puritan morality. In field and forest alone with his God, at night in the oil-smelling farmhouse alone with his Bible, the farmer kept his ideals. Right and wrong were absolutes. Sin was not justified by expediency. The farmer often sinned darkly; drunkenness, cruelty, sexual abnormalities, even incest were never wholly alien to American rural life in its dreary years, but the sins were admitted and condemned. There were no "alibis." Children did not blame their parents for their delinquencies because of "psychological" pressures. God would judge them in the end, and there was no earthly paradise sufficiently joyous to make them forget the heaven or hell ahead.

[2] Articles "Kansas" in *American Annual Cyclopedia,* 1874, 1875, cited in Nevins: *Modern America,* p. 160.

Where life depended on something that grew, always mysteriously, out of the ground, belief in the supernatural and devotion to a Deity whose smile is perennially hoped for is usually found. He was present, too, where danger dwelt beyond the doorstep. A great volume of prayer must have gone up from the frame houses, the log houses, the mud huts, and the wagons that were the homes of the wanderers for so long. When a preacher came, there was often an orgy of repentance followed by ecstasies of salvation. Always it was an event. The preacher could bring God to everyone. In the unsettled West he was still a great man.

The new religion, sometimes called the "Gospel of Wealth," that was growing round the giant millionaires of the eastern and far western cities had not yet softened the middle people. The urban ministers were telling their well-fed, well-dressed flocks that God was rewarding them because they were rich; the circuit-riders held the hope of God before the countrymen because they were poor. Perhaps more than any modern deity, the American Christian God was adapted to circumstances.

Much of the reading of rural Americans was in religious periodicals. When these had been read, they were kept and treasured. Scarcely a family was without one of these pious weeklies or monthlies—most of them published in New York or New England.

> Grandfather's favourite paper [wrote Caroline Richards in her diary in upstate New York] is the *Boston Christian Register*. He could not have one of them torn up any more than a leaf of the Bible. He has barrels of them stored away in the garret.[3]

In the '70's the greater part of the population still lived rural lives. But the change had already begun. Everywhere industry was encroaching on agriculture, on the agrarian society, on the rural economy. In increasing numbers boys were leaving the farms for the city. Almost without their knowing it, home-owners were becoming tenants; vast tracts were passing through foreclosed mortgages into the possession of large corporations. By the end of the 1870's the gates that closed the frontiers were already visible.

With the passing of the frontier an entire phase of American history would come to an end. It was the most formative phase of all. In it were molded most of the traits, good and bad, that are pre-

[3] Caroline Cowles Richards: *Village Life in America, 1852–1872* (New York, 1912), p. 81.

dominantly American today. If we are to break some of our worst habits, we must break with the frontier; if we are to regain some of the good we have lost, we must go back to the frontier to find it. Wasteful, destructive, cruel as life often was along "the hither edge of free land," there was, too, a positive vitality that has dissolved in our more saturate, our more rotary, our more organized, anonymous society.

Chapter XXIV

Mid-Victorian Behavior Patterns

ABETTED by the theories of twentieth-century psychologists, it has become the fashion among those Americans who do not blame the Puritans for their shortcomings to lay them at the door of the "mid-Victorian era." The restraint of sexual expression, the inhibitions upon sex education of adolescents, the unhealthy fashions in women's clothing, the ostrich attitude of the well-to-do toward the "other half," the hypocritical sentimentalism, and the submergence of the realities in romantic dreams of "sweetness and light"—these ways of American society in the last half of the nineteenth century are thought to have had far-reaching effects upon the generations of the twentieth.

Our failure to understand and enjoy the happiest relation of the sexes, our ignorance of the "techniques" of love, the fact that American males are notoriously poor lovers, the supposed prevalence of homosexuality and other perversions, and the acceleration of the divorce rate probably consequent upon this behavior pattern all stem—or so the legend runs—from mid-Victorian stultifications. It is, of course, a sop to the consciences of later Americans to feel that their present mistakes are not their fault but the result of pressures beyond their control. Perhaps the greatest comforter of conscience in twentieth-century society is Dr. Freud. Few Americans know what this revolutionary psychologist really said, but they know what they want to think he said, and that supplies an adequate set of alibis for most of their sins.

If, however, we make an objective study of that gaslit era when the dirt in the corners was so hardly visible, we may lose confidence in that belief. We can make such a study now. We are far enough away. Our view has become isometric enough to see not only the lambrequins, portieres, bedcurtains, carpets, statuary, bric-a-brac, bowls, pitchers, and chamberpots, the bustles, corsets, petticoats, hair transformations, and street-sweeping skirts of brownstone society, but also the bare shacks of lumbermen and miners, the wind-tortured outpost farmhouses on Kansas prairies where women and children were unshod, or the locomotives pushed through snowdrifts on the high curves of the Rockies by freezing engineers. We can see, too, the roaring railroad and mining camps, here tonight, gone tomorrow, with their mobile saloons, gambling palaces, and whorehouses; the gallows with their pendant horse thieves strung up by vigilantes after a drumhead trial; the soldiers pursuing and fighting Indians on the Great Plains; or the men and animals dying of thirst in the wide desert and leaving their bones to punctuate the trails.

But even below the surface of urban complacency there was a kind of volcanic unrest, cumulative, potentially eruptive. Women, having completed their fight for emancipating the Negro, were fighting to emancipate themselves. They were also fighting the Demon Rum, who had been and still was a demon indeed in America. They were fighting for moral, social, economic, and political equality with men. And they were beginning the crusade for humanitarian action. They organized charities and societies for the prevention of cruelty. They investigated and tried to reform prisons, hospitals, insane asylums, sweatshops, and slum areas. This last effort was progressing slowly, to be sure, and some of the women were more zealous for organization than for its results, but the impulse was there, and it upset the complacency of overfed men and overdressed ladies who were sure this was the best possible world and shut their eyes to all evidence of the reverse.

2

In this time, so static on the surface, religion prescribed strict conventions. Never had church-going been more necessary to respectability. The Protestant churches had adjusted themselves as best they could to the "gospel of wealth"; nevertheless, those parishioners who had acquired their fortunes in dubious ways buttressed their consciences and salvaged their reputations by regular appearance in church. And never was the Sabbath more rigidly observed. A British visitor found "the American Sunday . . . a day of tribulation." [1] Games, recreation of all kinds, and public entertainment were on the index, and the taboo was enforced in many places by the police. An occasional state law even made attendance at church compulsory. Sewing, even for charity, on Sunday put women beyond the pale of decency. In some cities there was no public transportation. For children, Sunday schools were nearly universal, but where they were lacking, unhappy youngsters were catechized at home; sinful boys and girls were shut in dark rooms and told to "examine themselves," sometimes with unexpected results; and even reading, except in sacred literature, was forbidden.

Thus, religious observance was apparently an inflexible form, and this, too, is held up as an example of the horrid conditioning of our forebears' psyches. Yet beneath the crust a religious upheaval was in preparation more seismic perhaps than any since the Reformation. Already by the '70's cracks were opening in the fundamentalist faiths all over the country, and countless young men and women were doubting the sermons they listened to because of the beautiful logic of a new science. At the same time the stanch believers in Scriptural exactness were so shocked by the picture of God's image hanging by prehensile toes and tails from the branches of trees that they consigned the new insurgents to the lowest depths of hell.

Charles Darwin published his *Origin of Species* in 1859. The Civil War prevented its extensive circulation in America until the 1870's. Meanwhile, however, the Darwinian theory had been expounded by Herbert Spencer and popularized by Edward Youmans, and, as Americans always prefer to get their information from secondary sources, the epidemic of "infidelity," as it was called, spread rapidly through the student bodies in the colleges. The college administrators, being usually of a sectarian cast of mind, tried to resist and were sometimes successful. Even at Harvard, which often led the way in intellectual movements and listed among its teachers such brilliant scientists as Wolcott Gibbs and Asa Gray, President Cornelius Felton, though a Unitarian, thought the evolutionary

[1] G. A. Sala: *America Revisited* (London, 1883), II, 58.

theory undermined young men's morals. He was particularly shocked by the views of the brilliant student John Fiske on Darwin, Auguste Comte, and Spencer.

> President Felton [Samuel Eliot Morison tells us] wrote to the lad's mother: "We never attempt to control the religious opinions of young men. But I consider it a great and lamentable misfortune to a young man, when, in the conceit of superior wisdom, he openly declares himself an infidel. . . ." And he adds that "any attempt to spread the mischievous opinions which he fancies he has established in his own mind" will require his removal.[2]

Felton's attitude showed a curious state of flux in the religious biases of New England. Unitarianism, the radical departure from Puritan doctrines that had been so deprecated a generation before, had now become conservative and, at Harvard at least, was shutting the door against new philosophies.

> There is something deliciously ludicrous [Morison adds] in the picture of President Felton, member of a cult that had almost reduced Christianity to an inspired system of ethics, looking down his nose at a disciple of Comte.[3]

But this very paradox indicates a ripeness for change. Fiske was not "removed," and he later became the pre-eminent American torch-bearer of evolutionary belief.

The impact of Darwinism on orthodox religion was quite different from that of the earlier Enlightenment. The eighteenth-century exponents of "nature's God" and the philosophers who hoped to discover a basis of worship against the background of science were vague in their idealistic pursuit of "reason," and the need of religion was inherent in their philosophy. But Darwin said nothing about God, and he dealt with man (presumably cast in the divine mold) as if he were merely a species high in the hierarchy. He shattered (as geologists were already doing) the entire Scriptural chronology. He excluded the creation of Adam out of the dust, and his suggestion that man arrived more or less by accident wiped out the dogma of original sin. His reasoning dealt with specific organisms and marked specific stages of evolution; there was nothing vague about it. And

[2] Samuel Eliot Morison: *Three Centuries of Harvard* (Cambridge, Mass., 1936), p. 308.
[3] Ibid., pp. 308, 309.

the worst of it was, it made such sense that prolonged prayer was necessary to combat it. Finally, parallel with the publication of the theory and interpretations of it, science was making such immense visible and tangible strides in the material world that the natural became far more exciting than the supernatural and thousands of young people were converted out of the "old-time religion."

Thus, in this time we think of as "stultifying," new vistas were opening for young minds, some of them so positive, so vital, and so realistic that no time was left for brooding on repression.

3

It is, however, questionable how much repression there was. The close, overstuffed drawing-rooms, where men paid court while the ladies hid their blushes behind fans and fainted at the slightest suggestion of coarseness, do not seem to us conducive to full sex expression. Also, the ever present chaperone, busy with her needlework but always ready to intervene in the event of liberties with her ward, would seem to discourage even an ardent lover—yet perhaps these barriers were goads. Perhaps they made possession seem more precious when it came. Perhaps the convention of coyness was more alluring than the hasty surrender of a later type known in our frank vernacular as a pushover. It is not certain that even the costumes of the time were not more provocative than the unmysterious bareness of a later day. Surely the hoopskirt of the '60's, giving occasional flashing glimpses of forbidden territory, was one of the most seductive sartorial creations ever invented.

In the post-war years, before economic stringencies delayed it, early marriage was expected. In the cities a girl was eligible at seventeen or eighteen; on the frontier, even earlier. In the "finishing" schools, although the intimacies of marriage were unmentionable, the general subject was ever present. One girl's diary, for example, tells of a teacher writing on a blackboard a proper letter of refusal to an ardent lover's written proposal.

> Although [Prudence Fleming wrote in her journal] Miss S's Lecture contained much enlightenment, [I] was consumed with curiosity regarding proper method to pursue if I should desire to *Accept* a Young Gentleman. Lacked courage to question Miss S. so confided

my complexity to E.J. [a fellow pupil] who shrugged her shoulders and replied: "Just swoon & let matters take their natural course." [4]

With young marriage so common and with the need for child-bearing enforced by the high rate of infant mortality, sex repression could hardly be a reasonable complaint. There was infidelity, to be sure, as always, but unsatisfied men usually chose the prostitute in preference to the adulteress. The statistics of known and estimated prostitution in the cities in the '70's were high, but many factors such as large immigration and rapid industrialization swelled them. That the brothels had as their main patrons tormented young Americans who had no normal outlet for their urgencies is unlikely. On the contrary, the standard of sexual morality among the native-born in most parts of the country was the subject of surprised comment by European travelers from Tocqueville to Bryce.[5]

In the South there was a special situation created by the presence of the "inferior" race. Interracial sexual relations were characteristic of the slavery period. These continued into late Victorian times. While white women were protected at gunpoint from the remotest suspicion of unchastity, Negro concubinage was common. It was even thought by some southern gentlemen that Negro "wenches" stood as a protection between "ouah daughters and the super-abundant sexual energy of ouah hot-blooded youth." [6] Perhaps more than anything else, this custom has weighed heavily on the consciences of southerners. It is something they cannot escape, as the presence of the mulattoes is a constant reminder. It was not, of course, unprecedented in social mores: it was the practice in ancient Greece and Rome and wherever slavery was an accepted institution. In America, however, it has seemed to non-southerners to be accompanied by a measure of hypocrisy. The boasts of the southern gentlemen about their "honor" have seemed empty in the face of this kind of liaison, especially when it comprehended both infidelity to a wife and the birth of bastard children. Southerners have sometimes retaliated with the argument that many mulattoes are the children of northern invaders, but in the face of statistics over the years this rarely carries full conviction. The accusation continues,

[4] Hazel Hunton: *Pantaloons and Petticoats* (*The Diary of a Young American*) (New York, 1940), p. 24.

[5] Alexis de Tocqueville: *Democracy in America*, revised edition (New York, 1951), II, 204, 214; Rhodes: op. cit., III, 97, 99.

[6] A. T. Morgan: *Yazoo* (Washington, 1884), p. 212.

buttressed by an increasing number of books, articles, and historical works by Negro authors,[7] and it is always salt in a wound northerners have never permitted to heal.

In the era of greater promiscuity which followed the Victorian age and is thought to be an excessive reaction from it, prostitution and Negro concubinage have relatively little place, and the distinction between "good women" and "bad women," which was universal and inflexible in Victorian America, has largely disappeared. The picture of the fallen woman clutching her infant as she is thrust into the blizzard by her unforgiving father has comic color today. Contraception, abortion, venereal prophylaxis and cure have passed from quackery to science, and thus the sexual conscience has been eased. That there is greater scope for normal sex expression than in the earlier years may be doubted. The postponement of marriage beyond the most urgent sexual period for economic reasons and the habits of promiscuity gained during that period often make for uneasy marriages. The equalization of sexual responsibility between men and women in defiance of biological exigencies is likely to have a deteriorating effect on family permanence. The per-capita divorce statistics of the United States—the scandal of the Western world in the mid-twentieth century—would seem to bear out these guesses, though, as always, there are other factors.

There are, indeed, so many other factors to account for the present flexibilities in sexual morals that it is unreasonable to blame Victorianism for the reaction. Two world wars, a catastrophic economic depression, contacts with European and Asiatic societies, immense population increase with consequent overcrowding, mobility due to industrial changes—these are but a few. They account for the delinquencies which we ascribe to Victorian "repressions." And whether there was actual repression beyond that of talk becomes more and more dubious, the more we probe beneath the plush surface.

Some American behavior of later years unquestionably had its origins in the period we call middle or late Victorian. But the evils for which we have been most criticized both by ourselves and by foreigners stemmed from conditions remote from the smugness, prudery, and escapism of the urban East. They are products of the frontier.

[7] A notable example is John Hope Franklin: *From Slavery to Freedom*, pp. 203, 204, 223.

4

Crime and extra-legal punishment were both inherent in frontier life. In mountain mines, along the construction lines of railroads, and in the prairies temptation was constant and escape easy. Vague and disputed claims invited "claim-jumping"; the judge of the rights and wrongs of it was Colt's revolver. Courts and police never quite caught up with the quick-moving frontiers. In the places where the horse was indispensable, horse-thievery was common, and as the horse thief endangered the life of his victim, he was punished by summary death. Lack of fences and barns for livestock invited the cattle thief. The quarrel of two men over a girl in country where women were few and necessary often led to family feuds extending over two or more generations, and even where there were a sheriff and a court, feud-murderers were rarely convicted. Both judge and jury knew that hands-off was the safest policy. Many a sheriff had been shot from ambush because he tried to carry out justice.

In California and the Nevada mining country, crime was to be expected because of the generally reckless character of the seekers after quick wealth, especially when their ventures had disappointed them. Conditions in California after the placer gold was gone were so lawless that the citizens had organized "vigilantes" to take the place of absent police; then, as so often happened, many of these self-appointed constables had become outlaws themselves. On the Great Plains the cattle barons with their herds were invading millions of acres of the public domain and defrauding government and homesteaders with equal abandon. In wild, sparsely populated country such lapses of conscience were natural. Yet even in parts of the settled Middle West the behavior of frontier times had become a sort of tradition.

It is instructive, in the light of the gang wars which in the 1920's distinguished the state of Illinois, to read of the bloody feuds between large coalitions there in the 1870's. Often these had trivial beginnings such as a dispute over the ownership of a cow or a parcel of land. This might grow into an exchange of insults, and that in turn led to the sort of brooding over injuries that characterized country where people were few and the elemental aspects of nature were present. William Hepworth Dixon, who has told a good many stories of these conflicts, thinks that the impulse of vengeance so usual among frontier folk had come from contact with Indians for whom "an eye for an eye and a tooth for a tooth" was the only code.

Invariably the neighbors would take sides. Sooner or later an incident—an open fight between individuals or damage to someone's property—would breed a thirst for vengeance. From this point an offender would be a marked man. He would be shot while sitting quietly in his house or, more often, in his farm wagon, after which the horses would take his corpse home. If someone had seen the killing, he or any number of other witnesses would be shot to forestall any testimony that might come to court. By this time any prospective jurymen would have been warned that unless a verdict of acquittal was brought in they would suffer the same fate. The only way to evade the vengeance was to leave the community—a common move which increased the general mobility of the population. On this trend, flight from justice or from revenge had a marked, continual effect in the formative years.

The parallel between these events and those of a later era when a gangster would be followed in his car through the streets of Cicero or Chicago until in a dark street the shot sounded and the victim would be "rubbed out" is vivid enough. It is true that later gang leaders were usually immigrants or second-generation Americans, but unless the tradition of lawlessness and the impotence of justice had been there, they could hardly have achieved such large success.

The English traveler Dixon reports a dialogue in Illinois in the 1870's which seems to sum up the case against the prevailing American attitude toward crime—an attitude we are only just beginning to appraise and correct.

> "A law abiding people!" says to me a magistrate of much experience on the bench in Illinois: "a jest, Sir, and a sorry sort of jest!"
>
> "Your codes," I interpose, "seem marked by much good sense, as well as highly liberal sentiment."
>
> "Oh the codes are well enough," he answers with a jerk, "if anybody would obey them; but our folks are spendthrifts who pay their debts with promissory notes. We make more laws and break more laws than any other people on earth." [8]

[8] William Hepworth Dixon: *The White Conquest* (London, 1876), I, 237, 238.

Have we not come full circle, here, from the earliest Puritan settlements where conscience was so often satisfied by the mere presence of a statute on the books?

5

There is one behavior pattern, sexual in its nature, that we may trace directly to the nineteenth-century frontier, but it has no connection with mid-Victorian convention. That is the open domination of women over men, unique in America, and with far-reaching consequences.

This is not a result of the suffrage movement or of any honest effort to achieve sex equality. It is the aftermath of a kind of deification of the female due, in the first instance, to frontier conditions, particularly in the far West. It has been nurtured by the default of husbands and the adoration of sons. Its latest manifestation is what Philip Wylie in his wickedest satire [9] has called "momism," and what psychologists have called the Œdipus complex or the "silver cord."

On all the frontiers women's behavior and status have always been quite different from those in the static communities. This was true even in colonial times. Where dangers had been overcome so that men could pursue their "callings" in serenity at home, it was easy to observe the decree of God as interpreted by Saint Paul and require women to "learn in silence with all subjection" [1] and to remain "discreet, chaste, keepers at home, good, obedient to their own husbands. . . ." [2] In the backwoods it was harder.

Where men were away from home for days at a time, a woman had to play a man's part. She kept a firearm ready for use and often used it against beasts or Indians. In floods or fire she must be ready for acts of strength and wisdom: the constant fight against nature kept her alert and gave her presence of mind and calmness in emergencies. In the qualities necessary to a frontiersman she was her husband's equal—sometimes his superior—and he came to regard her as his partner.

[9] Philip Wylie: *Generation of Vipers* (New York, 1946).
[1] I Tim. 2:11.
[2] Titus 2:5.

From Hannah Dustin, who, captured by Indians in 1697, escaped after killing and scalping nine of her captors,[3] to Guri Endreson, who, after seeing two of her sons shot, rescued two wounded men and effected their escape from an Indian fight in 1866,[4] there are incidents of heroism that can match any male exploit. These built an admiration that stood in sharp contrast to the urban attitude. In the cities women were admired for their weakness; on the frontiers for their strength. On the wilderness farms, where men were so badly needed, this strength was demonstrated—in addition to the endurance of hardship—by the multifold bearing of necessary sons.

In the West, therefore, sex equality was never the furiously fought issue that, well into the twentieth century, it remained in the East. Where civilization had caught up with the frontier and the people were no longer obligated to fight nature, savages, and loneliness, women, like men, engaged in every sort of civilized activity. Thus, the first higher education provided for women was in Ohio.[5] Once the gates of learning were opened, women entered business and the professions—even including the ministry, despite Paul's pronouncement that "it is a shame for women to speak in the church." [6]

> Women of the Middle West, who had enjoyed virtual sex equality in the task of conquering the frontier, refused to be demoralized by the leisure which came to them with increasing relief from domestic routine. They merely found larger opportunity for engaging in organizations with varying social objectives.[7]

Among other things, they reached out for "culture" and attained a far greater understanding of the arts and literature than the men. Here we see the first stage of man's default. Men were "too busy" with the business of making money and launching large commercial or industrial projects; thus, alone in the civilized world, the United States relegated cultural activity to the women. The result was increased feminine refinement and elegance; beside his wife a man became a sort of clodhopper. Of this, however, he came to boast: the "he-man" was properly a "roughneck"; he could not be both-

[3] "Dustin, Hannah," in *Dictionary of American Biography*.
[4] Theodore C. Blegen: Grass Roots History (Minneapolis, 1947), pp. 78, 79.
[5] Oberlin University in 1833, Antioch in 1852, Iowa State University in 1860.
[6] I Cor. 14:35.
[7] Arthur Charles Cole: *The Irrepressible Conflict, 1850–1865* (New York, 1934), p. 173.

ered with delicate matters such as painting and music, and the advancing women encouraged the total separation of the spheres. After a time men no longer read; the magazines and books of the later nineteenth century were adapted to women's taste. Although this trend stemmed from the vigorous West, it came, in time—though never wholly—to affect eastern society. The feminine possession of the arts persisted until very recent years; in parts of the country it still persists.

There is an undocumented story of the 1920's about a Yale professor of the fine arts who was offered the curatorship of a museum in a midwestern city. When he took up his new work, he was surprised to discover that, although he was invited to countless teas and meetings of the women's clubs, no men came to meet him and he was never invited to join a men's club. He was puzzled about this and asked the one man he knew—the president of the bank in which he kept his account—the reason for this strange behavior. The president told him with great embarrassment that the curator of an art museum was looked upon by the men of the town with suspicion as being, of necessity, effeminate. If, now, this easterner could show some sort of athletic prowess, things might change. On learning that he had considerable skill in horsemanship, the bank president suggested his joining the local troop. At his first bareback drill he performed the feat of riding standing up with each foot on a horse and a third horse running between his legs. After that he was invited to join all the clubs, became exceedingly popular among the men of the town, and broke the conviction that interest in art was impossible for a "he-man." In the same town a man was barred from society because when he was a guest at a house party a book of poetry was found in his room.

Next, primary and secondary education passed to the women. Boys, therefore, remained under female influence long after they had presumably untied their mother's apron strings. They grew to manhood, taught to obey a woman, and the mental compulsion caused a reversal in the older pattern of marriage. Men also came to feel that moral judgments—at least about themselves—were in the hands of their women. When women got the vote in Wyoming—the first state to give it to them—they immediately began cleaning up brothels, saloons, and gambling establishments—the last male escapes—in Cheyenne.

It is true that in European societies women have often exerted a commanding influence over their husbands. But they have done this in subtle ways. Seldom have the men admitted their domination, and the women have usually shown outward and public deference. But in the United States the woman's power has been freely admitted. Humorous writing has consistently played up the American man's fear of his wife. The classic cartoon shows the man coming home late and his wife standing at the door, rolling-pin in hand.

In the far West in the post-war decades there was a logical explanation of the American man's alternate worship and fear of women. This was their relative scarcity. In Colorado at war's end there were said to be twenty men to every woman, in Nevada eight, in Washington four, and in California three.[8] As Dixon wrote in 1876,

> White females are still too rare and precious on this coast; some cynics say too rare and precious for their own well-being, not to mention the well-being of the Commonwealth.[9]

His concern for the commonwealth was based on the fact that the rarity and preciousness of women had put them—however little some deserved it—beyond the reach of the law. He tells stories of bloody crimes committed by inflated California women. There was the history of Laura Fair, for example, which he thought typical.

> Having a secret with a married man, and finding that false love runs no smoother than true, Laura loaded her revolver, and in the presence of his wife and children, pistoled her paramour coolly and in open day. Laura is a heroine. Tried for murder, and acquitted on the ground of emotional insanity, she lives in style, gives balls, and speculates in stocks. Few ladies are so often named at dinner-tables, and the public journals note her doings as the movements of a duchess might be noted in Mayfair.
>
> Laura's torch has lighted many a fair sister on the way to murder; yet . . . no woman's life has yet been given in California to public justice.
>
> "No, we cannot hang a woman in this country," says a judge of the Supreme Court. . . . A judge will never get twelve men to find a female guilty of wilful murder in San Francisco; nor in any other city west of the Rocky Mountains.[1]

Bringing this frontier tradition up to 1919, Arthur Calhoun, historian of the progress of the American family through the centuries, writes:

[8] Nevins: op. cit., p. 377. [9] Dixon: op. cit., I, 166. [1] Ibid., I, 169.

> Even to the end of the nineteenth century, California was "essentially a man's state" yet it is precisely in such commonwealths that woman rises to sovereignty. Today woman is not exactly rare in America but the tradition endures and the deep-rooted effects of her scarcity value are ineradicable.[2]

This trend has provided the psychologists with more cogent material than mid-Victorian repression. They show a good deal of evidence that American women have tended to transfer their possessive impulses from husband to son. Whether this was because of their sexual frigidity or because American husbands have become (perhaps through intimidation) inadequate lovers makes little difference to the result. The "silver-cord" school believes that the transferred attachment is a sort of sublimated incest. If so, it accounts for a mother-possessed youth not marrying because the image of his mother has become such a rare ideal in his mind that all other women become unattractive or even repellent to him. If so, too, this would account for the alleged spread of homosexuality and other perversions among American men in late years, though certainly other factors may be considered here.

Although some rather obscenely sentimental demonstrations were put on as late as the Second World War by the "mothers of our boys"—frequently causing embarrassment to both generals and lawmakers—the tradition may be said to be breaking down. Perhaps the mom-softened youth finds it difficult to maintain his devotion through the family permutations that have become so common. But more probably the economic changes since the great depression have removed women from their pedestal. In every sense, the home has become more a partnership than it has ever been. Men and women work together in every phase of home life, including cooking and child care. It has also become usual for both to earn, either together or in separate jobs. In any case, the possibility of one partner achieving a conventional superiority over the other is becoming more and more remote. Finally, the wide publicity given to the "silver-cord" theory has given many a mother pause in her attentions to her growing boy.

[2] Arthur W. Calhoun: *A Social History of the American Family* (New York, 1917–19), III, 106.

6

As we review the American period that was synchronous with the middle of the little English queen's reign it seems anything but static. It was rather a transition period in which the trends toward today's way of life began. The tempo of life was stepped up beyond any precedent of acceleration in history. The railroads brought new concepts of speed; they and the network of the telegraph spreading with what seemed the rapidity of a spider's spinning brought all parts of the nation closer together. The Atlantic cable brought Europe to our doorstep. The telephone and the ticker quickened business transactions in the cities, and techniques were in the making that would extend these communications too. The incandescent electric lamp, subdivided current, and power distribution either arrived or were just across the threshold. The new light lighted the corners where the dirt was, and all kinds of concealment became harder.

Old myths faded. Geology and the evolution concept dissolved the belief that the Lord made heaven and earth in six days, and though men still rested on the seventh, it was less because the Lord had done so than because it was practical. The total Sabbath holiness began to break, and if men went to church in the morning, they might play later. The certainty that man had been born in sin and that the sexual act, however necessary, was sinful, was replaced by happier views of love, and, though baptism was still universal among Christians, enlightened people no longer thought that infants had been corrupted by their begetting.

Behind the deceptive façade of stolidity there was incessant turmoil as the old gods died. Conscience was turning practical. Franklin's opinion that actions were not bad because they had been forbidden in Scripture but rather that they had been forbidden because they were bad for us or commended because they were good for us gained acceptance some sevenscore years after he expressed it. Disquiet began to come to the public conscience because wealth seemed to rest on a foundation of poverty: that workers and servants were wickedly underpaid and driven; that all the "sons of Martha," sweating and hungering in the dark, were becoming a reproach to decent society. More and more, with better communications and better light, these evils were heard and seen, and action soon followed the brooding of the more sensitive listeners and watchers. Some of it, like the prohibition movement, may have been wrong-headed, but most of it was earnest.

What Clarence Decker has written of the Victorian age in England is largely true of America, though the creative impulse here ran in other channels than the English.

> If Mrs. Grundy looms large as the protector of the proprieties, she is more than matched by lusty and intransigeant rebels against her prudery. If there is smug convention, there is also courageous revolt. If there is pretension, there is also solid achievement. If there is much generally to regret, there is more to praise. When the ephemeral injustice of twentieth-century reaction has given way to the larger perspective of history, it is certain the Victorian Age will be finally remembered as one of the great creative ages of history.[3]

[3] Clarence R. Decker: *The Victorian Conscience* (New York, 1952), p. 12.

Chapter XXV

Reform

BETWEEN the ninth and tenth decades of the nineteenth century, the frontier, as Americans had always understood it, ceased to exist. At the beginning of his famous essay "The Significance of the Frontier in American History" Frederick Jackson Turner quotes the government announcement in a bulletin of the Superintendent of the Census for 1890:

> Up to and including 1880 the country had a frontier of settlement, but at present the unsettled area has been so broken into by isolated bodies of settlement that there can hardly be said to be a frontier line.[1]

At about the same time there were signs that the national conscience was returning after its long lapse. There being no longer an "area of free land" and an "advance of American settlement westward,"[2] there was an interval of pause after the reckless pursuit of opportunity. Now Americans could contemplate themselves and their nation, and the images they saw in the mirror were disturbing.

It was, in many ways, a peculiarly trying time for Americans. There was nothing historically unique about the American change from an agricultural to an industrial economy. Other nations—notably England—had passed through it before us, and the industrial revolution there had brought agonizing overtones. But the change had come slowly and without sudden shock to national ideals. In the vastness of North America land had been for more than two centuries the goal of ambition. It was wealth, it was opportunity, it was freedom, it was the ultimate and ideal way of life, it was Manifest Destiny. If new population from abroad flooded into the coastal

[1] Turner's paper, originally read at the meeting of the American Historical Association in Chicago, July 12, 1893, is conveniently reprinted in the volume of his essays, *The Frontier in American History* (New York, 1920 and 1947). The above quotation is on page 1 of this volume.

[2] Ibid.

cities, there was always the hope of escape from the congestion, and on the land one became an individual again, unbound by restraints of law and taxes. On the land there was opportunity to prove one's worth, and to be rewarded with the treasures God would pour out from the good soil.

Now there was no more land. Now there was no more empty West below the horizon. The arable parts of the public domain had been pre-empted and even the arid parts were being invaded by wishful thinkers. The migration had struck the wall at last—the wall that was not supposed to be there; the place where "endless opportunity" met its end—and the movement now was backwash. The movement was back now, into the cities, and the reversed migrants were seeking there new avatars, new kinds of wealth, new destiny. If in the '70's and '80's and '90's the adjective "un-American" had existed, this would have been an un-American trend.

That at least was the appearance of the nation as the Superintendent made his announcement, as the people paused to look at themselves, and as Turner led his studies toward his great essay. We know now that the appearance was sometimes mirage, never wholly true. There was still land that with the intensive cultivation that Americans had never tried could be lured into bud and blossom and burgeon. There was still a future even for the prairie farmers and the husbandmen of the plateaus, although from then on the economics and the way of life would change and there would be more and more violations of the economic "laws" to make an increasingly uneasy grave for Adam Smith.

But through the years from 1870 to 1890 the appearance grew more and more definite. And there was something about it that worked on the consciences of those who cherished the agrarian tradition. They wanted to find out why things had changed. When they found out they fought. Their fight at first was uncertain. The forces against them were vast and vague, nightmare forces. But the reform they began acquired a momentum that did not stop until the unbalance was balanced and order brought out of chaos. Like a rolling snowball, the reform gathered other reforms, and the result was a new conscience. The traditional agricultural economy was never, to be sure, restored. Industry was, in the end, triumphant. Government, which had so prodigally helped industry toward that triumph, then had to turn and help agriculture—not toward triumph but for survival. But in the meantime we had learned that "free enterprise" could never be wholly free, and restraint was essential to that kind of liberty which had been the ideal of the Enlightenment.

2

In later popular juvenile stories of the West, a rugged boy hero would leave home determined to lift the mortgage from the family farm. An earlier generation would hardly have known what this meant—at least in the West. In pre-war days or on the homestead settlements land was either owned free and clear or there was a government obligation that could be worked off in a few years. But to be shackled with debt and forced to pay extortionate interest to a private corporation—this was not the American way on a continent in which there was land for everybody.

Then, in the 1870's, farmers found themselves becoming impoverished by industrial encroachment. The leading encroachers were, as usual, the railroads. Welcomed at first by the farmers as providing means of reaching the eastern markets, they had grown, through alternate government subsidy and unbridled *laissez faire,* into giants of colossal stature, ruthlessly exploiting their power.

In vivid words the oligarchy was described by William Mason Grosvenor in 1873.

> Three men meet in a room in New York. They are not called kings, wear no crowns, and bear no scepters. They merely represent trunk lines of railway from the Mississippi to New York. Other points settled, one says,
>
> "As to the grain rate; shall we make it fifty from Chicago?"
>
> "Agreed; crops are heavy and we shall have enough to do."
>
> Business finished, the three enjoy sundry bottles of good wine. The daily papers announce that "the trunk lines have agreed upon a new schedule of rates for freight, which is, in effect, a trifling increase; on grain from forty-five to fifty cents [per hundred pounds] from Chicago to New York with rates to other points in the usual proportion." The conversation was insignificant, the increase "trifling." But to the farmers of the Northwest, it means that the will of three men has taken over thirty millions from the cash value of their products for that year, and five hundred millions from the actual value of their farms.[3]

[3] William Mason Grosvenor: "The Railroads and the Farms," in *Atlantic Monthly,* Vol. XXXII (November 1873), p. 591.

But this arbitrary upping of rates, gouging the farmer because of his urgent need to move his surplus, was only one of the abuses common under railroad domination. There was every sort of discriminatory tactics. One shipper would be charged one rate, another another, depending on which was the better customer. Rates were also based on the roads' convenience as to shipping-points, a short haul often costing the shipper more than a long one. Rates changed according to season: in winter when water routes were frozen and that competition removed, the freight charges would rise to exorbitant heights. Where there was competition between roads, rates fluctuated to a point at which the farmer's budgeting and bookkeeping were thrown into confusion. And, in addition to other pressures, the railroads bought up elevators and warehouses and charged the poor farmer what they liked for his grain storage.

After the railroads, other industries began to harass the cultivator of the land. A high tariff raised the price of his needed manufactured products. Also, he was constrained to buy his tools and machinery from traveling middlemen who charged what they thought the desperate traffic would bear.

Thus the farmer was pushed to the wall. His only recourse was to mortgage his precious lands. As effective usury laws had not penetrated the West, interest rates, seldom below ten per cent, often rose as high as twenty. One by one, owners became tenants. Sometimes foreclosures would force them to join the ever growing backward migration into the seething cities.

By 1880 more than a quarter of the nation's farms were tenant-operated. In 1890 this proportion reached more than 28 per cent.[4] In 1886, in Illinois, one of the most productive agricultural states, eight million acres were under mortgage, and in Michigan there were mortgages on half the farms.[5] In 1890, 66.4 per cent of the farms in Kansas were mortgaged up to 38 per cent of their value, and interest rates averaged 8.1 per cent. In Minnesota there were mortgages at 8.2 per cent on 46.4 per cent of the farms; in Iowa 53.8 per cent of the farmers paid average interest of 7.3 per cent.[6]

[4] Isaac Lippincott: "Farm Tenancy," in *Dictionary of American History,* II, 250.

[5] Roy O. Robbins: *Our Landed Heritage* (Princeton, 1942).

[6] Ida M. Tarbell: *The Nationalizing of Business* (New York, 1936), pp. 133, 134.

3

It was impossible to appeal to the consciences of the railroadmen. An ingenious device had been invented to liberate businessmen from that inconvenient encumbrance. This was the corporation. It was not a new invention, but its enormous popularity in the United States as a means of dissolving individual responsibility was of the nineteenth century—mainly of the gilded age and the age of the "robber barons."

By a legal fiction the corporation is called a "person" and treated as such. It assumes the liability which without it would rest upon the shoulders of those who own the business. Presumably it also takes over their consciences. Just as the stockholders of a corporation are not personally responsible for its debts, neither are they morally accountable for its deeds—or so, at least, they conveniently believed in the great nineteenth-century heyday of the institution.

But, argued the farmers, who were in the habit of direct and realistic thinking, the corporation is *not* a person, even if all the world's lawyers call it so; and, not being a person, it cannot have a conscience. And as the men who owned a railroad or an oil company or a stockyard had unloaded their consciences on a fictional creature incapable of conscientious scruple, conscience must have dropped entirely out of corporate business.

The farmers were truly frightened of this vague, soulless thing to which there was no appeal, yet which was capable of such evil works. As Edward Alsworth Ross later wrote in his extraordinary diatribe against the wickedness of the times when others beside the farmers had begun to protest,

> . . . the tropical belt of sin we are sweeping into is largely impersonal. Our iniquity is wireless and we know not whose withers are wrung by it. The hurt passes into that vague mass, the "public," and is there lost to view.[7]

Early in the 1870's the first American farmers' organization decided to attack the railroad's threat to their survival. The organiza-

[7] Edward Alsworth Ross: *Sin and Society, An Analysis of Latter-Day Iniquity* (Boston, 1907), p. 11. This little book, whose reiteration of the menaces to American morality in the dawn of the new century seems like the beating of a jungle drum, gives an incomparable picture of *laissez-faire* deterioration.

tion, "The Patrons of Husbandry"—more familiarly known as the National Grange—had been formed in 1867, not for political purposes, but

> To enhance the comforts and attractions of our homes, and strengthen our attachments to our pursuits. To foster mutual understanding and co-operation. . . .[8]

The sweetness and light of the Grange's Declaration was a thin veil over the insurgent bitterness of its members. As its growth, especially in the Midwest, was rapid, it soon became a society of considerable power.[9] Though it was the butt of sardonic attacks by the press in the eastern industrial centers, it was able to influence the legislatures of Illinois, Iowa, Wisconsin, Kansas, and California to put records of the farmers' conscience on the statute books. The farmers' attitude was this: If there is no conscience in the soulless corporation, we will call upon government to supply the deficiency. In all of these states laws were passed providing for some regulation of railroad rates or practices.

The repercussions were wide and immediate. The cry of "Socialism!" echoed in the city streets. Never before had government been allowed to interfere with the operation of that sacred American institution, free enterprise! This was the entering wedge! It would be a short step from here to Marxist communism. In 1873 when, along with the rest of industry, the railroads were depressed by the panic, many easterners held the farmers responsible.

The laws were short-lived. New legislators caused the repeal of most of them. The farmers and their rural lawyers had not known how to word them to make them workable. Even before the repeal they were largely ignored. But they were the opening gun in a war which continued through the rest of the century. They called the attention of Americans everywhere to the fact that, as the doors began to close on "endless opportunity," the faint light of a new dawn of national conscience was coming through the opposite windows.

And one direct result of the Granger laws was extremely far-reaching. In 1874 the railroads pleaded that one of these laws in Illinois relating to railroad-owned grain-storage facilities was un-

[8] The Declaration is given in full in National Grange, Proceedings, VII (1874), 56–60 and interpreted in Solon J. Buck: *The Granger Movement* (Cambridge, Mass., 1913), pp. 64, 65.

[9] Buck: op. cit., pp. 58 ff.

constitutional. It was "repugnant," plaintiffs said, to Section 8 of Article I on interstate commerce and to the fourteenth amendment, which ordains that no state shall "deprive any person of life, liberty, or property, without due process of law"—the railroad corporations, of course, being "persons." There was also some pleading about the sanctity of contracts and about state preferences.

In his famous decision Judge Waite said that the plaintiffs'

> business most certainly "tends to a common charge and is become a thing of public interest and use." . . . Certainly if any business can be clothed "with a public interest and cease to be *juris privati* only," this has been.[1]

Thus, for the first time, it was clearly stated in an American court that certain corporations could not take shelter behind the free-enterprise doctrine.

> It was a blow [Frederic L. Paxson writes] to the ideas that had hitherto prevailed in the conduct of private business in the United States, to have the public admitted as a partner in the venture, and it marked a great turning point in the development of American Government.[2]

From now on it would be found that more and more corporations would be "clothed with a public interest": gas-illuminating companies, telegraph and telephone corporations, street railways, and eventually electric-power distributors—all the "utilities," as we call them—would come under the restriction. Judge Waite's decision was the first victory of the public conscience in an age of moral dissolution. The railroads continued their evil practices for many years. But the stage was set for reform.

4

As communications improved, as the nation was knit more tightly together, and as the supreme effort turned from conquering more territory to the consolidation of the ground already gained, the farmers were able to effect other reforms. One with a wide effectiveness

1 Munn *v.* Illinois, 94 U.S. 113, abridged in Commager: *Documents of American History* (New York, 1935), II, 93.

2 Frederic L. Paxson: *History of the American Frontier, 1763–1893* (Boston, 1924), p. 531.

was aimed at the dishonest middleman on whom the people in the rural districts had long been dependent. These agents of farm machinery or tool companies charged what they pleased for their goods, and the remote farmer was unable to check on the prices. They also sold on credit, relying, as so many crooked salesmen had always done, on the farmer's conscience, a faculty developed partly from long communion with the inexorable facts of soil and growth—the work of God. The credit, of course, again upped the price.

In the disastrous post-war drop in farm prices, corn had fallen to the below-cost figure of ten to fifteen cents a bushel. Wheat would have brought more but for the manipulations of financial jugglers in Chicago, where "corners," short selling, and other games were being played with the product of the farmer's sweat. In the Iowa winters farmers burned their corn to keep warm because it was cheaper than coal.[3]

As the industrial consolidation went on, with mergers and monopolies removing the small friendly establishments in which the farmer had bought goods and services, his "closely girded habit of economy" [4] suffered.

> He saw with anxiety that the process of consolidation was beginning to touch the small neighborhood crafts on which he had depended. The grist mill was being put out of business by the great milling centers. The number of carpenter shops, of cooper shops, of blacksmith shops, decreased under his eyes. At the same time he saw the number of middlemen multiply. On them he blamed, in part, the high prices he was obliged to pay for the manufactured articles which he and his family needed. In all this the farmer sensed a concentration of the growing wealth of the community in fewer and fewer hands. . . .[5]

The National Grange could not help the farmer restore the local industries, but this organization used its power to circumvent the minions who were fleecing him. They did this by buying in quantity from the big producers and selling through co-operative stores. They paid cash for such things as "implements, parlor organs, sewing machines, wagons, scales, even groceries and dry goods." [6] The Grange

[3] Oberholtzer: op. cit., III, 97.

[4] Horace Bushnell: "Work and Play," in *Library of the World's Best Literature* (New York, 1896–8), V, 2921, quoted in Tarbell: op. cit., p. 132.

[5] Tarbell: op. cit., pp. 131, 132; *U.S. Compedium of Tenth Census*, Part II, 926–7.

[6] Oberholtzer: op. cit., III, 104.

and, later, the Farmers' Alliances thus were able to accomplish a reform that individuals could never have effected. We see here evidence of the collective necessity which was imposed by industrial organization—a necessity that was to continue through our late history. The group conscience—not of a community, as in older times, but of a producing body—was here beginning to fight the growing evils of licentious enterprise.

Of material assistance to this group's attack (or defense) was an immensely able merchant, one of the first in the era to see that business might also have a conscience and that, in the general atmosphere of disguised banditry, honesty might become profitable. Aaron Montgomery Ward's first clientele was among the Grangers. Seeing the desperate needs of the rural population whose backs were against the wall, he offered to supply the co-operatives with honest goods at honest prices. Then, taking advantage of improved postal facilities, he established the first great mail-order house. As his business increased, his prices became lower and lower, his catalogues larger and larger, and he adopted the unprecedented practice of guaranteeing his merchandise, not only replacing defective goods but actually returning their money to unsatisfied customers. Until the coming of rural free delivery, of automobiles, and of radio, perhaps no greater boon ever came to the remote country-dweller than the establishments of Ward and his competitors.

5

It is hard for us to realize how revolutionary was the practice of selling honest goods, truthfully advertised, guaranteed, and at prices that conformed to value, following the age of "buyer beware."

It is impossible to estimate the extent to which the public was swindled in this half-century or so of commercial fraud. In a sense we have always been a gullible people. Barnum used to think Americans liked to be fooled. The jokes about gold bricks and wooden nutmegs are part of American folklore. It is also a national failing to "try anything once." Another widespread national weakness, strange among a people so much of whose achievement depended on physical robustness, was hypochondria. Beginning with dyspepsia and the "flux," we ran the gamut of real or imaginary ills and became willing clients of every species of quackery. The classic Yankee remark that So-and-So was "enjoying ill health" had a certain validity, especially in rural America after the first pioneer ardors of settlement were over. It is therefore not accurate to say that the swindles were forced upon us wholly against our will. The game of *caveat emptor* implied a sly smartness, and the smart ones who had learned their lessons laughed at the victims who got "stung," but always with good nature, as if adding to their laughs the comment that "after all, we are all suckers of some kind." Also, in the gilded age even the mean swindler was not invariably unadmired.

But after chemistry and medicine had made the rapid advances characteristic of the 1890's, the practices of the cheaters became dangerous and often tragic. By food-processors, for instance,

> the new knowledge was welcomed with open arms. Improving on past practices, they found new and ingenious ways by which stale meat and rancid butter could be freshened and food artificially preserved for an indefinite time. . . . Not only were substitutes and adulterants freely used, but the chemicals employed were often harmful.[7]

Adulteration was general. Earth was mixed with chocolate, marble dust with sugar, alum with flour, and other pulverized waste with baking-powder. Food already partly decomposed was restored by chemicals and artificial color. Old eggs were deodorized with formaldehyde and sold in quantity for baking. Meat, kept for months in an inadequate cold storage, was sold as "fresh." Apples too old to sell "were made into a jelly which, mixed with flavoring substances derived by chemistry from coal tar, appeared on the market labelled 'currant,' 'blackberry,' 'plum jam,' 'pure apple butter.' "[8] Mr. Sullivan quotes Professor (later Senator) Edwin F. Ladd, Food Commissioner of North Dakota, as stating:

> Of cocoas and chocolates examined, about 70 per cent have been found adulterated. . . . Ninety per cent of the so-called French peas we have taken up in North Dakota were found to contain copper salts. Of all the canned mushrooms, 85 per cent were found bleached by sulphites. . . . Many catsups were made from the waste products from canners—pulp, skins, ripe tomatoes, green

[7] Harold Underwood Faulkner: *The Quest for Social Justice, 1898–1914* (New York, 1931), pp. 236, 237.

[8] Mark Sullivan: *Our Times* (New York, 1927), II, 503, 504.

tomatoes, starch paste, coal-tar colors, chemical preservatives, usually benzoate of soda or salicylic acid.[9]

According to another analyst, James H. Shepard, coal-tar dye, alum, salicylic acid, sodium sulphite, saltpeter, formaldehyde, boracic acid, methyl alcohol, borax, copperas, and sulphurous acid were daily taken into the stomach of the average American, but the manufacturers he accused "claimed the amount in the portion of a single meal was so small as to be harmless." In a menu comprising the common food eaten by a normal family, Professor Shepard found "forty doses of chemicals and colors." [1]

Through the whole post-war period the practice of quack doctors and the sale of "patent" medicines increased, and as medical science advanced, it was possible to use long, ominous words in the advertising that exploited these. In newspaper advertising, subjects which could not have found a place in the news columns were freely displayed. Cures for impotence, treatment for "loss of manhood," "female disorders," and venereal afflictions tormented the thousands of boys and girls who secretly devoured this shocking material. Unhappy lads were told that perfectly normal phenomena of adolescence "drained away their strength." Others who had contracted a disease were crippled for life when they responded to quacks who addressed them in "plain envelopes."

Of the medicines, most were as harmless as Lydia Pinkham's celebrated pink pills, the damage coming either in the cost of the fraud to the innocent victim or in keeping him from legitimate treatment. Simple concoctions of herbs and spices were advertised as cures for cancer, consumption, all kidney troubles, catarrh, and even yellow fever. But other widely advertised and freely sold medicines "soothed" babies to sleep with opium and stopped coughs with drugs that could not be obtained today without a prescription. Samuel Adams, who eventually exposed the whole swindle, included in one of his articles the facsimile of this Cincinnati newspaper report of a coroner's verdict on the death of a child:

> Deceased came to her death from the poisonous effects of drinking the contents of a bottle of Doctor Bull's cough syrup.[2]

[9] Ibid., II, 504. Statement made by Edwin F. Ladd at a meeting of National Association of State Dairy and Food Departments at St. Louis in 1904.

[1] Ibid., II, 506, 507.

[2] Samuel Hopkins Adams: "The Great American Fraud," in *Collier's Weekly*, January 13, 1906.

Most of the liquid medicines gave the sick person a sense of well-being because of their large content of alcohol. Many Americans who believed themselves strict teetotalers and zealously campaigned for prohibition became addicts through the use of such "medicine" as Peruna, a disguised whisky which was prohibited on the Indian reservations. It is diverting to look over some of the old newspapers and find an advertisement for Peruna juxtaposed with the announcement by a quack that he could "Cure Your Husband of Drinking."

The "patent"-medicine [3] advertisements were almost invariably bolstered by letters from grateful patients. The fictitious nature of one of these was exposed by Mr. Adams. He showed clippings from the same issue of a small-town newspaper. One, disguised as a news item, read:

> Mrs. Mary C. Adams . . . wants all stomach sufferers in Winsted to know that she owes her present good health to a course of treatment with Dr. Richards' dispepsia tablets. . . .

The other:

> Mrs. Mary C. Adams passed away at her home on Adams street Wednesday evening. . . .

In her letter to *Collier's* enclosing the clippings, Mary's friend and neighbor wrote:

> The lady died from the trouble she claims she was cured of, and the funeral notice is on the opposite side of the sheet from where they call attention to her good health.[4]

This account points the venality of the provincial press. In the later days of the era the better urban papers refused bribes to print advertisements as "news" items, but they were almost universal in the small-town papers; indeed, the editors complained that the papers could not survive without them.

The century had turned before the public conscience was aroused against this evil. The exposures came in the so-called muckraking era. They became possible when certain cheap magazines which had attained enormous circulations could afford to refuse fraudulent advertising. Edward Bok's *Ladies' Home Journal* was a pioneer in this negation; it and the immensely successful *Collier's* led the reform.

[3] "Patent" medicine was a misnomer. These concoctions could not be patented. Secrecy was essential to their preparation.

[4] Adams: op. cit., October 12, 1907.

Following these, Upton Sinclair's *The Jungle*, accusing the great slaughterhouses and packing plants, and the articles of Harvey W. Wiley, and provoked also by the painful memories of the "embalmed beef" scandal of the Spanish War, the first Pure Food and Drug Act was passed in 1906. Although the abuses have never been wholly eliminated, progressive legislation following the return of the national conscience has stopped the worst of them.

The uniquely American part played by the early large-circulation magazine in attacking the deeply entrenched group swindles and the depredations of fraudulent, monopolistic, or extortionist corporate enterprises was vital to the revival of conscience. It came only after the frontier doors had closed. It came after millions of people of all the strata had been hurt. It came when jobs were scarcer, when vast immigration from new European areas seemed to be pushing the native-born into dead ends of sub-subsistence pay and intolerable working conditions. It came when power had been almost feudally concentrated. It came when the American masses were seething with discontent. And it came when Americans lower in the scale than the readers of *Harper's* and the *Atlantic* could be reached. The promoters of the new cheap magazines sensed the revolt against power. With the great increase in both quantity and quality of legitimate advertising based on the surge of production, they had nothing to lose. The material was sensational and, once they could go over the heads of the tycoons on the subscription lists of the more expensive publications, they had, indeed, everything to gain. Added to all these factors was the new desire of lower-middle-class Americans in the pause from continental conquest to read and to reflect.

Chapter XXVI

The End of the American Dream

ONE OF THE signal achievements of the American people has been their course between the Scylla of monopoly and the Charybdis of socialism. The fear of these twin bogies has been with us from the earliest days. The course has been haphazard; the wake of our ship as we look at it today is so zigzag that it seems we must have hit, at some time, the shoal of one rock or the other.

We have usually steered nearer monopoly than socialism—though our fear of its peril has been consistently less. But as the nineteenth century drew toward its close, we came so near monopoly that the violence of our reaction seemed for a time to be taking us into revolution.

In the '70's and '80's there was no federal legislative check on the concentration of power aimed at the destruction of competition. As we have seen, the unbridled competition had been wasteful and sometimes deadlocking. The total *laissez-faire* policy had therefore produced the impulse to defeat that competition by any available means.

The good Adam Smith had predicated his policy of not interfering with the interplay of the economic "laws" upon the belief that men had consciences. His scheme took no account of the possibility that those engaged in business would use force and treachery to defeat their rivals and thus stop the interplay just as effectively as if government had stepped in. As his great work was published in the year in which the American colonies declared their independence of

Britain, he could hardly foresee what might happen in a nation enriched beyond all dreams by its natural wealth and protected by its isolation from outside attack and by its autarchy from the need of extensive international intercourse. Nor could he envision a government which, far from interfering with business, supported it with bounties never before possible and which would come to regard the progress of industrial enterprise as more important than that pursuit of happiness to which it had been formally dedicated.

In the '70's and '80's, more slowly than the farmers, the people in general began to realize what was happening. Waves moving out from the centers of concentration were beginning to touch ordinary folk here and there—gently, at first, to be sure. But in the tighter organization of society that had followed the closed frontier and with the new communications, such waves could not be dissipated in space.

In 1872 an Ohio corporation for refining petroleum calling itself the Standard Oil Company wiped out by a threat of sure defeat some twenty competitors.[1] Mr. Rockefeller did not hold a gun at the heads of the directors of these refining companies. His method was more subtle but no less effective. Before confronting his rivals, he had secured secret agreements with the key railroads to rebate from twenty-five to fifty per cent of the freight charges his company paid them and, in addition, to pay a so-called "drawback"—a large percentage of the charges paid by rival companies. This the railroads were glad to do in order to assure a heavy, steady traffic in refined oil. Mr. Rockefeller and his associates then explained to the officials of the competing companies what he had done and generously offered to buy their enterprises at a price to be determined by a board of appraisers. If they demurred, he patiently showed them that the alternative was certain ruin. The potency of this threat was indicated by the fact that one company in which $75,000 had been invested, and which had paid an annual average of thirty per cent on the investment, sold out at the appraiser's price of $45,000.[2]

Standard Oil received a setback when, as a result of a suit brought by the oil-producing state of Pennsylvania against the Pennsylvania

[1] Ida M. Tarbell: *The History of the Standard Oil Company* (New York, 1904), I, 67.
[2] Ibid.

Railroad, John D. Rockefeller and seven associates were indicted for conspiracy to secure a monopoly of the oil business through control of transportation. The men were never brought to trial. This failure was the consequence, their opponents thought, of railroad pressure on state authorities, but they were obliged to seek new ways of winning their monopoly. The way they hit upon was the way of the "trust."

The Standard Oil Trust was the first of that series of combinations which produced a cumulative public agitation lasting well into the twentieth century. The devices that came to be called "trusts" were so varied that the word soon lost any specific meaning and became in popular concept an indictment of every competition-restraining combination from the simple trust devised by the Rockefellers to the holding company, whose cradle was the state of New Jersey. The first Standard Oil Trust effected a transfer of all the capital stock of the constituent companies to nine trustees. The original shareholders received "trust certificates" as evidences of ownership.[3] By this and other devices through the years to 1911, when the combination was dissolved, Standard controlled more than ninety per cent of the nation's refining business and most of the production as well. At least until 1906 the monopoly was buttressed by secret railroad rates.[4]

Like a highly contagious disease, the trust idea spread. Whisky followed oil, bringing sixty-eight distilleries to an end; next came sugar and the closing of eleven refineries.[5] Rubber, coal, linseed oil, copper, and many other commodities began to rise in price due to monopolistic control. Throughout business, the pressure was felt. The public conscience brought the abuses into court via the suits of damaged businessmen against the trusts. This gave the unfair tactics of combination an airing before the public. There were investigations in two state legislatures and four states passed anti-trust laws before John Sherman in the spring of 1890 introduced a sweeping bill in Congress designed to end all combination in restraint of trade.

In the debate on the bill there were wholesale indictments of the trusts.

[3] Ibid., II, 136. Tarbell: *The Nationalizing of Business*, p. 76.

[4] E. L. Bogart: *Economic History of the United States* (New York, 1924), p. 480.

[5] Sullivan: op. cit., II, 307.

> They aggregate to themselves [said Senator George of Mississippi] great, enormous wealth by extortion . . . they pursue unmolested, unrestrained by law, their ceaseless round of peculation under the law, till they are fast producing that condition in our people in which the great mass . . . are the servitors of those who have this aggregated wealth at their command.[6]

The bill passed with only one dissenting vote. Yet it had little effect on the epidemic. The law was too slow, the lawyers too clever, the Supreme Court too vague, too halting in its interpretation. When the old simple trusts were dissolved under it, other devices were invented to give technical legal sanction to the ruthless practices. For fourteeen years the combinations increased until in 1904

> it was estimated that 318 industrial trusts with a capital of $7,246,000,000 and representing consolidations of nearly 5300 distinct plants existed in the United States; of this capital over one third was controlled by seven great organizations.[7]

But by 1904 the printed word had taken effect. President Theodore Roosevelt had heeded the tumult of the national conscience and the true reform had begun.

2

The United States had known three sorts of periodicals—not including the almanacs. There was the "literary" magazine interesting to those who could afford contemplation of the arts and letters. It derived much material from abroad and amused travelers and those engaged in such esoteric pursuits as archæology or exegesis. Then there was the type that reached its apex in Godey's *Lady's Book*—practical manuals instructive in the art of keeping up with the Joneses. Finally, there were the countless religious papers, several for each of the splinter sects plus interdenominational champions of sugar-coated righteousness. By 1900 some of the Christian magazines had fallen into disrepute from printing the advertisements of

[6] *Congressional Record*, 51st Congress, 1st Session, Vol. 21, Part 2, p. 1768 (Feb. 27, 1890).

[7] Bogart: op. cit., p. 477. Professor Bogart explains that this is a rough estimate. Henry D. Lloyd: *Wealth against Commonwealth* (New York, 1902), Appendix, p. 537, gives a "Partial List of Trade Combinations, or Trusts, Achieved or Attempted, and of the Commodities Covered by Them."

frauds and quacks; certain of them had stirred distrust from their part in the not strictly religious controversy over Theodore Tilton's charge that Henry Ward Beecher had seduced Tilton's wife.[8]

Periodicals concerned with current affairs maintained a policy of hands off business and were champions of *laissez faire,* contenting themselves with "deploring" crime waves and labor agitation. Alone as a courageous critic of American business stood Benjamin Orange Flower's *Arena*; but this was branded by the respectable as "shamefully radical," and Flower was erroneously called a socialist. Incidentally, its style was hardly a popular one. To the great lower middle class and to literate proletarians ripe for revolt, the *Arena* carried little appeal.[9]

Literate but "uncultured" Americans by 1900 were sick of milk-toast literature. At the same time they craved sensational exposition. They were swayed by yellow journalism, but the best of them thought it superficial and untrustworthy. They wanted something they could "get their teeth in," yet something also that entertained by chilling the spine. Above all, they wanted writing that articulated the jelling conscience of the masses: articles that said what they wanted to say in the same terms but better, of course, than they could say it. And they wanted these things at a minimum of cost. The sensational but authentic and thoroughly documented book by Henry Lloyd, *Wealth against Commonwealth,*[1] which led all the muckraking, expressed what they wanted to say, but it was a book and cost $2.50.

In the '90's four publishing geniuses appeared. They were of very different cast. John Brisben Walker, with a kaleidoscopic background of many endeavors and a won-and-lost fortune, was a vital, energetic zealot for democracy intent on the current scene and with a mission to popularize the burning issues. Samuel McClure, Irish, emerging out of poverty to self-education, was an editor with a genuine intuition about potentially successful authors. Frank Munsey was a calculating opportunist whose main contribution to the American conscience was his leadership in lowering the price of maga-

[8] Theodore Tilton *vs.* Henry Ward Beecher, Action for Criminal Conversation, etc., New York, 1875.

[9] Louis Filler: *Crusaders for American Liberalism* (New York, 1939), pp. 39 ff. This is the most thorough and readable review of the "muckraking" period. For a sympathetic view of Flower and the *Arena,* see C. C. Regier: *The Era of the Muckrakers* (Chapel Hill, 1932), pp. 17, 18, 23 ff.

[1] First published in New York in 1894.

zines so that others could expose the sins of society.[2] Finally, there was the Dutch immigrant Edward Bok, who presented a balanced combination of sincere impulse for uplift with an eye for the main chance. This brought him the reputation of a Philistine among those who thought they knew what the word meant. Unless all of these men had been closer to the vulgar multitude than to the armchair connoisseurs of culture there would have been no medium for the moral indignation of a whole people. Their success was the sure index of the existence of a solid, homogeneous national conscience for the first time in our history.

English critics sneered at the cheap American magazines these men started, but several English authors pocketed their pride along with the scarcely believable sums the vulgar editors paid them. McClure went abroad to ensnare Rudyard Kipling, Conan Doyle, and Octave Thanet, and these writers in turn ensnared large circulation among the new American reading public that was surprised at getting these expensive writers for ten or fifteen cents. But McClure's greatest discovery was in Paris, where he found an American girl who had left her native oil lands of Pennsylvania for a Sorbonne education. He did not start Ida Tarbell on petroleum; he let her build her public with popular biographies of Napoleon and Lincoln. Then, when she was famous, he turned her loose on Standard Oil. McClure's purpose, in 1897, was not mere muckraking. He thought of Standard Oil as a sort of symbol of business success. But when he saw what Miss Tarbell's five years of research had turned up, he knew intuitively that it was what his public wanted. Its serial publication in *McClure's Magazine* began in November 1902.

> *The History of the Standard Oil Company* [Louis Filler writes] was not really the work of an agitated investigator. . . . The agitation existed in the minds of the readers who were compelled to face the truth that Standard Oil was tangible, corrupt and inescapable; the monumental nature of the exposure lay in the fact that Tarbell had telescoped into a relatively few pages a history which had involved the nation as a whole and still involved it. . . . No wonder the series was news; no wonder the history of a business house was followed month after month as if it had been a romance! [3]

[2] We are indebted for these appraisals to the suggestions of Louis Filler: op. cit., Chap. 3.

[3] Ibid., p. 105.

This established the McClure pattern and led magazine "muck-raking." Less tempered was *The Inside Story of the Carnegie Steel Company*, which followed it. McClure's stable now contained real crusaders such as Lincoln Steffens, Burton Hendrick, and Ray Stannard Baker. Steffens's articles on political corruption in St. Louis waked the people of other cities to pursue reforms. Baker fearlessly attacked the railroads, and Hendrick found abuses in the business of life insurance that were startling indeed. In Walker's *Cosmopolitan* David Graham Phillips stirred the political conscience with his *Treason in the Senate*. Perhaps Frank Munsey's greatest contribution to the muckraking era was in providing the ladder by which Erman Ridgway climbed into publishing. After his success as Munsey's vice-president and general manager, he was able to start *Everybody's*, one of the most down-to-earth of all the exposing magazines. Its title gives a clue to its popularity. During its publication of Thomas W. Lawson's *Frenzied Finance* its circulation went from less than two hundred thousand to nearly three quarters of a million.

Bok, whose *Ladies' Home Journal* was on a more elevated level than most of the big-circulation magazines, fired the opening gun in the campaign against what Adams later called "The Great American Fraud" when as early as 1892 he refused to accept patent-medicine advertisements in his magazine. An exposure of that racket in the *Journal* in 1904 was the curtain-raiser for the devastating series by Samuel Hopkins Adams in *Collier's Weekly* in 1905.

It is said that whenever in history concerted public opinion reaches a certain temperature, a leader appears to turn hot words into cool deeds. With all his personal faults, Theodore Roosevelt was one of our greatest reforming presidents. When the unexpected death of McKinley put him into the White House, he already had his hand on the pulse of the people. He had read such complete diatribes as that of Henry Lloyd. As governor of New York he had seen much of the industrial dictatorship. He had already engaged in brushes with powerful bosses or lobbyists and left such Titans smarting. Egotistic, vain, tiresome with his robust outdoor philosophy, ruthless certainly, sometimes ludicrous (as when he led his "rough riders" on foot up San Juan Hill against the orders of his superior officers), Roosevelt nevertheless knew precisely where he was going and with unquestioned courage went there.

In his first term he revived the moribund anti-trust law of 1890 against the Northern Securities holding company, which had acquired the stock of all the larger railroads west of the Mississippi, doing away with railroad competition there. When the Supreme Court ordered this giant with its four million dollars of capital dissolved, the American business world knew that the new president had become champion of the new national conscience. From then on there would be more and more legislative restraint of business. The law against rebates was newly enforced. Suits were instituted against alleged trusts in coal, oil, tobacco, meat, and other things. The sardonic remark that "Wall Street is paralyzed at the thought that a President of the United States should sink so low as to try to enforce the law" [4] had general currency.

Finally, after the exposures of the patent-medicine swindles, the conditions in slaughterhouse and packing plant, and the horrors of food adulteration, and after the exhaustive analytical work of Dr. Harvey W. Wiley, the Pure Food and Drugs Act of 1906 began what, for the mass of the people, was the greatest reform of all.

Taft carried the torch Roosevelt had lighted. During his administration there were forty-three trust indictments—about double the number secured under Roosevelt. Wilson went further. Declaring that still "the laws of the country do not prevent the strong from crushing the weak," he attacked the ingenious devices which corporation lawyers had invented to salvage the trusts. By the time, then, of the First World War, the public conscience had reversed a disastrous trend and, for the first time, installed the people as a legitimate partner in business enterprise.

3

Manifest Destiny, which presumably had been fulfilled when the frontiers closed, took a sudden leap westward just as the century ended. This last tremendous jump was wholly unexpected, and it planted the American flag in a place most Americans had never heard of. It brought thrills of patriotism to the spines of millions of Americans and catches in their throats; it brought songs about ringlets of thin gray hair and a hot time in the old town; it made a fabulous hero out of a surprised mediocre admiral; and it set off a chain

[4] Sullivan: op. cit., II, 415.

reaction of conscience that has never stopped. When the thrilled Americans realized that their patriotism had been spurious, that this last spasm of Manifest Destiny was largely the result of an effort to sell yellow journals, and that the whole affair had saddled us with a remote, insoluble problem, they remembered that orgy of 1898 with shame. As time went on, they realized, too, that the incident had forever shattered our precious isolation.

Whether the explosion that destroyed the United States battleship *Maine* in Havana harbor on February 15, 1898, was part of a deliberate Spanish plot is a question Americans have been asking one another ever since. A sort of morning-after conscience over what has been called an *opéra-bouffe* war against a pitifully weak antagonist, set off by that explosion, has induced many remorseful people to wonder if perhaps the disaster had been self-contained within the ship. In any case, the death of two hundred and sixty-four American sailors and two officers was enough to fire the national rage, already long incandescent over Spanish treatment of Cubans. It is doubtful, however, that the war would have developed without the agency of the most vicious and cynical behavior of a part of the American press that our nation had yet seen.

Hearst's New York *Journal* and Pulitzer's *World*, competing for circulation, led the parade, but provincial papers throughout the country were quick to follow. Since the early 1890's they had been whipping up the expansionist impulse which had slept after the closing of the frontier. They had insisted on America's "mission" in the Caribbean; on the need for "far-flung" navies and therefore Pacific coaling stations; on the importance of a new American imperialism that should keep pace with British expansion. Especially they had urged the annexation of Cuba as a step toward an Isthmian canal and, since 1895 when the Cubans had begun their revolution against mother Spain, had printed a succession of atrocity stories showing the cruelty practiced on the Cuban underdog—a sure way to secure popular backing for any economic or political aggression.

But what has most distressed the after-thinking American conscience was the fact that the President let himself be swayed by the press-agitated frenzy. At the start McKinley had stood against war with Spain. Even after the *Maine* affair he tried to secure peace by making certain demands on Spain, including a cease-fire in Cuba. But then, when at the last moment Spain completely capitulated, acceding to every single American demand, McKinley, feeling the press-inflamed Congress, goaded by the press-inflamed people, breathing down his neck, was frightened into sending his war message. It was a compelling pressure, surely, but a strong leader would probably have resisted it. And his party in the cooling-off period might well have accepted his leadership. At least, that is what many repentant Americans and their historians have come to believe.

> Any President with a backbone [write Samuel E. Morison and Henry S. Commager] would have seized this opportunity for an honorable solution. McKinley, a veteran of 1861, was averse from war. Mark Hanna, Wall Street, big business, and the leaders of the Republican Old Guard backed him up. With such support McKinley needed less firmness than John Adams had shown in the XYZ affair or Grant in the *Alabama* case to preserve peace. But Congress, the press, and the country were clamoring for war. . . . McKinley became obsessed with the notion that if he did not give way, he would forfeit his leadership in the party. After much prayer and hesitation, he decided to yield to popular demand.[5]

War was declared on the 25th of April. On the 1st of May Americans were amazed to find that Manifest Destiny had taken the star-spangled banner some seven thousand miles west of San Francisco and planted it on an island that turned out to belong to Spain. Hastily looking up their atlases to discover where Manila was, they were entranced to discover that West had met East, that here was empire beyond the wildest dreams of continental conquest: suddenly, like Britain herself, we were a world power. As this war had from the start been an opera war, the song-writers rushed to their pianos and this brilliant contribution to the war effort emerged. It reflected the color and sounded the pitch of the entire war.

Oh, dewy was the morning
Upon the first of May,
And Dewey was the Admiral,
Down in Manila Bay.
And dewy were the Regent's eyes,
Them orbs of royal blue,
And dew we feel discouraged?
I dew not think we dew! [6]

[5] Morison and Commager: *Growth of the American Republic,* II, 330.

[6] By Eugene Ware ("Ironquill"). Quoted in Sullivan: op. cit., I, 322. Mr. Sullivan insists that Ware wrote "Them orbs" because he thought that such a colloquial form had a "peculiar value."

The war was meant to be boisterous, colorful, and gay. That it did not turn out so for many unhappy people was because of the pestilential fevers, the illness and death caused by the profiteering sale of rotten meat to the army, and the strange discontent of the Filipinos at being rescued from the hands of the Spanish into the hands of the Americans. After four months the end came; the poor Spanish hulks followed the *Maine* to the bottom, peace was concluded, and in the treaty the accusation of outright piracy was avoided by the payment to Spain of twenty million dollars for the Philippines.

The conscientious reaction set in immediately. Men who had opposed the war but had kept silence while the guns were firing now leaped into an anti-imperialist crusade. A destiny in the Pacific, it was now said, had never been manifest. The annexation of the Philippines without the consent of the Filipinos was declared contrary to all American tradition. The most truly distinguished Americans of the time, from Eliot of Harvard to Mark Twain and Mr. Dooley, joined the campaign. The decent press was filled with letters, editorials, and poems scathing the Pacific conquest on economic as well as traditional and humanitarian grounds.

The crusade made little immediate difference in the election of 1900. McKinley was reinstated under the banner: "Don't pull down the flag." But it must be remembered that the dubious Bryan was his antagonist. And the demonstration of national conscience at the turn of the century had later consequences when its extension effected the independence of Cuba and of the Philippines.

Never again, after the war with Spain, were we capable of complacency in our isolation. From now on we must engage in world politics. Our position in the Far East brought us into brushes with Germany and new contact with England. It prepared the way for the war with Japan which began in 1941. We must necessarily from now on progress from a national to an international conscience. As we shall come to participate in the two world wars, nothing we do can have its consequences only in our own walled and moated nation. Our behavior must be in new measure either the cause or the reflection of the behavior of other mankind; the influences that guide us in our day-to-day conduct will be forever complicated by movements, desires, or conflicts outside ourselves. Only the American core remains—the precious puritan substance forged and tempered on the frontier—and here must be the last criterion of our world judgments and the eventual arbiter of our world thought.

We entered, however, upon the larger scene with the greatest reluctance. Even after the armistice of 1918, when the peoples with whom we had been allied were applauding our first appearance on the world stage, we withdrew, frightened, into the wings—walking out on the lines of our president and mouthing the half-forgotten words of Washington about entangling alliances.

In the confused era that followed, we repudiated the exalted position to which we had attained. We did our best to pretend that everything was as it had always been. We ignored the wings spreading over the protective oceans—wings that day by day were rendering those classic moats less protective. Parrot-like, we repeated over and over the words that the war to end war had been fought and won. With our new little Fords we sought and found new unexplored sections of promised land. We told ourselves that there was still gold in them thar hills, and on that promise built enormous paper pyramids. We deceived ourselves back into the old belief that morale could be legislated and the oldest customs killed in the Capitol's halls.

It was a mad time, that decade. As we look back on it, it seems scarcely real, a disordered dream with a starkly tragic ending. From that ending we may never wholly recover, just as we may never wholly recover from the disaster of the 1860's. But the scar it has left will be a reminder that we dreamed too long, that the old glamour cannot be restored, and that the American conscience must somehow adjust to a new environment.

Chapter XXVII

"Our Most Wanton Orgy"

THE REFUSAL to accept the realities began the instant war was over. The nostalgic retreat—the escape—into romance characterized the first post-war year. The will to forget bewildered the late arrivals from overseas in the summer of 1919. Cheers and tears and ticker tape had greeted the first heroes. Then the public became bored: sick of uniforms and steel helmets and shouldered arms; sick of heroes and the everlasting sameness of the stories they had to tell.

At considerable sacrifice of comfort, we had "pulled Europe's chestnuts out of the fire." That was enough of Europe. Now it was time to get back to our own business unencumbered by foreigners. We had managed a good many years by ourselves. Europe, the isolationists said, ignoring the immigration, had not helped us in the continental conquest.

This retreat into the past was accompanied by an insistence that we keep unsullied the "pure" American stock. There began a movement, against all tradition, to close the gates to immigration. A wave of racial intolerance swept the country. A revived Ku-Klux Klan of large membership and great strength became militant not only against Negroes but against Jews, Catholics, and Orientals. In the first post-war year seventy Negroes were lynched, some while still in uniform. Interracial conflict was not confined to the South. There were race riots and anti-Negro mob violence in Chicago, Omaha, and Washington as the colored veterans came back from the war to look for new homes.[1]

Popular opinion turned against our allies—especially Britain; we

[1] John Hope Franklin: op. cit., pp. 471 ff., with sources given on pp. 616, 617; Sullivan: op. cit., VI, 178, 179.

must extricate ourselves quickly from any alliance that might jeopardize our future. The wily European politicians were lying in wait to ambush us, to involve us in their sinister "Machiavellian" politics. The powerful isolationist element repudiated the wartime president and his dangerous League of Nations.

With remarkable speed the army was demobilized and the boys sent home to their moms. As the veterans came out, they were absorbed into the new, powerful American Legion, an institution that presently adopted frontier methods in its dealings with "subversives." Here, to be sure, the war spirit was perpetuated, and men in the habit of hating but no longer able to hate the defeated Germans were encouraged to turn their loathing upon the Reds.

In such a mood the dominant portion of the American people led the United States into one of the blackest decades in its history. The people, to be sure, acted for the most part without evil intent. On the contrary, they clothed their behavior with the old adornments of virtue. There were still echoes from the wartime pulpits assuring congregations that killing the "Hun" had been a Christian act, that the war had been a crusade: Christian soldiers marching onward against the host of Satan "with the cross of Jesus going on before." Thus, in the first confusion of the peace we find many misdeeds executed for a cause: hatred of the "Christ-killer" Jew, of the atheist Bolshevik, of the heathen Oriental. Even the Ku-Klux Klan could not carry on its obscene brutalities without the background symbol of a flaming cross.

But as we look back on the era, the most prevalent state of mind is a bewildered confusion. Lacking any strong leadership, we let ourselves be led by the most ignorant, the most unstable elements. We can detect a low, half-heard drumbeat of conscience through the years, yet it seems as if this exacerbating accompaniment had been one of the things from which we were fleeing. We followed the crowd as it pursued its mirage of frontier Utopia. We broke the laws because "everybody" broke the laws. We forgot old moralities because the crowd said we had been liberated. If we occasionally looked over our shoulder and shuddered at some reality back there that we had feared to face, the crowd laughed at us and dragged us on into the brightly illumined celluloid synthesis of the new never-never world.

Year by year the lunatic fringe deepened. Year after year it caught more and more normal citizens into its meshes. Absolute standards gave way to expediency. In some areas respect for law reached an all-time low. Political corruption attained a level lower than that of the '70's. The nation was swept by epidemics of hysteria running the gamut from Red-baiting to dance marathons and flag-pole-sitting. Speculation made the reckless gambling of the frontier look like a church raffle. National prohibition forced millions of citizens to take the law into their own hands and relegated thousands of others to the underworld. Boys and girls, dazed by bathtub gin, sang, as they danced, dirges to the "lost generation" to the accompaniment of wailing saxophones.

In the effort to clarify this curious picture of a late frontier hang-over and fit it into our study of the American conscience, we must examine some of these aspects in detail. The probability is that the decade will then reveal itself as a throwback—a stopping of the clock and a turning back of the hands, a moment of dead-center, if you like—rather than an advance into any actual future. In this light the 1920's hardly seem to be a part of the twentieth century.

2

Woodrow Wilson, driving through the flower-strewn streets of Paris between the rows of kneeling, praying women, may have acquired an exalted notion of his mission. In the brief weeks that followed he was Messiah. No American—not even Franklin in 1777—was so worshipped on foreign soil. It is doubtful that this homage aroused in him any personal vanity. On the other hand it is probable that this Puritan sincerely believed himself to be an instrument of God, predestined to mend a broken world and to make that restored world "safe for democracy."

Neither this blind adoration, however, by war-weary Frenchmen, nor the concept of a new crusade for international harmony, greatly appealed to the legislators whom the President had left at home in Washington. Some, moved perhaps by jealousy, as no flowers had been strewn for them, wanted to repudiate the false Messiah for personal reasons. Others objected on stubbornly partisan grounds: the Republicans had not been consulted. Many of the opposition said, and perhaps thought, that it was beneath the dignity of an

American president to go alone on a triumphal march through alien lands. And there were those, too, who sincerely wanted a league of nations but not Wilson's League.

When the President returned, therefore, wearing his laurel crown, he had in his own country a reception quite different from that in Paris or Rome. As day after day he heard the voices of the diversely inspired opposition, he became more rigidly determined to accept no compromise. Yet, he was reminded, he had compromised abroad when he had accepted conditions opposed to his own convictions and the American interest. Yes, to save the League. But now the compromises asked for by the "wilful men" would destroy the League.

The battle that ensued was as devastating as any the Capitol had seen since the post-Civil War days. But more and more, as it progressed, the people attached themselves to the anti-League faction. There seems to have been widespread confusion as to what the League actually was. In the end it was widely felt that any league would destroy American isolation, would "entangle" us with the cynical politics of Europe.

The American people may never have witnessed a more poignant tragedy than the defeat of Woodrow Wilson. If any statesman ever died of a broken heart, that fate was his. For weeks he toured the country, moved by a deep faith in the righteousness of his own people. Obsessed by belief in his mission, he went over the heads of their representatives to speak directly to the crowds of American men, women, and children, who rarely could appreciate the measured beauty of his words. From Boston to Chicago to San Francisco he traveled, until his eloquence presented a macabre contrast with the sagging lines of his face, his gray fatigue, the fading light in his eyes. Then, on the way home, he collapsed; he was smuggled into Washington to shield his shattered mind from the public consciousness.

Whatever the rights and wrongs of his convictions, Wilson made a demonstration of sheer puritan conscience that became increasingly haunting as we passed through the later reverses of the epoch between the wars. Millions of remembering Americans still think of him with bitterness as a self-centered, bull-headed, would-be dictator. But as his story is revealed in the study of history apart from personal prejudice, it is likely to stand as an evidence of that tough puritan core, built layer by layer through the centuries from the earliest beginnings, that still survived in our most amoral years.

While Wilson lingered on in his darkened room, a small group of Republican politicians in desperate search for a total throwback hit upon a largely unknown mediocrity in an obscure Ohio town and nearly frightened him to death by assuring him that he would be the next president. Handsome in face and figure, kindly, amiable, weak, and without the faintest understanding of statesmanship, he was the ideal contrast to the deep-thinking, scholarly incumbent. He was the perfect symbol of the reaction. He spoke the vernacular of the frontier. He was the negation of "culture," of the high learning that had taught Wilson to explore the international mind. He was the exponent of smiling ignorance, of innocent stupidity, of credulous faith in his fellow man.

Warren Harding rode to overwhelming victory on the shoulders of the nostalgic isolationists.

3

Soon after the United States had entered the war, Russia, which had been in it from the beginning, withdraw. In October 1917 began "the ten days that shook the world," from which Russia emerged as a communist state with the avowed Marxist purpose of bringing about revolution among the workers of the world. As a result, Russia became America's number-two enemy. After the armistice she became number one.

Atrocity stories told of the Germans during the war paled beside those emanating from Bolshevik Russia in the 1920's. The carcasses of bourgeois victims of the civil war were said to hang in the butcher shops of Moscow. Most horrible of all, there had been a campaign of militant atheism in which churches had been desecrated and little children were taught the evils of Christianity. Traitors to their Czar, their flag, their allies, and their God, they had imbued millions in the proletariats of other countries with their debased doctrines, and the chances were, thought many a wealthy American property-owner, that they would soon produce a revolution here too and hang tycoons to the lampposts of Chicago and New York.

"Hun," the fighting word of 1918, was replaced a year later by "Bolshevik." As usual, the tag was generally fixed in the wrong places. Not only the avowed communists, members of the party, and International Workers of the World were persecuted, but mobs fell upon law-abiding socialists and upon those critics of Wall Street and big business who a few years before had enjoyed applause and limelight. Accustomed to the indiscriminate behavior toward suspect German-Americans in the war, the super-patriots of the peace took even less care to accord justice to the so-called Bolsheviks.

The post-war economic and industrial background gave plausibility to the Red scare. Prices that had risen like rockets in 1919 had not been compensated by adequate wage rises or amelioration of working conditions. The result was a rash of strikes, some of them very crippling. As always in such circumstances, there were agitators working with labor, pressing sometimes for the socializing of the coal and steel industries, sometimes advocating revolution. To point the unrest, these troublemakers—often real communists, usually cranks or fanatics—distributed bombs in government offices or mailed them to prominent capitalists. Only a few went off, but the reports of those that did resounded and re-echoed through the nervous nation. The press, always quick to seize on sensational news material, did little to allay the almost universal fear or to underestimate the "peril."

But the alarm was not confined to the ignorant or the inflammable or to still bloodthirsty American Legionnaires. The soberest people, as Frederick Allen recalls,

> seriously thought—or at least millions of them did, millions of otherwise reasonable citizens—that a Red revolution might begin in the United States the next month or next week. . . .[2]

Thus, what would normally be rated as criminal acts were applauded in the drawing-rooms of Beacon Street and Fifth Avenue, in the country clubs of Evanston, Grosse Pointe, and Sewickley.

> It was an era of lawless and disorderly defense of law and order, of unconstitutional defense of the Constitution, of suspicion and civil conflict—in a very literal sense, a reign of terror.[3]

But because such high principles were at stake, consciences were not hurt. Not, that is, until later. Later it turned out, as it so often does, that it was the principles that suffered the damage.

[2] Frederick Lewis Allen: *Only Yesterday* (New York, 1931), p. 45.
[3] Ibid., p. 46.

Those who remember "McCarthyism" during the cold war of the 1950's will not be surprised to read that the terror extended to schools and colleges, where teachers were accused of subversive instruction, to publishers charged with printing treasonable books, and to preachers who did not conform their sermons to the day's patriotism. But that legislatures, the high offices of government, and the courts should take a hand in the indiscriminate prosecution subverting the most elementary practices of justice suggests that the Red scare of 1919 and 1920 was far more damaging to our national morals than anything that has occurred since. Yet precisely this happened.

In 1920 five duly elected socialist representatives to the New York legislature were prevented by vote of the Assembly from taking their seats. Shortly before, the United States House of Representatives had voted 309 to 1 to unseat Victor Berger, socialist congressman from Wisconsin.

In December 1919 United States Attorney General Mitchell Palmer began a series of raids on alleged Reds throughout the nation. In the same month he summarily deported 249 men and women on a U.S. transport. On New Year's Day 1920 he conducted simultaneous raids in dozens of cities, arresting and imprisoning men without warrant, searching communist or socialist offices without warrant, seizing and impounding every sort of documentary evidence. "Over six thousand men were arrested in all, and thrust summarily behind the bars for days and weeks," [4] and many were not told of the specific charges against them.

> In Detroit, over a hundred men were herded into a bull-pen measuring twenty-four by thirty feet and kept there for a week under conditions which the mayor of the city called intolerable. In Hartford, while the suspects were in jail the authorities took the further precaution of arresting and incarcerating all visitors who came to see them, a friendly call being regarded as *prima facie* evidence of affiliation with the Communist party.[5]

In the cold gray dawn after these orgies little evidence could be found on which these suspects could be convicted of conspiracy to overthrow the government, but Palmer's frontier methods were roundly applauded. It did not seem to occur to the serious headshakers that few exploits of California vigilantes, Carolina regu-

[4] Ibid., p. 57. [5] Ibid.

lators, or amateur posses in pursuit of cattle rustlers had exceeded Palmer's performance in disregard of the orderly processes of the law.

In the same year of terror—1920—occurred an incident which has disturbed the American conscience ever since. A commonplace crime took place on an April day in South Braintree, Massachusetts. A factory paymaster carrying his payroll was held up, murdered, and robbed. Suspected of this murder were two Italian "radicals," Nicola Sacco and Bartolomeo Vanzetti. Sacco was a worker in a shoe factory; Venzetti was an occasional fish-peddler. Both men were students of socialism and philosophical anarchy, followers of the Galleani school, which, in turn, followed Tolstoian precepts.

The men were tried before Judge Webster Thayer at Dedham, Massachusetts, in June 1921. The atmosphere of that trial, as we read about it in the 1950's, seems curiously reminiscent of the Massachusetts Bay Colony in the time of the seventeenth-century trials of heretics and witches. The mood of prosecutor, jury, and court was one of resentment against men who appeared to be dissenters from the accepted doctrines of the commonwealth rather than robbers and killers. The popular feeling outside seemed to be pressing against the walls of the courthouse. The hysterical fear, as in the summer of 1692 at Salem, was at its peak. The marked difference from the witch-trial days was in the support of the public conscience by the enormous Catholic population which so bitterly hated the Russians for their atheism.

Later, calmer reviewers of the evidence against the two men have found it largely circumstantial and insufficient for conviction. Defense evidence including alibis has convinced even conservative minds of the innocence of the accused. They were nevertheless found guilty of murder in the first degree on the 14th of July, and all applications for a retrial—even when fresh evidence was uncovered—were denied.

The verdict had repercussions all over the world. There were violent demonstrations in Paris and Rome—that in Paris was accompanied by a bomb explosion killing twenty people. Attempts were made to bomb the homes of the American ambassador in Paris and the consul general in Lisbon. There were a general strike and a boycott of American imports in Montevideo, and editorials in the radical press in most of Europe and South America. This international celebrity, added to liberal dissent in America, made the case a sort of American Dreyfus affair.

Sacco and Vanzetti spent seven years in prison. During this time a criminal under arrest for other offenses confessed a part in the Braintree murder and his confession exonerated Sacco and Vanzetti. The confession, said the inflexible Judge Thayer, was a fabrication. All appeal was denied because Massachusetts law did not permit a review of the facts by the state supreme court.

Meanwhile, the behavior of the prisoners aroused more and more sympathy throughout the nation as the fever cooled. Vanzetti, especially, despite his low estate, showed himself, in letters written in prison, a high-minded intellectual wholly without avarice or the greed for material gain that could have prompted a part in the sordid robbery and murder for which he was held. Studying English until he could write it, he was able to compose an eloquent statement when his death sentence was finally passed. In it he hailed Sacco and himself as martyrs to their cause.

> Now we are not a failure. . . . Never in our full life could we hope to do such work for tolerance, for joostice, for man's understanding of man as now we do by accident. Our words—our lives—our pains—nothing! The taking of our lives—lives of a good shoemaker and a poor fish-peddler—all! That last moment belongs to us—that agony is our triumph.[6]

Nothing availed against the new theocracy of Massachusetts. The conviction by syllogism stood. The Russians denied God; the Russians were communists; Sacco and Vanzetti were radicals; therefore they denied God; anyone who denied God would probably murder a factory paymaster while robbing him of his payroll. The Massachusetts witch-hunters withstood the appeals of Tomáš Masaryk, Albert Einstein, Anatole France, and Romain Rolland; they set at naught the powerful arguments of their own conservative lawyer William G. Thompson and accepted the final judgment by a committee of three famous Yankees whose distrust of foreigners had been inherited from the Winthrops, the Endecotts, the Cottons, and the Mathers of an early day.

President Lowell of Harvard, President Stratton of the Massachusetts Institute of Technology, and Judge Robert Grant, despite their other excellent qualities, have never been wholly forgiven by the

[6] H. B. Ehrmann: *The Untried Case* (New York, 1933), p. 245.

American conscience for their judgment against Sacco and Vanzetti. Year after year that conscience, becoming at last a historical conscience, has grown increasingly unhappy. It has been goaded by uncounted volumes, articles, tracts, novels, and plays. The story was told in Upton Sinclair's *Boston*; it was the theme of Maxwell Anderson's play *Winterset*; it was savagely satirized in *The Big Money* and *U.S.A.* by John Dos Passos; it was retold in James Farrell's *Bernard Clare*. Sacco and Vanzetti have become, not martyrs, but symbols: tragic memorials to the sacrifice of civil rights through mass hysteria; perpetual reminders to the national conscience in times of stress.

4

Prohibition had frontier origins. Drunken debauches were characteristic of mining, construction, and lumber camps. In earlier days when the frontier was only a jump from the coast, drunkenness was a besetting American sin, often punished in the cities but given license in less-settled areas. Down the Ohio, as we have seen, it ran riot in the flatboat days. It was a scourge in Kentucky. Even in the sedate, Yankee-settled Northwest Territory it presented a problem.

The temperance movements may have started in the eastern cities; they gained their greatest momentum as they followed the frontier. When in the West women became the dominant element, they sought the defense of their families among the lawmakers. It was the women and children who had suffered most from the men's habits. Their zeal, therefore, had primitive, savage impulses.

There was, however, another factor, not primarily concerned with intemperance. In the latter half of the nineteenth century the liquor interests had become powerful instruments of political corruption. The saloon had become the headquarters for the buying and selling of votes, for the breeding and instruction of ward "heelers," and the extensive undercover operations of such dominant institutions as Tammany Hall. The saloon was thought to have been an aid to the Tweed ring in New York and the Whisky Ring in St. Louis. This was quite natural, apart from questions of intemperance, as the saloon was the natural gathering-place of lower-bracket voters—

of the uninformed, the gullible, the easily corruptible men who had to rely on the bosses for political instruction. The saloon was the only "poor man's club."

The liquor-interest scandals put an additional tool into the hands of the temperance workers. At the same time the interests were able to prevent prohibition in the thickly settled, urban-dominated eastern states. Thus, the temperance fight became legally effective mainly in the West, where the pressure of sentiment was also greatest. With the exception of the state of Maine, then, the first prohibitory legislation appeared in the West. Kansas led the procession in 1880. By 1905 Nebraska and North Dakota were prohibition states. At the outbreak of the World War in 1914 the southern states of Georgia, Mississippi, and North Carolina had joined the parade for the special reason of their colored populations; before the year was over, the list included Oklahoma, Virginia, Arizona, Colorado, Oregon, and Washington. By war's end Arkansas, Idaho, Iowa, South Carolina, Alabama, Michigan, Montana, Nebraska, South Dakota, Indiana, New Hampshire, New Mexico, Utah, Wyoming, Florida, Ohio, Nevada, and Texas were legally "dry." [7]

This astonishing wave of "reform" was the product of pure conscience plus efficient, powerful organization. There can be little question that the proponents of the sumptuary laws were sincere in their effort to abolish a destructive force in society. They envisioned a resulting prosperity, a disappearance of poverty, a return to religion, an increase in the productiveness of labor, a decrease in industrial accidents—endless were the green pastures down which they saw a triumphantly abstemious American people marching toward a new dawn of civilization. But in order to achieve these glorious ends they resorted to the oldest puritan practice of putting statutes on the books, indulging an illusion which had persisted through American history and which had repeatedly proved false, especially on the frontier.

The hopeful champions of prohibition ignored the long history of lawbreaking beginning with colonial smuggling against intolerable British law and developing through the successive stages of frontier advance the most ingenious techniques of evasion ever evolved in civilized society. They ignored the ancient precept that it is impos-

[7] Preston W. Slosson: *The Great Crusade and After, 1914–1928* (New York, 1930), p. 105 and 105 n.

sible to legislate against established custom. Finally, they ignored the nullification that was going on under their eyes in their own communities.

The war exaltation spurred the drive toward national prohibition. The picture of "mom's boys" marching forward into battle clear-eyed, with no taint of alcohol on their sweet young breaths, drew tears of joy from the super-patriots. Also, the absence of those boys—of voting age—left the ballot in the hands of industrialists who wanted to remove temptation from their workers and of those women who had already been enfranchised. And the war brought also the patriotic argument that the distilling of whisky consumed large quantities of grain which ought to go into foodstuffs for the armies.

Before the boys returned, therefore, the notorious eighteenth amendment, prohibiting the "manufacture, sale, or transportation of intoxicating liquors" for beverage purposes, had been ratified. It became law, therefore, and on the effective date in January 1920 the concurrent congressional legislation known as the Volstead Act joined the other evidences of mass hysteria.

The subversive forces were ready. Through the succeeding thirteen years they built more powerful nullifying machinery than had ever been dreamed of, even during the lurid years of colonial piracy. Finding themselves now outside the law, the forces subverting an earlier liquor traffic found themselves free to build a new underworld Utopia.

The prohibition breed of lawbreakers included variations on the old theme. Rum-runners and hi-jackers were highly organized under new dictators—gang leaders with the power of kings. The community of Cicero, Illinois, became a feudal manor with an Italian named Al Capone as overlord. His rule there and in Chicago was extra-legal; he operated outside the pale of courts and police. Tributary to him were lesser lords practicing rackets in other cities. These gentlemen corrupted police and even occasionally revenue agents into affording protection for their criminal activities. The "speakeasy," sometimes called a "blind pig" or a "blind tiger"—also so effectively protected that it could operate practically in the open—became an urban commonplace. The itinerant bootlegger was usually a gentle Italian, warm and friendly to his customers, intimidated by the higher-ups in the liquor racket and by the racketing police. In no town could a citizen find himself unable to get a drink; often the patrolman on the beat could tell him how.

The failure of national prohibition—once called a "noble experiment"—was a peculiarly American debacle, tragic in many of its aspects. It inflicted a deep scar on the American conscience. The wave of crime it precipitated was one of the lesser moral obliquities. It bred individual hypocrisies, parallels to which we may find in long-dead puritan society. Tycoons, industrial magnates, wealthy businessmen—many of whom had promoted the amendment—adopted the Pharisaical attitude that they were "not as other men." Prohibition had not been meant for them. They knew how to handle liquor—"to take it or leave it alone"—to drink decently at home or in their clubs. It was quite all right for them to continue to drink: they could afford it; it did not produce poverty or sordidness in their families, nor dent their business efficiency. But the worker who, they said, had always abused alcohol, who now could not pay bootlegger prices, would enormously increase his productivity and thus enrich the tycoon. This class discrimination was, of course, intolerable in a democracy, and it became the strongest argument for repeal.

The truly high-minded citizens—judges, lawyers, doctors, educators, and occasional statesmen—were never free from conscientious torment. They almost all continued to drink, as it became a compelling custom. But they shuddered as the clandestine purveyor of contraband brought the packages to the back door. They knew that each of the packages might have cost lives or necessitated crime. They chafed at the need of sneaking to a club locker. Finally, as a sop to tortured consciences, they drank as a patriotic gesture: wrapping their bottle of gin in a figurative American flag, they drank in magnificent protest, toasting the Statue of Liberty, the Founding Fathers, and the ancient Constitution as it had stood before its desecration. All these things were wholly, characteristically American—frontier products. But the mature minds thought it was time we outgrew infantilism and stopped making ourselves the laughing-stock of the world.

Fortunately, national prohibition was repudiated with such righteous indignation and then forgotten with such avidity that today it is thought of, if at all, as one of the nightmares of a lunatic era. There remains, of course, the ironic fact—a tragedy to the sincere advocate of abstinence—that it markedly increased American drinking and spread the habit among the young.

5

One of the happy aspects of the era came with the discovery of new frontiers. This had begun with that beautiful instrument of individual freedom, the bicycle. The cheap automobile, a uniquely American product, extended it to a point at which the decade of the '20's became a repetition of the more glorious frontier days. Much of the progress of Tin Lizzie over the muddy and rocky trails of almost unexplored regions was rugged, too, recalling covered-wagon adventure. There were no Indians, to be sure—they had been relegated to reservations or to the back yards of the American conscience—but there were still weather and the unknown properties of gasoline.

The cheap car changed the social geography of the country. Millions of new pioneers penetrated to lands too far from the railroads to encourage settlement; good roads followed the cars, and suddenly there were new, thriving towns. Moribund hamlets became prosperous villages. As tourists followed the pioneers, they brought new markets. In many places where men had carried their goods long distances to markets, the buyers now came to them. Gay new stores, restaurants, taverns, inns profited from a transient population. Roadside stands became a new industry, filling-stations gave jobs to rural men, and eventually, in a later decade, the tourist camp or "motel" became a source of profit and pleasure in outlying country that had been a virtual desert a generation before.

The automobile may have made only minor contributions to the moral scene. Its main function in the morale of the '20's was in compensating the homesickness for a vanished frontier. Here it provided a balance for many of the evil features of the time. Instilling a love of adventure, it led youth away from the darker urban shadows into free and fresh spaces. It was a healthy thing.

It was said that it led to free love. Parents shook their heads and said that the Lord only knew what happened on the moonlit roads so far from home. The car was thought to provide a perfect sanctuary for that much-touted practice of the era, "necking" or "petting"—the consequence of which, of course, was deep sexual iniquity; yet, surprisingly, such consequences were far from certain. To the boys and girls of the jazz age, petting seems to have been a sort of sport grouped in many young minds with tennis or swimming. But the puritan conscience is always active about youth and quick to seize upon every novelty as a new tool of Satan. Movies, radio, comics, and television have all come under the disapproving scrutiny of an American search for sin.

The car, to be sure, facilitated elopements, kidnapping, seduction, and every sort of crime. But it did not cause these things. The impulse to sin in such ways had always been there. The old frontiers offered as easy escape as the new. Gangs, feuds, and casual killings had long antedated automotion in America: these things had increased in automotive days, but so had the population. The cheap automobile of the '20's—before the days of giant horsepower, of fantastic speed and horrendous accidents—can hardly weigh heavily on the American conscience. It was a harmonious accompaniment to a dissonant melody.

6

Woodrow Wilson was still alive when Harding was borne to his grave by the burdens of conscience. By 1923 the house in H Street and an even less reputable establishment in K Street had done their work. Behind a front of "normalcy," of super-patriotism, of mounting prosperity, corruption like termites was eating at the foundations of government.

The American people, when Harding died, knew nothing of this. But he had known in his last weeks that the boys with whom he had played so many cheerful games of poker had finally betrayed him. On his last journey to Alaska in the summer of 1923 he had puzzled companions and reporters by his nervousness and haggard fatigue. He died, presumably, of ptomaine poisoning brought on, it was said, by crabmeat, but the subsequent stories by Samuel Hopkins Adams [8] that he had committed suicide by poison and by Gaston B. Means [9] that his wife, knowing that he was at the end of his rope, had mercifully murdered him were both plausible.

[8] Samuel Hopkins Adams: *Revelry* (New York, 1926).

[9] Gaston B. Means: *The Strange Death of President Harding* (New York, 1930).

The facts which emerged after his death were, many of them, of a sordidness that has since been highly repugnant to the better American taste if not to the American conscience as a whole. When they first came out, however, as Frederick Lewis Allen so significantly points out, public opinion turned against the investigators rather than against the culprits. The public did not want to be shocked out of its complacency at the "normal" atmosphere to which they hoped the nation was returning. Even such ordinarily intelligent editors as those of the New York *Times*, *Tribune*, and *Evening Post* called the senators who uncovered and proved the scandals "assassins of character," "scandalmongers," and "mud-gunners."

> In these and other newspapers throughout the country one read of the "Democratic lynching-bee" and "poison-tongued partisanship, pure malice, and twittering hysteria" and the inquiries were called "in plain words, contemptible and disgusting." [1]

But the public that was revolted by the investigations lived to discover that it was the answers, not the inquiries, that were contemptible and disgusting.

As we read the lurid tales of the "gang," as Harry Daugherty proudly called it, surrounding President Harding from 1920 to 1923, we are almost surprised that the United States survived those three years. That we recovered, that we reversed the trend, that we regained the respect of the outside world, is testimony to the existence of a strong basic morality. But it is evidence, too, that the lapse was largely due to a perverse effort to fall back into a dream, to convince ourselves that we were still isolated and that frontier manners were still the truest American manners.

A small-town political manipulator who believed that anything was right that worked made Harding president. Harry Daugherty was never able to get any elective office for himself, but he was one of those king-making forces that always lurk in the wings of any political stage set. When he first met the small-town editor Harding, he liked his looks. "What a president he would make!" he is reported to have said. He presently learned enough about Harding to know that if he could be maneuvered into the White House, he would be big-hearted enough to take the home-town boys to Wash-

[1] Allen: op. cit., pp. 154, 155.

ington and put them in jobs that would be not only "cushy" but powerful and lucrative as well.

That, with effective guidance, Harding should have been elected to the United States Senate in 1914 is not surprising. The Senate has always contained many such nonentities boosted into the nomination by small-town machines. But that he should have been nominated for president testifies to the frantic search for a mediocrity to compensate for Wilson's educated and powerful vision that had antagonized so many bitter-end isolationists. Yet even the little group that chose him in that "smoke-filled room" at 2:00 a.m. were frightened for a moment at what they had done. Rumors of his loose living, his steady, genial drinking, his relations with women, compelled them to demand his solemn declaration that there was nothing in his past that could be used against him. Asking for time to think it over, Harding managed to adjust his conscience even in the matter of Nan Britton, the mother of a child she claimed as his daughter—conceived, she maintained, in the Senate office building. He returned to say that his conscience was clear.[2]

On his heels as he journeyed to Washington for the inauguration March 4, 1921, came the Ohio gang, the rag, tag, and bobtail of office-seekers, the vulgar, dishonest, drinking, poker-playing, grafting camp-followers. To take care of this crowd and keep their genial amusements from polluting the White House, the two extra-curricular resorts were acquired: the "House of Mystery" on H Street and the "Little Green House" on K Street. In point of fact, there were warm evenings even in the executive mansion itself, upstairs, where the prohibited liquor flowed freely and men took off their coats and got down to the serious business of high-stakes poker.

But it was in the K Street house that the boys really got back to the frontier. The H Street house, Mr. Adams tells us, was a semi-respectable front for the K Street one. Some quite formal parties alternated there with late poker evenings, and even Mrs. Harding was an occasional visitor. But the "Little Green House"

> became quite a social centre. Senators, Congressmen, and Cabinet members dropped in to have a drink from the supplies obligingly furnished by Government officials who diverted confiscated wet goods thither and to play in the sky-limit poker game. . . . It was

[2] Willis F. Johnson: *George Harvey, "A Passionate Patriot"* (New York, 1929), p. 282; Nan Britton: *The President's Daughter* (New York, 1931), p. 69.

> a port of call for big liquor operators, office-buyers, jobbers in bribery and all the sorry, furtive drift of political underworld.[3]

When Harry Daugherty was appointed Attorney General, it was unlikely that the wayward behavior of the Ohio gang would be disturbed by the Justice Department. To their hearts' content, then, its members

> traded in liquor withdrawal permits, protection to bootleggers, appointments to office, illegal concessions, immunity from prosecution, pardons, paroles, privileges and general graft.[4]

It is probable that the President himself was not fully aware of what was going on in these clandestine quarters. He never inquired too closely. He trusted all his old friends and Daugherty's friends—even that shadow of Daugherty, the slippery Jesse Smith, whose conscience finally drove him to suicide. With the exceptions of the front men in the Cabinet—Hughes, Mellon, Hoover, and Weeks—he appointed old cronies, men for whom he had personal affection, to jobs for which they were wholly unfit either from incompetence or dishonesty.

Behind the cheap, petty, cigar-chewing, drinking, and shyster-dealing performance in the White House annexes on H and K streets there were enacted some of the most corrupt "big deals" in modern history. There was the so-called Teapot Dome affair in which the President transferred vast naval oil reserves from the Navy to the Interior Department at the behest of his friend Albert Fall, Secretary of the Interior. Harding was ignorant of the fact that he had no constitutional right to do this. Nor did he know that Fall had been bribed to persuade him so that he, Fall, might then lease this government property to two private oilmen. Nor did he know that his trusted appointee to the office of Alien Property Custodian, Thomas W. Miller, had engaged in "wholesale looting" for which he was later convicted of criminal conspiracy to defraud the government.[5] He was reported to have discovered the mammoth graft of his fair-haired boy on whom he and Mrs. Harding had showered affection and hospitality, Veterans' Bureau Administrator Charles R. Forbes, and to have bitterly cursed this favorite and

[3] Samuel Hopkins Adams: *The Incredible Era* (Boston, 1939), p. 235.

[4] Ibid.

[5] Allan Nevins: "Harding, Warren Gamaliel," in *Dictionary of American Biography*; Morison and Commager: op. cit., II, 518.

"laid violent hands upon him." [6] Whether he knew of the lesser "betrayals" by the Ohio gang, he was sufficiently shaken by what he did learn to lose the will to live.

Perhaps there has never been a greater contrast between a president and his successor than that between Harding and Coolidge. A deep-dyed Puritan from the heart of New England, close-lipped, laconic, cold, unfriendly, suspecting all pleasurable activity, despising liquor, play, idleness, and good humor, Calvin Coolidge was almost a burlesque of the inflexible Yankee. Yet Coolidge could not restore the national conscience that had suffered in the first post-war years.

In the Republican convention that nominated him, Theodore E. Burton pointed a finger of scorn at those who were inquiring into the scandals of the Harding administration. William Allen White, reporting Burton's opening speech, wrote:

> Great applause greeted him when he criticized the investigation at Washington. If Fall or Daugherty had appeared after that declaration the convention would have given either an ovation.[7]

But there were several reasons for the delayed reaction of the national conscience. In spite of the revelations in Washington there was an increasing motive for keeping the *status quo* and enjoying it. Through the last years of the decade there was much to occupy the minds of the people. As golden a future as ever glowed over the Sierras seemed to light the American sky in these nostalgic days. For the second time the American dream was coming true.

7

The difference between the gold of the 1850's and 1860's and the gold of the 1920's was the difference between hard, solid, precious metal and paper facsimiles of it. The vision of wealth that the American people saw in what we now regard as the terrible spring and summer of 1929 capped the climax of that dream decade. It was a mirage of promise, a reflection of times long past. In October, when the happy dream turned to nightmare, we began to pay the price of all our follies with usurious interest.

[6] William Allen White: *Masks in a Pageant* (New York, 1928), p. 430.

[7] William Allen White: *Politics: The Citizen's Business* (New York, 1924), p. 33.

Never in our history had there been as great a shock to our faith in ourselves and in what till then we had thought of as the "American way." The actual house of cards that fell in the autumn of 1929 may have been only a decade in its building. It is all very well to say that the structure was composed of pieces of fiction held together by imaginary cement. Nevertheless, the fall brought down with it hopes and beliefs hundreds of years in the making. In a sense the whole of American history had been a sequence of fictions—but fictions based on extremely solid facts. Nearly every dream of new wealth, of new frontiers of space or thought or science, or of the conquest of enemies had come true twofold. Often our dreams had fallen short of the latent, underlying realities. Our wildest fancies, for instance, had failed to guess the fertility of western soil, the abundance of western gold, the prodigality of forest wildlife.

The centuries of fulfillment had addicted us to dreaming our futures. Now, in the depression following the crack, we could see no future. Destiny had ceased to be manifest. All our thoughts turned to the past. How did it happen? What was the first mistake? Were the roots in war, in overproduction, in the ruthless pyramiding of corporations by financial magicians in the attempt to get something from nothing?

All over the nation there came a wave of conscience far more real, more tangible, and more ubiquitous than any before it. Hardly an American escaped some sense of guilt—often vague, usually inarticulate or wholly silent. From the high financier who, goaded by intolerable remorse, found death below his window, to the office boy who had put his savings into shares of fabulous stock, all felt a personal part in the catastrophe: hardly an American could look at his hands and know that they were clean. From the weeks before when there had been "no ceiling" to the months and years after when the overcast of guilt had come so low above our heads, the contrasting values were those of a nonsense world. We would hear, from time to time, cries and imprecations, accusations or curses against God and man, but they were stilled as if some voice had said: "Hush, we are all in it: no one can be sure who threw the first stone."

The children of the depression years seemed a new breed. In their adolescence they craved security. The impulse to adventure was gone. In them the old American flair for gambling, for attempting the impossible, had dissolved. It was far more desirable to hold what you had, to become imbedded in a *status quo* that was real, than to "take a chance" on a chimerical future.

The mood changed somewhat, of course, with better times. The wounds are healed; only the scars remain. It is too soon to guess whether the scars will ever disappear. It is too soon to know how completely the "American way" has been changed. Since the disaster many new frontiers have opened. We have seen new vistas of science, new horizons of wealth. Again there are opportunities for dream and action, greater perhaps than before. Whether we shall meet them in the high mood of our great building days or, instead, lose the advantage that in those days we gained is perhaps a futile question in our present state of flux and myopia.

We only know that during the long hangover after our most wanton orgy—specifically, from 1929 to 1934—there came our greatest disillusion. It is possible, however, that that interval of introspection will prove a means of future salvation. It has left a residue of doubt in the most wishful minds. In the years after, when communications multiplied, our ears have become attuned to voices crying in the wilderness. The troubles of other consciences than ours have been in constant procession across our threshold, and all the singing commercials we could muster have been unable to keep them out.

One of the effects of the depression was to show us the tightness of our integration with the rest of the world. We became aware of our importance in foreign eyes. We realized what a body blow it had been to other faiths when our financial citadel had fallen. But we came to know, too, the part that world-wide operations had played in the disaster. Never again could we face threats from the outside with our old scornful laughter. Never again could we plan a great and brave future without first looking abroad to Russia or China or the Middle East or to one or more Germanies. Our national conscience, in short, was beginning to merge with an international conscience, diverse and uncertain as that might still be.

Unhappily, we have shown ourselves, to date, afraid of that merging. The long isolation has bred a distrust of the world outside. For three decades of the twentieth century while that isolation was in fact breaking down, we were able to pretend to ourselves that we were still a world apart and a world ahead—a leader who could make decisions that the rest must follow or be damned. We still believed that, as Kipling said, we were able

> *To shake the iron hand of Fate*
> *Or match with Destiny for beers.*

Then, after the depression had weakened our faith in ourselves and a second world war had proved beyond all pretense that we were no longer separate, we discovered that we actually were the world's leader, that the tired, broken nations of Europe and Asia looked to us for salvation; and the realization terrified us into paralysis.

Has conscience, then, made cowards of us? This is a question the historian cannot answer.

Epilogue

WE HAVE DEFINED public conscience as the body of opinion that judges moral behavior in a community. What we call the American conscience is the dominant body of opinion in the nation. As we have reviewed our history we have seen this national conscience emerge from a long evolution through the many diverse and dangerous phases of our growth. We have seen first those moral controls that were limited to a province and were usually deeply involved with religion; we have seen the rigid theologies—especially the dark, inexorable Calvinist patterns—transmuted in the New World out of their mysticism and dialectics into warm, intimate, human, and practical faiths that for a time united the colonial peoples; we have seen the new unity that came with the passion for liberty and was illuminated by the enlightened philosophies of Locke and Jefferson.

We have seen, then, as the people moved toward continental conquest, the gradual dissolution of that unity in the original provinces and the spread of a divided conscience westward. We have seen this phase as one dominated by regional consciences. The divisive questions were two. The first asked: Was the United States a nation or were the United States a league of nations? The second asked: Can Negro slavery be permitted in a society dedicated to the proposition that all men are created equal and possess the unalienable rights of life, liberty, and the pursuit of happiness? In the American climate these questions inevitably became moral issues.

The first question was answered in fact before the theory was resolved. The outcome of the conflict proved that through the operation of the integrating forces of communications, industry, and interregional commerce, the sections had, as Lincoln had foreseen, become indissolubly dependent on one another. The answer to Negro slavery had also been given—not of its right or wrong—but of its economic feasibility. Yet conscience demanded that the war be fought. Unhappily, that cruel conflict, with its residue of bitterness, posed new problems of conscience that have never been wholly resolved. We are learning—all mankind is learning—that war never really solves problems of conscience; on the contrary, it usually multiplies them. At least, however, the recognition, after the smoke had cleared, of the factual national unity laid the basis for the eventual coming of a national, an American conscience.

We have seen the slow, painful emergence of this body of moral standards, through a succession of peculiarly American conditions. The need for the restoration of decent government and the opportunity for new prosperity in the desolated South; the need for justice in wild, underpoliced communities in the overexpanded West; the need for humanitarian regulation of the coastal cities glutted with indiscriminate immigration; the constant need to control corruption in government—a chronic disease inherited from enforced colonial lawbreaking and nurtured by an environment of apparently unlimited wealth; the need to cleanse commerce of fraud and deception; the need to purify a press whose freedom had run amuck; the need to co-operate in world problems—all these and many other urgencies have led through trial and error, mistake, disaster, and conflict to the building of a public sense of right and wrong that has no sectional boundaries.

This is the progress, elusive, syncopated, passing over high peaks and through deep valleys, that we have tried to trace against the background of unique conditions.

2

But why, the reader may well ask as he pursues his reading, why all this history? Are not chapters of the story records of mere political events, of the working out of economic designs or social complexes? The answer lies in the peculiar American compulsion to assign moral values to every historical event, economic theory, or social trend. There is hardly a thought or deed in our story that has not been clothed with virtuous or vicious intent or religious significance. Scarcely a political step has been taken without an appeal for justification to the Almighty or a reference to a Christian ideal, a spiritual abstraction. In earlier days Scripture was quoted to prove every point. The effectiveness of Tom Paine's *Common Sense* depended on Biblical citations proving the fallacies of divine right.

Paine may have been a "free-thinker" himself, but he knew the necessity for an American public of pointing to the word of God. Throughout the nineteenth century nothing moved Americans more immediately than a religious allusion or metaphor. As late as 1896 William Jennings Bryan achieved enduring celebrity because in the advocacy of a purely economic program he pointed an accusing finger at the consciences of his listeners and told them:

> You shall not press down upon the brow of labor this crown of thorn. You shall not crucify mankind upon a cross of gold.

The Declaration of Independence may have been a political document, but its words moved far beyond the politics of empire into what appeared to its framers and signers to be the moral rights of all mankind. Its preamble transcended the traditions of government and focused upon the product of Protestant thinking since the Reformation—the exaltation of the individual. It stated its "self-evident truths" as absolutes imposed by nature's God and beyond the reach of human dialectic. And the conclusion called the Supreme Being to witness its sincerity.

Ever since, despite storms of analytical criticism, the Declaration has remained, to the great body of the American people, an instrument of conscience replete with ideals as sacred as those of the Gospels—immune even to the incisive logic of a Calhoun or the erudite scorn of a Rufus Choate.

All our wars have had conscientious apologists or opponents. Madison, in his war message of June 1812, spoke of committing "a just cause into the hands of the Almighty Dispenser of Events." The Mexican War produced a conflict of moral judgment between the believers in Manifest Destiny and those whose conscience warned against the extension of slavery, and conscience-stricken historians have been deploring it ever since as a cynical predatory operation. In the Civil War political and economic backgrounds were all colored with conflicts of conscience over slavery, and no issue has made more abundant use of Scriptural testimony on both sides than that of emancipation.

The war with Spain was fought, in the common mind, with the unselfish moral objective of liberating unhappy Cubans from diabolic Spanish cruelty, and if in the process we were forced to suppress the Filipinos in their struggle for liberty, the fact so hurt our conscience that we were never afterward content until we had made retribution by granting them independence. With apparent cynicism one president provoked the revolution of Panama from Colombia in order to establish a canal under American control, but this so weighed upon the conscience of a later generation and of a later puritan president that we gave reparations for the incident to the injured nation. Finally we entered both world wars as "crusaders."

A front of virtue has even been deemed essential to commerce. Few Americans are willing to concede that they are in business to make money. Publishers and advertising men are educating and enlightening the human race, bankers are promoting the virtue of thrift, soap manufacturers are advancing the ideal of cleanliness (second only to godliness). Everyone is "doing good" in some manner, and if in the process excessive fortunes have been accumulated, the sons of the money-makers, under pressure or fear of the public conscience, often feel constrained to turn over the excess to charity. The younger generations of Rockefellers, for instance, whose progenitor was under fire from the American conscience, became the greatest philanthropists in history.

Europeans have watched these things with amazement. Statesmen of nations allied with us in the First World War whose understanding of international politics was based on the precepts of Machiavelli's *Prince* were baffled by the moral aspects of Wilson's approach to peace. Like the framers of the Declaration, he seemed more concerned with the benefits of victory to mankind than with its rewards to Americans. They could scarcely believe his rejection of territorial aggression, they saw practical danger in his policy of the self-determination of peoples, and they were frankly frightened by his insistence on "open covenants openly arrived at." But the tired people of western Europe—of France especially—dubious about the benefits they had derived from the traditional operation of balances of power, looked upon America glittering in its crusading armor with awe and, for a brief time, thought Wilson might be the new Messiah.

In America, then, the history of conscience is scarcely separable from the rest of its history, and no record of moral behavior and moral judgment that ignores the political, the economic, and the social trends can ever be wholly intelligible.

3

This peculiarly American disposition to seek moral reference points for American aims and deeds is evidence of the persistence of a conscience that has remained puritan. How this has survived our headlong, reckless, wasteful, expansive drive is difficult to explain. How it has endured the influx of immigration—unique on its scale—from every part of the world and from every moral climate is seldom understood even by the immigrants themselves. There were times, as we have seen, when it seemed forever lost. There were long intervals when moral decay appeared to have eaten away the very foundations of our republic. Yet always, in the critical instants when the extremes of our conduct have brought us to the very verge of moral bankruptcy, the voice has spoken and the American soul has been saved again.

Perhaps the answer has been in the bigness of our spaces and the tenuous communications across them. We thought we had lost that puritan thing, only to find that it had merely been somewhere else. Under the first industrial dictatorship when the railroads were letting the public be damned, it spoke in the Grange. It has spoken repeatedly in our silent moments of disillusion. It spoke when the frontiers closed and we looked in vain for free land. It spoke in the silence following the crash of 1929. It has spoken after every war, once the echo of the martial music has died and the glory has faded from the battle flags: the greater the victory, the louder the voice calling for repentance, self-flagellation, forgiveness of the enemy, and "no more war." Like all conscience, it has slept in prosperity and waked in tribulation—but in America in greater degree, in tune with the violence of our ecstasies of pleasure and misery.

The voices we have heard have not always been right—as later voices have sometimes told us. The several voices, however, may come from the same conscience. The body of opinion that made us abandon national prohibition contained many of the minds that had forced us into it—but wiser in the knowledge that in fleeing from one evil we had found ourselves surrounded by others. With the nation, the American conscience has matured. Tempered in the fires of catastrophe and transgression, it may have become, like saw steel, more flexible but no less tough.

And now? From the moral point of view our land looks sterile enough. Now that mass communication has scanned every corner of our nation and revealed what it has found to every other corner, is there any place where the conscience that again seems to be lost can be hiding? Not in forest or prairie, surely, not on any lonely frontier farm. There are no lonely spots any more in America the Beautiful. But in some area, perhaps, of the American mind? It may be that only after another disaster will the noise die down to the point where the voice can be heard.

We are prosperous. We are complacent. Religion has become, for the most part, a social convention—convenient in time of trouble but devoid of responsibility. Skill is anonymous, thought is under pressure to conform, security has replaced venture as a dominant aim, intellect is in the discard, and politics are dictated by a cult of mediocrity.

The historian of a century hence may say all this of us; he may add that these mid-century years, this morally arid interval, was followed by a long and fruitful season. Have we not discovered, in all this history, that such times as these may be the most pregnant? Is it not possible to feel, in an hour of quiet darkness when we have turned off the television, the old forces rallying round us?

But perhaps now we are playing a game even more dangerous than that of the if's of history. Of one thing only can we be certain: the American destiny is no longer manifest—if, indeed, except in minds too wishful for conscience, it ever was.

Bibliography

Abridgement of the Debates of Congress. From 1789–1856. Thomas Hart Benton, editor. In sixteen volumes (New York, 1857–61).

Adams, Charles Francis: *Antinomianism* (Boston, 1894).

——: *Three Episodes of Massachusetts History*. In two volumes (Boston, 1892).

Adams, John: *Works*. Charles Francis Adams, editor. In ten volumes (Boston, 1850–6).

Adams, John Quincy: *Memoirs*. Charles Francis Adams, editor. In twelve volumes (Philadelphia, 1875).

Adams, Samuel Hopkins: "The Great American Fraud," a series of articles in *Collier's Weekly*, 1905–7.

——: *The Incredible Era* (Boston, 1939).

——: *Revelry* (New York, 1926).

"Address to the People of Great Britain," approved Oct. 21, 1774, in *Journals of the Continental Congress*, I, 87, 88.

Albion, Robert G.: *The Rise of New York Port* (New York, 1939).

Allen, Frederick Lewis: *Only Yesterday* (New York, 1931).

American Archives. Peter Force, editor. In nine volumes (Washington, 1837–53).

American State Papers. Documents Legislative and Executive of the Congress of the United States. Selected and edited under the authority of Congress by Walter Lowrie and Matthew St. Clair Clarke. The volume referred to in the text is Class II, *Indian Affairs*, Vol. I.

Andrews, Charles M.: *The Colonial Period of American History*. In four volumes (New Haven, 1936).

Andrews, Ethan Allen: *Slavery and the Domestic Slave Trade in the United States* (Boston, 1836).

Annals of Congress. The full, correct title of these volumes is *The Debates and Proceedings of the Congress of the United States; Annals of Congress, being the popular abridgement of that title*. In forty-two volumes (Washington, 1834–56).

Ballagh, James Curtis: *A History of Slavery in Virginia.* Johns Hopkins Studies in Historical and Political Science. Extra volume XXIV (Baltimore, 1902).

Bancroft, Frederic: *Slave-Trading in the Old South* (Baltimore, 1931).

Barce, Elmore: "Tecumseh's Confederacy," in *Indiana Magazine of History* (Indianapolis, 1916), XII, 169, 170.

Barck, Oscar Theodore, Jr., and Nelson Manfred Blake: *Since 1900: A History of the United States in Our Times* (New York, 1947).

Barlow, William: *The Somme and Substance of the Conference . . . at Hampton Court, Jan. 14, 1603* (London, 1605).

Barnes, Gilbert Hobbs: *The Antislavery Impulse 1830–1844.* A Publication of the American Historical Association (New York, 1933).

Barrett, Jay A.: *Evolution of the Ordinance of 1787* (New York, 1891).

Beale, Howard K.: "On Rewriting Reconstruction History," in *American Historical Review,* XXV (July 1940), 807–27.

Becker, Carl: *The Declaration of Independence: A Study in the History of Political Ideas* (New York, 1953).

——: *Freedom and Responsibility in the American Way of Life.* With an introduction by George H. Sabine (New York, 1953).

——: *The Heavenly City of the Eighteenth Century Philosophers* (New Haven, 1932).

Bemis, Samuel F.: *The Diplomacy of the American Revolution* (New York, 1935).

Benét, Stephen Vincent: *John Brown's Body* (New York, 1928).

Biddle, Francis: *The Fear of Freedom* (New York, 1952).

Bill, Alfred Hoyt: *Rehearsal for Conflict* (New York, 1947).

Bishop, George: *New England Judged by the Spirit of God* (London, 1793).

Blegen, Theodore C.: *Grass Roots History* (Minneapolis, 1947).

Bobo, William M.: *Glimpses of New York by a South Carolinian* (Charleston, 1852).

Bogart, Ernest L.: *Economic History of the United States* (New York, 1924).

Bolton, C. K.: *The Private Soldier under Washington* (New York, 1902).

Book of Common Prayer. Church of England.

Boucher, Jonathan: *Reminiscences of an American Loyalist.* J. Boucher, editor (Boston, 1925).

Bowers, Claude G.: *The Tragic Era: The Revolution after Lincoln* (New York, 1929).

Bradford, William: *Of Plymouth Plantation.* New Edition: The Complete text with notes and an introduction by Samuel Eliot Morison (New York, 1952).

Brockmeier, S. H.: *The Irrepressible Democrat, Roger Williams* (New York, 1940).

Buck, Solon J.: *The Granger Movement* (Cambridge, Mass., 1913).

Buckle, Henry Thomas: *History of Civilization in England.* In two volumes (New York, 1924).

Burke, Edmund: *Works of the Right Honorable Edmund Burke.* Fourth Edition. In twelve volumes (Boston, 1871).

Burlingame, Roger: *Benjamin Franklin: The First Mr. American* (New York, 1955).

Burnet, Jacob: *Notes on the Early Settlement of the Northwest Territory* (Cincinnati, 1847).

Burnett, Edmund C., editor: see *Letters from Members of the Continental Congress.*

Calder, Isabel M.: *The New Haven Colony* (New Haven, 1934).

Calhoun, Arthur W.: *A Social History of the American Family.* In three volumes (Cleveland, 1917–19).

Calhoun, John Caldwell: *Works.* Richard K. Crallé, editor. In six volumes (New York, 1851–6).

Calvin, John: *Institutes of the Christian Religion.* Translation by Henry Beveridge (Edinburgh, 1845).

"Candidus": *Plain Truth, Addressed to the Inhabitants of America. An answer to Thomas Paine's* Common Sense (Philadelphia, 1776).

Cannon, Carl L.: "Sutter's Fort," in *Dictionary of American History,* V, 212.

Carman, Henry J., and Charles H. Mueller: "The Contract and Finance Company and the Central Pacific Railroad," in *Mississippi Valley Historical Review,* XIV (December 1927), 326–41.

Cartwright, John: *American Independence the Interest and Glory of Great Britain* (Philadelphia, 1776).

Cartwright, Peter: *Autobiography* (New York, 1857).

Cassirer, Ernst: *The Philosophy of the Enlightenment* (Princeton, 1951).

Clarendon, Edward Hyde, 1st Earl of: *History of the Rebellion in England.* In six volumes (Oxford, 1826; reprinted Boston, 1827).

Cleveland, Catherine: *The Great Revival in the West* (Chicago, 1916).

Colden, Cadwallader: *Letter Books,* New York Historical Society *Collections* IX–X, L–LVI (1918 and 1923).

Cole, Arthur Charles: *The Era of the Civil War.* Vol. III of *The Centennial History of Illinois* (Springfield, 1919).

——: *The Irrepressible Conflict, 1850–1865.* Vol. VII of *A History of American Life.* Arthur M. Schlesinger and Dixon Ryan Fox, editors (New York, 1934).

Colonial Records of North Carolina. W. L. Saunders, editor. In ten volumes (Raleigh, 1886–90).

Colton, Calvin: *A Voice from America to England by An American Gentleman* (London, 1839).

Commager, Henry Steele: see *Documents of American History;* see also Morison, S. E., and H. S. Commager.

——, editor: *America in Perspective: The United States through Foreign Eyes.* With an introduction and notes by the editor (New York, 1947).

Congressional Record, 51st Congress, 1st session, Vol. 21, Part 2 (Washington, 1890).

Connecticut Colonial Records: see *Public Records of the Colony of Connecticut.*

Corwin, Thomas: *Speech Delivered in the Senate of the United States, February 11, 1847* (Washington, 1848).

Crawford, J. B.: *The Credit Mobilier of America* (Boston, 1880).

Dana, Richard Henry, Jr.: *Two Years Before the Mast: A Personal Narrative.* With a supplement by the author and additional chapter by his son (Boston, 1911).

Dangerfield, George: *The Era of Good Feelings* (New York, 1952).

Decker, Clarence R.: *The Victorian Conscience* (New York, 1952).

De Voto, Bernard A.: *The Course of Empire* (Boston, 1952).

Dick, Everett: *The Dixie Frontier* (New York, 1948).

Dickens, Charles: *American Notes.* Vol. II of *Works.* Autograph Edition, Richard Garnett, editor (London, 1899).

Dickerson, O. M., editor: *Boston under Military Rule as Revealed in a Journal of the Times* (Boston, 1936).

Dictionary of American Biography. Allen Johnson, editor. In twenty volumes (New York, 1928–36).

Dictionary of American History. James Truslow Adams, editor. In five volumes (New York, 1940).

Dixon, William Hepworth: *The White Conquest.* In two volumes (London, 1876).

Documents Illustrative of the Formation of the Union. House Doc. No. 398, 69th Congress, 1st session (Washington, 1927).

Documents of American History. Henry S. Commager, editor. Two volumes in one. (New York, 1947).

Dow, George F., and John Henry Edmonds: *Pirates of the New England Coast* (Salem, Mass., 1923).
Downes, Randolph C.: "Land, Indian Conception of," in *Dictionary of American History,* III, 253.
Dwight, Timothy: *A Discourse on Some Events of the Last Century, Delivered in New Haven, Jan. 7, 1801* (New Haven, 1801).

Early Western Travels. Reuben G. Thwaites, editor. In thirty-two volumes (Cleveland 1904–7).
Edwards, Jonathan: *Sermons by Jonathan Edwards* (Boston, 1785).
Ehrmann, H. B.: *The Untried Case* (New York, 1933).
Ellicott, Andrew: *Journal, 1796–1800* (Philadelphia, 1814).
Ellis, George Edwards: *The Puritan Age and Rule in the Colony of the Massachusetts Bay 1629–1685.* Third Edition (Boston, 1891).

Faulkner, Harold Underwood: *The Quest for Social Justice, 1898–1914.* Vol. XI of *A History of American Life.* Arthur M. Schlesinger and Dixon Ryan Fox, editors (New York, 1931).
Federalist, The. Modern Library Edition (New York, 1941).
Filler, Louis: *Crusaders for American Liberalism* (New York, 1939).
Fitzpatrick, J. C.: *The Spirit of the Revolution* (Boston, 1924).
Flanders, Ralph B.: "Slavery," in *Dictionary of American History,* V, 94.
Fleming, Walter L.: *Documentary History of Reconstruction.* In two volumes (Cleveland, 1906).
Flint, James: *Letters from America* (Edinburgh, 1822).
Flint, Timothy: *Recollections of the Last Ten Years* (Boston, 1826; New York, 1932).
Franklin, Benjamin: *Writings.* Collected and edited with a life and introduction by A. H. Smyth. In ten volumes (New York, 1905–7).
Franklin, John Hope: *From Slavery to Freedom: A History of American Negroes* (New York, 1952).
Friedrich, Carl J.: *The Philosophy of Kant.* Modern Library Edition (New York, 1949).

Gallaher, James: *The Western Sketch Book* (Boston, 1860).
Garrison, Wendell P. and Francis J.: *William Lloyd Garrison, 1805–1879, The Story of His Life as Told by His Children.* In four volumes (New York, 1885–9).
Garrison, William Lloyd: see *Liberator.*
Giddings, Joshua R.: *Speeches in Congress* (Boston, 1853).

Gipson, Lawrence H.: *The Coming of the Revolution, 1763–1775* (New York, 1954).

Graydon, Alexander: *Memoirs of His Own Times* (Philadelphia, 1846).

Green, John R.: *A Short History of the English People* (New York, 1894).

Grosvenor, William Mason: "The Railroads and the Farms," in *Atlantic Monthly,* XXXII (November 1875), 591.

Hansen, Marcus Lee: *The Immigrant in American History* (Cambridge, Mass., 1940).

Harris, Thaddeus Mason: *The Journal of a Tour into the Territory of the Alleghany Mountains. Made in the Year 1803* (Boston, 1805). Reprinted in *Early Western Travels.* Reuben G. Thwaites, editor (Cleveland, 1904).

Harrison, William H.: *Governors Messages and Letters* in *Indiana Historical Collections.* Logan Esarey, editor, Vol. I (Indianapolis, 1922).

Hart, Albert Bushnell: *American History Told by Contemporaries.* In four volumes (New York, 1897–1901).

Hawley, Joseph: *Commonplace Book* in collection of Joseph Hawley Papers, Manuscript Division, New York Public Library.

Heckewelder, John: "History, Manners, and Customs of the Indian Nations Who Once Inhabited Pennsylvania and the Neighboring States," with an introduction and notes by the Rev. William C. Reichel of Bethlehem, Pa., in *Memoirs of the Historical Society of Pennsylvania,* Vol. XII (Philadelphia, 1876).

Henry, Robert Selph: *The Story of the Mexican War* (Indianapolis, 1950).

Hinsdale, Burke A.: *The Old Northwest* (New York, 1888).

Historical Collections Relating to the American Colonial Church. W. S. Perry, editor (Hartford, 1870–8).

Hughes, John T.: *Doniphan's Expedition. Containing an Account of the Conquest of New Mexico. Illustrated with Plans of Battlefields and Fine Engravings* (Cincinnati, 1848).

Hulbert, Archer Butler: "The Methods and Operations of the Scioto Group of Speculators," in *Mississippi Valley Historical Review,* I (March 1915), 508.

Hunton, Hazel: *Pantaloons and Petticoats: The Diary of a Young American* (New York, 1940).

Hutchinson, Thomas: *Diary and Letters.* In two volumes (Boston, 1884–6).

——: *The Hutchinson Papers* Prince Society Edition (Albany, 1865).

——: *Strictures upon the Declaration of the Congress at Philadelphia: In a Letter to a Noble Lord* (London, 1776).

Jenkins, William S.: *Pro-Slavery Thought in the Old South* (Chapel Hill, 1935).

Jensen, Merrill: *Articles of Confederation: An Interpretation of the Social-Constitutional History of the American Revolution, 1774–1781* (Madison, Wis., 1940).

——: "The Cession of the Old Northwest," in *Mississippi Valley Historical Review,* XXIII (1936), 27–48.

——: "The Creation of the National Domain, 1781–1784," in *Mississippi Valley Historical Review,* XXVI (December 1939), 323–42.

——: *The New Nation: A History of the United States During the Confederation, 1781–1789* (New York, 1950).

Johnson, Charles A.: "The Frontier Camp Meeting: Contemporary and Historical Appraisals," in *Mississippi Valley Historical Review,* XXXVII, 91–110.

Johnson, Willis F.: *George Harvey, "A Passionate Patriot"* (New York, 1929).

Journals of the Continental Congress, 1774–1789. Library of Congress Edition. In thirty-four volumes (Washington, 1904–37).

Josselyn, John: *Two Voyages to New England* (London, 1675).

Kane, Murray: "Some Considerations of the Safety-Valve Doctrine," in *Mississippi Valley Historical Review,* XXIII (September 1936), 169.

Koch, G. Adolph: *Republican Religion* (New York, 1933).

Labaree, Leonard W.: Note on George Whitefield in *William and Mary College Quarterly* (Williamsburg, Va.), VII (October 1950), 590, 591.

Laurens, Henry: *Correspondence of Henry Laurens of South Carolina.* Frank Moore, editor (New York, 1861).

Lecky, W. E. H.: *England in the Eighteenth Century.* In seven volumes (London, 1918–25).

Letter from Ebenezer H. Cummings to a friend in Augusta, dated July 7, 1802, printed in *Augusta Herald,* July 28, 1802.

Letter from New England, A, by "J. W." George Parker Winship, editor. Reprinted from 1682 Boston edition as the Second Publication of the Club of Colonial Reprints (Providence, 1905).

Letter to the People of America, lately printed at New York, now republished by an American. With a postscript by the Editor addressed to Sir W. . . H. . . (London, 1778).

Letters of Junius. C. W. Everett, editor (London, 1927).

Letters of Members of the Continental Congress. Edmund C Burnett, editor. In eight volumes (Washington, 1921–36).

Liberator, The. William Lloyd Garrison, editor. A periodical (Boston, 1831–65).

Lincoln, Abraham: *Complete Works.* Gettysburg Edition, J. G. Nicolay and John Hay, editors. In twelve volumes (New York, 1905).

Lippincott, Isaac: "Farm Tenancy," in *Dictionary of American History,* II, 250.

Lloyd, Henry D.: *Wealth Against Commonwealth* (New York, 1902).

Locke, John: *Essay Concerning Human Understanding* (London, 1690).

Lowell, James Russell: *Complete Poetical Works.* Cambridge Edition. In one volume (Boston, 1896).

Lyman, George D.: *The Saga of the Comstock Lode* (New York, 1937).

Madison, James: *Letters and Other Writings.* In four volumes (Philadelphia, 1865).

Massachusetts, Colonial Society of: *Publications.* In thirty-seven volumes (Boston, 1895–1954).

Massachusetts Historical Society: *Collections.* In seventy-nine volumes (Boston, 1806–1941).

Mather, Cotton: *Magnalia Christi Americana or, The Ecclesiastical History of New England, from its First Planting in the Year 1620, unto the Year of Our Lord, 1698.* First American Edition. In two volumes (Hartford, 1820).

Mather, Increase: *Pray for the Rising Generation* (Boston, 1678).

Maxson, Charles H.: *The Great Awakening in the Middle Colonies* (Chicago, 1920).

"McGready's Narrative of the Record in Logan County," in *New York Missionary Magazine* (1803), p. 192.

McLaughlin, Andrew C.: *A Constitutional History of the United States* (New York, 1935).

McNemar, Richard: *The Kentucky Revival* (Cincinnati, 1808).

Means, Gaston: *The Strange Death of President Harding* (New York, 1926).

Michaux, Francis A.: *Travels to the West of the Alleghany Mountains.* Volume III of *Early Western Travels,* Reuben G. Thwaites, editor (Cleveland, 1904).

Miller, Perry: *The New England Mind: From Colony to Province* (Cambridge, Mass., 1953).

——: *Roger Williams* (Indianapolis, 1953).

Mitchell, Mary Hewitt: *The Great Awakening and Other Revivals in the Religious Life of Connecticut.* A Tercentenary Pamphlet (New Haven, 1934).

Moore, George: *Notes on the History of Slavery in Massachusetts* (New York, 1866).

Morgan, A. T.: *Yazoo* (Washington, 1884).

Morgan, Edmund S.: *The Puritan Family* (Boston, 1944).

Morison, Samuel Eliot: *Builders of the Bay Colony* (Boston, 1930).

——: *The Maritime History of Massachusetts, 1783–1860* (Boston, 1923).

——: *Three Centuries of Harvard* (Cambridge, Mass., 1936).

—— and Henry Steele Commager: *The Growth of the American Republic.* In two volumes (New York, 1937).

Motley, John Lothrop: *The Rise of the Dutch Republic.* In three volumes (London, 1904).

Myers, Gustavus: *History of the Great American Fortunes.* In two volumes (New York, 1936).

Narragansett Club Publications: see Williams, Roger.

Narratives of Early Virginia. Lyon G. Tyler, editor (New York, 1907).

Narratives of the Witchcraft Cases 1648–1706. George Lincoln Burr, editor (New York, 1914).

Nevins, Allan: *Emergence of Modern America.* Vol. VII of *A History of American Life,* Arthur M. Schlesinger and Dixon Ryan Fox, editors (New York, 1927).

——: "Harding, Warren Gamaliel" in *Dictionary of American Biography,* VIII, 252.

——: *Ordeal of the Union.* In two volumes (New York, 1947).

New York Association for Improving the Condition of the Poor: *Annual Reports,* 1852, 1858.

Oberholtzer, Ellis P.: *History of the United States Since the Civil War.* In five volumes (New York, 1937).

Odegard, Peter: *The American Public Mind* (New York, 1930).

Otis, James: *A Vindication of the British Colonies against the Aspersions of the Halifax Gentleman* (Boston, 1765).

Paine, Thomas: see Pearson, Hesketh.

——: *Common Sense.* With preface by William M. Van Weiden (New York, 1928).

——: *Writings.* Moncure D. Conway, editor. In four volumes (New York, 1896).

Palfrey, John G.: *History of New England.* In five volumes (Boston, 1858–90).

Parker, Theodore: *A Sermon of War* (Boston, 1846).

Parrington, Vernon: *Main Currents in American History.* In three volumes (New York, 1927).

Parton, James: *Life and Times of Benjamin Franklin.* In two volumes (Boston, 1867).

Paxson, Frederick L.: "The Gateways of the Old Northwest," in Michigan Pioneer and Historical Society *Collections,* XXXVIII, 139–48.

——: *History of the American Frontier, 1763–1893* (Boston, 1924).

Pearson, Hesketh: *Tom Paine, Friend of Mankind* (New York, 1937).

Peck, Epaphroditus: *The Loyalists of Connecticut.* A Tercentenary Pamphlet (New Haven, 1934).

Pennsylvania Archives. Compiled and edited by Samuel Hazard, John B. Linn, William H. Egle, George E. Reed, Thomas L. Montgomery. Nine series, one hundred and eleven volumes (Harrisburg, 1874–1935).

Perry, Ralph Barton: *Puritanism and Democracy* (New York, 1944).

Perry, William Stevens: see *Historical Collections . . . American Colonial Church.*

Peyton, John Lewis: *Over the Alleghanies.* Second Edition (London, 1870).

Pickering, Timothy: *A Letter from the Hon. Timothy Pickering . . . Exhibiting to his Constituents a View of the Imminent Danger of an Unnecessary and Ruinous War* (Northampton, Mass., 1808).

Pike, James S.: *The Prostrate State: South Carolina Under Negro Government.* With introduction by Henry S. Commager (New York, 1935).

Pitt, William: *Correspondence with Colonial Governors and Military and Naval Commissioners in America.* Gertrude S. Kimball, editor. In two volumes (New York, 1906).

Plymouth Colony Records. Full title: *Records of the Colony of New Plymouth in New England, 1620–1692.* N. B. Shurtleff, editor. In twelve volumes (Boston, 1855–61).

Pro-Slavery Arguments. A collection of essays by James H. Hammond, William Harper, Thomas R. Dew, and William Gilmore Simms (Philadelphia, 1853).

Public Records of the Colony of Connecticut. Compiled by J. H. Trumbull and C. J. Headly. In fifteen volumes (Hartford, 1850–90).

Quincy, Josiah, Jr.: "Journal, 1773," in Massachusetts Historical Society *Proceedings,* XLIX, 424–81.

Randall, James Garfield: *The Civil War and Reconstruction* (New York, 1937).

Randolph, Edward: *His Letters and Official Papers from the New England, Middle and Southern Colonies in America . . . With Historical Illustrations and a Memoir.* Robert Noxon Toppan, editor. In five volumes. A Prince Society publication (Boston, 1898).

Records of the Colony of Rhode Island and Providence Plantations. Compiled by J. R. Bartlett. In ten volumes (Providence, 1856–65).

Records of the Court of Assistants of the Colony of Massachusetts Bay. In three volumes (Boston, 1901–28).

Records of the Governor and Company of the Massachusetts Bay in New England. N. B. Shurtleff, editor. In five volumes (Boston, 1853–4).

Records of the Virginia Company. Susan M. Kingsbury, editor. In nine volumes (Washington, 1933).

Regier, C. C.: *The Era of the Muckrakers* (Chapel Hill, 1932).

Respective Pleas and Arguments of The Mother Country, and of the Colonies distinctly set forth (London, 1774).

Rhode Island Colonial Records: see *Records of the Colony of Rhode Island.*

Rhodes, James Ford: *History of the United States from the Compromise of 1850.* In seven volumes (New York, 1893–1906).

Richards, Caroline Cowles: *Village Life in America, 1852–1872. Including the Period of the Civil War as Told in the Diary of a School-Girl* (New York, 1912).

Riis, Jacob: *The Making of an American* (New York, 1902).

Robert, Joseph Clarke: *The Road from Monticello: A Study of the Virginia Slavery Debate of 1832.* Historical Papers of the Trinity College Historical Society, Series 24 (Durham, N. C., 1941).

Ross, Edward Alsworth: *Sin and Society, An Analysis of Latter-Day Iniquity* (Boston, 1907).

Savelle, Max: *Seeds of Liberty: The Genesis of the American Mind* (New York, 1948).

Schlesinger, Arthur M.: *The American as Reformer* (Cambridge, Mass., 1950).

——: *The Colonial Merchants and the American Revolution 1763–1776* (New York, 1917).

—— and Dixon Ryan Fox, editors: *A History of American Life.* In twelve volumes (New York, 1927–44).

Schlesinger, Arthur M., Jr.: *The Age of Jackson* (Boston, 1945).

Schoolcraft, Henry R.: *Information Respecting the History, Condition, and Prospects of the Indian Tribes of the United States.* Collected and prepared under the Bureau of Indian Affairs. Volume VI, referred to in the text, is entitled *Archives of Aboriginal Knowledge* (Philadelphia, 1860).

Schortemeier, F. H.: *Rededicating America: Life and Recent Speeches of Warren G. Harding* (New York, 1920).

Schurz, Carl: *The Reminiscences of Carl Schurz.* Frederic Bancroft and William A. Dunning, editors (New York, 1908).

Seldes, Gilbert: *The Stammering Century* (New York, 1928).

Sellers, Coleman: *Lorenzo Dow: The Bearer of the Word* (New York, 1928).

Shafer, Joseph: "Some Facts Bearing on the Safety-Valve Theory," in *Wisconsin Magazine of History,* XX (December 1936), 216.

Shannon, Fred A.: "The Homestead Act and the Labor Surplus," in *American Historical Review,* XLI (July 1936), 637.

Smith, Bradford: *Bradford of Plymouth* (Philadelphia, 1851).

Smith, Captain John: *Generall Historie of Virginia* (London, 1624).

——: *Works.* Edward Arber, editor (Birmingham, 1884).

Stearns, Raymond P.: "The Great Migration," in *Dictionary of American History,* II, 418.

Stoddard, Solomon: *An Answer to Some Cases of Conscience Respecting the Country* (Boston, 1722). Reprinted in *Magazine of History With Notes and Queries,* Extra Number 55 (1917), 189.

Stowe, Harriet Beecher: *Uncle Tom's Cabin, or Life Among the Lowly.* In two volumes (Boston and Cleveland, 1852).

Strachey, William: *Historie of Travaile into Virginia Britannia.* A Hakluyt Society Publication (London, 1849).

Sullivan, Gov. James: *Interesting Correspondence between His Excellency Governor Sullivan and Col. Pickering* (Newburyport, Mass., and Boston, 1808).

Sweet, William Warren: *Revivalism in America* (New York, 1944).

Swift, Lindsay: "The Massachusetts Election Sermons," in Colonial Society of Massachusetts *Publications,* I, 388–451.

Swisher, Carl Brent: *American Constitutional Development.* Second Edition (Boston, 1954).

Tarbell, Ida M.: *The History of the Standard Oil Company.* In two volumes (New York, 1904).

——: *The Nationalizing of Business 1878–1898.* Vol. IX in *A History of American Life.* Arthur M. Schlesinger and Dixon Ryan Fox, editors (New York, 1936).

Tawney, R. H.: *Religion and the Rise of Capitalism* (New York, 1926).
Theodore Tilton *vs.* Henry Ward Beecher. Action for Criminal Conversation, etc. (New York, 1875).
Tocqueville, Alexis de: *Democracy in America.* The Henry Reeve text, revised by Francis Bowen and further corrected and edited with introduction, editorial notes, and bibliographies by Phillips Bradley. In two volumes (New York, 1951).
Trexler, Harrison Anthony: *Slavery in Missouri, 1804–1865.* A Dissertation Submitted to the Board of University Studies of The Johns Hopkins University (Baltimore, 1914).
Trollope, Frances: *Domestic Manners of the Americans* (London, 1832).
Turner, Edward Raymond: *The Negro in Pennsylvania: Slavery—Servitude—Freedom 1639–1861* (Washington, 1911).
Turner, Frederick Jackson: *The Frontier in American History* (New York, 1947).
Tyler, Moses Coit: *Literary History of the Revolution.* Second Edition. In two volumes (New York, 1898).

U.S. Congress: 34th Congress, 1st session, 1856, House Report No. 359. 42nd Congress, 3rd session, House Report Nos. 77 and 78.
U.S. Department of Commerce, Bureau of Statistics: *Historical Statistics of the United States, 1789–1945* (Washington, 1949).
U.S. Statutes at Large. George P. Sanger, editor (Boston, 1863).

Van Doren, Carl: *Secret History of the Revolution* (New York, 1941).
Van Tyne, Claude Halstead: *The Causes of the War of Independence* (Boston, 1922).
——: *The Loyalists in the American Revolution* (New York, 1902).
Virginia: A Guide to the Old Dominion. Compiled by Workers of the Writers' Program of the Work Progress Administration in the State of Virginia (New York, 1940).
Virginia: Committee of Correspondence "Proceedings . . . 1759–1770," in *Virginia Magazine of History and Biography,* X–XII.
Virginia: Magazine of History and Biography.

Washington, George: *Writings.* W. C. Ford, editor. In fourteen volumes (New York, 1891).
Weber, Max: *The Protestant Ethic and the Rise of Capitalism* (London, 1930).
Weeden, William B.: *Economic and Social History of New England.* In two volumes (Boston, 1890).

Weinberg, Albert K.: *Manifest Destiny, A Study of Nationalist Expansion in American History* (Baltimore, 1933).

Wertenbaker, Thomas Jefferson: "Pocahontas," in *Dictionary of American Biography,* XV, 18.

——: *The Puritan Oligarchy* (New York, 1947).

White, William Allen: *Masks in a Pageant* (New York, 1928).

——: *Politics, the Citizen's Business* (New York, 1924).

Whitefield, George: *Works.* Rev. John Gillies, editor. In six volumes (London, 1771).

Williams, Roger: *The Writings of Roger Williams.* Narragansett Club Publications. In six volumes (Providence, 1866–74).

Winslow, Ola Elizabeth: *Jonathan Edwards* (New York, 1940).

Winsor, Justin: *Narrative and Critical History of America.* In eight volumes (Boston, 1884).

Winthrop, John: *Winthrop's Journal.* James K. Hoskins, editor. In two volumes (New York, 1908).

Wish, Harvey: *Society and Thought in Early America: A Social and Intellectual History of the American People through 1865* (New York, 1950).

——: *Society and Thought in Modern America: A Social and Intellectual History of the American People from 1865* (New York, 1952).

Woodburn, Albert: "The Missouri Compromise," in American Historical Association *Annual Report,* 1893, 251.

Woodson, Carter G.: "The Negroes of Cincinnati Prior to the Civil War," in *Journal of Negro History,* I (1916), 1–22.

Wylie, Philip: *Generation of Vipers* (New York, 1946).

Index

A NOTE ON THE AUTHOR

ROGER BURLINGAME *was born in New York City in 1889. After graduation from Harvard in 1913, he returned to New York to work for a year on the editorial staff of* The Independent. *From 1914 to 1926 he was associated with a large New York publishing firm, first as publicity manager, later as an editor. While there, he began writing fiction, and published two novels before leaving the firm in 1926.*

Mr. Burlingame lived in Italy from 1927 to 1931, continuing to write and publish novels. He returned to America shortly before publication of his first book of nonfiction, a short book called Peace Veterans (*1932*). *He had published six novels in all before he turned his full-time attention to American history and biography and to his special field: the role of a changing technology in shaping democracy's social pattern. In 1938 he wrote* March of the Iron Men, *which gave a new slant on American history by tracing the industrialization of American life from the arrival of the printing press down to 1865.* Engines of Democracy (*1940*) *continued this narrative through the twentieth century, revealing the staggering impact of such inventions as radio, telephone, photography, and the automobile on the contemporary scene. In* Backgrounds of Power (*1949*) *Mr. Burlingame met squarely the controversial issue of the human effects of the assembly line in describing the development of mass production in American industry.*

With these and other books Mr. Burlingame established himself as a first-rank interpreter of industrial history. At the same time, he has been the most versatile of writers. Of Making Many Books (*1946*) *told the story of one hundred years of the Scribner publishing house. He wrote an outstanding life of* Henry Ford (*1955*), *and his* Benjamin Franklin, The First Mr. American (*1955*) *won the Poor Richard Almanack Award in 1956.*

A NOTE ON THE TYPE

The text of this book was set on the Linotype in a face called Times Roman, *designed by* Stanley Morison *for* The Times *(London), and first introduced by that newspaper in the middle nineteen thirties.*

Among typographers and designers of the twentieth century, Stanley Morison has been a strong forming influence, as typographical adviser to the English Monotype Corporation, as a director of two distinguished English publishing houses, and as a writer of sensibility, erudition, and keen practical sense.

In 1930 Morison wrote: "Type design moves at the pace of the most conservative reader. The good type-designer therefore realizes that, for a new fount to be successful, it has to be so good that only very few recognize its novelty. If readers do not notice the consummate reticence and rare discipline of a new type, it is probably a good letter." It is now generally recognized that in the creation of Times Roman *Morison successfully met the qualifications of this theoretical doctrine.*

Composed, printed, and bound by The Plimpton Press, Norwood, Mass. Paper made by S. D. Warren Co., Boston.

Typography and binding design by

WARREN CHAPPELL